MW01037274

The Twinship Sourcebook

Your Guide To Understanding Multiples

COMPILED BY THE EDITORS OF **TWINS®** MAGAZINE

Copyright **TWINS**® Magazine, Inc., 1984, 1985,
1986, 1987, 1988, 1989, 1990, 1991, 1992.
First Printing 1992
Second Printing 1993
Third Printing 1997
Revised 1997

Library of Congress Catalog Card Number 93-60586
ISBN 0-9636745-4-4

All rights reserved. No part of this book may be reproduced or transmitted in
any form or by any means, electronic or mechanical, including photocopying,
recording or by any information storage or retrieval system without written
permission from:

TWINS® **Magazine**
5350 S. Roslyn Street, Suite 400
Englewood, Colorado 80111-2125

Publisher: Donald E.L. Johnson
Editor-in-Chief: Susan J. Alt
Managing Editor: Marge D. Hansen
Assistant Editor: Heather White
Art Directors: Valri Blasi Kaleda/Shelly Whitmore
Proofreader: Geri David
Cover Illustration: Valerie McKeown

Table of Contents

Chapter 1
Twins in the World

Many unique biological and psychological circumstances affecting identical and fraternal twins have long been the subject of myths, leading to an often irrational and even sensational perception of twins by the general public. Although it has been true that the striking similarities between genetically identical twins continuously feed the world's hunger for stories relating the sometimes eerie duplication of experiences, the truth is that identical twins are not exactly alike in every way. In fact, many people are often disappointed to learn that a variety of environmental influences, operating either before or after birth, may result in physical and behavioral differences between co-twins!

To further shatter the stereotyped definition of "twin" as "same," it is important to note that fraternal twins are not biologically closer than ordinary siblings; both share half their genes, on average, by descent. Another myth to be shattered: Fraternal twinning runs in certain families but, contrary to popular opinion, does not "skip generations". In contrast, identical twinning appears to occur with equal frequency among most families.

This chapter cogently dispels these and other myths and substitutes them with a look at the reality of raising twins. In short, the stories here give fuel to the fires of truth that multiple-birth advocates are responsible for igniting in their families, neighborhoods, communities and schools.

Chapter 2
The Importance of Twintype

When understanding twinship, it's essential to start with the basics-the two types of twins and how they are formed.

Fact #1: Identical twins share all their genes, having split from a single fertilized ovum between one and 14 days following conception. Differences between these twins can be explained only with reference to differences in experience.

Fact #2: Fraternal twins result from the separate fertilization of two ova by two spermatozoa, which explains why they share only half their genes, on average. Differences between these twins may be associated with genetic and/or environmental factors.

Knowing without a shadow of a doubt the twintype of a pair of co-twins is critical for understanding and appreciating their similarities and differences, as well as each of their own particular behavioral and physical changes in each stage of growth.

This chapter enables readers to learn not only how to determine their multiples' twintypes, but also how to become familiar with the unique qualities of each kind of twin by sex.

Chapter 3
Temperament and Personality: Why They Do What They Do!

Multiples, especially identicals, are often envied for the special intimacy they share. At the same time, the conflicts that arise due to their having common birthdays, joint possessions, and divided parental attention may lead some non-twins (and often some twins!) to prefer life as a singleton. Many parents of multiples find pleasure in the constant companionship that each child enjoys, a situation that many parents of non-twins find appealing. At the same time, additional effort and expense are associated with the successful rearing of twins and triplets. On balance, it is important to note that most twins enjoy the special circumstances of their birth, and parents of multiples delight in watching their children develop!

This chapter explores the many variations of temperament and personality that each type of multiples can, and do, exhibit, as well as ways that parents can help each flourish.

Chapter 4
Death of a Twin

The social bonds shared between twins, especially identical twins, have been described as the closest of human relationships. Recent research demonstrates that many surviving twins experience the loss of their sibling as a more devastating event than the loss of other close relatives. Until recently, the psychological consequences of twin loss have gone almost unnoticed by health professionals and by the general public. However, there is an urgent need to develop appropriate support systems to assist bereaved twins and their families.

One mother of twins, Eileen Vinnola, shared her feelings about the loss of one of her twins with **TWINS**® Magazine. Her words reflect the many emotions both multiple-birth families and their friends experience concerning twin loss and how both can be supportive of each other: "I have learned that friends and acquaintances had a much harder time dealing with the death of my son than our family did. They would not bring up the death; or if I did, they would change the subject. I know why-they did not want to remind me of our son's death. But I really resented this reaction.

"I now know how I would handle this situation if it should happen to someone I know. I would ask the person how he or she would like me to react, whether that person would like to talk about it or if he or she would rather not be reminded. I feel it should be that person's individual decision."

This section looks at ways co-twins and their families can cope with this tragic experience.

Chapter 5
Twin Studies

Although both identical and fraternal twins are being born and thriving in record numbers throughout the world, twinning rates, as well as attitudes and beliefs about twinning and the rearing of twins, show important cross-cultural differences that warrant attention by those for whom this information has the most relevance—parents of multiples. Twin research conducted on a multi-national level reveals meaningful information for all multiple-birth caregivers about how cultural practices affect the experience of twinship, both for the co-twins and for their families. Comparing resemblances between identical and fraternal twins from different ethnic and social backgrounds can enhance the understanding of the relative contributions of hereditary and environmental influences to human development, another essential body of knowledge that can support multiple-birth families in their childrearing challenges.

This chapter translates the findings of twin studies around the world into usable, practical information designed to enhance parents' day-to-day lives with their multiples, as well as help multiples of all ages and twintypes better understand themselves.

Chapter 6
To Separate or Not to Separate

Decision-making strategies concerning how co-twins can learn to navigate as individuals-in class, with friends, with family-as well as how these separation struggles are perceived by singletons, are perhaps, the most fundamental issues that need to be faced by multiples and their caregivers from even before the multiple-birth event through the entire lifetime of twins.

Separation may prove difficult for twins who have not experienced time apart from one another. The challenge is one of guiding young twins toward making choices that allow them to enjoy their special relationship, but also guide them toward opportunities that provide for individual growth and interaction, as well as alone time, and individual time with family members and friends. A concern that twins may fail to develop a sense of themselves as individuals can lead their caregivers to unnecessarily separate them, and, consequently, create distress about their twin identify on the part of some co-twins. Older twins may even feel compelled by this imposed pressure to set different educational or career goals if made to feel self-conscious about pursuing common paths.

Therefore, appreciation and respect for the natural similarities and differences of identical and fraternal twins should be a high priority for anyone who is interested in the healthy development of multiple-birth children.

This chapter explores these issues, addressing both the "how-tos" and the theoretical questions families of multiples face concerning the question of whether to separate or not to separate in formal school and family life.

Acknowledgements

All of us at **TWINS**® Magazine respect and treasure our readership families who share *their* families' hopes and dreams with us each day in the most compelling ways. Due to heartfelt requests for information from these individuals-teachers, parents, medical professionals and multiples themselves-we have dedicated many months to putting together this one-of-a-kind resource, compiled from the past eight years of special **TWINS**® Magazine editorials.

This book, therefore, belongs to these friends around the world who are not only hungry for information, but have also entrusted us with the responsibility of teaching and sharing multiple-birth research with them and the entire world.

Thanks to them and multiples everywhere for the practical and spiritual lessons they teach us. May we never stop growing, loving and learning together.

Dedication

This book is born with heartfelt appreciation to all of our readers who have loved **TWINS**® Magazine since its birth in 1984. Because of their respect for multiples, and their interest in supporting their healthy growth and development as multiples and individuals, we are continuously motivated to bring them together as a family, a family as diverse and passionate as the subjects about which they care so deeply.

Introduction

Twins* have long captured the interest and imagination of everyone from behavioral and medical science professionals, journalists and artists, to families and even strangers who do a double-take when multiples pass their way. As published research reports demonstrate, identical and fraternal twins offer scientists convenient methods for exploring the relative contributions of nature and nurture that underlie human behavioral and physical characteristics. For individuals in creative arts, twins facilitate elaboration of concepts such as duality, interdependence and related themes.

The profound impact a multiple birth has upon a family has, unfortunately, remained an aspect of twinship that has been generally neglected in the popular media. But all families of multiples can attest to the fact that the arrival of multiples changes a family forever because the psychological and biological circumstances of multiples differ from those of non-twin children. Furthermore, special developmental characteristics are uniquely associated with the different varieties of twinship, thus precluding the formulation of a single philosophy or set of rearing practices regarding twins.

Success in raising and educating twins and other multiple-birth children is most likely when parents and educators engage in informed decision-making. Choices made during early infancy may significantly affect developmental events during childhood or adolescence. Issues surrounding placement at school or manner of dress pose considerable challenges to multiple-birth parents as they attempt to assist twins in celebrating both their twinship and their individuality. Members of the community who hold misconceptions about twinship may unknowingly jeopardize twins' positive adjustment by offering inappropriate comparisons or advice. Parents, thus, assume an immense responsibility as they must educate themselves, as well as others, about the numerous aspects of growing up as a twin.

Multiple-birth issues have increasingly engaged both professional and public interest in recent years. Twins methodology has been incorporated into the research programs of a wide variety of disciplines, including psychology, anthropology, economics and the health sciences. International societies and workshops bring twins researchers together to discuss and disseminate current findings on

*Note: The words "twins" and "multiples" are used interchangeably in this book when referring to multiple-birth children.

multiple-birth. Local and national organizations involve twins and their families in discussions or parenting and other topics with special relevance to twinship. Several books targeted at academic and general audiences have also become available.

Nevertheless, parents and other individuals closely associated with twins remain hungry for timely information on unique developmental aspects of raising multiple-birth children. The public must, therefore, be provided with greater access to twin research findings on an ongoing basis. **TWINS**® Magazine, by presenting comprehensive treatments of a broad variety of topics as they relate to multiples at different ages, is uniquely able to fill this need.

It is, in addition, extremely important to establish meaningful links between parents of multiples who share special interests or needs. Twins are, for example, more likely to be born prematurely than non-twins, an event that can result in early health difficulties. The raising of twins may pose considerable financial and emotional strain for some families. Newborn twins may prove stressful for singleton children in a family, given the high level of attention that twins typically attract.

A community of families who has experienced these various unique circumstances associated with twinship can best support those in similar situations. **TWINS**® Magazine has already facilitated contacts among tens of thousands of families requiring special information or assistance, thus contributing to the successful developmental outcomes of many pairs of twins, and the positive attitudes of parents of multiple-birth children concerning their caregiving role.

The Twinship Sourcebook brings together selected articles on issues of particular concern to multiple-birth families. These articles span a period of nine years during which time the readership of **TWINS**® Magazine has steadily increased as a result of heightened awareness of the significance of twinship. This special effort represents a direct response to our readers' requests for a single source of timely information. The Twinship Sourcebook is designed to meet the information resource needs of parents, as well as physicians, educators, social service professionals and others dedicated to the successful rearing and well-being of twins.

Nancy L. Segal, Ph.D.
Professor of Psychology
Director of Twin Studies
California State University, Fullerton, CA

PREFACE

More Than One— Amazing Multiples

by Marge Hansen

The birth of a baby is always a special event. But when two, three or more arrive at one time, the management of pregnancy and delivery becomes an ensemble performance.

Everyone is fascinated with multiple birth children. They are the subjects of newspaper and magazine articles. We see them on television. They turn our heads in public places and turn our thoughts to the reasons we seem to be seeing or hearing of duos, trios, or even larger sets of children much more often these days.

Multiple births in the United States have topped the 101,000 mark. The 1994 figures, representing the latest statistics available from the National Center for Health Statistics, show 97,064 twin births, 4,233 triplets, 315 quadruplets, and 46 quintuplets. (These numbers refer to individual babies, not sets.) We are even beginning to hear about sets of sextuplet miracle babies that have survived and are thriving.

Factors Influencing Multiplicity

Several factors have contributed to the significant rise in multiple births over the last 15 years. As women delay childbearing and the age of the mother increases, the possibility of multiple fetuses increases. Extraordinary advancements in fertility treatment and assisted reproductive procedures help couples previously unable to conceive. Improved medical technology makes it feasible to detect multiple fetuses early on, monitor their development and even carry out fetal surgery to correct anomalies in utero. Physicians are better able to prolong high-risk pregnancies, helping babies born in sets to survive in greater numbers. High-tech neonatal intensive care units and specially trained caregivers make survival not only possible but increasingly probable for even the smallest at-risk infants.

Doctors are advising women who are pregnant with multiples to improve their nutrition and to even purposefully gain extra weight. Bed rest is often prescribed, and a higher number of Cesarean sections are being performed to ensure successful deliveries.

When a woman who has given birth to multiples gets pregnant again, her chances of giving birth to another set increase greatly. Based on this biological fact, the rising birth rate of multiples has the potential to continue to climb, resulting in even more multiples being born.

Twinning

Throughout history, twins-and higher order multiples-have been the subject of myth, mystery and superstition. Fortunately, most societies have dispelled age-old fables surrounding twins. In most cultures around the world, the birth of twins is now valued and accepted with joy as well as great curiosity.

Different parts of the world have varying incidences of multiple births. Asian populations have the lowest rates of twin births and West Africans the highest. There are about 125 million twins worldwide.

In the United States, during 1992-1994, twins were born at a rate of 24 babies per 1000 births. Another way of viewing this is that one in every 50 births is a twin baby. Twinning rates were the highest in Connecticut and Massachusetts and lowest in the mountain states of the West.

Biologically, multiples may have identical genes (identical twins) or familial genes (fraternal twins). About two-thirds of all twins are fraternal and one-third are identical.

Twins: Identical vs. Fraternal

Identical twins come from the same egg that has split, and are always the same sex. They always look very much alike. Often they act alike and develop very similar behaviors and personalities as they grow up.

Fraternal twins come from two separate eggs that are fertilized at or about the same time. They may or may not be the same sex, and they are no more identical in appearance, temperament or behavior than any other siblings. It's not uncommon, however, for same-sex fraternal twins to look very similar-though frequently they have little resemblance.

• Characteristic	Identical	Fraternal
• Sex	Same	Same or different
• Appearance	Identical	Many similarities, but not identical
• Placenta	One	Two
• Chorion bag	One or two	Two
• Amniotic sac	One or two	Two
• Blood types	Identical	May be identical or different

Source: American Academy of Pediatrics

Triplets and Higher Order Multiples

Triplet deliveries tripled between 1980 and 1994. Remarkably, the triplet birth rate (number of babies born per 1,000 births) increased more than 200 percent during this period. Some 4,233 triplets, 315 quadruplets, and 46 quintuplets were born in 1994, which means that one of every 860 babies born was a higher order multiple. This compares with only about one in every 3,500 births in the early 1970s.

Triplets and other higher order multiples are usually a combination of identical and fraternal types. There is often a set of identical twins, with the other child or children in the set being fraternals.

It is extremely rare for all the children in a higher order set to be identical. Amazingly, however, in March 1997, healthy identical female quadruplets were delivered at Long Island Jewish Medical Center in New Hyde Park, New York. Statistically, the chance of quads being identical is only about one in 11 million.

The rarest of multiple births are sextuplets. An April 1997 newspaper story announced, "Mail carrier addresses her biggest delivery: six kids." The two boys and four girls weighed in at between two and three pounds each when they were born at State University Hospital in Stony Brook, New York.

There are 34 sets of surviving quintuplets in the U.S., and 3 sets of surviving sextuplets. Women have been pregnant with septuplets, but medical records indicate all seven babies have never survived the birth.

Advances in Reproductive Medicine

When infertility is an issue, couples often turn to reproductive medicine to help them conceive. The principal techniques used today are in vitro fertilization (IVF), gamete intrafallopian transfer (GIFT) and zygote intrafallopian transfer (ZIFT).

According to The American Society of Reproductive Medicine, IVF is a process in which an egg and sperm are combined in a laboratory dish to facilitate fertilization. When fertilized, the resulting embryo is transferred to the woman's uterus. In 1994, 28.3% of IVF deliveries were twins, 5.9% were triplets and 0.6% were higher order multiples.

GIFT is the direct transfer of a mixture of sperm and eggs into the fallopian tube. Fertilization takes place inside the tube. Of the GIFT babies born in 1994, 29.2% were twins, 6.5% were triplets and 0.6% were higher order multiples.

ZIFT is a process in which an egg is fertilized in the laboratory, and the resulting zygote (fertilized egg) is transferred to the fallopian tube at the pronuclear stage—before cell division takes place. On one day, the eggs are retrieved and fertilized, and the next day the zygote is transferred to the mother. In 1994, births of babies using ZIFT alone or combining it with another procedure resulted in 27.7% twin births, 4.8% triplet births and no other higher multiples.

Sharing Knowledge and Resources

One of the largest data banks of information pertaining to multiple births is managed by the National Organization of Mothers of Twins Clubs. Multiple Birth Data Forms have been completed by 11,000 mothers representing 22,000 multiple birth children. A wide range of interesting facts is contained in the 1900 surveys that make up a subset of the NOMOTC data base. Of the 1,854 sets of twins, 38 sets of triplets and three sets of quadruplets represented:

- 1% of the mothers adopted their sets of children
- 18 mothers had two sets of multiples, one had three sets and one had four sets
- For 40% of the mothers, their first pregnancy resulted in a multiple birth
- 66% of the mothers were age 26 to 35; 14% were 36 to 40; 5% were 41 or older

- 15% of the mothers had taken fertility drugs; less than 1% were involved in in vitro fertilization procedures
- 20% gained more than 50 lbs. during the pregnancy; 47% gained 31 to 50 lbs.; 22% gained 21 to 30 lbs.
- 33% of the twins, 80% of the triplets and all the quads were delivered by C-section
- 22.5% were fraternal boy/girl twins, 18.1% fraternal boys, 16.6% fraternal girls, 18.6% identical girls, 17.6% identical boys, 1.9% triplets, and 0.2% quads.

J. Susan Griffith, M.D., research vice president of the NOMOTC, emphasizes that this is a membership-based study, not a sampling of all mothers of multiples in the general population.

A Monumental Challenge

When most people think of twins, triplets and other higher order multiples, they find the very idea of more than one baby at a time to be overwhelming. Understanding the psychology of raising multiples and the issues that confront parents of multiples is of great interest to academics and researchers. Despite what parents of singleton children may think, the issues related to raising multiples are very different from those of other families, even when families have singleton children who are close in age.

Should we dress them alike? Is it better to keep them in the same classroom or separate them? How do we foster individuality? What about equal care and equal love? How do we encourage healthy competition while preventing destructive self-comparisons and comparisons by others? Is it possible to avoid having one child in the set become dominant while the other(s) assumes submissive roles?

Just keeping up with the day-to-day routine of busy schedules, household tasks, emotional challenges and inevitable upheavals results in extra responsibilities that unbalance the accepted concept of family life.

The Fascination Continues

The wonderful world of multiples is filled with percentages, odds, ratios and other statistics not all of them applying to numbers of babies born. On the practical side, these terms describe stacks of diapers, quantities of changes, ounces of formula, and loads of laundry. The lowest numbers are the precious few hours of sleep parents of multiples manage to squeeze into their busy days and nights.

A great many families with twins, triplets and more feel extremely blessed, especially when their children are healthy and happy in the face of high-risk pregnancies and deliveries. The challenges and rewards of being a family with multiples add a dimension to parenting most people will never experience. There are lots of questions and not enough answers. But, as we see, hear and learn more about these amazing multiples we can only say we truly live in amazing times.

CHAPTER 1

Twins in the World

How the World Views Twins

by Alice M. Vollmar

Today, parents of multiples often enjoy a measure of status (and pity!) not normally accorded to other parents. But in some parts of the world, and in some people's minds, twinship folklore lingers. Some people still believe that eating a twin food, such as a double apple or double-yolked egg, will cause one to have twins. In the southern United States, if a first child's umbilical cord has two knots close together, it supposedly predicts that the next birth will be twins. And it is said that if one identical female twin has a baby, the other will be barren.

Some of the twinship myths of our era, such as the misconception that twins always run in families, are familiar to most people. According to Drs. Judy Hagedorn and Janet Kizziar in the book, *Gemini: The Psychology and Phenomena of Twins*, "Although many families have histories of several multiple births, twins frequently occur where there has been no previous history of multiples. Another myth is that if one's grandparents had twins, one is more likely to bear them. Occasionally twins do occur every other generation, but this is not usually the case."

Although some myths persist, most of us live in a time and a place not ruled by myths and superstition. Twin myths now seem like fascinating remnants of a remote era or tales from far-distant regions.

Where twin births are rare, for example, cultures tend to accord them little acceptance. Asians are less prone to twinning than people elsewhere, and in Manchurian Tunguses culture, it has always been bad luck to buy or borrow something from a mother of twins. Twin researchers say that even today, twins are an embarrassment to Japanese families.

Where twinning is common, histories are rich in twinship customs, for better or worse. Africa has perhaps the highest twin birth rate, and among tribes such as the Yoruba, twins are revered. However, that was not always the custom. Twins in that culture were killed, until an oracle told them to stop the killings if they wanted to be free from mysterious deaths among their people. Mothers then began to worship twins. Consequently families with twins prospered, and twins' births came to signify good fortune.

In Upper New Guinea, twins receive special houses, clothing and tasks and are set apart from the populace. In yet another sect, twins are said to be born with bad character, and poor behavior is tolerated if one is a twin. But in the Niger Delta, "May you be the mother of twins" is the worst insult a mother can be given.

Clearly, the Greeks and Romans were fascinated with twinship. Their mythology is laced with twin images-Apollo and Diana, Hercules and Iphicles, Castor and Pollux, Romulus and Remus. The supreme Greek deity, Zeus, plays a heavy role, fathering more than one of these immortal combinations.

Interestingly, in one grandiose legend, the Greeks awarded twins supernatural powers and control over natural elements. They wrestled with questions about the paternity of twins, the unusual circumstances of twin births, the possible part played by a powerful god, and the twins' relationship with one another.

In the "hold-onto-your-hats, folks" myth of Castor and Pollux, Zeus disguised himself as a swan and impregnated the fair Leda with twins, Pollux and Helen. That very same eve, the lucky Leda was impregnated with another pair of twins, Castor and Clytemnestra, by her mortal husband. Subsequently, these four children were hatched from two giant eggs-a happening that is immortalized in Leonardo da Vinci's painting, *Leda and the Swan*. Deeply devoted to one another, Castor and Pollux became military heroes and were also given power over the weather and the oceans by Neptune. Some accounts of the legend say the brothers alternately lived on earth and in the heavens due to the mortal/god variance in their origin. However, when Castor was killed in battle, the twin brothers reunited in the sky as the twin stars of the Gemini constellation.

Although Castor and Pollux felt affinity for one another, some mythological twins didn't. Romulus and Remus were fathered by the Roman god Mars and cared for by a wolf after being abandoned. Mythologists speculate that twins probably were abandoned often in that culture. These twins went on to found Rome, but Romulus killed Remus in the ensuing struggle for power.

Nor was twinship harmonious in the Old Testament Bible stories. Perhaps best known is the story of Jacob and Esau, in which the younger twin, Jacob, tricked Esau out of the blessing rightfully due the elder son, and then fled to keep an angry Esau from doing him in. God had warned their mother before their birth that "the elder shall serve the younger" (Genesis 25:23), and the dispute over who should be first-born evidently began in the womb.

Often, the question of birth rights and birth order is complicated by twin births, and in many cultures the first-born twin is considered the younger twin. Such is the case in Africa's Yoruba tribe where the first-born supposedly is sent by the older twin to check things out.

Most primitive tribes used to try in some way to reconcile the puzzle of twin births. The Northwest American Indians decided that twins actually were salmon and they took pains to keep them away from water lest they revert to being salmon and swim away. The Mohave Indians credited twins with being able to read minds, and the Iroquois thought one twin was good and one evil. In the myth believed by the tribes of the Plains Indians, "monsters" came and took the younger twin away-forever.

As in Greek and Roman mythology, twins in primitive cultures often were linked to the gods or supernatural beliefs. North American Mohave Indians believed twins controlled thunder, rain and lightning. During droughts, the

Indians poured water over the graves of twins. The British Columbian Kwikutal Indians rejoiced when twins were born; to them, twins predicted a year rich in hunting and fishing, and twins were thought able to cure diseases with the aid of their wooden birth ceremony rattles. Parents of twins in many cultures were asked to conduct rites to stimulate livestock and crop productivity. Some Hindus in India painted the buttocks of twins black and white, and then exposed them to the weather to protect the crops from rain and hail.

Twins in the above cultures could be considered lucky. Multiples fared less well when they were thought to cause crop failures and natural disasters such as floods and drought. In Bali, elaborate purification rites were administered to twins to maintain nature's balance. In other cultures, one or both twin babies were killed and the mother ostracized for fear she might contaminate the crops. Or she was killed to curtail the "evil" twinning phenomenon.

Where two babies posed economic hardships, twins were dealt with harshly. Often it was impossible for a mother to feed and care for two babies and survive herself. Australian aborigines often killed one twin to safeguard scanty resources. At one time, Eskimos thinned the elderly from their ranks if they became a burden, and the same fate often befell at least one twin.

Moral beliefs dictated the fate of some twins. If the twin relationship was believed to be an incestuous one initiated in the womb, twins often were sacrificed or male/female twins were forced to marry one another. However, in ruling Egyptian dynasties where brothers and sisters married to keep the family line exclusive, a match between fraternal twins was thought the best of all pairings.

Many people, including some primitive African, Brazilian, and American Indian tribes, saw twinning as a step backward in human development, a regression to animal birthing of young in a litter. Sometimes the mother was suspected of being an animal in disguise or of having mated with an animal. In West African Dahomey, it was believed that twins might later revert to being monkeys if not protected by rituals.

The paternity of twins was a riddle in cultures as diverse as African, American Indian, and Japanese; surely two babies must have two fathers, they reasoned. In one African tribe, it was thought that one father was the wife's husband and the other a wizard. Then came the difficulty of deciding which twin was legitimately fathered. If no answer came through tribal witchcraft, both babies were killed. Often twins were thought to be evidence of adultery. In some Brazilian and American Indian cultures, the mother was rejected or killed-as well as the twins.

Modern peoples may have transcended the limitations of such legends, but the twin mystique is inextricably bound to the cement of our civilization.

AN INSIDE LOOK:
THE YORUBA PEOPLE OF WEST AFRICA

Imagine how you'd feel if you believed your newly born twins not only shared the same soul but also had the power to bring either good or disaster. Such is the case among the Yoruba people of West Africa, who have the highest rate of twin births in the world.

They celebrate the birth of twins as many cultures do, but accord twins special favors. The Yoruba treat twins with respect and loving care, for they can bring special blessings to the family-health, happiness, prosperity-or they can bring about disaster, disease or death. Thus twins receive the best food, clothes, and jewelry. Their upbringing is far more permissive than that of other children. They are spoiled and coddled to prevent them from using their power for evil.

The twinning rate among the Yoruba-one twin birth to every 22 or 24 single births-is four times that of the United States and England. The Yoruba also hold the world record for twin mortality. Because many twins are born prematurely or are even physically stronger if born full-term, 75 percent of all twins die there. That is five times the high mortality rate for single births among the Yoruba.

Just as the birth of twins is greeted with rejoicing, everyone is saddened when a twin dies. Since the Yoruba believe twins have a combined, inseparable soul, the minute one twin dies, the life of the other is in danger because the balance of his soul has been disturbed.

To restore the unit of the soul, the parents commission an artisan to carve a small wooden figure called an ibeji as a symbolic substitute where the soul of the deceased twin will reside. Should both twins die, a pair of ibeji is commissioned.

The ibeji is given ritualistic attention based mainly on the fear that those who do not follow the prescribed procedure are threatened with misfortune. For living or dead, the twins have the power to cause sickness, even the death of parents and siblings. If the ibeji is not properly honored, a woman may be unable to bear more children or the surviving twin may be beckoned to the spirit world by its mate.

The mother decorates the body of the ibeji with camwood powder and trinkets and the hairdo with indigo or-more recently-Reckitt's laundry bluing. Makeup sometimes is applied to the face.

At first, the care of the ibeji is entrusted to the mother. If the living twin is a girl, she will care for it as soon as she is old enough. All families have a special place where they keep the ibeji.

The twin figure is clothed, fed, washed, put to bed at night, and honored as if it had lived. The facial features of many images are worn smooth from feeding and washing. When the survivor receives a new garment, the ibeji will also be given a new one. It will take part in all rites of passage of the living twin. When the twin marries, the twin figure may also be given a wood-carved mate.

In modern times, traditional Yoruba dolls called "children of wood" are sometimes used in place of ibeji in some areas of Yorubaland. These dolls have simplified, flat bodies and naturalistic heads.

In some cases, plastic dolls are taking over the ritual functions. The most recent development is the use of photographs to represent the deceased twin. After the surviving child is taken to a studio to be photographed, two copies of the picture are made and hung together in a frame on the wall. Weekly food offerings are placed on a table beneath the photographs.

Despite the variety of images used today, the traditional carved figures are still prominent even though the number of carvers capable of producing them is declining.

by Judy Clouston

DID YOU KNOW?

- About one in every 80 births in the U.S. is a twin birth. The twinning rate for African-Americans is approximately one in 73 births. For American whites it is nearly one in 93 births.

- In Ireland, twins occur about once in every 77 births.

- Asian peoples tend to have twins only about once in every 155 births.

- Fraternal twins occur more frequently than identicals in general. However, in Japan there are two sets of identicals born for every set of fraternals.

- The fraternal/identical ratio for American whites is about 65 fraternals for every 35 identicals. For American blacks, there are about 70 fraternals for every 30 identicals.

- The worldwide individual twin count is close to 125 million.

- The twinning rate for identicals is about the same throughout the world, ranging from 3.5 to 4.0 for every 1,000 births.

- One in every four identical twin babies are mirror-image twins because of a delayed splitting of the egg.

- For every 80 sets of twins, one set of triplets is born.

- The chance of having quadruplets is literally one in a million.

- Quintuplets are very rare indeed, occurring once in every 20 to 40 million births.

- The likelihood of a mother having fraternal twins increases as she ages, reaching a peak at age 35.

- In general, identical twins are believed to be a chance event not caused by hereditary factors. However, it is now thought that a tendency to have identical twins could be hereditary in a few cases.

Post Card Pairs from the Past

by Marjorie W. Uhrich

Imagine having twins 80 years ago, before the many modern baby-care conveniences and the advanced medical technology we enjoy today were available. It was a time when twins were born less frequently and were usually unexpected.

It was also a period known as the Golden Age of the Picture Post Card. Between 1898 and 1915, post cards were published by the tens of thousands for virtually every holiday, topic, town, and event. They commonly sold for a penny, could be mailed for the same amount, and were proudly displayed in albums in family parlors. These cards, preserved today by collectors, provide a glimpse into our society during that time, including its curious and often humorous attitudes toward those rarely born babies called twins.

My fraternal twin sons were born in March 1987. I will admit that for many months, my 25-year-old hobby of post card collecting, called deltiology, took a definite back seat to diapers, feedings, and sleep-when I could get some! But as I gradually found the time and opportunity to renew my collecting actively at flea markets, post card shows, and post card club meetings, I focused my interest on a new category-post cards about twins-and my collection has now grown to over 100 such cards.

In the early 1900s, the story about the baby-delivering stork provided a popular theme for birth announcement post cards. Many cards from those days depict the faithful stork carrying bundles, buntings, or baskets filled with two infants, frequently balanced on his back in a yoke or saddle-like arrangement. Occasionally, the stork chose to ride an old bicycle or drive an automobile.

One card shows the stork returning to his nest with a bandaged bill and exclaiming to his wife, "A hard day, my dear-five twos, two threes and fourteen singles! Gee! How my bill aches!" Another pictures the stork and two babies on a rooftop, with the stork calling down the chimney, "Hello! Are you there? I've brought you twins."

In addition to delivery via stork, there are numerous old post cards which present a more realistic picture of birthing practices of the time. Those pertaining to twin or other multiple births are usually comic in style, with the expectant father being told the surprising extra news by the nurse in attendance. One card keeps the verbal caption short and simple-"Two!!"-and lets the frantic expression on the father's face tell the rest.

It is very interesting to note that although the fathers were not usually participants in infant care, numerous cards feature Dad while his wife sleeps or pushing them in double strollers with greetings such as, "Cheer up, it might be worse" and "May your trouble never come in doubles." He feeds them with old-fashioned baby bottles, or rocks them by the fireplace and dreams a romantic picture of his courtship days long ago. One of a series of cards featuring poetic verses and harassed fathers with increasing numbers of infants shows the father holding his quiet twins and states, "Two little darlings! The die is cast, Happy they are now-how long will it last?"

Post cards showing happy, peaceful twins are the exception, however. There are a few with twins sharing a bottle, but most multiples are depicted as a fussy, crying duet. As one card so accurately describes it, "Two of anything make a pair...but two of these make a howling mob!" A card featuring wailing triplets in an old tin bathtub has a humorous verse, "They grew in beauty side-by-side; they fill'd one home with glee."

In contrast to the comic images are, perhaps, the even more interesting ones captured on real photo post cards. Just as we take and send photographs today, these sepia or gray-tone black-and-white photo cards provide excellent pictures of twins that were sent to friends and family to keep in touch.

Photo cards of older twins are less common, but my collection includes one of little twin girls labeled on the message side as "Dorothea and Doris-age 2 years, 5 months." Another shows twin boys about 4 years old with buttons on their short pants, bows at their necks and true soup-bowl haircuts.

Hazel and Helen at age 12 appear on yet another card, dressed in identical clothing with high-button shoes and bows in their ringlet-curled hair. A most unusual real photo post card is of elderly twin ladies taken in September 1906 labeled "age 76."

Several other types of post cards highlight "special" sets of twins. For example, two series of cards were published in 1906 featuring the still-popular Sunbonnet Twins who always wore blousey red dresses and white bonnets which obscured their faces. The first of the series was of the days of the week and the other was of various popular phrases such as "Should Auld Acquaintance Be Forgot."

A card published in 1907 pictured "The Happy Baldwin Twins," two apple-headed boys playing leap-frog. A puzzle-type card labeled "Simple Arithmetic" illustrates two parents, minus one daughter, plus one boyfriend, married by one preacher, equals twins!

Another interesting card presents a nurse holding boy-girl twins dressed in long gowns with blue and pink ribbons. This card reads, "When upon this event your thoughts are intent, if to make up your mind you feel loath; which would give you most joy, a girl or a boy, this will settle the question-Have Both. A Double Event."

Perhaps my favorite verse appears on an "Award for Patience" card showing twins on an old ribboned-medal: "I hope as your most Treasured Gift this medal you'll preserve it, and if you haven't won it yet, let's hope you'll soon deserve it."

Just as patience is important when raising children, it is also important when pursuing a collecting hobby. I often look through hundreds of post cards, organized by the sellers under such categories as children, comic, and real photo, before finding one or two cards with twins.

Today's prices for twin-related post cards can range from $0.50 to over $15 each. For those interested in learning more about the subject or starting their own collection, there are many books available about post cards.

I recommend *The Book of Postcard Collecting* by Thomas E. Range, an introductory reference which includes a listing of post cards collectors' clubs and a helpful bibliography.

In some ways, people's fascination with twins hasn't changed much in 100 years. They still find twins to be a source of humor and curiosity, and exclaim the familiar phrase, "Double trouble!" In fact, old post cards, while illustrating just how different things were so many years ago, are some of the clearest evidence

I've seen of the fact that the more twins change, the more people's reactions to them stay the same!

———————————————————— ❦ ————————————————————

Oh! The Things People Say!

By Anne Hancock Kirley

All twins and their parents live with the simple fact that multiples routinely elicit comments, often very personal comments, from total strangers as well as casual acquaintances. They discover, if they did not already know, that there is a fascination about twins that crosses all economic, social, and ethnic barriers. The similarities and differences between twins and the special closeness they share make them intriguing not just to the professionals who study twins, but to the general public, as well.

People also appear to assume a certain familiarity with twins making conversation with them or their parents upon sight-even though they don't know the family. Maybe you can remember commenting on someone else's cute twins before you became a parent of multiples. I can. But I was never aware of the truly incredible things people say to or about twins until I was the one pushing my own twins in their double stroller.

Since I've been a mother of twins for eight years, I've answered what must be thousands of questions about my identical sons. I began to wonder about the effect of all of these comments on twins, in general, and my sons, in particular. I wondered about the effect of all of the extra attention twins received from strangers. Of particular concern to me were the possible negative effects of comments that compare one twin unfavorably to the other. After I could not find anything published on the subject, I contacted a child psychologist, asking him how twins would be affected by being the subject of all these "twin-type" comments.

He told me that my concerns were unfounded and assured me that all siblings were compared with one another, usually with no lasting ill effects.

I still wasn't sure whether or not I believed him. So, I decided to ask twins themselves, as well as their parents. I interviewed identical and fraternal twins (and one set of triplets) of all ages-some I'd known for years, while others I met through friends, in the checkout line in the grocery store, or movie theaters. The twins, of course, were each unique, but their responses were all surprisingly similar.

Twin-type comments can conveniently be divided into the following three categories: **General Interest, Comments, and Questions** cover almost anything that is neutral or positive that an interested passerby says or asks about twins.

"Are they twins?" is the typical questions in this category. That question sounds so innocent, but it can be annoying to a new twin mother who has been up half the night consoling two colicky babies who couldn't possibly look like anything *but* twins.

Often, "Are they both boys?" is the next question. And then, "Well, then they are identical." I've always found it surprising that people assume that same-sex twins must be identical. But one hardly wants to explain the difference between fraternal and identical twins to the lady at the grocery store who stopped on her way to the cottage cheese to admire the howling infants in the cart of their bedraggled-looking mother.

One mother of twins said that she got so tired of question-and-answer sessions that she would cut the conversation short by denying that her fraternal twin sons were twins at all! No one ever knew what to say after that, she claimed, and she would not be detained any longer by that curious passerby.

I seriously considered attaching a posterboard placard to the front of my sons' double stroller with answers to the most frequently-asked questions printed in bold letters-"Yes, they're twins," "No, they were not simultaneously breastfed," etc. (I was always shocked by the number of total strangers who would ask me that last questions.) This placard idea is not original though, as I once saw a small sign affixed to a double stroller simply proclaiming, "Yes, they're twins."

Many of the people who make a general interest comment, or who ask twin-specific questions, turn out to be a twin themselves or somehow related to twins. Occasionally, I even pick up a valuable twin-parenting tip from these conversations.

Of course, the comments about twins change somewhat as the subjects grow older. For instance, no one now has to ask me "Are they boys?", or even, "Are they identical?" since the answers to these questions have become more apparent as my sons approach their eighth birthday. Once my sons graduated from the twin stroller at age 2 1/2, their twinship became less obvious to the untrained eye, and the frequency of the general-interest comments diminished. About the same time, I stopped dressing them alike, which I had done until that time so that they wouldn't "clash" as they were perched side by side in their twin stroller. (It is embarrassing to admit that!) The elimination of matching outfits further reduced the number of general-interest twin comments.

However, as my sons left the "adorable baby stage" and entered the "wild-child stage," a new type of comment began to predominate. These comments make up what I call the second category, the **"Double-Trouble Genre."** Typically brief, these comments are usually trite and almost always negative. Saying that twins must be "double trouble" is a prime example. Among all of the twins and parents of twins whom I talked to, this was one of the most prevalent, and least liked, of all of the comments. Perhaps it is because there is the obvious threat of the self-fulfilling prophecy that "double trouble" entails; what parent wants her twins to think of themselves as really being "double trouble"?

Certainly, there are other comments in this category. All parents of twins can recite various versions of the following negative comments: "Boy, have you got your hands full"; "I don't envy you"; "What do you do with your spare time"; and "I'm glad they're yours and not mine." These comments may make twins and their parents bristle, but few parents admitted that they made any retort to them.

One mother of 15-month-old identical twin sons said that she always answers negative comments with a positive comeback. Some of her examples were, "No, they're double pleasure," or "I'm glad they're mine and not yours, too."

A mother of twins may roll her eyes or groan inwardly when she hears her twins called "double trouble" for the one-millionth time that day, but there is another type of comment that all parents of multiples especially dread hearing, and having their children themselves hear. I am referring to the third category, the **Comparative Comment.**

In any family it is hard, and even impossible, to avoid comparing siblings. It is a common parental fear that often-repeated sibling comparisons may damage the siblings' relationship and the self-image of the habitual "loser" of the comparison. All comparisons do have "winners" and "losers." "Jake is so much taller than Brian," "Elisa is a better student than Erika," or "Bobby is so happy and involved in school, but Jack just stays off to himself" are three such examples. Parents may carefully avoid making such comparisons in front of their children, but others often are not as thoughtful. No matter how guarded parents may be to avoid making these verbal comparisons in front of their twins, the twins often will be with peers, relatives, and even teachers who are quick to pick up some performance, growth, or behavior discrepancy between them.

While many parents of twins will try to negate these remarks, as the twins themselves mature, each co-twin often takes on this job himself. Many twins also told me that they had purposely developed different interests and pursued divergent areas of study that, ultimately, lead to diverse careers just to limit these almost constant comparisons.

Based on my research, I found that parents of twins worry more than their offspring about the effects of these comparative comments, possibly because they fear showing favoritism themselves. In fact, it has been suggested by some researchers that parents may foster perceived differences in their twins to make them seem less alike and more like siblings than twins so that comparisons are less valid.

Relatively speaking, twins (and their parents) did not react as adversely to being quizzed regarding the general and more intimate aspects of their twinships as they did to comparative comments. Several twins and their parents said, in an embarrassed sort of way, that they often enjoy the comments directed at them concerning twins. The things people say, it seems, contribute to the "special" feeling of being a multiple.

My sons' pediatrician once told me that all of the interest people have in twins (and the comments that come from this interest) compensate for some of the *individual* parental attention that young twins must forfeit because of their parents naturally divided time. Certainly, parents of young twins are made to feel special and, thus may feel compensated for the extra labors of love that they perform for their young charges. On especially hectic days, it would be nice to make it through the supermarket without giving a narrative on the joys of twin parenting, but then maybe *that* is what "double trouble" is all about.

"THE ONLY WAY I COULD COPE..."

I didn't want to leave the house ever again. I couldn't face going into public with my babies and answering those questions one more time. For me, it began when my triplets were about 4 weeks old.

I had heard about all the commotion at the nursery windows but experienced very little of it firsthand. For seven days, I was protected by a very loving nursery staff. My super healthy babies weighed a total of 18 1/2 pounds and were "trouble free." The nurses would tell me what people at the nursery window would discuss about the babies and me. "I heard the mother was very tall; that's why she could carry them so long," one person would say. Another might comment, "She must have had very good nutrition." At the time, I thought it humorous for perfect strangers to be discussing my life, but now I believe it was the beginning of the "invasion."

We all came home after being in the hospital for seven days, and everything was wonderful. So wonderful that, after several days, I thought it was time to get back to resuming a semi-normal life. Making a few short trips to run to the doctor's office and the department store, for example, seemed a logical place to start.

Of course, crowds formed everywhere we went. And then the questions began. You know which ones. Ones to which people won't remember the answers, ones that are none of their business, and ones that are plain ignorant-like asking if having triplets was a surprise. I should have worn a sign: "No, I planned this from the beginning."

Somewhere between the crowds and the questions, I went crazy. The emotion came gradually, but strong. From that point on, every time I needed to go somewhere with the babies, I would almost get sick to my stomach. More than the annoyance of the questions, I was afraid I would get somewhere and the babies would all start to fuss. It had happened before. People would still gawk and ask questions above the screams as if they couldn't hear the babies cry. I'd feel so trapped.

The obvious answer to the problem was not to leave the house. I knew it was crazy, but it seemed to be the only way I could cope just then.

Luckily somewhere between the babies' 6- and 9-week birthdays, those desperate feelings went away as gradually as they had come. I don't know exactly when, but I have a good idea how.

During that time, my family and some friends of ours went on a vacation, of sorts. (Does anyone vacation with seven children?) We had many family members and friends with us wherever we went. They each knew that I was experiencing problems with this "going into public" situation. So between my husband and everyone else, I never had to push the stroller, answer questions, or talk to anyone.

More often than not, passersby would assume that the person "behind the wheel" was the parent, and I usually faded into a store or someplace else depending on where we were. If people asked where the triplet's mother was, a general nod and an, "Over that way," became the standard answer. My "stand-ins" all enjoyed the attention and didn't mind talking to everyone, or being stared at, and I thoroughly enjoyed being anonymous.

I remember one specific incident where my brother, sister and I were in a toy store, and my niece was outside in the mall with the stroller. I had been telling my brother earlier about feeling mobbed wherever I went. We walked out of the store and saw at least 15 people crowded around the stroller. In my state of mind, it looked more like 50! We stood and observed. You'd think people had nothing better to do, I thought to myself. I was just fine until someone asked, "Where's the mother?" My niece pointed to me and grinned. I smiled and walked quickly past the crowd, jabbering at my brother so as not to be addressed. I knew then that being one of the crowd, instead of the center of it, would get me through this hard time.

I have on several occasions in my life been in the limelight or the focus of attention, but I never felt like a circus act before. I was neither prepared for my emotions, nor well-equipped to deal with them. I'm sure there were times that I appeared rude in public, but most of the time it was an inner battle. Some people have been kind; most are overwhelmed wondering how I manage my multiples. Of course, I don't know how I "do it." I only know that it isn't easy, and handling the public is more difficult than all of the diaper changes and feedings put together!

As I write this, my two girls and boy are only 12 weeks old. I know there are so many new experiences waiting for us, but at least I've adjusted some to taking my babies out. I'm confident that the worst is behind me. I have learned that when I'm in a hurry, if I walk quickly and do not make eye contact with anyone, I can go uninterrupted for the most part. If I stop to answer questions, I might as well set up a booth and sell tickets! Even so, it's still comforting to take someone along who is willing to answer all those questions.

by Kree Manchan

More Than One Set of Twins: The Odds and Odysseys

by Judy Westman, M.D.

The two questions asked of every parent with more than one set of twins (and worried about by every parent of a single set of twins) are, "What are the odds of having two sets of twins in the same family?" and "Do twins run in your family?"

Identical twins are not normally conceived more than once in a family except by pure coincidence. The odds of having two sets of identical twins are at least one in 70,000. There have been a few families reported, however, who do seem to have identical twins as a familial pattern.

The likelihood of the same family conceiving fraternal twins in many generations is greater, however. In other words, fraternal twins are more apt to "run" in families. Fraternal twins occur as a result of several eggs being released by the mother at the same time, an event controlled by the level of follicle-stimulating hormone (FSH).

The tendency to have high FSH may be passed along in a family, but would only affect twinning if it occurred in women. Female fraternal twins have an increased chance to have fraternal twins at an actual rate of one in 60 births or more. Male fraternal twins are not at any increased risk for having twin children. Sisters of fraternal twins also produce twins at a high rate. Brothers do not, though their daughters may. Daughters of female and male fraternal twins are more apt to have twins themselves, though this is not necessarily so for the sons of female and male fraternal twins. Because the daughters of male fraternal twins are more likely to have twins themselves, it appears that twins "skip" a generation, but this also is not necessarily the case.

Once a woman has had a set of fraternal twins, her risk of having another set is three times that of the general population. The odds of having two sets of fraternal twins is therefore one in 3,000.

The incidence of fraternal twinning also increases in older mothers, just as the incidence of Down Syndrome increases. Women between 35 and 39 years have a 10-fold higher chance of having twins than teenage mothers. Women who take fertility drugs have an increased chance of having fraternal twins and other fraternal multiples because these drugs stimulate FSH and therefore produce more eggs to be fertilized.

Going off the birth control pill also stimulates FSH and therefore promotes fraternal twinning. Most physicians recommend the use of an alternative form of birth control for three to six months after stopping oral contraceptives if the woman wants to become pregnant, but also wants to decrease the risk of having twins.

Twins in the Spotlight

by Alysia Lewis Harris

Hollywood...the glitter...the glamour...the sparkle of the silver screen. Maybe it seems like a fairy tale or a dream, but for some, dreams do come true.

Even when my identical twin sons, Jarret and Garrett, were only one month old, I dreamed of seeing them on television. So, when they were 5 months old, I began submitting their pictures to agents. A few weeks after my first submission, a girlfriend told me about an open interview she was attending with her daughter. I decided to go with my twins, but when we arrived at the casting office, my heart sank-approximately 200 children were waiting in line!

We took our place in line, but I didn't expect to stay long enough to take pictures or talk to anyone. One of my girlfriend's daughters began walking around with one of my twins just to pass the time. A few minutes later, she came back with the casting director. He told us that the producer of the made-for-television movie, "Shattered Vows," needed twins, and he wanted to send my sons' pictures to the production company.

My twins did get the part! They even had their own dressing room with "Harris Twins" and a star on the door.

I soon learned that twins are often requested by producers because production time is expensive and minors can only work for a limited time, especially when they are under 6 years of age. When using identical twins, one child is filmed for a while, then the children are switched and nobody ever knows the difference. In one scene for the movie, for example, even I had a hard time trying to tell the difference between my own twins.

According to Marilyn Schoeman of the Shoeman Talent Agency, being parents of twins who are in entertainment is a stressful situation. "Often the production company will have a morning call for one child and an afternoon call for the second child. Just this separation of the twins for three or four hours is difficult," she explained.

Rules and regulations governing the hours minors can work in the entertainment industry are categorized by age groups. Infants who are 15 to 180 days of age are limited to two hours on the set-20 minutes at work and one hour and 40 minutes of recreation time. Of those 20 minutes, a baby can only be under the lights for 20 seconds at a time. Babies who are 6 months to 24 months of age can only be on the set for a total of four hours, work and recreation time is divided equally. Children who are 2 to 5 years old can work three hours of the total of six hours on the set. Children 6 to 18 years old have a total of eight hours on the set-four hours at work, three hours for school work, and one hour for recreation. Rules also stipulate that when a minor is on the set, a studio teacher must be provided.

Until about 20 years ago, no laws existed to regulate the money made by minors in the entertainment industry. Now the Jackie Coogan Law provides for a percentage of the money (around 25 percent, and not to exceed 50 percent of the net income) to be placed into a "box account" for the child. This law states that the remaining percentage is to be controlled by the parents of the young actors. This law also applies to any work on videotapes, such as a television series or soap opera.

Currently, there are no laws for work done for commercials or advertisements; the entire amount made is controlled by the parents. Commercials on an average can pay $15,000 to $20,000 each. Compensation for commercials is based on a sliding scale divided into cycles. Residuals are paid each time the commercial is aired. In the case of multiples, each child appearing in the final production is paid; however, if one child is edited out, he does not receive residuals. Each child also receives pay for interviews and production time. In commercial advertising, children cannot appear simultaneously in advertisements for similar products.

My advice to any mother who wants to pursue a career for her child is for her to be *absolutely certain* that she wants to do it. It's hard work, especially when there are two or more children involved.

DOUBLEMINT GUM TWINS: A CASE HISTORY

When a nationwide talent search for twins to appear in a commercial for Doublemint gum was announced over radio stations in nine U.S. cities, the stations were inundated with phone calls and photos from 1,500 sets of twins.

At stake was a fleeting appearance in a television commercial in which identical twins have been showing consumers how to "double your pleasure, double your fun with Doublemint gum" since 1959.

Sifting through hundreds of photographs, the casting agencies called in the most promising candidates for auditions to identify the twins with the best combination of looks and talent.

Final auditions were held in Los Angeles where twins vying for one of the spots in the cast found there was an art to chewing gum on camera.

After an unusually long auditioning process, four sets of twins had not only demonstrated their ability to have fun while chewing gum, but they also had met the specialized requirements for the commercial's cast, which was developed around a bluegrass theme.

"We had four callbacks; it was really nerve-wracking," said Liz and Jean Sagal afterwards. Professional dancers, the Sagals had just completed dance parts in the movie, "Grease 2." Their youthful vitality, which never flagged during the lengthy auditioning process, won them the double kicking part in the Doublemint commercial.

Tom and Bob Holst also survived four callbacks before they were picked as the banjo players. In their thirties, the Holsts had their last acting roles when they were infants double cast in a Barbara Stanwyck movie.

Blond and beautifully photogenic, Randi and Candi Brough have been performing in tandem since they were three-year-old youngsters growing up in Indiana. "Coordinating our movements is second-nature," said the Broughs, who were cast as the "double-howdy" twins.

Reprinted with permission.
Courtesy of the Wm. Wrigley Jr. Company

CASTING DIRECTORS AND AGENTS SAY...

According to Pamela Campus, an independent casting director and head of Campus Casting, parents need to help their twins be outgoing, responsive, smart, "with it" kids, in order to prepare them for casting calls. A number of agents recommend giving children acting classes or commercial workshops. These classes reduce shyness, instill confidence, and help children know what to expect when they are called upon to show off during auditions.

As all parents of multiples are aware, each child is different. When trying out for a role, one twin may make a better impression on the casting director than his co-twin. "We often meet one twin who is real quiet and one who is real outgoing," remarked Carolyn Thompson, a children's agent with Caroline Leonetti Talent in Hollywood. "I represent one set of twins. When they go out together, the one twin with more sparkle is always chosen over the other."

"Sometimes one twin is almost a star type of personality, and the other one is rebellious," Campus noted. "A parent needs to be aware of each child's individual personality. If a child doesn't show interest, don't push him into performing."

Casting director, Margery Simkin of New York, offers the following additional advice to parents of multiples:

1) Be wary of unscrupulous people. Anybody who says you have to spend hundreds of dollars to get your children into commercials should be avoided. Obtain a list of franchised agents from your local office of the Screen Actors Guild, or in Southern California, send $3 (check or money order payable to SAG--no cash, please) plus a business-sized self-addressed stamped envelope to Screen Actors Guild, Attn: Receptionist, 5757 Wilshire Blvd., Los Angeles, CA 90036.

2) It's not necessary to immediately get expensive pictures taken. For twin infants, a color snapshot showing the children's hair and eyes is sufficient. Get professional photos, first an 8 x 10, and later composites, for children over 4 years of age. Plan on spending up to $200 a year on photos, once your children are seriously involved.

3) Decide if you're willing to have your multiples take roles separately. They have very individual personalities, of course, so prepare yourself and your twins for the possibility that one may get more work than the other.

4) Understand that there is not an enormous amount of work for multiples. Your best bet is to approach it as a special, once-in-a-while thing, and enjoy it for the entertainment value.

5) Realize that having children in show business is a tremendous commitment for the parents. You have to be available, sometimes on short notice, and willing to drive your kids all over town for auditions and work. Once they get jobs, you (or someone you designate) need to spend hours on the set with them.

6) Although your children are very special to you, they will not always be right for the part. Prepare yourself and your children for disappointment.

Most show business work is found in major cities such as Los Angeles, New York, Chicago, Dallas, Atlanta, and San Francisco. Be sure to let your local Mothers of Twins club know of your interest; agents and casting directors often contact them as a resource.

by Susan Perry

The Unusual Single Child

by Carey Winfrey

For three-and-a-half years after my twin sons, Graham and Wells, were born, my wife, Jane, and I wondered-on those rare occasions when we found a second or two to wonder about anything-what we'd gotten ourselves into. We were zombies living in a permanent state of sleep deprivation; there always seemed to be at least one baby awake, and one's wails or upsets acted on the other like a catalyst.

Then, miraculously, the tide turned, and our burdens changed into...well, not angels exactly, but manageable, sweet-tempered, very individual boys. Boys who slept through the night. Boys who actually liked playing together. Boys who could keep themselves occupied for hours at a time.

Ah, twins, we said (and still say). How could we be so lucky? The only liability is the world's tendency to treat them as a unit, as curiosities or freaks. It's understandable, of course, but it's also enough to set one to musing about what things might be like if twins were the norm. How would an average person look at the unusual single child?

I've always been fascinated by singletons. I was introduced to the mother of a singleton at a cocktail party the other day, so of course the first thing I asked was, "Do singletons run in your family?" The answer to that one was yes (it usually is); but contrary to popular belief, she told me, singletons don't necessarily skip a generation-in fact, her husband was a singleton, too. I guess there's as much misinformation going around about singletons as about multiples.

The next thing I asked was, did they know they were going to have a singleton beforehand, or did it come as a surprise? These days, with sonograms and amniocentesis, most do know in advance. Good thing, too-imagine buying a double stroller and double crib and having people give you two sets of rompers, and then having only one baby to use it all!

So then naturally I inquired, "Unsplit or blighted?" And she didn't even know. It's amazing how many parents don't know whether their singleton resulted from a fertilized egg that failed to split or from a twin conception that didn't fully develop.

You'd be surprised how many famous people are singletons. President Bush is a singleton. So is Vice President Quayle. Sonny and Cher, both. Margaret Thatcher, Muhammad Ali, even Yasser Arafat (not to mention Ariel Sharon). It's quite a list. This woman tried to tell me that Elvis Presley was a singleton, but I knew better. Technically he's not; his twin brother was stillborn.

After a while, she seemed to be put off by all my questions; you can't be too careful, because some parents of singletons are like that. I don't know why-you'd think they'd be flattered by my interest. I mean, it's not as if a singleton is a freak. Like the time I asked my friend Ed, "How's the singleton?" He got all huffy. "Look," he said, "my daughter has a name. It's Alice. I'd prefer that you use it."

If I sense that the parent of a singleton doesn't mind my questions, I keep asking them. I just can't help it. The whole idea of singletons is so...mysterious. And so inefficient. I mean, one man, one vote, that's one thing. But one pregnancy for each kid?

What must their home be like. With twins, it's a front-row seat at the circus; they're always on, caroming off one another, riffling, giggling, egging one another on, them against us. And the fighting! Sometimes I feel more like a referee than a father. But there's never a dull moment, that's for sure.

Oh, there are a lot of questions I ask.

"Doesn't he get lonely?"

"Who does he play with?"

"Do you have to entertain him all the time?"

"Is he different from any older or younger sets of twin siblings, in appearance or temperament or both, as with my boys?" Sometimes that question gets me a look that says: "Whatsamatta you?"

And how does a singleton parent know how he's doing? It must be hard. When a singleton acts up, the parent doesn't know if it's his fault or not. The twin parent, with a control child for comparison, knows he's blameless.

No wonder singleton parents seem so serious. Sometimes I tease them. "Single schmingle!" I say. Okay, maybe it's not as cute as "Double Trouble!" But it's catchy.

Singletons themselves are sometimes touchy, too. No wonder. All the other kids are always being asked, "Which one are you?" But the singleton has to stand alone; there's no equivalent question for him, unless it's the "unsplit/blighted" query. And the kids are usually no better than their parents on that one; they don't have a clue.

I guess I shouldn't be surprised, since not much is known about singletons, even by scientists. No one is certain why some eggs fail to split into identicals, or why, in the rarer women who produce two eggs at a time and have fraternal twins, only one egg gets fertilized or the second fertilized egg fails to develop.

But there I go again, turning into a singleton bore. You'll have to forgive me. It's just that I've always found singletons so...*singular*.

CHAPTER 2

The Importance of Twintype

"Now I Know They're Fraternal!"
by Kenneth Ward, M.D.

Most twins are fraternal, otherwise known as non-identical or dizygotic twins. Fraternals are the result of two different eggs being fertilized and resulting in two completely distinct and separate pregnancies in the womb at the same time. On rare occasions, the two conceptions even occur one month apart! Identical or monozygotic twinning, on the other hand, occurs when a single conception splits into two around the time that the pregnancy is implanting in the womb (between the fourth and twelfth day of development). Monozygotic twins are identical in the sense that they have the same genetic makeup, but they may not be identical in all their behavioral and physical characteristics. (See "They're Identical? No Way!", **TWINS**® Magazine November/December 1994.)

The Parent Trap

Parents are frequently mistaken about the twintype of their children. Studies show that parents have a 10 percent chance of being incorrect in determining twintype based on the degree of similarity between their twins (whether they and others never could or always could "tell the twins apart" as they were growing up).

Errors in the twintyping occur because dizygotic twins can look incredibly similar, since, after all, they are siblings with many genes in common. Monozygotic twins sometimes look very different, especially at birth, when their weights tend to vary more than dizygotic twins'. Many traits, such as whether or not the twins are both right-handed, simply are not reliable indicators of twintype. (Handedness is different in 25 percent of monozygotic twins and in 25 percent of dizygotic twins.)

Sometimes parents are misled by their doctor or midwife, who reports the twintype based on an incomplete or erroneous examination of the placenta. Unless the twins are of different sexes or inside a single bag of water (amniotic sac), examining the babies or the placenta with the naked eye is not very helpful.

Certainly, the number of placentas does not predict zygosity, since two-thirds of monozygotic twins have one placenta, and 42 percent of dizygotic twins have a single fused placenta. Many obstetricians try to guess the zygosity based on how thick or thin the membrane between the two amniotic sacs is, or by how easily it can be peeled apart.

However, microscopic examination of the placenta, usually by a pathologists, is the only accurate way to use this intervening membrane to determine zygosity. Unfortunately, even with a detailed examination, the placental membranes can reveal the zygosity of only 35 percent of same-sex twins.

Why You Need To Know

Why go to all of this trouble to determine twintype? Most twins and their families want to know about the twins' zygosity simply out of curiosity. However, accurate determination of zygosity is critical in genetic research which uses twin methods to determine the relative importance of environment versus heredity.

Knowing the twintype can also be important in some medical situations. Medical research is revealing that genetic disease and genetic predisposition to disease are common. If a monozygotic twin exhibits a serious genetic trait, his or her co-twin should be watched carefully for that same trait.

Certainly, developmental differences between the twins might be evaluated differently depending on the twintype. Certain birth defects are more common in monozygotic twins and might be searched for more diligently when zygosity is known. Finally, when transplantation of bone marrow, kidney or other tissue is necessary, monozygotic twins are perfect "matches" while the blood types of dizygotic twins may not match at all. (Of course, doctors may not want tissues from one monozygotic twin to treat his or her co-twin if the disease being treated is genetic.)

Zygosity can also be determined by examining various, simple-inherited traits like blood groups, HLA types, protein markers, DNA markers, and physical characteristics and measurements. If the twins differ for any two traits, they are classified as dizygotic. If all traits examined are the same, monozygosity is not proven, but the probability that the twins are monozygotic is not proven, but the probability that the twins are monozygotic can be calculated.

For decades, twin testing was performed by testing dozens of major and minor blood "types" in both twins. Blood types are determined by the chemicals which cover our red blood cells. If twins match for every blood type tested, then a calculation is done to determine if this occurred by chance alone. Unfortunately, these tedious calculations depend on knowledge in the frequencies of each "type" in the twins' particular ethnic group. Even after many blood groups are examined, the probability of erroneously classifying twins as monozygotic can be five to 10 percent. Eventually, HLA tests and protein-typing were added to the battery of tests to make blood analysis more accurate, but this also drove up the cost of twin testing.

Twintyping Advances

The use of DNA polymorphisms has improved twin zygosity determination. DNA is the chemical of which our genes are made. The four-chemical subunits of DNA are strung together in a chain like a four-letter alphabet spelling out our genetic instructions. The human instruction manual is made up of roughly three billion letters. Any two individuals have millions of differences in their codes, unless they are monozygotic twins.

DNA polymorphisms are sites in the DNA chain which are extremely variable from one person to the next-sometimes there are dozens of different spellings of the DNA-code in a polymorphic region. Like several other twin-typing techniques, most DNA tests require that a blood sample be drawn on the twins, but DNA polymorphisms are more efficient and more accurate than blood, HLA and protein-typing. Unfortunately, DNA testing is also more expensive, with prices ranging from $200 to $900.

The newest type of DNA markers which have been developed for twin testing are called STAR (short tandem amplifiable repeat) markers. Similar DNA markers are now widely used for genetic research and diagnostic testing. Only small amounts of DNA are required, greatly simplifying DNA purification and sample handling.

For instance, enough DNA can be obtained by swabbing the inside of the cheek, so there is no need to draw blood-an obvious advantage when testing young children. Relatively degraded DNA samples can be used for testing, so samples can be sent by regular mail, thus lowering the cost.

DNA-STAR probes can offer practical advantages over other DNA probes that have been used for twin testing. Tests can be carried out rapidly, in a highly automated fashion, greatly lowering the cost (currently about $90). The results are easy for the lab to interpret, meaning fewer errors. Precisely defined patterns are obtained, and the statistical interpretation is very simple. If the twins match completely, they can be classified as "monozygotic" with greater than 99.98 percent probability, regardless of the particular pattern obtained.

Parents no longer have to wonder if their twins are identical or fraternal. Genetic research has proved efficient and accurate methods for typing twins. DNA tests can now be performed without blood being drawn from the twins, and the cost of testing is finally decreasing as the technologies improve.

What Is The DNA-STAR Test?

My colleagues and I have developed a lower-cost DNA test to accurately determine twin zygosity. The test uses tiny quantities of DNA which can be obtained by gently brushing the inside of a child's cheek with a sample collection brush. For more information, contact Affiliated Genetics, Inc. (801) 298-3366.

Kenneth Ward, M.D., of Salt Lake City, Utah, specializes in high-risk obstetrics and genetics and directs the DNA Diagnostic Laboratory at the University of Utah School of Medicine. He is the father of two.

Males from Opposite-Sex Pairs
by Nancy L. Segal,Ph.D.

Unlike parents of same-sex twins, parents of opposite-sex twins have the advantage of knowing the twintype of their children (fraternal) with complete certainty. However, opposite-sex pairs have been less well studied by twin researchers; consequently, less information about them is available.

Available research does suggest that the experience of twinship for male-female pairs is unique. However, the considerable normal variation in development observed among both male and female children similarly applies to male-female twins. Some male twins may, for example, perform less well on verbal tests than other male twins or non-twins. In contrast, some young male twins may show earlier intellectual or social progress than their sisters. Developmental sex differences may appear exaggerated for male-female twins because the children are the same age.

It is very important for parents to appreciate the individual interests and talents of each child, and in the case of opposite-sex twins, to engage in only very cautious comparisons.

A critical milestone in the lives of all children is entry into nursery school or kindergarten. This may be stressful for those male twins who twin sisters show relatively greater social, intellectual and/or physical progress. Parents and educators need to be especially sensitive and responsive to these kinds of differences in young opposite-sex twins.

Biological Basis

Fraternal twins (opposite-sex and same-sex) occur with approximately equal frequency; so that each represents about one-third of all twins among Caucasian populations. Both types of fraternal twins form from the separate fertilizations of two ova by two spermatozoa. These twins on average share half their genes by descent the same as ordinary brothers and sisters.

The behavioral and physical implications of sharing a prenatal environment with an opposite-sex twin partner have been of considerable interest to psychological and biological researchers. A phenomenon known as the freemartin effect has, for example, been observed among opposite-sex twin cattle, but not among humans. Shared intrauterine circulation between cattle twins leads to sterility in the females, but not the males, a result associated with the females' exposure to circulating male hormones. Prenatal exchange of blood, known as chimerism has, however, been documented in approximately 20 pairs of human fraternal twins, some of which were opposite-sex.

The late Professor Norman Geschwind, Ph.D., at Harvard University, speculated that there might be a relationship between left-handedness and intrauterine exposure to testosterone. He also suggested that this relationship might partly explain the increased incidence of left-handedness observed among twins. He reasoned that a female fetus would be affected by the testosterone produced by her twin brother, thereby increasing the chances that she would become left-handed. Gerschwind's hypothesis remains to be confirmed, but has encouraged further investigation along these lines. A study examining the possible effects of early exposure to cross-sex hormones on the mental abilities of the female members of opposite-sex twin pairs will be discussed in a future article in this series.

Physical Characteristics

A 1966 twin study by Helen Koch, Ph.D., at the University of Chicago, included 19 pairs of opposite-sex twins. Male twins were delivered first in 87 percent of the cases, even in the few cases in which they were not the heavier pair member. This observation has not, however, been confirmed in other investigations. Koch raised the possibility that though a higher death rate among second-born twins indicates that they are at a higher risk of birth trauma, they are not at a higher risk for prenatal mortality. It is important to note that the modest size of her sample may not have produced results representative of opposite-sex twin pairs in general.

The late Ronald S. Wilson, Ph.D., at the University of Louisville Twin Studies, periodically compared mean weight and height among the different types of twins, between the ages of 3 months and 9 years. The sample initially included 231 newborn identical twin pairs, 151 newborn fraternal same-sex twin pairs and 94 newborn opposite-sex twin pairs. (The number of pairs included in each twin group varied at each time of measurement.) Opposite-sex fraternal twins were similar in weight to same-sex fraternal twins until the age of 6 years, after which the opposite-sex pairs averaged 5 kilograms heavier. Height measures were quite similar across the different types of twins.

The extent to which opposite-sex twins may resemble one another in weight and in height may vary with the age at which they are measured. Male and female twin partners had comparable weights at birth, but the male twins gained weight more quickly during the first year of life. Their twin sisters did, however, catch up by the age of 2 years, thereby reducing this difference. Weight differences between male and female twin partners were equal to, or smaller than, weight differences between same-sex fraternal twin partners during the third year of life.

Height differences between fraternal twins increased fairly steadily after birth for both types of fraternal twins. Opposite-sex twins showed larger height differences than same-sex fraternal twins only between the ages of 9 and 24 months. Wilson concluded that "any sex differences in growth were far overshadowed by other factors leading to concordance in opposite-sex pairs."

Studies comparing the physical growth of opposite-sex twins and unrelated non-twin male and female pairs during puberty have been completed by Siv Fischbein, Ph.D., from the Department of Educational Research, at the Stockholm Institute of Education. Participants in this study were part of a Swedish longitudinal twin study, initiated in 1964, when the twins were 10 years of age. Analyses of height and weight, measured yearly between the ages of 10 and 18 for boys and 10 and 16 for girls, have recently been summarized by Fischbein. The twins were consistently more similar in both weight and height than the non-twins, findings that reflect both shared inheritance and environment.

Twin similarity in height was greater than twin similarity in weight at ages 11, 12, 13 and 14 years, but not at age 15 years, at which time a substantial sex-based difference in height was observed.

David R. Shaffer, Ph.D., at the University of Georgia, has defined the term growth spurt as a "rapid acceleration in height and weight that marks beginning of adolescence." The typical female growth spurt occurs between 10.5 and 13.5 years of age, while the typical male growth spurt occurs between 13 and 15.5 years of age. By the age of 15 years, the males' generally greater height and weight, relative to females, is apparent. The unrelated non-twin pairs also showed increasing differences in height after age 15.

Weight differences between twins seemed to level off after age 14 years, while differences between non-twins widened. Fischbein concluded that "sex differentiation at puberty exerts a very powerful influence overshadowing the hereditary and environmental similarities existing for twins." She suggests that Wilson's comments concerning opposite-sex twins similarity in physical growth may apply prior to puberty, but not afterwards.

Mental Abilities

Information on mental abilities has also been gathered on twins enrolled in the Louisville Twin Study. Measurements were taken every few months when the twins were between the ages of 3 and 30 months, and annually when the twins were between the ages of 3 and 6 years. A comparison of within-pair similarity was reported by Wilson in 1981. With the exception of measurements made at 9 months, differences in the magnitude of similarity between same-sex and opposite-sex fraternal twins were not detected. These data are consistent with several previous studies of same-sex and opposite-sex twins and sibling pairs. It is interesting to note that the sex differences in verbal and non-verbal scores were not detected at ages 5 and 6 years.

Wilson notes that his findings are unable to resolve the issue of whether or not parents provided differential encouragement or experiences to male and female children. He does suggest, however, that any sex differences in treatment did not significantly impact upon the test measures. A reanalysis of Wilson's data (complete through 1985) by R. Darrell Bock, Ph.D. and Michelle Zimowski, Ph.D., at the University of Chicago, did detect the expected female advantage in fluent language production, and the male advantage in spatial ability.

Fischbein's work with Swedish twins is informative with respect to their intellectual development during childhood and puberty. Opposite-sex twin and non-twin pairs completed tests of verbal ability, inductive reasoning and clerical speed at the age of 12 years. Differences within both types of pairs were modest, with the exception of the clerical speed test in which the females outperformed the males. The twins were, however, more similar than the non-twins, an effect that Fischbein associated with both shared genes and shared rearing environment. Other studies have revealed a female superiority in verbal skills, so that the results reported here may be somewhat surprising. As Fischbein points out, however, sex differences in linguistic skills become smaller after 3 years of age until 11 years of age. It may be that continued study of this sample will eventually reveal relative female verbal superiority.

Social Behavior

Opposite-sex twin pairs provide a convenient research design for studying the emergence of sex-related differences in behavior. In 1982, Marilyn DeBoer, a graduate student at the University of Chicago, used opposite-sex infant twins to examine sex differences in response to physical play. The study included 10 twin pairs and two triplet sets located in the Chicago area. Infants ranged in age between 4.5 and 6.5 months. Interactions of each twin with the mother and with a stranger were videotaped for analysis.

The results showed that the male twins looked at their mothers' faces more often during physical play than their twin sisters looked at their mothers. This finding was relevant only for periods during which physical play occurred. The majority of the infants smiled more frequently during physical play than during non-physical play. Smiling occurred slightly more often among the males (26.3 percent) than among the females (24.8 percent) during physical play, while smiling occurred more often among the females (12.5 percent) than among the males during non-physical play (7.8 percent). It was also observed that "younger" boys (12-21) weeks, as compared with "older" boys (24-29 weeks) were more attentive to their mothers and smiled more during physical play than their twin sisters. However, the mothers did not engage in more physical activity with the males than with the females. Other investigations have also observed that parents more frequently use physical actions to gain the attention of young infants than older infants.

During periods of both physical and non-physical play, both male and female infant twins looked at the stranger more than at their mothers. Both males and females smiled more at the stranger than at their mothers during non-physical play, but this difference was pronounced for males only. Younger males looked at the stranger more often than did their twin sisters during physical interaction. DeBoer emphasized the importance of considering the context (such as physical activity) in which behavior is being expressed. She suggested that the increased attention to mothers and strangers shown by the males may reflect their higher degree of arousal during physical play, relative to females. Further research is needed to explain the observed sex differences in smiling.

Koch reported differences in social development in the members of 5- and 6-year-old opposite-sex twin pairs. She suggested that some males from opposite-sex twin pairs show less sex-typical behaviors than males from same-sex fraternal twin pairs. For example, these male twins were judged to be less dominant than their twin sisters, and appeared to be somewhat less active than other male twins. Interviews with the children revealed that these male twins were less close to their twin siblings than were other male twins. In addition, they liked the protection and guidance offered by the female twin, but felt somewhat threatened by her social maturity. These male twins did, however, display superior speech ability, relative to other male twins. Koch suggested that members of opposite-sex twins may exert a "tempering effect" on each other's sex-role learning and attitudes."

David A. Hay, Ph.D., and Pauline J. O'Brien, Ph.D., at La Trobe University in Australia, noted that birth order was commonly associated with twins' behavioral differences by parents of identical twins, only rarely by parents of same-sex fraternal twins and never by parents of opposite-sex twins.

Females from Opposite-Sex Pairs

by Nancy L. Segal, Ph.D.

The following story completes **TWINS**® Magazine's exclusive series dedicated to examining the biological and psychological characteristics associated with the various types of twins, and focuses on females from opposite-sex pairs. Because of the many meaningful developmental differences among twintypes, it is inappropriate to formulate principles or practices regarding the rearing of twins in general. It is useful, however, to formulate policies with reference to specific twintypes, insofar as that specific twintype relationship is distinct from both other twintype relationships and sibling relationships in general.

For example, female twins from opposite-sex pairs are most often seen as members of a "hidden" twinship. This is because of one obvious reason-sex differences in appearance. In addition, their interests, peer preferences and style of dress also often contribute to the camouflage of their identify as co-twins. An unfortunate consequence of this situation is that the special circumstances affecting male and female twin children from these twin pairs are often overlooked.

However, there is considerable normal variation among twins of a particular type. Some females from opposite-sex twin pairs will display many of the characteristics described below, while others may appear to be less "typical." Diversity among the female twin population is to be expected and is not a cause for concern. Appreciating the diversity, as well as the commonality, among these special twins is a first step toward ensuring their developmental success.

Biological Basis of Opposite-Sex Twinning

Fraternal twins, whether opposite-sex or same-sex, result from separate fertilizations of two ova by two spermatozoa. These twins share half their genes, on average, by descent, and so are genetically the same as non-twin brothers and sisters. Specific fraternal twin pairs may have relatively higher or lower proportions of shared genes. As a result, some twins may look or behave more alike than others.

Fraternal twins represent approximately two-thirds of all twins among opposite-sex pairs. Fraternal twinning occurs more frequently among black populations and less frequently among Oriental populations, relative to Caucasian populations.

A 1966 twin study conducted at the University of Chicago by Helen Koch, Ph.D., revealed that female twins were born second in 87 percent of the cases and the majority weighed less at birth than their twin brothers. More recent research at the Louisville Twin Study has revealed that birth weight differences between members of opposite-sex and same-sex fraternal twin pairs were similar.

In contrast, opposite-sex twins show larger differences in weight than same sex fraternal twins from 3 to 18 months of age. After 18 months, however, the difference disappears. This was explained by the more rapid early weight gain by males, followed by a gain in weight by females at approximately 2 years of age. Early height differences between opposite-sex twins tend to be most pronounced between the ages of 9 and 24 months, relative to same-sex twins.

Sex differences in physical development are well known to child development researchers. For example, male children generally maintain a height advantage over female children during infancy and childhood. The adolescent growth spurt usually occurs two years earlier for females than for males. At approximately 11 years of age, females become taller and heavier than males. This situation is reversed at about age 14, at which time the adolescent male growth spurt typically begins. These sex differences in growth patterns become quite obvious to families with opposite-sex twins. The female's size advantage at 11 may prove difficult for her male co-twin; efforts should be made to avoid twin comparisons, and male twins should be assured that the situation is likely to change.

Intellectual Abilities

Researchers associated with the Louisville Twin Study compared resemblance in mental ability between same-sex and opposite-sex fraternal twins. Twins were tested between the ages of 3 months and 6 years. Differences were not larger between opposite-sex twins, as compared with the same-sex twins. At 3 months of age, female twins scored slightly lower than their brothers, but at 18 months, female twins outperformed their brothers. At all ages, however, differences between male and female twins were not meaningful.

These findings are generally consistent with studies of intellectual resemblance that have used older opposite-sex twin pairs. The investigators suggested that even if parents provide differential encouragement or experiences to members of opposite-sex pairs, these rearing differences are not substantially impacting upon twins' similarity in overall mental performance.

The psychological literature includes numerous studies demonstrating sex differences in special mental abilities. It appears that females show greater average performance in verbal skills, while males generally excel in tests of spatial ability and mathematical reasoning. It is, therefore, possible that while males and females may not differ in overall level of intellectual ability, their structure or profile of abilities may differ.

Opposite-sex twins offer informative tests of hypotheses concerning influences on special skills. Dr. Shirley Cole-Harding and associates at the University of Colorado compared differences in spatial ability between opposite-sex twins and same-sex fraternal twins. It was of particular interest to compare the performance of females from these two types of fraternal twin pairs. The investigators reasoned that females from opposite-sex pairs might score higher than females from same-sex pairs, due to prenatal exposure to the male hormone testosterone.

Females from opposite-sex twin pairs did, in fact, show superior spatial skills, relative to females from same-sex pairs, and showed greater improvement across trials. Following the last trial, male-female twin differences in performance were not detected. These findings are, thus, consistent with the view that prenatal hormonal influences may be associated with various intellectual skills. Further research is needed, however, to confirm this hypothesis and to consider the possibility that differential rearing experiences for males and females may partly explain the pattern of findings.

Studies of Swedish twins have been extremely informative with respect to identifying the various intellectual strengths of males and females, as well as the bases of these differences. Siv Fischbein, Ph.D., at the Stockholm Institute of Education, has compared the performances of 12-year-old male-female twins and opposite-sex unrelated pairs on tests of verbal ability (a series of words are provided; the opposite of each word must be supplied), inductive reasoning (four groups of letters are presented; the group which does not follow a common rule must be identified); and clerical speed (two-digit numbers are presented; numbers appearing more than once must be detected).

The twins scored lower on all three tests, relative to the non-twins, a finding that was associated with biological prematurity and/or the twin relationship. The only test that showed a genuine advantage for females was the clerical speed test, a finding consistent with previous studies. Females scored higher than the males on all three tests, but the differences were not marked.

Dr. Fischbein collected additional data on these twins when they were 13 years old. These data were additionally examined with respect to social class. Opposite-sex twins from the highest social class group showed the greatest resemblance in verbal ability, while those from the lowest social class group showed the least resemblance. In contrast, resemblance in mathematics achievement was similar across social classes. Dr. Fischbein suggested that verbal ability may be more dependent upon family treatment than mathematics achievement. Additional research in this important area would be welcome.

Social Behavior and Social Relationships

Dr. Koch's study provides a number of findings that help to clarify the behaviors expressed by 5- and 6-year-old females from opposite-sex twin pairs. These female twins in her study felt less close socially to their twin brothers than the fraternal female twins felt toward their twin sisters. The differences were not large, but were noted in several area. Female twins indicated that they were not similar to their twin brothers, nor did they wish to be similar. In addition, they preferred not to have their twin brothers in the same class with them at school. They were less inclined to play with their brothers than fraternal females were to play with their twin sisters. They were also more likely to identify friends of their own than were their twin brothers. These females also indicated an absence of parental impartiality, in that they sensed that their fathers favored them over their twin brothers. Finally, they were judged to be the dominant member of the pair.

The foregoing findings may be explained, in part, with reference to the different developmental patterns of male and female children. These differences have been recently summarized by Laura E. Berk, Ph.D. Females show greater early proficiency in language skills than males. In addition, females outperform males in every area of school achievement, beginning in kindergarten and lasting until third grade.

In contrast, young male children are typically more aggressive and assertive than young females. It is possible that the female twins' increased dominance, as observed by Dr. Koch, may be partly explained by their superior educational performance; this could boost their self-esteem over and beyond that of their brothers. It may also be that prenatal exposure to male hormones may partly influence their social behavior (as well as their spatial ability, as proposed above), although this hypothesis has not been scientifically examined. Clearly, a great deal remains to be understood with regard to the maturational histories of females with male twin partners.

Research Contributions

Opposite-sex twin pairs are largely underrepresented in the psychological twin literature. This is most unfortunate, since these twins have a great deal to reveal about sex differences in development. Social-interactional aspects of these unique twinships may also have important implications for near-in-age, opposite-sex non-twin sibling pairs. The observation that female members of these twin pairs tend to display increased assertiveness relative to their brothers is intriguing, and warrants additional analysis. Clarification of this situation will require the combined efforts of experts representing diverse disciplines.

Research comparing the intelligence test scores of female and male twin partners is currently in progress in Sweden. These studies should prove of considerable interest in the future as the young twins are assessed over time.

Fraternal Male Twins

by Nancy L. Segal, Ph.D.

The successful rearing and educating of multiple-birth children can be best assisted by paying careful attention to features uniquely associated with each type of twins-fraternal and identical. There is, however, considerable normal variation among fraternal male twins. In other words, some of these twin pairs may look and/or behave in ways that are more typical of identical male twins.

A departure from what is considered "typical" does not imply a departure from what is considered "normal." Appreciation of the diversity within twintypes is just as meaningful to parents, educators and researchers as diversity between twintypes.

Biological Basis

Fraternal twins result from the separated fertilization of two ova by two spermatozoa. As a group, these twins share half their genes, on average, by descent. Individual fraternal twin pairs may, however, share relatively higher or lower proportions of common genes.

Genes are present in pairs located on the chromosomes, and each pair member is called an allele. Each fraternal twin has a 50 percent chance of inheriting the same gene (or allele) from each of his or her two parents. Some twin partners will each receive the same gene from each parent; some twins will receive the same gene from one parent and a different gene from the other parent; while other twins will receive different genes from each parent. This process works similarly for all of the genes in the human genome.

While it is theoretically possible for some fraternal twins to share all of their genes, or to share none of their genes, both of these events are virtually impossible. It is estimated that fraternal twins may vary in genetic relatedness between 25 to 75 percent. Genes, thus, explain both similarities and differences between fraternal twins. This same biological relationship also applies to singleton brothers and sisters. In fact, members of some fraternal twin pairs may resemble other siblings in the family more than they resemble each other.

Types of Fraternal Twins

There are several types of fraternal twins, including a third twintype, known as polar body twinning, that has been presented in both the scientific and popular literature. It is thought that equal divisions of the egg prior to fertilization may result in this type of twin. (Polar bodies are produced as the egg undergoes the unusual processes of division before fertilization. Polar bodies are typically smaller than the primitive or mature ovum and are not fertilized.) This type of twin may show unusual genetic similarity of dissimilarity, depending upon embryological events. In 1979, Karen M. Fischer, at the University of Pennsylvania, and Dr. Herbert Polesky, Director of the Minneapolis War Memorial Bank, in Minneapolis, Minnesota, reported an association between the use of clomid (a fertility drug) and polar body twinning.

Fraternal twins occasionally display chimerism, or the presence of more than one distinct red blood cell population. This situation is explained by connections between fused (or joined) placentas. Dr. Victor A. McKusick, at the Johns Hopkins

University, in Baltimore, Maryland, has indicated that either one, or both, pair members may show this condition. These unusual cases pose important implications for the objective determination of twintype. In other words, blood exchanges between fraternal twins might result in similar blood-typing, which would lead researchers to classify them as identical. Superfecundation refers to the conception of fraternal twins, following separate coital acts during the same menstrual cycle. Thus, fraternal twins could conceivably have different fathers, a situation that has been demonstrated in some cases, following extensive blood group examination. Such superfecundated twins are genetically "half-siblings." Superfecundation may cause marked development discrepancies between twin partners.

Finally, superfetation may result from multiple conceptions occurring during different menstrual cycles. Evidence of this process includes delivery of full-term infants separated by weeks or months, and the birth or abortion of twin infants displaying differential developmental status. In 1976, Drs. Sam Rhine and Walter E. Nance studied a family which included six twin pairs born in four consecutive generations, all of which included one normal twin and either a macerated fetus, stillborn or premature infant, and suggested superfetation as an explanation. This work was completed in the Department of Medical Genetics at the Indiana University Medical Center in Indianapolis. The frequency of this type of twinning is unknown.

Language Abilities

Comparisons between twins and singletons help to identify meaningful differences in ability that may be associated (at last in part) with membership in a twin pair. The language abilities of fraternal male twins were contrasted with those of identical male twins and singletons as part of a larger investigation documented by Helen Koch, Ph.D., at the University of Chicago, in 1966. Language skills were assessed by four measures: mothers' estimate of language progress at school entry; teachers' ratings of speech form and structure; tape recordings of children's stories told in response to a picture series (Children's Apperception Test, or CAT); and the number of errors in form and structure detected in these stories.

Males, in general, did not perform as well as females in linguistic abilities, a finding that has been implicated by many child development researchers. Relative to singleton males, fraternal male twins were rated lower in articulation and showed a higher frequency of structural errors. They were also described as "less talkative" at school than singleton males.

Differences between the fraternal male twins and non-twins were, however, not detected on the other language measures. Dr. Koch suggested that various biological hazards associated with twinning may partly explain the performance of the fraternal males. This group (as well as the identical males and females) scored lower in general intelligence than the fraternal females who proved quite skillful in language abilities.

A 1973 study of reading disability in twins by Harry Bakwin, Ph.D., from the New York University School of Medicine, included 152 fraternal male twin individuals. Twenty-seven children, or 17.8 percent of these twins, were classified as "poor readers," based upon interviews and questionnaires completed by families. The percentage of "poor readers" among the identical and fraternal male twins was the same. In contrast, both twins in only 42 percent of the fraternal male pairs showed reading difficulties, as compared with both twins in 84 percent of the identical male twin pairs. Weight at birth was not related to reading performance. A genetic influence on reading disability was, thus, suggested.

Social Behavior and Social Relationships

Dr. Koch's study provides insightful contrasts between fraternal and identical male twin pairs with respect to social behavior and social relationships. Fraternal male twins said they recognized dissimilarities between themselves and their twin brothers and did not enjoy the same high degree of social closeness nor like to dress alike-two typical characteristics of identical male twins. Dr. Koch suggests that tensions associated with the twinship may be linked to the greater aggressivity and gregariousness displayed by fraternal male twins, relative to identical male twins.

A more recent twin study of Jilla Ghodsian-Carpey, Ph.D., and Laura A. Baker, Ph.D., at the University of Southern California in Los Angeles, examined genetic and environmental influences on aggression using 4- to 7-year-old children. Mothers completed two checklists describing their twins which included behaviors such as teasing, yelling and verbal threats. The results showed that males and fraternal twins displayed greater aggression than females and identical twins.

Interestingly, fraternal and identical male twin pairs did not differ in their degree of aggressivity. The size of the sample was, however, quite modest so that additional analyses are required before definitive conclusions concerning the presence of aggressive behavior across twin groups can be reached.

Research Contributions

Fraternal male twin pairs are critical components of the twin research design, providing important insights into genetic mechanisms associated with various behaviors. David T. Lykken, Ph.D., in the Department of Psychology at the University of Minnesota, has described a process called emergenesis. This process characterizes traits that show a very high degree of resemblance between identical twins, but very little resemblance between fraternal twins. Observations of this kind suggest that the trait in question may be influenced by unique configurations of genes; identical twins share identical configurations which would explain their resemblance, but it would be rare for fraternal twins to inherit the same complex gene configurations. Specific types of brain waves appear to be emergenic traits, for example.

My own studies of cooperation and competition using twin children and adolescents are currently nearing completion. Two fascinating cases have recently come to attention: Families who have adopted non-twin males very close in age and essentially raised them as twins have recently participated in the project. These special pairs of young boys are not twins, but the unique circumstances of their rearing make them excellent choices for evaluating the effects of a common environment upon completely different sets of genes. This is because, like twins, they have been exposed to the same family environmental influences at the same time. Additional cases such as these will, hopefully, come to my attention; females and opposite-sex children would also be welcome.

WHEN IT COMES TO PARENTING...

The unique biological and psychological aspects of fraternal male twins are important to appreciate, both for the purpose of research and for the well-being of the twins themselves. Greater attention to factors affecting language development among fraternal male twins should be a high priority among parents and educators. The possibility that only one pair member may display a language disability is not unexpected in view of their genetic relationship.

In fact, marked differences across many behavioral and physical domains are not atypical for fraternal twins. Loyalty and harmonious relations should be encouraged among all family members, but occasional (even frequent) friction between some fraternal twins is not unusual. In such cases, parents may wish to foster appreciation and respect for each twin's own special talents and preferences.

Some fraternal male twins may physically resemble one another to the point that they are confused by others. Other fraternal male twins may display a close social relationship, preferring each other as social partners relative to other children. Parents of such pairs may question whether the twins are truly identical or fraternal. Doubts about twintype can best be resolved by extensive blood-typing analyses, and parents are encouraged to complete this procedure. Decisions concerning childrearing and development are most effective when based upon the greatest quantity of information

Fraternal Female Twins

by Nancy L. Segal, Ph.D.

There is enormous diversity within the fraternal twin population with respect to resemblance in behavior and appearance. Some fraternal twin partners may show considerable physical resemblance, even to the point of being confused for one another by others, while other fraternal twins may display marked differences in height, weight and facial features. Some fraternal twin partners may show similar intellectual or personality traits, while others may appear to be "opposites." There is, in addition, considerable variation in the closeness of the social bonds shared by the members of fraternal twin pairs.

In short, fraternal twins should not be expected to be alike jut because they are twins. The study of fraternal twins teaches that individual differences among family members are to be respected. Appreciation for the range of fraternal twin "types" is, thus, critical for parents, teachers and social service professionals, who must render informed decisions about the rearing and educating of twins.

This close-up look at fraternal female twin pairs represents the fifth article in a special series on the unique psychological and physical characteristics of the various types of twins. The biological bases of fraternal twinning are explained below. A review of key findings from twin research that specifically apply to female fraternal twins follows.

Biological Bases of Fraternal Twinning

Female fraternal twins represent approximately half the number of same-sex fraternal twins born among Caucasian populations. On average, fraternal twins share half their genes by descent; this is exactly the same genetic relationship shared by non-twin siblings. Fraternal twins result when two separate eggs are fertilized by two separate sperm. The degree of relatedness of these twins varies along a spectrum of genetic relatedness; that is, some fraternal pairs may share relatively higher or lower proportions of genes in common. It is estimated that individual fraternal twin pairs may vary in genetic relatedness between 25 and 75 percent (although, again, *on the average*, fraternal twins share 50 percent of their genes).

Genetic factors underlie similarities *and* differences between fraternal twins. Fraternal twins who share higher proportions of genes in common may, thus show greater resemblance for some traits than fraternal twins who carry relatively fewer genes in common.

The tendency to produce fraternal twins (but not identical twins) appears to be genetically transmitted within families. The pattern of transmission has not, however, been determined. Other evidence to support a genetic influence of fraternal twinning comes from a comparative analysis of twinning rates across different human populations. According to Martin Bulmer, who authored *The Biology of Twinning in Man* in 1970, the fraternal twinning rate is lowest among Oriental populations (approximately 2/1,000 births), intermediate among Caucasian populations (8/1,000 births) and highest among Black populations (as high as 57 per 1,000 births in parts of Nigeria).

It is also of interest that mothers of fraternal twins are taller and heavier, on average, than mothers of identical twins and non-twin children. These physical differences may partly reflect hormonal variations associated with multiple ovulations.

Furthermore, the tendency to have fraternal twins increases with the age of the mother (especially after age 35), and with the number of children to which she has previously given birth.

Examining relationships among families with twins has yielded some fascinating kinships, such as "genetic fraternal twins." For example, there are cases in which identical twins are married to identical twins. The children from these marriages, while legal first-cousins, are also "genetic full siblings" because both sets of parents are biologically equivalent. In the event that the two mothers delivered infants on the same day, these children would be genetically equivalent to fraternal twins!

Handedness

The elevated incidence of left-handedness among twins has long been of interest of psychological and biological researchers. Approximately 12 percent of individuals in the non-twin population are left-handed, while 18-20 percent of twins are left-handed. This figure applies equally to fraternal and identical twins. Furthermore, 25 percent of both fraternal and identical twin pairs include one left-handed member and one right-handed member.

Handedness differences have been associated with late zygotic splitting and adverse birth events among identical twins. Among fraternal twins, opposite handedness has been associated with genetic differences and with differential birth events. Many studies, including those conducted by this author, have observed a greater frequency of left-handedness among male twins than female twins. Left-handedness is also observed more frequently among males than females in the general population.

Verbal Abilities

The verbal skills of fraternal female twins were compared with those of other male and female twins and singletons as part of a major study conducted by Helen Koch at the University of Chicago in 1966. In this study, mothers were asked to estimate twins' language progress at school entry, and teachers were asked to provide ratings of twins' speech form and structure. The researchers provided additional assessments of speech based upon tape recordings of stories told in response to pictures included in the Children's Apperception Test. Teacher and examiner ratings revealed that fraternal female twins outper-formed identical twins, males (but not females) from opposite-sex twin pairs and female non-twins in phonetic, morphological and syntactic features of speech. (Phonology refers to the comprehension and production of speech sounds; morphology refers to the use of grammatical indicators of gender, tense, etc.; and syntax refers to the rules by which words appear in sentences.) It was also found that fraternal female twins told more imaginative stories than fraternal male twins. Overall, the fraternal twins displayed the most advanced language skills of all the twin and non-twin groups.

In reviewing her findings, Dr. Koch suggested that the increased social close-ness of identical twins, relative to fraternal twins, coupled with the high level of sociability of the fraternal females, may underlie the observed twin group differ-ences in verbal abilities. It is, however, also necessary to consider biological prematurity and birth events as possibly influencing twins' mental skills, and leading to differences among twin types; birth histories may prove more difficult for identical twins.

Finally, it is important to recall the considerable behavioral diversity within all twin groups; the findings reviewed above may describe twin groups as a whole, but individual pairs may show significant departures from these general tendencies.

Social Behavior and Social Relationships

The fraternal female twins in Dr. Koch's study were described as the "most vivacious, outgoing subjects." In contrast to the identical female twins, they were less likely to want to be similar to their co-twin, more likely to prefer solitary play to play with the co-twin, more distressed about sharing possessions, and less likely to feel accepted by their co-twin's friends.

These findings capture the generally less intimate social relationships shared by fraternal twins of both sexes, relative to identical twins. The specific mechanisms underlying these differences have not yet been fully identified, but may be associ-ated with the reduced behavioral and physical resemblance of fraternal twins.

A twin study of genetic influences on behavioral deviance was completed in 1985 by Dr. Philip Graham from the Institute of Child Health in London, and Dr. Jim Stevenson from the University of Surrey. Parents of twins were interviewed at home, then were asked to complete a series of questionnaires. The twin sample included 102 identical twin pairs, 111 same-sex fraternal twin pairs and 72 opposite-sex fraternal twin pairs.

Twins from homes with poor marriages tended to show elevated rates of behavioral deviance; this finding was especially true for fraternal girls, though an explanation was not provided. Genetic influences on behavioral deviance were supported by greater identical than fraternal twin resemblance among the males, but not the female twins. It was suggested that parents who misjudged their fraternal twins to be identical rated them more alike than parents who accurately judged their twins to be fraternal.

Research Contributions

Studies of fraternal female twin pairs offer valuable contributions to scientific research. Comparisons between fraternal twins and same-sex sibling pairs may be informative with respect to the effects of arrival into the family at the same time. In the event that social or financial conditions in the family may differ somewhat for each child, this may explain why fraternal twins may be more alike than siblings, despite the same proportion of shared genes. Like their male counterparts, fraternal female twins are often underrepresented in volunteer twin studies. Professor David T. Lykken, in the Department of Psychology at the University of Minnesota, has indicated that fraternal twins who do volunteer for research may be more similar in some ways than those who do not participate.

Triplet sets composed of an identical twin pair and same-sex fraternal co-triplet can be very informative in behavioral science investigations. It becomes possible to arrange three twin pairs from these triple sets: one identical pair and two fraternal pairs. Comparisons of behavioral and physical similarities among the identical and non-identical dyads can highlight the relative contributions of genetic and environmental influences on development.

These sets are rare, though an identical/fraternal female triplet set recently participated in a twin study of cooperation and competition at the University of Minnesota. A similar case was included in the Minnesota Study of Twins Reared Apart, in which identical twin sisters were reunited with each other and with an older sister from whom they had also been adopted away as infants. By pairing the older sibling with each identical twin, two pairs of "pseudo-twins" were created.

Summary

The special psychological and biological features of fraternal female twins are important to appreciate. In view of their genetic differences, these twins should not be expected to be alike in every way (or at all!). Nevertheless, some female fraternal twins may look and act very much alike. It is also the case that some fraternal twins may *not* share close social relationships; in fact, occasional friction between some fraternal twins is not atypical. In contrast, other fraternal female twins will relate in ways that are more typical of identical twins. Research with fraternal females who have lost a twin, and interviews with fraternal twin survivors of the Nazi Holocaust reveal that fraternal twins can be quite close.

Diversity among female fraternal twinships was given considerable emphasis at the beginning of this article. Appreciation and respect for the individual talents and predispositions displayed by each twin is critical to her successful development.

Fraternal twins can best be assisted by parents and teachers remaining sensitive to their individual behavioral styles. A surprising number of people are not fully aware of the important differences among twintypes. Parents can best help their twins by staying alert to these differences, and by seeing to it that others do as well.

Identical Male Twins

by Nancy L. Segal, Ph.D.

Identical twins, which occur in approximately one in 240 births, result from the splitting of a single fertilized egg within one to 14 days following conception. Representing about one-third of the Caucasian twin population, male and female twins occur fairly equally, although there are slightly more male twins at birth. (This observation is also true of the non-twin population; it is thought that the greater vulnerability of male infants than female infants explains their relatively reduced survivability during their early years.)

The additional hazards associated with twinning may place some male twins at elevated risk for birth difficulties or survival. As a result, more females have been observed among triplets sets than males, and fewer males than females have been survivors of monoamniotic multiple-birth pregnancies. (In these pregnancies, identical twins are carried in a single amniotic sac.)

Elizabeth M. Bryan, M.D., has indicated that monoamniotic pregnancies, which are a rare occurrence, may pose a number of intrauterine difficulties for the two fetuses, such as entanglement of the umbilical cords.

Physical and Medical Characteristics

Only a few twin studies of children have reported separate physical characteristics data for males and females. A study of physical and behavioral development in twins was conducted by Helen Koch, Ph.D., at the University of Chicago in 1966. This study included 36 identical male twin pairs, in addition to other groupings of twin and singleton children. The research participants ranged from 5 to 6 years of age.

All the twins, regardless of twintype, were somewhat shorter and lighter than the singleton children. The identical male twins, however, were substantially shorter. This was interpreted as reflecting the prematurity associated with multiple births. The identical male twins were significantly heavier than the males from fraternal twin pairs. It is important to recognize that growth norms for twins, because of their unique prenatal and perinatal circumstances, differ from those that are established for singleton children.

Many identical co-twins, both male and female, show striking similarities in physical characteristics, such as facial structure, dental pattern, and hair color and texture. In addition, some researchers have found that genetic influence on body weight is more pronounced among identical male twins than among identical female twins, especially during the adult years. This may reflect the greater susceptibility of females to hormonal and dietary effects, as well as to various sociocultural influences relevant to body weight.

A recent study by Claude Bouchard, Ph.D., and colleagues at the Laval University in Canada, looked at 12 pairs of identical male twins to examine genetic influences in response to long-term overfeeding. These college students were studied for 100 days, during which time their dietary and exercise regimens were carefully monitored and controlled. The results indicated that while the different twin pairs showed considerable variation with respect to weight gain and fat distribution, the resemblance between co-twins was striking. It was concluded that genetic factors are implicated in response to overfeeding.

Reversals in selected physical characteristics, such as hand preference or fingerprint patterns, are known as mirror-image reversals, and have been observed in approximately 25 percent of identical twin pairs. These effects are associated with delayed splitting of the fertilized egg, a splitting that occurs after approximately days 7 or 8 post-conception. The direction in which the hair grows at the crown of the head (hair whorl) is another example of a physical feature which may display mirror-image reversal. This feature occurs with equal frequency in males and females, although its presence in identical male twins may be more obvious because males typically cut their hair shorter than females.

Studies using identical male twins have been especially informative in investigations of genetic and environmental influences on selected medical conditions. Beth Newman, Ph.D., from the division of research at the Kaiser Permanente Medical Care Program in Berkeley, California, and colleagues studied 250 identical male twin pairs to determine if co-twin differences in obesity were related to co-twin differences in risk for cardiovascular disease. It was reported that obesity and pattern of weight change were, in fact, related to blood pressure and other risk factors associated with cardiovascular difficulties. This analysis does not, however, rule out the possibility of genetically influenced predispositions toward heart disorders; rather, it is suggested that the chances of actually developing such a condition may be modified by appropriate interventions.

The study by Newman was facilitated by the availability of identical male twins enrolled in the National Academy of Sciences-National Research Council Twin Panel. These twins were identified due to their service in the United States Armed Forces from World War II through the Korean War. Other on-going studies using identical male twins are also made possible through the existence of such registries. John Breitner, M.D., at Duke University, is conducting twin studies of Alzheimer's disease, having located twins from the same source. The Vietnam Era Twin Registry, which includes 4,774 male twin pairs born between 1939 and 1957, will also enable numerous studies of medical and psychiatric characteristics.

Language Abilities

The verbal deficit observed among some twins is well-known among twin researchers interested in child development issues. A major study of the language skills of identical and fraternal boys was recently undertaken by Hugh Lytton, Ph.D., and colleagues at the University of Calgary in Canada. The sample included 17 identical male twin pairs, 29 fraternal male twin pairs and 44 singleton males, whose mean age was 2 1/2 years. The children were studied by means of multiple measures: naturalistic home observation, interview and experiment.

A key finding was that fewer verbal exchanges were observed between parents and twins than between parents and singletons. Twins, furthermore, received fewer displays of affection compared to singletons. It was observed that while mothers of twins intervened more often than the mothers of singletons, they directed nonverbal behaviors at their twins more frequently than verbal ones. An interesting finding was that identical twins were less skillful than fraternal twins in vocabulary and speech rate.

The prediction of reading disability in twin boys has been a major interest of Australian researchers Carol Johnston, Ph.D., Margot Prior, Ph.D., and David Hay, Ph.D. Thirty-six twin boys between the ages of 9 and 13 who were enrolled in the La Trobe Twin Study completed a number of tests to assess language and reading skill. It was determined that male twins are at a high risk for developing and that reading disability could best be predicted by preschool language skills. The relative risks associated with being either an identical or fraternal male twin were not provided, most likely due to the modest size of the sample.

Social Behavior

Koch provided some useful insights into the social behaviors of young identical male twins. Twins in her study were compared by means of parent and teacher interviews, teacher ratings, and interviews and mental ability tests completed by twins. Many identical co-twins were described as displaying passivity, low levels of aggressivity and high levels of dependence upon each other. It was suspected that their close social relationship might be associated with their generally passive behavioral styles.

Temperament refers to the "how," or style or manner in which a given behavior is expressed. For example, one child may converse in a lively, animated fashion, while another may speak in a slower, more controlled manner. Robert Plomin, Ph.D., at the Pennsylvania State University in College Park, Pennsylvania and Arnold Buss, Ph.D., at the University of Texas in Austin, Texas, developed the EASI (Emotionality, Activity, Sociability, Impulsivity) Temperament Survey. This survey has been administered in several studies involving young twin children.

Jim Stevenson, Ph.D. and Jane Fielding, Ph.D., from the University of Surrey in England obtained EASI ratings on 576 twin pairs who ranged in age from early infancy to 5 years. Rating scales were completed by their parents. Identical and fraternal male co-twins showed little resemblance in emotionality, indicating an absence of a genetic influence on this behavior. Activity did show evidence of a genetic contribution, especially as twins aged. Sociability showed a similar pattern of results, though a slight contribution from genetic factors was suggested. A very modest influence of genetic factors on impulsivity was suggested for males between 2 and 5 years of age, but it should be noted that in later versions of his temperament survey, Plomin eliminated the impulsivity scale due to the absence of a genetic influence for females in his twin sample.

The underpinnings of behavioral deviance (inappropriate behavior) have also been of considerable interest to parents, psychologists, and educators. Understanding the causes of behavioral difficulties is a critical first step toward identifying appropriate treatments and interventions. A twin study of genetic influences on these behaviors was undertaken by Dr. Philip Graham at the Institute of Child Health in London, England.

Questionnaires completed by their parents and teachers revealed that among identical twins, there was a tendency for boys to receive higher behavioral deviance ratings than girls. In addition, there was a slight, but inconsistent, tendency for identical twins to receive lower ratings than fraternal twins.

As described in this article, many identical male twins may display certain characteristic physical and behavioral features. At the same time, it is important to emphasize that there is a great deal of overlap in the behavioral features and degree of resemblance expressed by the different types of twins (identical and fraternal).

In other words, contrary to what may be generally expected of their twintype, some identical male co-twins may show little resemblance in some areas, such as reading ability, as well as little dependence on each other. Such occurrences need not cause alarm, though if parents are concerned about these or any aspects of their children's growth, they are advised to consult health and/or educational professionals. Parents' knowledge about their twin children is the best way to ensure their healthy physical and behavioral development.

Identical Female Twins

by Nancy L. Segal, Ph.D.

Female identical twins have always fascinated the general public. In addition, they continue to be of considerable interest to psychological and medical researchers, who report that female twins are the most willing and enthusiastic twin participants in the research process. David Lykken, Ph.D., and colleagues in the department of psychology at the University of Minnesota have observed that in most twin studies involving volunteers, two-thirds of the participants tend to be identical twins, and two-thirds tend to be female.

As with male identical twins, some identical female twin pairs may display none, or only several, of the features that generally characterize these twins. It is important to appreciate that there is considerable normal variation within twin types, so that departure from what is considered "typical" should not cause concern.

Biological Bases of Identical Female Twin Differences

Identical twins occur in approximately one of 240 births among Caucasian populations. These pairs result from the division of a single fertilized egg between one to 14 days after conception. Male and female twins are fairly equally represented in the population, but there are slightly more male twins at birth. This is also true of fraternal twins, as well as the non-twin population.

Identical twins share all genes in common, a fact which contributes to similarities in physical characteristics and in various behavioral traits. Researchers have observed, however, that identical twins are less alike than the general public tends to believe. Unusual prenatal and perinatal events, such as shared intrauterine circulation, delayed splitting of the fertilized egg, and/or type of delivery, have been associated with identical twin differences in various traits.

In addition to these events, female identical twins may differ in specific ways due to a process called *lyonization*, or the *Lyon hypothesis*. This process was named after May Lyon from Harwell, England, who first described it in 1961. Lyonization refers to the inactivation of one X chromosome in each cell of a female at, or about, the time that the embryo implants in the uterus.

All human females receive one X chromosome from the mother and one X chromosome from the father, while human males receive one X chromosome from the mother and one Y chromosome from the father. Female twins are thus identified as XX, while males are identified as XY. Inactivation of one X chromosome in each female cell occurs randomly and prevents expression of information in that chromosome; but, because the process occurs following the splitting of the fertilized egg, which X chromosome is inactive can vary even between identical twins.

Several case studies involving identical female twin pairs demonstrate differences between the twins that may be linked to lyonization. Some of these cases are reviewed in the section following.

Case Studies

A study called *Twins and Twin Relations* was completed in 1966 by Helen Koch, Ph.D., a professor of psychology at the University of Chicago. This study included measures of intellectual, social and physical development. Seventeen pairs of 5- and 6-year-old female identical twin pairs were identified, in addition to other groups of twin and non-twin children. The 17 twin pairs were shorter in stature than the non-twin females, but all twins (regardless of twintype) were somewhat shorter and lighter than the non-twin children.

Several studies using adult twins, both reared apart and reared together, have demonstrated that the contribution of genetic factors to body weight is less for identical female twins than for identical male twins. This finding may be associated with the greater susceptibility of females to the effects of dietary regimes, hormonal influences and/or various sociocultural factors relevant to body weight.

Female identical twins have proven especially useful in medical research because, given that identical twins share all their genes in common, any differences between them must be attributed to environmental factors. Medical studies using identical female twins have detected genetic influences on a wide range of conditions, but the strength of that influence appears to be less than might be expected. In some cases, twin differences may be associated with lyonization. In other cases, environmental factors may be necessary to "trigger" a given genetic susceptibility that both twins share. In the event that these environmental factors differ within a twin pair, the twins will show differences for the trait or condition in question.

The recently published book, *Nature and Nurture*, by researcher Robert Plomin, Ph.D., provides some important information concerning the fragile X syndrome, a condition that has received considerable attention in recent years and may be another cause of differences within a twin pair. Some individuals have an X chromosome that, for unknown reasons, may break in a certain region during the process of cell preparation. Males have only one X chromosome; if the fragile X is present, it is expressed in the form of mild mental retardation. In contrast, females are less likely to display the fragile X syndrome because they have two X chromosomes in each cell, only one of which is inactivated. (Should a female carry the fragile X on both X chromosomes, she would display retardation. This event would, however, be quite rare.)

In 1985, E. Tuckerman, T. Webb and S.E. Bundey of the Infant Development Unit at the Birmingham Maternity Hospital in England described a pair of identical female twins who showed marked differences in level of intelligence. It was determined that the level of fragile X was equal for the two sisters. However, the twins differed in the percentage of active fragile X chromosomes; this percentage was substantially lower for the twin of normal intelligence, supporting the suggestion that lyonization took place after the fertilized egg divided.

Still another possible cause of differences between twin females was documented in 1987 by Craig S. Kitchens, M.D., from the College of Medicine at the University of Florida in Gainesville. This case involved identical female twins who differed in their level of factor IX deficiency. (Factor IX is a characteristic of the blood.) The genetic information concerning factor IX is carried on the X chromosome. The researchers concluded that the twins differed in this characteristic because different X chromosomes underwent inactivation.

Women's Diseases-Female Identical Twin Research

Female identical twins are very valuable participants in medical research concerning diseases that affect women. A study of risk factors associated with breast cancer was completed in 1984 by Dr. D. J. Odenheimer and colleagues at the University of California-Berkeley. The two participant groups consisted of 90 female twin pairs, in which one twin had a history of benign breast disease and the twin partner had no such history, and 48 female twin pairs, in which one twin had been clinically diagnosed with fibrocystic benign breast disease and the twin partner was disease-free at examination.

Coffee consumption was found to correlate with the onset of breast disease; that is to say, the twin affected with breast disease drank more coffee than her twin sister. In contrast, the use of oral contraceptives and larger body mass (body weight in pounds/height in inches squared) were found to decrease the chance of breast disease. These relationships were stronger in identical female twin pairs than in fraternal female twin pairs, but this particular finding was not addressed by the investigators. It is important to appreciate that the onset of breast cancer may be associated with numerous life history factors, so the findings in this study may not apply in all cases.

Language Abilities

Sex differences in verbal skill have been documents by a number of psychological investigators. Females, on average, tend to out-perform males on tests of verbal ability. (This does not imply that all females will perform better than all males; it means that if the average scores of male and female groups were compared, the score for females would most likely be higher.)

The verbal deficit observed among some twins, relative to non-twins, is well-known among child development researchers. In Dr. Koch's study, the identical female twins scored lower than the non-twin females on the verbal section of a general mental ability test, but the difference was not large. In contrast, differences in verbal between identical male twins and non-twin males in her study were fairly pronounced. Identical female twins also scored somewhat lower than the non-twin females in speech articulation; but again, the degree of difference was modest.

Several case studies involving young identical female twins have contributed substantially to information concerning children's language development. Dr. J.E. Douglas from The Hospital for Sick Children in London, England, and Dr. A. Sutton from the Parent and Child Centre in Birmingham, England, discussed a case concerning young identical female twins who showed a severe delay in the onset of normal speech. At the time of psychological assessment, the twins were 4 years, 11 months of age. They showed normal physical development, but displayed unintelligible speech and underdeveloped play. These behaviors were associated, in part, with the twins' early social isolation and the fact that their mother suffered from depression.

The girls were given a training program specially designed to teach them the function of speech, increase their sentence complexity and increase their vocabulary. They were assigned to different classes after remaining together for one term. Initially, they visited one another often, but visits decreased in frequency as the term progressed. After one year, both twins showed impressive gains in verbal areas. Follow-up assessment at a later date revealed, happily, that the twins' improvement in language had been maintained.

Social Behavior

Dr. Koch's study has offered some valuable information concerning the social behaviors of young identical female twins. First, it is interesting that the identical female twins were judged to have a greater number of interests than the singleton females. They were also regarded by the examiners as more confident and socially involved. The latter may be explained, in part, by the additional observation that the identical female twins appeared to share a close social relationship. This is consistent with the finding that many adult identical twins emphasize feelings of security and well-being, which they attribute to the company of the twin.

Genetic and environmental influences on aggressive behaviors have been of recent interest. A study by Jilla Ghodesian-Carpey, Ph.D., and Laura Baker, Ph.D., at the University of Southern California-Los Angeles obtained mothers' ratings and observations of the behaviors of 4- to 7-year-old twins. Aggressive behaviors included yelling, verbal threats and destructiveness. Females and identical twins were rated as lower in aggression than males and fraternal twins. It was of special interest that, as a group, the identical females were much less aggressive than the fraternal females. Additional research in this area is needed, however, in view of the small sample sizes.

THE IMPACT ON PARENTING

Biological and experiential differences vary considerably among the various types of twins. Knowledge of the true twintype of your twins is the most effective means of ensuring healthy physical and behavioral development. Information about twintype is most reliably obtained through extensive blood-typing analyses. Examination of the placenta could be misleading in some cases, because early-splitting identical twins and fraternal twins both have separate placentas.

As indicated elsewhere in this article, variation within twintypes is frequently observed; that is to say, some identical female twin pairs may behave more like fraternal twin pairs in some areas of behavior. For example, fraternal twins, on average, tend to be less close socially than identical twins. Should a particular pair of identical females display preferences for peers outside the twinship and/or select differing educational programs or career choices, this should not be viewed as cause for alarm.

The most important consideration should be whether or not the children are happy and healthy as individuals and as twins. Indications to the contrary should be dealt with by discussion with the twins and/or consultation with trained professionals, if necessary. Twin children are just like non-twin children with respect to emotional and physical needs; however, being an identical twin poses unique psychological circumstances that may affect development. The best way to foster healthy physical and behavioral development is to stay as attuned to your twins as possible.

Are Multiple Births Multiplying?

by Nancy L. Segal, Ph.D.

In her 1983 book, *The Nature and Nurture of Twins*, Elizabeth M. Bryan said that the fraternal twinning rate "has been falling over the past decade, or at least in developed countries...from developing countries we have only reports from Nigeria. Here the rates are still increasing, possibly due to improved nutrition."

United States government statistics show an age-adjusted drop of 11 percent in total twinning, from 11.5 per 1,000 births in 1936, to 10.2 per 1,000 births in 1964. This represents a 17 percent decrease in the birth of fraternal twins. (The frequency of fraternal twinning, but *not* identical twinning, has been on the decline.) French researcher Denis Hemon and his colleagues found that the fraternal twinning rate decreased by 25 percent in France between 1901 and 1968. Michael Mosteller and co-investigators at the Medical College of Virginia, Richmond, identified the early 1960s as the time of the greatest decline in the rate of twinning in the United States, Canada, several European countries, Japan and Australia.

A 1946 "twinning peak" was, however, observed in the U.S. by Gordon Allen and Joseph Shacter from the National Institute of Mental Health, Bethesda, Maryland. They suggest that this may be associated with the return of American servicemen at the end of World War II and their desire to establish families quickly. (Both twin and non-twin births increased during this period.)

The reasons underlying these observations are varied and are, as yet, not firmly established. It is widely agreed, however, that the fraternal twinning rate is falling. In contrast, the rate of identical twinning (3 to 4 per 1,000 births) appears to be both uniform and stable throughout the world.

Knowledge of the factors associated with the birth of identical and fraternal twins allows greater understanding of the observed patterns of the two types of twinning. It is also important to consider why, despite the apparent decline in twinning, general interest in twins and twin-related topics continues to soar.

Identical and Fraternal Twinning

Identical twins result from the splitting of a single fertilized egg, or zygote, from one to 14 days after conception. Why this division occurs is unknown. Tendencies toward identical twinning do not generally run in families; it seems, instead, that zygotic splitting represents a random biological event. There have, however, been several reports of families in which many sets of identical twins are born, many of whom also are opposite-handed or left-handed.

The important points, however, are that the worldwide incidence of identical twinning has remained unchanged for many years, and that there are no clearly-recognized factors associated with the occurrence of identical twins.

Fraternal twins result from the fertilization of two separate eggs by two separate sperm. Fraternal twinning has been associated with advanced maternal age, increased number of births prior to the birth of the twins, increased height and weight of the mother, use of fertility drugs and oral contraceptives, as well as social class membership.

Genetic factors also are responsible for variation in the fraternal twinning rate, across both families and populations. The pattern of transmission of the "twinning trait" within families is not known. Fraternal twins are more frequent in black populations than Caucasian populations, and least frequent in Oriental populations.

Byan reported that the chances of a fraternal twin birth for a Nigerian (Yoruba tribe) mother are eight times greater than for an Oriental mother, and five times greater for a Nigerian mother than for a Caucasian mother. Finally, the observation that some very isolated villages, such as Eftimie Murgu, Romania, show an extremely high twinning rate further underlines the importance of genetic influences on twinning.

Fraternal Twinning: Why Is It Decreasing?

Researchers know that older women have an enhanced probability of producing fraternal twins relative to younger women. The ages of 35 to 39 have been identified as the period of "greatest risk" for fraternal twinning. French researchers reported that 30 percent of the older mothers (35 to 39 years) in their study (which surveyed all births in France between 1901 and 1968) gave birth to fraternal twins. The chances of having fraternal twins does, however, decrease after age 39. Given the current trends toward postponing the childbearing years, an increase in the rate of fraternal twinning might seem more likely. The situation is, however, more complex.

Fraternal twinning also is more likely if a woman has previously given birth to other children. Fraternal twins are, in fact, found most frequently among families with lower social status, probably due to the generally-larger family size.

Another finding is that the relationship between the number of previous births and twinning increases the birth order of the twins. Evidence shows that levels of the pituitary hormones FSH (follicle-stimulating hormone) and LH (lutenizing hormone) influence the probability of having fraternal twins. In fact, the average peak levels of these hormones differ amongst populations and those with the highest peak levels (blacks) have the highest twinning rate. Dr. S. Milham has hypothesized that increases in the levels of FSH and LH, with both a mother's age and number of pregnancies, might explain the influence of mothers' age and twins' birth order on the frequency of fraternal twinning.

Maternal age and number of pregnancies are factors that are clearly related. Older mothers would have greater opportunities to raise larger families than younger mothers. Younger mothers, however, also improve their chances of a fraternal twin birth if they have produced a large family. The effects of birth order may, in fact, be more important than maternal age, as revealed by twin studies in Nuevo Leon, Mexico.

Current practices in the United States and other western nations include not only postponing the child-bearing years, but also reducing family size. Some women who have inherited the tendency to produce fraternal twins might not, therefore, have the opportunity to re-express it. These changes in family planning have been facilitated by the availability of effective methods of contraception. The Virginia researchers observed that the decline in twinning that occurred in this century appears to have stabilized since 1960, as indicated by data obtained from residents of that state. In other words, while the age of the mother is increasing, the number of births is decreasing, which are factors that tend to cancel each other out. This still leaves unanswered the question of why a decline in fraternal twinning occurred prior to the 1960s.

Factors Affecting Fraternal Twinning

A number of researchers have confirmed that the mothers of fraternal twins are both heavier and taller than the mothers of identical twins and non-twins. Mothers of identical twins and non-twins do not differ from one another in these characteristics.

The fraternal twinning rate also may be affected by changes in the food supply. It is, therefore, not surprising that Martin Bulmer, author of, *The Biology of Twinning in Man*, reports that during World War II, the twinning rate fell in France, Norway, and the Netherlands, areas in which the nutritional supply was scarce.

In this country, women have become increasingly weight-conscious and have been dieting with greater frequency. The additional health benefits associated with physical fitness have encouraged more active participation in a variety of sports. Both of these activities lower weight and body fat, factors that would reduce the probability of fraternal twinning, and conception, in general. This may explain why the twinning rate seems to be increasing in developing countries— there, the food supply is growing. Only limited statistics are currently available from such countries, however, so that additional data are required to fully comprehend the changing patterns of twinning around the world.

Studies that address the effects of oral contraception upon the fraternal twin-ning rate have yielded conflicting findings. Hemon and his colleagues compared 673 mothers who had used oral contraceptives with those who had not. They found that fraternal twinning declined in frequency among the users. They cited examples of birth defects in the spontaneously-aborted fetuses of pill users, evidence that could explain the lowered rate of fraternal twinning. However, the researchers said that they recognized that multiple factors influence the rate of twinning, so their findings must be viewed with some caution.

In contrast, Dr. Kenneth J. Rothman, at the Harvard University School of Public Health, found that the use of oral contraceptives increased the chances of having fraternal twins among mothers who conceived during the first months following termination of "the pill." He found, in addition, that fraternal twinning occurred with even greater frequency if contraceptives had been used for six months or longer. Clearly, additional research is needed to resolve the relationship between oral contraceptives and twinning.

The factors reviewed above, neither individually nor collectively, provide a satisfactory answer to the question of why twinning is on the decline. It is, therefore, necessary to search for additional explanations. W.H. James, at the Galton Laboratory, Great Britain, has suggested that the introduction of pesticides and other chemical agents into the environment may have reduced the sperm count in males, thereby affecting the twinning rate.

Mosteller has proposed that "unusual social events may have an overriding influence on twinning rates." He refers to the marked declines in twinning during the Depression years—1930s— and the period just prior to World War II. He and his colleagues emphasize that emotional stress can reduce the sperm count and motility in males, lead to the cessation of menstruation in females, and cause a reduction of sexual desire among both males and females. These events could serve to lower birth rates, in general, and fraternal twinning, in particular. Environmental stress would seem an integral part of life in industrialized societies and, as such, may be closely linked with current patterns of twinning in this country.

Statistics on Twinning

In recent years, the accuracy of twinning rates has been challenged by the "vanishing twin" phenomenon. In 1982, Helain Landy and Louis Keith, of the Northwestern University Medical School and Center for the Study of Multiple Birth, Chicago, and Donald Keith, also from the Center for the Study for Multiple Birth, reported that, "the number of twins observed at delivery was significantly less than the number of twin conceptions identified by ultrasound during the first trimester." Their findings were based on data from nine study centers located in the United States and abroad. The rates of disappearance ranged from 0 to 78 percent across the nine centers.

The most common explanation given for this observation is resorption of the second gestational sac. Other explanations include the occurrence of blighted ova (empty gestational sac) and, more rarely, fetus papyraceous (compression of the second fetus and its embedding in the placenta of the normal twin). Slight vaginal bleeding is the only physical symptom so far associated with the vanishing twin event.

The investigators concluded that the incidence of human twinning is probably higher than the figure (one per 80 births) that is generally reported. It is, however, difficult to determine the twinning rate with complete accuracy because many mothers do not routinely seek ultrasound early in their pregnancies.

Increased Focus on Twins

Interest and attention to twins and their special concerns has increased within recent years. This seems ironic in light of the falling twinning rate. It is important to recognize, however, that while the frequency of twin births may be on the decline, *the proportion of surviving twins is higher*, due to improved prenatal and postnatal medical care.

In other words, the occurrence of fraternal twin births per year is falling, but a higher percentage of twins born are surviving. Statistics provided by the United States Department of Health and Human Services show that the number of live births in twin deliveries has been on the rise since 1975. Premature infants, both twins and non-twins, are enjoying greater chances for survival, as well.

Twinship brings with it a varied array of unique and fascinating biological and social circumstances. It is very fortunate, both for twins and their parents, that medical, psychological, and educational professionals are devoting greater attention to such issues. This, in turn, helps to stimulate public interest in twins, a trend that is becoming increasingly apparent. Manufacturers are showing an increasing sensitivity to the needs of twins and their parents, as evidenced by the greater availability of products (for example, strollers, dolls) designed especially for multiples.

Twin themes are beginning to figure more significantly into books, movies, and other works of fiction. Most importantly, the increased focus on twinning has made the public aware that twins are not "oddities" but "specialties," with their own sets of needs and concerns.

Who Is a Twin?

by Nancy L. Segal, Ph.D.

In 1986 "… a baby girl was born to a 38-year-old mother here (Stoke-on Trent, England) 18 months after the birth of the baby's twin sister." This report, which appeared in *Medical World News*, explained that this unusual event was accomplished by means of in vitro fertilization.

The United States' first set of triplets, born 21 months apart via in vitro fertilization, was later announced in November 1988 by physicians at the AMI South Bay Hospital in Redondo Beach, California. In both of the above cases it is, however, appropriate to ask: Are the individuals resulting from these procedures *really* twins and triplets? Mothers of twins attending the 1986 Minnesota State Convention were clearly reluctant to accept this novel conceptualization of twinning. As a researcher of twins, I share their concern.

Sophisticated medical technology is now providing opportunities for some otherwise infertile couples to have children of their own. One consequence of these procedures (as demonstrated by the cases cited above) has been increased attention to the definition of a twin, as well as to the various types of twins and normal variations on ordinary twinning processes. This information is extremely important to parents, educators, physicians and the concerned public with respect to fostering the optimal well-being of multiple birth individuals.

Future advances in medical technology will most likely create additional unusual types of kinships, many of which cannot be anticipated at present. These events will increasingly challenge existing definitions of twinship and encourage the development of new classification schemes. Even today, decisions as to who may be appropriately classified as a twin, triplet or quadruplet can be quite complex.

In the absence of established guidelines that permit assignment of individuals as twins or non-twins, it seems most appropriate to regard twinship as a set of classes, falling along a continuum, with some pairs coming closer to resembling ordinary twins than others. Understanding twinning processes and in vitro fertilization techniques are important steps in considering who is a twin.

Types of Twins

There are two broad classifications of twins: identical and fraternal. Identical twins result from the splitting of a single fertilized egg between one and 14 days following conception. Members of identical twin pairs share all their genes in common and must always be of the same sex.

Observed differences in behavioral and physical traits within identical twinships are explained by environmental events which may occur before, during or after birth. Identical twins might, for example, differ in birth weight due to differences in the amount of nutrition received in the womb.

Some identical twins show differences in behavioral style such as dominant vs. submissive, partly associated with the social relationship that evolves between them. The differential exposure of twin partners to illnesses or other unfavorable life events may also lead to co-twin differences in health or behavior.

Fraternal twins result from the fertilization of two separate eggs by two separate sperm. Fraternal twins share half their genes in common, on average, by descent. Their genetic relatedness is exactly the same as that shared by non-twin brothers or sisters.

Fraternal pairs may be of the same or opposite sex, events which occur with equal frequency. It is possible to think of fraternal twins as representing a "spectrum of relatedness," in that some pair members may share a large percentage of their genes in common, while other pair members may share a small percentage of their genes in common.

Differences between fraternal twins are associated with both genetic and environmental influences. For example, to the extent that fraternal twins display unique talents, parents may respond by providing opportunities designed to "match" these talents, thereby enhancing the twins' natural differences.

Methods of Determining Twintype

The classification of twin pairs as identical or fraternal may be accomplished in a variety of ways. David T. Lykken, Ph.D., at the University of Minnesota, has shown that comparative analyses of 18 blood characteristics (eight blood group systems, four serum proteins and six red blood cell enzymes) provide the most accurate, objective method for determining if twins are identical or fraternal. Differences in blood groups identify fraternal twins with complete certainty.

Similarity across all measured blood groups indicates identical twins with very high, but incomplete, certainty. This is because fraternal twins, on rare occasion, may share all their blood groups in common, an event that is possible because they share the same parents. (Non-twin siblings may also show identity across all blood groups for the same reason.)

Blood group information, in combination with co-twin comparisons of various physical characteristics (such as fingerprints), can improve accuracy. Physical resemblance questionnaires, specially developed to determine twintype, have generally proven to be quite accurate when compared with bloodtyping. Fingerprint studies alone show variable accuracy; unusual prenatal influences may be associated with discrepancies between identical twins on these traits.

The presence of one or two placentas is *not* informative with respect to classifying twins as identical or fraternal. This is because early-splitting identical twins (those resulting from the division of the embryo before approximately day six post-conception) and all fraternal twins have two placentas. Late-splitting identical twins (those resulting from the division of the embryo after approximately day seven post-conception) have a single or shared placenta. It is possible, however, that separate placentas may fuse, yielding a misleading impression of single placentation and inaccurate diagnosis of twintype.

M.G. Bulmer, professor and author of *The Biology of Twinning in Man*, cited studies showing 43 percent of identical twin pairs with two separate chorions and 42 percent of fraternal twin pairs with fused placentas. Early-splitting identical twins and all fraternal twins have two chorions, two amnions and two placentas. Amnions are the inner membranes and chorions are the outer membranes that surround the fetus during gestation. Knowing that your twins have "two of everything" is, therefore, not informative with respect to twintype.

The timing of the split is associated with the number of shared fetal membranes for identical twins: The later the split occurs, the greater are the chances that fetal membranes will be shared. Approximately one-third of identical twins have separate chorions and amnions, while the remaining two-thirds have a single chorion, but separate amnions. Only a very small percentage of identical twins have a single chorion *and* single amnion.

For the reasons above, parents are encouraged to challenge assignments of twintype solely based upon the number of placentas.

The opinions of experienced observers of twins have proven to be extremely accurate. The late James Shields, a professor who studied twins at the Maudsely Institute between 1947 and 1978 in England, provided judgments of twintype that strongly agreed with the results from bloodtyping laboratories.

My own judgments of twintype were accurate for 96 percent of the identical and fraternal twin pairs I studied at the University of Chicago in 1982. I found that mothers of twins were less accurate than I was! I suspect that this reflects parental sensitivity to very subtle differences between identical twins, differences which an experienced investigator may discount as unrelated to diagnostic accuracy.

My colleagues and I have, however, encountered several twin pairs for whom judgments of twintype are difficult to make, due, for example, to the near (but not complete) physical likenesses between them. On very rare occasions, laboratories make errors in analyses of blood, as well. Should laboratory results be at odds with a parents' or an expert's strongly-held opinion, it is advisable to repeat the tests.

In Vitro Fertilization Techniques

In vitro fertilization involves the extraction of eggs from a female to be fertilized outside her body. The resulting embryos are then implanted into the womb.

Physicians implant several embryos at a given time because of the high probability that some implantations will fail; multiple implantation increases the chances that at least one embryo will be successfully carried to term.

Fertilized embryos that are not implanted may be preserved, by freezing techniques, to be used at a later date. Thus, children may be conceived at the same time, but born months or years apart.

In the case of the British family mentioned at the beginning of this story, Dr. Patrick Steptoe had removed 10 ova from a woman in 1984 for fertilization by her husband's sperm. A first attempt at pregnancy proved unsuccessful, but six embryos were frozen. A year later, a successful pregnancy was achieved. The following year, two more embryos were implanted, resulting in a successful multiple-birth pregnancy.

Twins vs. Non-Twins

Despite simultaneous conception by in vitro fertilization, infants who develop from separate pregnancies do *not* qualify as members of twin or triplet sets. Twins, triplets and other higher-order multiple births experience both common prenatal and postnatal environments. These special birth and life history situations uniquely distinguish such sibships from ordinary sibling pairs.

Embryos implanted at different times *and* which, consequently, experience differential developmental condition, lack several key characteristics which uniquely define twinship. It is the case, however, that ordinary siblings and siblings born through in vitro fertilization do share the same genetic relationship as fraternal twins, which is half their genes in common, on average, by descent.

In the future, scientists might possibly be able to artificially induce identical twinning in embryos fertilized outside the human body. It would then be possible to implant one embryo inside the mother and preserve the other one for implantation at a later date. Are these individuals twins? The answer would be no, because the developing individuals would not share the same intrauterine environment and would differ in chronological age.

Other issues remain: What if the two embryos (provided by the same family) were implanted in two different women at the same time and shared the same birthday? Classification of these individuals as twins would *not* be possible, given the different intrauterine environments.

It is important to note that even ordinary twins do not necessarily share exactly the same intrauterine environments due to the transfusion syndrome, unequal nutritional supply, etc. However, the intrauterine environments of ordinary twins would, in all likelihood, be more similar than those experienced by individuals formed from separately implanted embryos.

It is worth noting that two ordinary siblings born several years apart could (theoretically) share close to all of their genes in common, depending upon which genes are passed on from the mother and which genes are passed on from the father. Most everyone knows siblings who display striking physical and behavioral resemblance, but would not refer to them as twins.

In the world of animal research, some scientists develop many generations of genetically identical laboratory mice or other organisms to study the effects of environmental differences on development. These animals, while genetically identical between generations, are not termed twins, but members of inbred strains.

Variations on Ordinary Twinning Processes

Polar Body Twinning: Cases thought to demonstrate the existence of polar body twinning (the "third twintype") have been described. It is thought that equal divisions of the primary or secondary oocyte (primitive ova) prior to fertilization may result in twins that might show unusual genetic similarity or dissimilarity.

Bulmer has explained that twins sharing all their maternal inheritance, but half their paternal inheritance (on average), may be more alike than most fraternal twins, but less alike than most identical twins. Depending upon the precise timing of these events, the twins could be even less alike than typical fraternal twins, but would be more alike than unrelated individuals.

Chimerism: The presence of more than one distinct red blood cell population has been occasionally detected in members of fraternal twin pairs. Elizabeth Bryan, M.D., in Queen Charlotte's Maternity Hospital in England, notes that this condition, known as chimerism, is associated with placental anastomoses (interconnections between the blood vessels) in a fused (dichorionic) placenta.

According to Dr. S. Gilgenkrantz and colleagues at the Centre de Transfusion Sanguine d'Hematologie in France, this condition has been frequently observed among some mammalian species (it is evident in 90 percent of fraternal calves, for example), but has been observed in only about 20 cases involving human twins.

Other intriguing evidence of chimerism has been provided by Dr. Gordon Dewald and associates at the Mayo Clinic in Rochester, Minnesota. They describe an individual thought to have arisen from the fertilization of an ovum and a polar body by separate sperm, which then fused.

Superfecundation: Dr. Bryan explains that superfecundation refers to fraternal twins who result from separate coital acts occurring in the same menstrual cycle. Evidence of different fathers, provided by examination of red blood cell groups and biochemical analyses, has been reported. In one instance, fathers were of different racial origins. According to Dr. Vandeplassche, superfecundation may result in marked developmental discrepancies between co-twins, although this could also be associated with delayed implantation of one embryo.

Superfetation: Superfetation refers to multiple conceptions occurring during different menstrual cycles. Evidence to demonstrate this process has been cited in both human and non-human mammalian species. Superfetation may include delivery of full-term infants separated by weeks or months and the birth or abortion of twin infants discordant for developmental status.

While at Indiana University in 1976, Drs. Sam Rhine and Walter E. Nance reported a family which included six twin pairs born in four consecutive generations, all of which included one normal twin and either one malformed fetus, stillborn or premature infant. They proposed the transmission of a gene for superfetation on either the maternal or paternal branches of the family.

Vanishing Twin Phenomenon: The "vanishing twin" phenomenon refers to the disappearance of one fetus in a twin pregnancy, an event usually detected during the first trimester, but possibly detected early in the second trimester. One proposed explanation is absorption of the fetal tissue by the mother, although other explanations have been suggested. The use of ultrasound has provided an informative picture of this phenomenon, as it can monitor development of a fetus by bouncing ultrasonic waves off a fetus during gestation.

The vanishing twin phenomenon has received attention only recently, given improvements in ultrasonic technology. In 1982 and 1986 papers, Helain J. Landy, M.D., in the department of obstetrics and gynecology at the George Washington University Medical Center in Washington, D.C., and colleagues reported that the number of twin pairs delivered at birth was less than the number of twin pregnancies diagnosed by ultrasound.

The vanishing twin phenomenon is estimated to occur in 0 to 78 percent of diagnosed multiple pregnancies, depending upon the patient population and timing of ultrasound.

Precise figures are difficult to obtain, because not all women routinely undergo ultrasound procedures. An important implication of the vanishing twin phenomenon is that the true rate of twin conceptions is probably higher than today's overall incidence of twins in the United States (one in 80 births).

Interruption of a twin pregnancy due to the vanishing twin phenomenon may be understandably stressful to a mother. I am unaware of studies specifically addressed to this issue, but related research is relevant.

A study by Ann L. Wilson, Ph.D., and colleagues demonstrated that parents who lose one twin early in life grieve just as much as parents who lose a singleton child. This finding dispels the misconception that the parents of twins may grieve less than the parents of the singleton baby because they still do have one infant for whom to care.

The vanishing twin phenomenon also raises critical issues for the surviving individual: Is this child a twin? Should the child be informed that he began life as part of a twin pair? The answer to the first question would seem to be yes; it now appears that the loss of one twin early in gestation is a normal variation of twinning that occurs with greater frequency than was previously suspected. Certainly the initial biological processes unique to twinning were operative in the case of such twins.

The answer to the second question would also seem to be yes. These special survivors should be informed as to familial tendencies toward twinning, as it may help them in their own family planning. Furthermore, these individuals may, in some cases, serve as constant reminders of the lost twin, a situation which may prove difficult to their parents. Knowledge of their birth histories may help these individuals to better understanding of their parents' attitudes and reactions.

Mirror-Imaging in Twins

One variant of the typical processes associated with identical twinning is "mirror-imaging" of some physical traits. According to Sally P. Springer, Ph.D., at the University of California, at Davis, and Georg Deutsch, Ph.D., at the University of Texas Medical Branch, at Galveston, mirror-imaging has been observed among approximately 25 percent of identical twin pairs; it results when splitting of a single fertilized egg occurs fairly late (approximately on, or following, day seven post-conception). One twin develops from the original left half of the embryo, and the other twin develops from the original right half of the embryo.

Mirror-imaging is held responsible, in part, for the relatively increased incidence of left-handedness observed among twins, as compared with non-twins (20 percent vs. 12 percent), and the observation that one-fourth of both identical twins are opposite-handed. It may be that left-handedness in twins associated with delayed splitting represents a qualitatively different characteristic than left-handedness observed in non-twins.

Examples of other "reversed" features in identical twins include dental characteristics, fingerprint patterns, birthmarks and moles, and direction of hair whorl. In very rare cases, reversals of some (situs inversus) or all (situs inversus totalis) internal organs may occur in identical twins.

It is, therefore, not surprising that an overrepresentation of midline neurological malformations have been observed among identical twinships. Jerre Levy, Ph.D., at the University of Chicago, emphasizes that not all features will be affected in a given twin pair—the affected features and their number are, presumably, influenced by the timing of the twinning event and the location of the split on the embryo.

It is also recognized that unusual birth traumas, such as fetal crowding and breech delivery, that are associated with left-handedness in non-twins may partially explain the high frequency of left-handedness among twins. This is because twin births, in general, tend to be at greater risk for adverse influences, as compared with singleton births.

This may also partially explain why 25 percent of fraternal twins also show opposite-handedness. Charles Boklage, Ph.D. at the University of East Carolina, has proposed that the higher frequency of left-handedness among fraternal twins may be associated with polar body twinning, as well, in particular the relatively equal splitting (and fertilization) of the primitive ova.

Left-handedness runs in families, though the genetics of hand preference are not well understood. The finding that left-handedness may be hereditary may also explain opposite-handedness in some pairs of twins. One member of a fraternal twin pair may inherit this tendency from a parent(s), while the other twin might not.

It is also possible that both members of an identical twin pair might inherit a familial tendency toward left-handedness, but that birth trauma to one twin might result in altered handedness (in this case, right-handedness). This event would be unusual, however, because of the general rarity of identical twinning.

In 1925, Dr. C.E. Lauterbach suggested that non-twin left-handers may be survivors from identical twin pairs. Dr. Springer has, however, indicated that there is little evidence to either support or dismiss this idea.

Dr. Boklage found an increased frequency of left-handers among parents of identical and fraternal twins. Louise Carter-Saltzman, Ph.D., at the University of Washington in Seattle, reported an excess of left-handed individuals among the relatives of opposite-handed identical twins.

Conjoined Twins

Conjoined twinning is a rare event in the lives of twins and their families. It is a rare form of identical twinning which results from the incomplete splitting of a fertilized egg.

Dr. Bryan, in her book, *The Nature and Nurture of Twins*, indicates that conjoined twins occur in approximately one in 200 identical twin births. Recent advances in medical technology have allowed for the successful separation of a number of such pairs.

A moving account of one such pair, Lisa and Elisa Hansen reported in the *Chicago Tribune*, November 9, 1980, documents the special closeness that may develop between such twins: "When they were joined, they acted almost like one person...They were amazingly coordinated and learned to crawl together. Their bond has continued even after separation."

Dr. Bryan cites examples of conjoined twins who have married and raised children. It is revealing that in two well-known pairs, the survivor refused surgical separation from his co-twin following the death of the co-twin, only to die several hours later. These special cases of twinning provide unusual insights into the nature of the identical twin relationship: a special closeness and a special caring that is maintained despite extraordinary circumstances.

Knowledge of Twintype Is Important

Knowledge of twintype may provide critical clues toward understanding the physical, intellectual and social development of twins. Identical twins, on average, are expected to show similarities in *many* behavioral and physical characteristics throughout the course of the life span.

Some identical twins may, however, display differences in size and/or vigor, effects that might reflect differences in their intrauterine environments. (It is possible, for example, for co-twins to receive unequal nutritional supplies during gestation.)

As indicated above, identical twins may also show differences in dominance and submission, possibly associated with their special twin relationship. Identical twinships often provide a unique advantage to the co-twins, and to their parents because, in most cases, each twin can potentially demonstrate the skills and talents expressed by the other. (I am acquainted with identical female twins who work in different areas of fine arts. Both claim that they could just as easily assume the tasks performed by the co-twin.)

Parents are advised to stay alert to pronounced behavioral or physical differences between identical twins, but should appreciate that identical twin pairs may vary with respect to degree of resemblance.

Observed differences between a pair of fraternal twins would not, however, cause this type of concern because fraternal twins are expected to differ physically and behaviorally due to their genetic makeup. It should be recalled that these twins share only half these genes in common, on average, and so are no more alike genetically than ordinary brothers and sisters.

Robert Plomin, Ph.D., at Pennsylvania State University, and Denise Daniels, Ph.D., at Stanford University, have pointed out that siblings raised in the same family show less personality resemblance than has generally been believed. Attempts to minimize co-twin differences between fraternal twins, in the belief that they are identical, may thus prove incompatible with the natural predispositions of the children.

Most studies agree that identical twins, on average, share a closer social bond than fraternal twins. (There are exceptions, in that some identical twins are not as intimate as some fraternal twins.) The reasons for this difference have not been fully determined; but an explanation may reside, in part, in the greater behavioral and physical similarities between identical twins. These similarities, in turn, appear to be associated with the genetic commonality of identical twins.

This information, together with knowledge of twintype, may help parents understand the nature of twins' interactions with one another. Finally, in the unfortunate event of an illness affecting one twin, knowledge of twintype may be a useful guide to determining the chance that the twin partner may become affected, enabling preventive measures.

Disruption of the Twin Bond

The following events may interfere with, but do not negate, one's status as a twin or triplet:

- One fetus may undergo spontaneous abortion during pregnancy, while the other may be carried to term.
- A multiple pregnancy may eventuate in a healthy newborn infant and a still-born co-twin.
- Twins may be separated at birth and raised in different families such as participants in the Minnesota Study of Twins Reared Apart.
- Untoward events may handicap, or cause the untimely death, of one twin in childhood or adulthood.

The unfortunate events named above clearly disrupt the shared prenatal and/or postnatal environments of multiples, but are imposed only after the natural processes of twinning have begun. Dr. Bryan encourages parents to inform singleton twins of the loss of their co-twins, regardless of how the loss occurred. She explains that knowledge of a lost twinship may help to understand feelings of loneliness. Some individuals may feel anger toward the physician and/or guilt toward themselves for the loss of the twin, and need to express these feelings openly.

I am aware of singleton adult twins who continue to introduce themselves as twins, despite the loss of a co-twin at birth. These individuals emphasize that they were part of a special relationship and wish others to appreciate this, as well. Many twins who have lost their co-twins during adulthood firmly maintain that "they are still twins."

Physical and situational similarities among people have yielded a wide variety of "twin-like" relationships. Communality between individuals in similarly stressful situations, such as hospitals, orphanages and concentration camps, has been described as twin-like.

Dr. Bruno Bettelheim, at the University of Chicago, Orthogenic School, has drawn parallels between twin relationships and the social relationships established among kibbutz children in Israel who are raised together from birth. He finds that their most remarkable qualities have been the "deep dependence, reliance on each other and the feeling that no one but their twin can ever fully understand them."

I recently tested a pair of unrelated boys who are five days apart in age and who were raised together from one week of age. They clearly display social-interactional qualities that are typically associated with fraternal twins.

In Great Britain, a pair of identical twin women married identical twin men— both couples had children on exactly the same day! These children, while legal first cousins, are genetically equivalent to fraternal twins because the two sets of parents are genetically the same and the children are the same age.

Is there potential damage to referring to these unusual dyads as twins? In some cases, the individuals in question may perceive their "twinship" as amusing. In other cases, expectations of similarity or social closeness may be incompatible with the children's unique personalities and skills.

Twin-like relationships are of high interest because they highlight many of the treasured qualities shared by twins, especially shared experience and social intimacy. Continued psychological and medical studies of identical and fraternal twins may bring us closer to identifying and understanding those features which uniquely define members of multiple births.

So Happy Together!

by Alice M. Vollmar

From their earliest years, male/female twins are immersed in a firsthand lesson of sexual identity, learning about the opposite gender's physiological and behavioral characteristics simply through their daily interaction with each other.

"I've noticed that my twins, Amanda and Jarrod, who are now 8 years old, are more at ease with friends of the opposite sex than children who have not spent much time around opposite-sex playmates," observed their mother, Julie Schmidt.

During my interview with several sets of male/female middle-years co-twins, many of their parents made similar comments as did the parents of adolescent and adult twins.

Indeed, having an opposite-gender twin can demystify the opposite sex and furnish a good foundation for each twin's sense of his or her own sexual identity. This is particularly true if the twins' parents use toddler and preschool bathing and dressing times to name body parts correctly and talk about male/female differences, notes Gary Best, Ph.D., a professor of education at California State University-Los Angeles and certified sex educator of the American Association of Sex Educators, Counselors, and Therapists.

"Our sexual identity is really who we are, how we behave and how we communicate that to other people," Best notes. "This includes both external designators such as names, manner of dress and behavior, and the physiological designators of basic body anatomy."

Male/female twins generally view themselves as distinct from each other, though it's fairly common for one twin to briefly "try on" aspects of his co-twin's sex role. For example, during the toddler years it's common for male and female co-twins to imitate the opposite-sex twin in dress, toileting and other behavior, as well as examine each other's body. Experts concur that in the young preschool years, these behaviors are simply the playing out of children's natural curiosity.

Parents should respect each of their twin's need for modesty. They should not "force the issue"; not take sides with either child; and not make a "big deal" out of one co-twin's need for more privacy, advises Best. In addition, they should ask their child who is experiencing this normal stage of development what he would like to do to feel more comfortable around his co-twin, reassuring him that they will find a way to honor his privacy needs.

Friendships

Along with it being developmentally normal for 6-to-12-year-olds to desire more privacy, it is also normal for them to prefer same-sex friends. Typically, when male/female twins enter kindergarten or first grade, they will form strong same-sex friendships based on shared interests, as do any siblings at this age, asserts Best.

This transition may or may not occur without conflicts. For example, one twin may reach the "I don't play with girls" or "Boys are yukky" stage before his co-twin, usually resulting in hurt feelings. Best recommends that parents tell their left-out twin, "There are times when girls want to be only with girls and times when boys want to be only with boys. Right now, your sister (brother) is feeling like that, and you need to honor her (his) feelings."

In cases like the one above, as well as in daily play experiences, it is helpful if both co-twins have access to a variety of activity alternatives, so that they don't rely just on each other for company, notes Best. "Each co-twin also needs to have a chance to be with his (her) friends exclusively at times without his (her) co-twin interrupting in order to help each co-twin get practice in developing social skills outside of the twinship."

Sex Education

During the middle years, children's interest in and questions about body development naturally become increasingly sophisticated. According to Betsy Weisman and Michael Weisman, M.D., in their book, *What We Told Our Kids About Sex*, the middle years offer an opportunity for parents to discuss not only body changes, reproduction and sexual intercourse, but also a chance for parents to share with their children their views on premarital sex, homosexuality, contraception and other sexually-specific topics.

"(Our kids) needed sex education as preteens, before they reached adolescence themselves," write the Weismans. According to these authors, children from ages 9 to 12 are "interested and receptive to information, but are not personally involved. Discussions can still be objective and factual. Talking with your kids about sex at this age is not talking about their having sex."

At this in-between stage, "Children are most absorbed in what is happening and what is going to happen to them, but they are also interested in the bodies of siblings and friends," writes Joae Graham Selzer, M.D., in her book, *When Children Ask About Sex*.

Dr. Selzer suggests using children's questions about a friend's or sibling's physical development as an opportunity to give them information on body development. A parent might ask her child's opinion about the developmental changes of his friends ("How do you feel about...?") and reassure him that such changes are normal, adding that each person's development is unique and never exactly the same as someone else's.

Dr. Selzer relates a story about a mother who knew that her 9-year-old son and his older friends had been looking at *Playboy* magazine. She and her son bought an issue and looked at it together. The mother answered her son's questions about adult female bodies and why teenage boys sometimes like to look at pictures of nude women. In other words, she used *Playboy* as an opportunity for solid sex education and diffused its appeal as something forbidden.

By using such an approach, parents of middle-years children can lay the groundwork for later, more personal discussions about the value choices inevitably facing adolescents. Often, as twins approach the older end of the middle years, one twin is likely to surge ahead of his co-twin in sexual development. Suddenly, for example, Jane may tease her co-twin, John, about acting like a nerd or a baby, while John may accuse Jane of acting like a snob or a flirt. Best suggests that parents explain to each child privately about different rates of maturation and the physiological and emotional changes of adolescence, talking about what is happening or about to happen to each twin.

"Both children should have the same knowledge," Best emphasizes. "If a female twin is maturing faster and there is a need to talk with her about physical and sexual changes, her male co-twin is going to be observant and has the same right to know what is occurring with his sister—or vice versa."

Often children of pre-junior high or junior-high age signal a desire for information by teasing, name-calling or asking a question. Best says, "If your son tells you that his twin sister is a flirt, you might ask, 'What do you mean? Why does that bother you?' Give him a chance to talk it out with you. It's likely that he doesn't understand why she's acting that way, and he may even wish he was more like that.

"Of course, if children do bring up the subject with you, it's usually at a time when they feel comfortable doing so, which may not be convenient or comfortable for you, such as when you are eating dinner or adding soap to the wash," Best remarks. "In fact, your children's timing in broaching these topics may be purposeful—it may have a built-in component of avoiding a face-to-face confrontation with you!"

Generally, experts say that sexuality questions are more likely to be directed to parents if they have established a history of discussing body development comfortably with their children and can be counted on to really listen. It's wise to address a pre-adolescent's initial questions as honestly as possible and then set aside time for a more complete discussion.

How can adolescent development information be delivered to male/female twins in their late middle years? Best suggests the following as an ideal or optimum model:

Dad talks with John, then Mom talks with John, followed by Mom and Dad talking with John. Mom talks with Jane, then Dad talks with Jane, followed by Mom and Dad talking with Jane. After that, Mom, Dad, Jane and John talk together.

"Ideally, both children should get an equal share of both parents' information," Best says. Of course, that may not be possible given varying family situations and the willingness of both parents. However, it is important that a parent be involved in offering accurate information. It's far better for one parent to talk to both twins than no parent at all.

Talking to middle-years twins about body development and giving them accurate information is important, but parents' actions also have a strong impact on their children. Authors of books on sex education say that whether parents are aware of it or not, they are constantly conveying non-verbal lessons and sexuality role modeling to their offspring, just as female/male twins learn about their sexual identity as they interact with each other.

In fact, through their kisses, hugs, pats and smiles (or lack of them) and their interactions with each other and other family members, parents are helping each of their twins form a healthy sexual identity every day of their lives.

A parents' listening to her twins and asking them how they feel about a particular difficulty, such as self-consciousness or the societal male/female inequities, can help twins cope with the problem, according to Best. However, if a problem is disrupting a twin's activities or causing extreme anguish, he recommends that a parent seek advice from child-development professionals.

WATCHWORDS TO GROW BY

What contributes to the development of each twin's healthy sexual identity? The following guidelines are offered by Gary Best, Ph.D.:

- Each twin needs the opportunity to be his or her own person and to express his or her individual identity.
- Each twin needs the opportunity to express his or her own characteristics of sexual identity without comparisons being made to his or her co-twin.
- Parents should respond to the sexual identity of their twins in the same way that they respond to the sexual identity of their singletons.

Same-Sex Fraternal Twins

by Nancy L. Segal, Ph.D.

People seem to be most often impressed with the striking behavioral and physical similarities of identical twins. Equally intriguing, however, are the diverse qualities displayed by same-sex fraternal co-twins despite their common rearing situation. The fact that some of these twins maintain close relationships with each other shows that the differences between people need not serve as barriers to their forming strong social bonds. In fact, same-sex fraternal twins have a great deal to teach us regarding the appreciation of individual styles.

It may be surprising to learn that, in Caucasian populations, the frequency of same-sex fraternal twinning is equal to that of identical twinning. (Same-sex fraternal twins and identical twins each represent one-third of the twin population; opposite-sex fraternal twins represent the remaining one-third.)

Why, then, are the social and experimental aspects of same-sex fraternal twins often overlooked? This observation may be explained, in part, by the fact that these fraternal twins are not identical in appearance and, consequently, do not always attract the fascinated attention that is often directed toward identical twins. Some same-sex fraternal twin partners, in fact, show such little physical or behavioral resemblance that it may be surprising to learn that they are twins! In contrast, the members of other fraternal twin pairs may look and behave very much alike.

Another explanation for the apparent "neglect" of same-sex fraternal twins may relate to their role in the classic twin research design. Twin researchers typically compare the behavioral or physical resemblance between identical co-twins to the resemblance between same-sex fraternal co-twins.

Relatively greater resemblance between identical co-twins is consistent with a genetic influence on the trait(s) under study. Researchers typically regard same-sex fraternal twins as a comparison or control group for identical twins, thereby focusing more exclusively on the latter.

Similarities at Birth

In some respects, same-sex fraternal twin infants may originally appear more alike than identical twin infants. The Louisville Twin Study, in Louisville, Kentucky, found that same-sex fraternal twins were more similar in birth length than identical twins. The fraternal twin pairs became increasingly dissimilar, however, when their heights were measured at selected ages, from 3 months to 8 years.

In contrast, the same-sex fraternal twins in the study were only slightly more similar in birth weight than the identical twins. As was true for height, the fraternal twins became increasingly dissimilar in weight, while the identical twins became increasingly similar over time. Early differences between identical twins may reflect unusual intrauterine effects, such as transfusion syndrome, to which these twins may be especially susceptible.

The Fraternal Twin Bond

A considerable amount of clinical, experimental and biographical data has demonstrated that, in general, same-sex fraternal twins do not share the same degrees of social intimacy as identical twins. This does not imply, however, that some of these twins cannot be as closely affiliated as identical twins or that all identical twins necessarily enjoy a close social bond. There does appear, however, to be greater variation in the quality of social relationships shared by same-sex fraternal twins than by identical twins.

Research studies conducted after reunions between adult twins who were raised separately from infancy are enormously revealing with respect to the nature of these relationships. The Minnesota Study of Twins Reared Apart, at the University of Minnesota, has been administering twin relationship interviews to participants in an attempt to better understand the experience of meeting a twin for the first time. Questions concerning the search for the twin, initial and current impressions of the twin relationship, and judgments about the future of the relationship are included.

The majority of twins in these studies were raised by adoptive families, and many were unaware until late in life that they were part of a twinship. A striking observation is that, in general, most searches for biological relatives by adopted individuals are generally launched for the purpose of locating a parent, most often the mother.

But once the individual learns that he is a twin, his search most often becomes focused upon locating his twin sibling. His twintype (identical or fraternal) is unknown at this stage in his search process and may be regarded as inconsequential by the individual; identification of the multiple-birth partner is the primary goal. The existence of other biological brothers and sisters is sometimes revealed during a search, but these siblings do not appear to command the same degree of excitement and investment as one's co-twin.

Preliminary analyses suggest that reunited identical twins tend to experience greater feelings of closeness and familiarity during the initial meeting than same-sex fraternal twins, a finding possibly associated with their generally greater physical and behavioral resemblance.

However, a number of the reunited same-sex fraternal twins have pursued close, loving relationships with each other. A pair of male twins, Dewayne Gramley and Paul Forbes, met for the first time when they were 69 years old. These twins are aware of many differences in their lifestyles and behaviors. They are, however, currently enjoying their newly-found twin relationship and have embarked upon several trips to their place of birth in search of information about their early histories.

Comparing Same-Sex Fraternals to Singleton Siblings

Very few studies have systematically compared social relationships between same-sex fraternal twins and singleton siblings. An important exception is a study conducted by Helen Koch, Ph.D., in 1966 at the University of Chicago. The study included 18 identical male twin pairs, 17 identical female twin pairs, 18 fraternal male twin pairs, 17 fraternal female twin pairs, 19 opposite-sex fraternal twin pairs and 432 singleton children.

All of the twins were the only children in their families, while all of the singletons came from two-sibling families. The participants were between 4 and 7 years of age. Interviews with the children, parents of the twins and teachers of the twins addressed various aspects of the twin relationship and social adjustment. Twins and non-twins additionally completed a mental ability test battery and the Children's Apperception Test (CAT) to assess verbal skill, as well as family attitudes and perceptions.

Both groups of identical and fraternal twins were closer to their twin siblings (co-twins) than the matched singletons were to their siblings. Closeness was determined by the amount of time spent playing together, the number of shared friends and possessions, and the degree of conflict.

Results of the study showed that the twins from the same-sex pairs (identical and fraternal) more often believed that their parents treated them impartially than did the singleton siblings. Furthermore, the same-sex co-twins maintained a less critical opinion of each other and indicated that they had a better social relationship than did the singleton siblings. The twins also showed a reduced desire to change places with their co-twins, as compared to the singleton siblings.

These results demonstrate that same-sex fraternal co-twins share more interests in common and receive more similar treatment from parents than singleton siblings, a finding that is a likely consequence of their common age and developmental level. In addition, unlike singleton siblings, fraternal co-twins come into the family together so that one is not "upstaged" by the other due to their birth order.

RESEARCHERS SAY...

- R. Darrell Bock, Ph.D., at the University of Chicago, and colleagues provided evidence that similarity in a greater number of blood groups (increased genetic relatedness) may be associated with increased behavioral and physical resemblance. Several mental ability scales were administered to fraternal twins for whom some blood-typing information was available. Twins whose blood groups were the same showed reduced variation on the mental ability scales compared to twins whose blood groups differed. This finding was replicated by Andy Pakstis and colleagues at the University of Minnesota.

- A more recent study conducted by Marilyn Dumont-Driscoll, Ph.D., and Richard J. Rose, Ph.D., at Indiana University, used same-sex fraternal twins to determine if twins' perceived similarity in physical appearance was associated with genetic similarity. Extensive blood-typing information was obtained on twins and on their family members, enabling estimates of the degree of genetic relatedness between the twins. Twins who were uncertain or mistaken about their twintype had a higher proportion of genes in common than twins who correctly identified themselves as fraternal. Furthermore, twins who expressed uncertainty about their twintype were rated as more similar by their mothers than twins who were sure of their twintype.

- Emergenesis, a relatively new concept in the study of human behavior that has arisen through the study of fraternal twins, is a term coined by David T. Lykken, Ph.D., of the University of Minnesota. Lykken has noted that for some traits that are each influenced by more than one gene, such as certain brain wave parameters, identical twins show a high degree of resemblance while fraternal twins "are no more alike than pairs of unrelated persons."

This finding suggests that some traits may be influenced by many different interacting genes. Therefore, identical twins would have the same gene combinations, but it would be rare for fraternal twins to inherit common configurations of many genes. This explanation helps us to understand how some traits may be genetically influenced, but do not appear to run in families.

PRACTICAL ANSWERS TO POPULAR PARENTING QUESTIONS

1) How can I help my same-sex fraternal twins adjust to their individual differences, especially when people expect them to look the same, as well as learn skills at the same time; reach developmental milestones simultaneously; and have the same interests, temperaments and personalities?

The psychological "plague" usually attached to the twin situation is that a pair of co-twins will be fused together so much that each twin's individuality will suffer. In this respect, dissimilar same-sex fraternal co-twins have an advantage if people give up the popular notion that "twins" means "same." In fact, the scientific study of twins is but one aspect of the study of individual differences which, if measured carefully, exist for everyone.

When their same-sex fraternal co-twins are young, parents can help them adjust to their individual differences by stressing and rewarding their unique qualities—the same advice often given to parents of identical twins. Each twin's adjustment to being a twin is an outgrowth of the importance that his parents place on the twin's own individuality.

2) What can I say when people see my same-sex fraternal twins for the first time and exclaim, "Are they really twins?" and "They can't be twins! They're so different from each other!"

Parents can handle comments like these by giving a short summary of what being a twin means from a genetic and an obstetric perspective. Of course, there is a social risk attached to educating the uninformed, so a better strategy might be to fend off such comments with a smile and a light comment about being lucky enough to have a little variety out of one pregnancy!

3) How can I adjust to being so disappointed that my same-sex fraternal twins do not get much attention because they don't look or act alike? I really don't feel like a parents of twins!

Given the difficulties (and expense!) of raising twins, it is no wonder that some parents feel cheated because their same-sex fraternal twins receive less attention than they would if they were identical twins.

However, infant twins appearing together in public almost always receive at least twice the attention that people give to singletons. The problem is that when twin differences become more obvious as the twins age, their parents' celebrity status may not last. With or without regret, most parents seem to adjust to the marked individuality of their dissimilar twins. The real "trick" is for parents to see that each of their twins gets a full share of their parental love and care as a person, whether or not their twins bring attention to the family via their twinship.

4) Should I encourage my same-sex fraternal twins to accentuate their twinship (tell people they're twins, always stick together, etc.) so that they will not lose their identity as co-twins? Or should I simply treat them as I would any of my singletons?

A balance has to be struck between overly encouraging the similiarities and highly exaggerating the differences between same-sex fraternal co-twins.

In some cases, same-sex fraternal co-twins' differences can be so overemphasized that the twins may become polar opposites as a result of the co-called "contrast effect": One twin is quiet and his co-twin is noisy; one twin is shy and his co-twin is outgoing, etc.

Parents may fall into the trap of treating or labeling their same-sex dissimilar co-twins as more different from each other than from the other siblings in their family. This "contrast effect" may ultimately force a pair of twins to fit highly inflexible roles in their family.

It is important that parents of same-sex fraternal twins let their twins' behaviors instruct them about when their twinship "matters" and when it doesn't. Twins can be encouraged to accentuate their twinship when it is appropriate and when they feel comfortable doing so in a given situation, just as they can accentuate their gender, family or nationality, for example, at certain times.

Do Twins Really Run in Families?

by Alice M. Vollmar

In the book, *Having Twins*, author Elizabeth Noble, former director of the Maternal and Child Health Center in Cambridge, MA said, "The cause of identical twinning remains a mystery—some chance factor favors a delay in the division process of the fertilized single egg. As a result, the chromosomes, which carry the genes and are fixed in quantity (46), decide to double in number and the egg splits into equal halves."

Evidently, the why of identical twinning is, as yet, an unsolved puzzle. The rate of identical twinning remains fairly stable worldwide, regardless of race and culture—four or five per 1,000 births, according to Elizabeth Noble in the 1991 edition of *Having Twins*. However, Louis Keith, M.D., director of the Medical Center for Study of Multiple Births, has reported some correlation between identical twinning and older mothers.

Interestingly, Noble mentions a 50 percent increase in monozygotic (identical) twinning in Sweden and northwestern Europe since the 1970's, and makes note of instances of identical twins bearing identical twins and a family with four sets of identical twins in the family line. Despite this circumstantial evidence, however, researchers have yet to determine the role of genetics in identical twinning.

Fraternal Twinning Tendencies

In contrast, researchers have determined that heredity does play a part in fraternal twinning. Harvard Medical School bio statistician Grace Wyshak, Ph.D., "found that the gene favoring fraternal twins passes along the family line," Noble reported in *Having Twins*. "If a woman has a history of fraternal twins in her family on her mother's side, or if she is a twin herself, her chances of conceiving twins are increased." On the other hand, "the influence of heredity through the paternal line, or with monozygotic (one egg) twinning, is unclear." Noble also said that having one set of fraternal twins quadruples a mother's chances of conceiving another set, and the incidence of fraternal twinning increases with the number of pregnancies.

However, many factors affect fraternal twinning. Race is one of the variables. For example, white Americans have 20.4 fraternal twins per 1,000 births; African Americans, 25.3 in 1,000 births; Japanese and Chinese populations, about four in 1,000 births; Nigerians, particularly the Yoruba, about 45 per 1,000 births. (Interestingly, the rate of triplet pregnancies for white Americans is one in 84,000; for African Americans, one in 98,000 births.)

Another variable is age. Older mothers are more likely to conceive fraternal twins, with peak twinning years between 35 and 39 for white and African Americans—due to higher levels of hormones which can result in more eggs being matured and released. After age 40 for white Americans and age 49 for African Americans, twinning rates generally decline.

Some studies link frequency of sexual intercourse with twinning. In seeming contrast to statistics on older mothers and twinning, this research shows that "twins are most frequently conceived within the first three months of marriage, presumably because of the higher levels of sexual activity," said Noble. These studies contend that increased orgasms trigger double ovulation.

An eclectic array of factors are believed to affect the conception of twins, including where one lives and the time of year. It has been suggested that exposure to light after long northern winters may stimulate double ovulation; fertility in the Northern Hemisphere is highest in February and March, according to Noble. She also told of a study showing that California has the highest rate of twinning in the United States; however, another and more recent study found an increase in twinning among whites in northeastern states. As Noble noted, studies on twinning related to geography and seasons offer "a mixed bag of conclusions."

Additionally, the use of fertility drugs which stimulate ovarian function and new techniques such as in vitro fertilization can result in multiple births. Although oral contraceptives have been linked to increased twinning, other studies found a decline or no difference in multiple births among oral contraceptive users.

Good nutrition increases the incidence of twinning, as does being a taller and heavier than average woman in her later childbearing years with several previous healthy births. However, since so many factors play a part in twinning, not every woman with a hereditary predisposition to fraternal twinning actually gives birth to fraternal twins.

Twinning Perplexities

Then there are the unexplained-by-research twinning events that nature tosses into the twinning picture, such as families with numerous sets of identical twins in their history, identical twins who father or give birth to identical twins or families with fraternal twins only in the male's family line.

Clearly, exceptions to the unknown predicators of twinning exist. The phenomenon continues to pose unanswered questions.

In pursuing an answer to "Just who has twins anyway?", one winds up with a substantial body of research, some actual facts and figures related to twinning—and some mysteries.

IDENTICAL AND FRATERNALS: THE DISTINCTION

Identical twins develop from one egg. All the genetic material in the fertilized egg first doubles and then divides in half so that each half receives the same genetic potential. Identical twins' heredity, therefore, is the same.

When two eggs are produced at the same time and are fertilized at the same time, fraternal twins develop, and each has his own assortment of genes. Two-egg twins may look and be as much alike or as unlike as any sisters or brothers.

If the terms "one-egg twins" and "two-egg twins" were substituted for "identical" and "fraternal," respectively, the differences between twintypes might be much clearer.

UNDERSTANDING THE TWINTYPING OPTIONS

Type of Test	Sample	Cost	Comments
Placental Exam	Placenta	$150-400	Gives answer only 35% of the time. Accurate if performed correctly. Only at birth
Blood Typing	Blood	$100-300	Less accurate than DNA tests
HLA	Blood	$150-350	Less accurate than DNA tests
DNA Fingerprinting	Blood	$200-900	The two most accurate methods
DNA-STAR Test	Cheek Swab	$80	

WILL BLOOD-TYPING GIVE ME A "FOR SURE" ANSWER?

Blood-typing is the most accurate, objective method of determining twin-type. Blood samples are taken from each pair member and are compared across various blood group factors. Blood group differences identify fraternal twins with complete certainty.

In rare cases, however, fraternal twins (and singleton siblings) may have all measured blood group factors in common because they share parents in common. Some investigators (myself included) have classified twins as fraternal, despite results from the blood-typing laboratory indicating identical twinning. These decisions were prompted by observing pronounced twin differences in characteristics that are substantially influenced by genetic factors, such as height, hair color or eye color.

I believe that it is important to know with certainty if twins are identical or fraternal in order to better understand their developmental differences and to assess their risks of contracting certain diseases that are influenced by genetic factors.

by Nancy L. Segal, Ph.D

STEP-BY-STEP:
HOW MY GRANDCHILDREN WERE TWINTYPED

My family wondered whether my twin granddaughters, Alyssa and Rachel, were identical or fraternal. We assumed, almost from their births in 1988, that they were fraternal because of our own observations, as well as those of my daughter's obstetrician who based his judgment on the fact that the babies were carried in two separate placenta (both double layered) separated by a thick membrane.

I remembered a story I had written about Cellmark Diagnostics and thought that testing my grandchildren's blood through the process of DNA Fingerprinting could settle the matter of Alyssa and Rachel's zygosity.

Once we decided to go ahead with the tests, it was a relatively simple procedure. When Enrique and Juli took their babies to their pediatrician for a routine examination, they asked him to draw extra blood. He obtained about six milliliters from each child, and Juli and Enrique mailed the samples to Cellmark Diagnostics.

When blood samples such as Rachel and Alyssa's arrive at Cellmark's laboratory, the lab assistant logs them in and starts the process of tracking the samples by computer. Next the samples are sent to a staff molecular biologist who draws the amount of blood that is needed for testing. The remainder is placed in a freezer, where it is stored for at least a year. The procedure is witnessed, as are all the steps in the process, by another molecular biologist.

At this point in the procedure, the desoxyribonucleic acid (DNA) is extracted from the blood samples. Then a process called restriction is applied, in which the DNA segments are then separated by size in a process called electrophoreses. The segments are placed on a gelatin-like material, and an electrical charge is passed through them. The negatively-charged segments spread out as the smaller ones move farther toward the positive end of the gelatin; the gelatin acts as a sieve.

For quality control, so-called known DNA standards are placed on the gelatin as well. This is done, according to Mark Stolorow, manager of forensic services, so that if something goes wrong in the process, the problem will be readily noted and can be corrected.

In its normal state, DNA looks something like a twisted ladder, which is called a double helix. For the DNA Fingerprint, the strands are separated or unzipped, in a process called denaturing. Once finished, the separated strands are placed through a step called Southern Blotting; this transfers the unzipped DNA segments from the gelatin to a permanent nylon membrane, which can be used repeatedly for testing.

The membrane is then placed in a soupy mix of chemicals and introduced to the radioactive probes of DNA. The probes are short strands of DNA, radioactively charged, that attach themselves in a predictable way to the unknown DNA. The molecular biologist then exposes the membrane to a piece of X-ray film, on which the emulsion is set up to react to radiation. It is run through a film processor that produces the DNA Fingerprint.

After completing a preliminary analysis and comparison, the molecular biologist turns the film and her findings over to the staff geneticist, who does the final analysis and scoring, and sends the final report regarding twin zygosity to the twins' parents.

Our report revealed that Alyssa's DNA Fingerprint contained at least 36 bands and that Rachel's DNA Fingerprint also contained at least 36 bands, all of which matched the bands in Alyssa's Fingerprint. The report continued, "The probability that the DNA Fingerprint of Alyssa Navarrete has by chance 36 of the 36 bands found in the DNA Fingerprint of Rachel Navarrete is one in 4.7 x10^{21}. The population of the world is approximately 5.2 x 10^9. Conclusion: "Alyssa Navarrete and Rachel Navarrete are identical twins."

Now that's the kind of certainty that parents (and grandparents!) of twins can savor!

by Frank Aukofer

How to Tell Twintypes Apart

by Nancy L. Segal, Ph.D.

Identical twins are not identical in every way. It is, in fact, somewhat surprising to realize that they may differ on a considerable array of physical and behavioral characteristics. Identical twins share identical genes, but unique pre- and post-natal circumstances may underlie differences in some cases.

Fraternal twins, in contrast, share the same genetic relationship as ordinary brothers and sisters, that is, half their genes in common, on the average, by descent. They are, therefore, expected to differ, both physically and behaviorally, due to genetic *and* environmental influences. These differences may be a matter of quality *and* degree. Some fraternal pairs, however, *do* show striking similarities in certain features.

This observable "overlap" between the two types of twins has caused some parents to seriously question the diagnosis of *identical* or *fraternal* given to them by their physicians at the time of birth. Some parents, for example, might suspect that similar developmental patterns in their children are more consistent with identical twinning, despite a physician's report of fraternal twins. This also explains why researchers prefer the terms *monozygotic* (one-egg twins) and *dizygotic* (two-egg twins) for classifying twin pairs.

This article will review some key characteristics that can differ in identical twinships, despite genetic identity, and that can be alike in fraternal twinships, despite genetic non-identity. The most effective available methods for determining twin type will be explained, as well as why this information is important for parents of twins, and for twins themselves.

Identical and Fraternal Twins: Similarities and Differences

1) The Placenta: It is a common misconception that twin type can be accurately determined by the number of placentas observed at birth. It is, for example, incorrectly assumed that one placenta *always* signifies monozygotic (identical) twins, while two placentas *always* signify dizygotic (fraternal) twins. Monozygotic twins can have one or two placentas, depending upon the time at which the fertilized egg undergoes division. Two placentas are associated with "early-splitting" twins (egg splits on, or before, the fifth day after conception; this occurs in about one-third of identical twins).

One research study determined, however, that 43 percent of this group of identical twins may show fused placentas. This can occur when the two fetuses implant closely to one another in the uterus. Fusion of the placenta may be partial or complete, resulting in the appearance of a single structure. A single placenta is associated with relatively "late-splitting" twins (egg splits between five and 10 day after conception; about two-thirds of identical twins.)

Dizygotic twins *always* have two placentas. Approximately 42 percent of fraternal twin births, however, show fused placentas. It is, therefore, understandable that errors in diagnosing twin type may be likely from examining the placenta alone.

The additional analysis of other fetal membranes, namely the amnion and chorion, is informative. These membranes surround the fetus during its prenatal stages, and also provide clues as to the time that splitting occurs to form identical twins.

Early-splitting identical twins have two separate amnions and chorions. The majority of relatively late-splitting twins share a single chorion, but have separate amnions. Only about 4 percent of identical twins share a common amnion. In contrast, fraternal twins *always* have individual membranes. It should be easy to see that, based on fetal membranes, one might confuse fraternal twins with early-splitting identical twins.

2) Birth Weight: Approximately 10 to 15 percent of identical twins are seriously affected by "fetal transfusion syndrome." This results from intrauterine blood transfusion between identical twins who share a common chorion or outer fetal membrane. (Shared intrauterine blood circulation has, however, been observed among 85 percent of twins in this group.) A common effect of this condition is a marked difference in the birth weights of the two twins. Other effects may involve differences in general health and vigor.

Dr. Daniel G. Freedman, at the University of Chicago, reported a case study of identical twins whose birth events and contrasting behavioral styles at 6 years old were probably associated with this condition. (It is possible that some pairs may display more subtle differences in size and health that are not immediately detectable at birth.) Fraternal twins are not subject to this syndrome because fetal membranes are not shared.

It is striking that identical twins, on average, show *greater* birth weight differences than fraternal twins. This twin group difference is, however, not maintained when weight is measured periodically during the first year of life. Dr. Ronald Wilson, former director of the Louisville Twin Study, explained that, beginning at 3 months old, identical twins become increasingly alike in birth weight and fraternal twins become increasingly different with the "rapid convergence of each twin on his genetic growth curve."

3) Height: Identical twins, on the average, show greater resemblance in height than fraternal twins. At birth, however, fraternal twins are more similar in height than identical twins. By 3 months old, and throughout the early childhood years, however, identical twins become increasingly more alike in height than fraternal twins. As adults, identical twins are expected to differ by no more than two inches, while fraternal twins, on average, may differ by three inches, or more. Particular pairs of identical twins may, however, show differences ranging between three to five inches. The larger differences may reflect the influence of unusual intrauterine factors, such as the transfusion syndrome mentioned above.

I observed 8-year-old identical females who differed in height by five inches. The smaller twin displayed the effects of a marginally attached placenta that prevented her from receiving sufficient prenatal nutrition. In contrast, some fraternal twins will resemble one another in height to the same degree as typical identical twins because they share genes for that specific trait. The important point is that resemblance or non-resemblance in height alone does not accurately identify twin type.

4) Handedness: About 25 percent of identical *and* fraternal twins differ in hand preference. Unusual prenatal influences, such as fetal crowding, may be associated with these differences for both types of twins. Delayed splitting of the fertilized egg may further explain opposite-handedness in identical twins only. Fraternal twins also may differ in hand preference if one child should inherit this tendency from a parent. (Handedness has been shown to be genetically transmitted, although the pattern of transmission is not well understood.) The message here is that the resemblance, or lack of resemblance in traits such as handedness cannot be used to determine whether or not twins are identical or fraternal.

A variety of other features also may show the "mirror-imaging" effect, due to delayed splitting in *identical* twins only. They may include opposite-eyedness (such as in eye preference when looking through a camera), opposite birthmarks or moles, or opposite dental characteristics, for example. Situations exist in which identical twins may not be strictly identical in every way! Fraternal twins also could display reversals for these traits, but the source of these differences would be associated with their genetic differences.

5) Personality: Psychological researchers have determined that identical twins show greater resemblance than fraternal twins across a variety of personality characteristics. Observable differences can, however, emerge in the behavioral styles of identical twins, due to their social interactions with one another. One twin may, for example, display greater extroversion than his or her twin, a feature of the relationship that may change across time or situations. Rene Zazzo, twin researcher, refers to this phenomenon as the "couple effect."

Identical twin partners have been nicknamed the "active" twin and the "passive" twin, and the "doer" and the "clinging vine" by various investigators. These roles may be most apparent when the twins are together. Fraternal twins also may show distinctive behaviors, but their characterization along a common dimension may be less likely. James Shields, a British researcher, referred to members of a fraternal pair as the "terror" and the "professor." It is likely that fraternal twins will maintain their respective roles apart from the twinship, as well as when they are together.

Methods for Classifying Twins

A comparative examination of twins' blood types is the most accurate method of determining if twins are identical or fraternal. In comprehensive studies, approximately 20 to 24 red blood cell characteristics, as well as other blood constituents, are examined. If differences are detected, it is certain that the twins are fraternal. If all blood groups match, this indicates identical twinning with a very high degree of certainty. Researchers cannot say for sure that the twins are identical because fraternal twins could inherit exactly the same blood characteristics from their parents. This event would, however, be quite rare.

The cost of blood-typing is variable among hospitals and health centers, but averages $35 per child. Some research studies can offer a reduced fee, or free services, if the twins are participants in a study. (Parents should note that tests for certain blood groups may be less reliable than others, introducing a very small degree of error even into a blood analysis. In several cases, I have requested that laboratories repeat their tests, which then agreed with my impression of twintype!)

When Are Identical Twins Not Identical?

by Alice M. Vollmar

Answers to the above question confound many parents of identical twins who wonder just what is "wrong" with their babies who display opposite hair whorls and opposite dominant hands but are twintyped as identical.

Learning that mirror-image twins display characteristics such as these twins do can be reassuring and useful information for all family members.

"When Matthew and Aaron started to feed themselves and draw with crayons, we noticed they used opposite hands," said Teri Polzin, mother of 3-year-old identical boys. We also noticed that their cowlicks and natural parts are opposite and that each twin has one slightly smaller eye – and that's opposite, too."

The Incidence Of Mirror-Imaging

Up to 25 percent of identical twins exhibit mirror-image features, according to Elizabeth Bryan, M.D., vice president of the International Society for Twin Studies and medical director of the Multiple Births Foundation. In her book, *Twins, Triplets and More* (St. Martins Press, 1992), Dr. Bryan offered this description of mirror-imaging: "If the features on one twin are reversed, then the mirror-image thus created will be most similar to the appearance of the second twin."

Dr. Bryan listed hair direction and placement of hair whorls, fingerprint patterns, and dental patterns as commonly reversed features. The reversed location of internal organs, such as the heart or liver, is less common, she said, and noted that "mirror-imaging rarely causes any problems."

Other Mirror-Image Phenomena

In addition to opposite side/direction hair whorls, identical twins Benjamin and Samuel Brodsky, 18 months, used opposite arms to pull them along when they learned to crawl, and received opposite-side new teeth, ear infections in opposite ears and sores on opposite big toes. Interestingly, Benjamin has a birth-mark on his left armpit, and Samuel has one on his right thumb.

Mirror-image features in 3-year-old identical twins, Joshua and Jacob Hooper, include not only opposite hair whorls, handedness and ear infection occurrence, but also dimples! In a **TWINS**® article on mirror-image twins (March/April 1985), Candy Schock, R.N., observed that congenital malformations, such as inguinal hernias and curvature of the spine, also can manifest on opposite sides. She noted that some twin pairs have more mirror-image traits than others. Why this is so remains one of twinship's mysteries—as does the impact of mirror-imaging on personality and temperament.

The socialization process—helping children learn how to get along with others—can be affected by some mirror-image characteristics, as it did for mirror-image co-twin Lori Stewart, 50. "My twin sister, Lynn Long, is right-handed, and I should have been left-handed; but my mom encouraged me to use my right hand," recalled Stewart. "I ended up being ambidextrous, which is great today. I can write and, as a hairdresser, cut hair and wrap perms with either hand."

In her article, Schock suggested the possibility that a mirror-image twin who does not use his dominant foot to kick a ball may do so because that's the way he was taught to kick. Hence, some mirror-image functional traits may be affected and perhaps altered by the "environment" rather than genetics.

How Does Mirror-Imaging Happen?

The cause of mirror-imaging remains largely a matter of speculation. According to Dr. Bryan, "The explanation that used to be given for mirror-imagery was that the division of the fertilized egg took place after the left and right sides of the developing embryo's body had been designated. This now seems an unlikely explanation, because when the egg splits, the embryo is still a mass of undiffer-entiated cells. However, no more likely explanation has been put forward."

Schock commented that it has long been thought that mirror-image twins result when "the embryo suddenly splits at a later date than non-mirror-image twins...and since conjoined (Siamese) twins exhibit a high degree of reversed asymmetry (mirror-imaging), some feel that mirror-image twins escape being born conjoined by a short span of time."

If division of a fertilized egg happens between 10 and 13 days of development, the result may be mirror-image identical twins, according to Edward Ziegler in his Reader's Digest article "The Mysterious Bonds of Twins" (January 1980). When division occurs after the 13th day, the twins may be conjoined, said Ziegler.

Does Being Mirror-Image Twins Affect Twins' Lives?

Stewart believes that being a mirror-image twin has not had any impact on her relationship with her co-twin. Nor do the parents of twins whom I inter-viewed think that mirror-imaging had any effect on their parenting, other than serving as a way for telling their twins apart and being a minor challenge when right-handed parents teach a left-handed child to tie a shoelace, or use scissors and eating utensils.

However, Brodsky identified a potential plus. "Benjamin and Samuel should be able to play tennis doubles well," she quipped. "They should make a great team."

The Special Challenges Faced by Families of Conjoined Twins

by Jillian Bosman

The recent explosion in scientific knowledge and subsequent understanding of human genetics and the early stages of human embryonic development has provided answers to many important questions about conjoined twins (commonly known as Siamese Twins).

"An expectant mother and father are anticipating entering a relationship with one or more individuals," noted clinical psychologist Teria Shantal. "If the outcome of the pregnancy is twins and those twins are conjoined, the parents often become confused. They wonder how to relate to two babies but, at the same time, to one unit."

A somewhat natural contradiction may then arise for the parents of these special twins—a need to bond emotionally with the children, yet a fear of doing so, and of developing a relationship that may well be short-lived.

Shantal explained, "Obviously, a predominant question in the parents' minds when a major organ is involved is whether one or both twins might die. They don't want the relationship to end. This often causes severe stress, particularly if they have cared for the babies for months or years before the operation."

Not all separations of conjoined twins are successful; in some instances, they are not even attempted. If major organs such as the brain, liver or cardiovascular system are involved, it is often preferable to delay separation for months or years, giving the babies' systems time to mature. In many situations, the separation may involve various meticulously planned stages, allowing time between operations for full recuperation.

In a very small minority of cases—usually if one of the fetuses is tiny, dead, and attached to the other by pliable soft tissue—the separation may be done intrauterine. Since risk of maternal injury is high, however, this is not a common procedure. When small areas and no major organs are shared, separation might be undertaken as soon as the newborn babies are strong enough to undergo the operation.

Thirty-nine-year-old American craniopagus twins, Yvette and Yvonne Jones, who are still joined at the crown, profess that they would not like to be separated. A strong reason for their feelings is their fear that one or both might not survive the procedure.

"It's understandable," said Percy Miller, a senior member of the Baragwanath Hospital neurosurgical team in Soweto, South Africa. "After 20 to 30 years of being together, one must grow so used to one's partner that perhaps each becomes an integral part of the other."

Shaltall supports this view. "There must have been periods of great stress for the Joneses, especially during the formative years," she remarked. "Although their personalities may differ markedly, rather than developing authentic independent selfhoods, they have probably become each other's framework, since they have always been subject to one another's wishes and demands."

According to medical professionals, survival of the twins after separation is not synonymous with success. In a 1968 *South Africa Medical Journal* editorial, pediatric surgeon M. Dinner quoted A.W. Franklin's comment that, "Success demands tissues and organs for two independent, normal persons. In some cases, the decision may be made to leave the twins in their conjoined state. In others, one twin might be sacrificed to save the life of the other."

ARE CONJOINED TWINS ON THE RISE?

At the 1986 International Congress of Twin Studies, Denis Viljeon, M.D., of the department of human genetics at the University of Cape Town, South Africa, noted that there had been a marked increase in the number of births of conjoined twins in South Africa during 1974 and 1975. Suggestions have been made that a similar rise in incidence is apparent at the present time.

"One must analyze the data over a five-or 10-year period," cautioned pediatric cardiologist Solly Levin, who was closely involved in the case of the first successful South African separation of craniopagus twins, Shirley and Catherine O'Hare, performed in 1968. They were only the second pair of craniopagus twins recorded to have survived and develop normally after separation.

Levin explained, "Six or seven sets of craniopagus twins may be born over a period of one or two years. This might give the impression of an increase in the average proportion of craniopagus twins. However, if the data were examined over a longer period, it may be found that those five or six pairs were the only craniopagus twins born over the entire 10-year period; so the statistics average out within expected parameters. This also applies to the general rate of conjoined twinning.

THE LONGEST-SURVIVING CONJOINED TWINS

The term Siamese was derived from the well-documented and astonishing pair, Chang and Eng Bunker.

Born in 1811 in Meklong, Siam (now Thailand), Chang and Eng were joined by a cartilaginous band at the chest and remained joined until their death. Laymen flocked to see them when they became an exhibit in P.T. Barnum's circus. Controversy raged in medical circles over whether they could be safely separated.

Achieving fame and fortune touring the world with the circus, Chang and Eng settled in America and married sisters. Chang fathered 10 children, and Eng fathered 12. The co-twins died within hours of one another, shortly before they were to turn 63 years old—the longest-surviving conjoined twins on record.

HOW CONJOINED TWINS ARE CREATED

1) Conjoined twinning occurs in one in 50,000 to one in 100,000 births, or at a rate of one in 200 to 1 in 400 monozygotic twin births.

2) Although the anomaly appears to be independent of the mother's pregnancies, age, race and heredity, three times more girl than boy conjoined twins are born.

3) In the 1987 *British Heart Journal*, Martinez Barra Rossi and colleagues explain the creation of conjoined twins by comparing the event to the extreme end of a "time continuum of fission." These twins are formed by a very late separation of a monozygotic twin conception. At the other end of the continuum are identical twins who are in separate sacs (dichorionic monozygotic twins).

It is more likely that twins will have two separate amnions the closer to conception that the separation occurs. The longer after conception that the separation occurs, the more likely they will share one amnion (monochorionic monozygotic twins).

In rare instances, for reasons unknown, separation halts altogether or goes awry, causing not only the amnion, but also the body parts, to be shared. This may involve anything from a small area of shared skin and tissue to a shared body with two heads, four arms and two legs.

4) Duplicatas completa, or diplopagus, refers to cases in which infants' component parts are equal and symmetrical.

5) Duplicatas incompleta, or heteropagus, describes conjoined twins who are unequal and asymmetrical.

6) Craniopagus (joined at the head) is the rarest form of diplopagus twins—occurring in about one in 2.5 million births.

7) Thoracopagus (joined at the chest) is the most common form of diplopagus twins, found in 70 percent or more cases.

8) Pygopagus (joined at the back) account for about 20 percent of all diplopagus twins.

THE MATHIBELA TWINS

Sophie Mathibela of South Africa wept when told that her twins were joined at the back of their heads. She was too afraid to see them. Sophie, a single mother with two older children, believed that God was punishing her for bearing the children out of wedlock. As with most conjoined twins, their condition was undiagnosed until their births by Cesarean section on December 7, 1986.

Surprised to learn that she had given birth to twins, she was even more shocked and bewildered upon learning that they were conjoined. Yet, when persuaded to visit the babies, Sophie experienced an overwhelming love and named the girls Mpho and Mphonyana—"Big Gift" and "Little Gift" from God.

On May 4, 1988, 17-month-old Mpho and Mphonyana were finally separated in the gruelling third of a series of operations at Baragwanath Hospital in Soweto, South Africa.

Interviewed before the Mathibela separation, Robert Lipschitz, M.D., head of the Baragwanath neurosurgical team, explained why, apart from obvious physical restrictions and consequent development delay, the twins were ready for separation.

"Intensive psychological assessments indicate that Mpho and Mphonyana are beginning to suffer from a deprivation syndrome," he said. "The pressure of the two brains against one another may cause some sort of atrophy. This could lead to problems because they are joined at a vital area of the brain."

The apparently successful separation of the Mathibela twins was due not only to meticulous planning, practice runs and superb teamwork, but also to lessons learned from earlier cases; the Mathibela twins' separation involved three phases. In the first operation in October 1987, the vein was clamped in one child's brain just before it converged with the shared section. The clamp was then tightened gradually during the following week prior to the second operation, in the hope that the blood flow in that child's brain would be redirected via alternative channels.

During the second operation, however, the smaller and weaker of the pair, Mphonyana, unexpectedly bled profusely and almost died. Seven months later, on May 4, 1988, when successfully separated, one twin retained the intact clamped vein, while the other had a redirected blood flow.

Sophie was obliged to contribute only a token amount of money toward the entire cost of the hospitalization of her children. A trust fund also was established for her twins. Without this assistance, Sophie, an unemployed domestic worker, would have been destitute when she and her babies eventually left the hospital.

"I feel so happy," wept an elated Sophie after the operation. Overcome, she paused and then added quietly, "I want to sleep a little, pray and thank God for all he has done."

THE BENNIE TWINS

Pam and Dugal Bennie, who live near Johannesburg, South Africa felt an overwhelming love and tenderness when they first saw their twin boys, Cameron and Andrew, who were born on April 2, 1986, joined from the coccyx to a third of the way up the back.

"It made me realize how parents can accept their handicapped children. I felt no rejection whatsoever," remembers Pam.

Pam learned that she was carrying twins when she was almost seven months pregnant. The babies, delivered by Cesarean section four weeks later, were five weeks premature.

Describing her initial reaction when told that the twins were conjoined, Pam says that she wasn't surprised. "I knew all along that something was wrong with the pregnancy. When they told me, something had been confirmed, subconsciously. I was just grateful that it wasn't something worse."

The Bennies were fortunate. Medical specialists reassured them after intensive exploratory tests that it was unlikely that there would be major complications in the process of separating Cameron and Andrew. They shared no vital organs—only tissue and muscle. The twins were successfully separated three days after their birth.

Showing courage and determination, Pam breastfed the babies—even while they were joined. "I would position one at the breast and support the other," she laughs. "It wasn't easy, but I was determined to feed them if I could."

Coping with two premature babies, as well as a 13-month-old toddler, can be difficult enough under normal circumstances. Pam and Dugal had also to cope with Cameron and Andrew each having one leg, from knee to foot, in a plaster cast in an attempt to correct their club feet.

Like many other separated conjoined twins, Cameron and Andrew still face years of therapy and perhaps further surgery. Apart from the club feet, each child also has a 36 percent scoliosis of the spine. It's too soon yet to determine whether they will need foot or spinal surgery.

Pam remarks, "It's not over. We've got a long road to travel."

As Pam speaks, 2-year-olds Cameron and Andrew and 3-year-old Claudia race past. "I'm very positive about the future," she says. "We're doing all we can to give our children the best possible chance in life."

CHAPTER 3

Temperament and Personality: Why They Do What They Do!

Who Was Born First?

by Elinor Davis

"Which one is the older?" This is one of those often-asked questions that twins and their parents must learn to handle. Young twins may react with discomfort, amusement or bewilderment, depending on whether this matter is an issue for them. Their answers can vary from the straightforward ("We're the same age, silly!" or "Jennifer is nine minutes older, but I'm 1/2-inch taller!") to the delightfully elaborate.

Fraternal twin, Mike Marsh of Los Angeles, explained it this way. "When we were about 8 years old, my brother and I created an imaginary story about our life in the womb and what happened at our birth. We imagined we were millionaires getting ready for a ball to which we were already late. Then my brother found he had forgotten his cane and he had to go back to get it. That's why I was born first, and he was born second."

Mike said it always gave him pleasure to tell people that he was the elder. "Before we were old enough to understand that there was a logical explanation, we would battle out the question of who was older. Whoever was stronger or whoever had won the last fight was the 'oldest.' Later we found we could look at it from two perspectives—the one who is born first is older or the one who is in the womb longer is older."

Ancient Themes on Birth Order

In their struggle to assign meaning to their nearly simultaneous debuts, Mike and his brother, who grew up in the 1950s, unknowingly recapitulated several major themes in the evolution of ancient societal attitudes about twins and birth order.

Most societies operated under the belief that the older twin had the rights of the firstborn. Others said the secondborn was the true elder because he was conceived first.

The Biblical story of Esau and Jacob illustrates the historical importance of birth order and portrays it as a source of twin rivalry. Their mother Rebekah, who had been barren for many years, suffered tortuous pain during her pregnancy because the twins had already begun their life-long quarrel in utero. God said to her, "Two nations are in thy womb and two manner of people will be separated from thy bowels. One people will be stronger than the other and the elder shall serve the younger."

The twins were very different at birth. Esau, the firstborn, was red and hairy. Jacob, who reached out and grabbed Esau's heel, was smooth and white. One day, a near-starving Esau came to Jacob, who had made some lentil soup. Jacob refused to share unless Esau sold him his birthright. With hunger being more immediate than his inheritance, Esau complied. When the time came for the first-born to receive his blind father's blessing, Jacob connived, with his mother's help, to fool his father by covering his hands with goat skin to resemble the hairy Esau.

The mythical Romulus and Remus, abandoned at birth, came to fatal blows partly because they did not know which was born first. Not knowing which was the elder, they looked to the gods for an omen to determine which of them should name and govern the new city they were building. Each claimed to have received an omen. They fought and Remus was killed. So their city was named for Romulus—the city of Rome.

Many peoples have attributed divine origins to twins and have seen them as symbols or incarnations of the dualities in human nature—the "good twin/bad twin" dichotomy. According to Kay Cassill in her book *Twins: Nature's Amazing Mystery*, certain American Indians believed that a firstborn twin was fathered by the sun, a heroic emissary of God. The secondborn twin was the child of under-ground waters representing evil. This second twin might be dragged down into the underworld (die), or, if lucky, would become a wise and powerful magician or medicine man. In some cultures, where twins were perhaps feared as a threat to a mother's energy, nutritional reserves and ability to contribute to the tribal work, secondborn twins were routinely killed at birth. Whether the arrival of twins was viewed as fortunate or ominous, the secondborn seemed usually to have been seen in a less favorable light.

Implications in Today's World

During this century, much has been observed and written about the impli-cations of being a firstborn, middle or youngest singleton child. Researchers have convincingly linked particular personality traits and roles within the family to birth order, although some social scientists downplay the relative importance of this factor when compared to overall patterns of family interac-tion, and to socio-economic, biochemical and other factors which relate to child development.

But what, if anything, has all this got to do with present day twins? With the exception of royalty, for whom the inheritance of crowns and titles may hinge on the few minutes separating the deliveries of twin princes, does it really make a lasting difference which infant wriggled through the birth canal first?

As you might expect when discussing twins, there are two ways of approaching the answer to this question about birth order. First, researchers can find out if there are any differences between first- and secondborn twins based on objective physical and psychological measurements. Next, parents, teachers and the twins themselves can discuss their perceptions of each twin and the researchers can determine if there are any consistent correlations between these attitudes and birth order.

Health Differences

While there is not a great deal of data presently available, several studies—from Australia, Finland and the United States—confirm each others' findings.

Firstborn twins are usually (but, of course, not always) heavier at birth than their secondborn wombmates. According to a Chicago survey of 588 pairs, secondborns are more likely to die at birth or to experience medical complications, such as prolapsed umbilical cord. Second twins more often have health problems after birth—general physical immaturity, respiratory distress and other problems associated with low birthweight and prematurity. Thus, secondborns are also more likely to remain in the hospital intensive care nursery after the mother and first twin go home.

The La Trobe University Study

A large, on-going study at La Trobe University in Australia has investigated, among other things, the role of parental attitudes in the development of twins' temperaments. On questionnaires, mothers rated their firstborn twins as "more dominant," "more independent," "better coordinated," and "less loving." (With other characteristics, such as "intelligent," "competent," and "likeable," there was no correlation with birth order.)

The La Trobe research has found that both parents generally "feel closer" to the firstborn and perceive the first twin as "easier to manage, less fussy and healthier." In the Louisville Twin Study, secondborns had more feeding and "temper" problems, but fewer sleeping problems. However, secondborns were also reported as laughing and smiling more readily, coinciding with the La Trobe finding that secondborns were rated by parents as "more affectionate."

Commenting on the practice of keeping a more fragile secondborn twin in the hospital longer than the first, the La Trobe study observes, "There may be permanent effects on how the family accepts that second child, resulting not from the biological event which necessitated that hospital stay so much as from the reactions of the family to this event. Similarly, while birthweight in itself may not be a major determinant of subsequent behavior, parents may show more positive responses and less anger and rejection to the higher birthweight twin, with the exception of low-birthweight sons to whom the mother responds the most."

Worldwide Research Reports

Research in Finland involving adult male twins also found a number of statistically significant differences related to birth order, based on interviews and psychological tests. Firstborns were more frequently physically stronger and more dominant in childhood, and were less reserved, less introverted and less disturbed as adults.

Another interesting, and as yet unexplained, finding from the Indiana University School of Medicine is that among identical twins who develop opposite "handedness," the firstborn is much more likely to be the left-handed one of the pair, with the secondborn being right-handed. No such correlation with birth order has been found for fraternal twins.

None of the researchers cited here have found birth order differences on conventional intelligence tests, though firstborns scored better on certain individual cognitive tasks. It is interesting and important to note that most researchers have found "birth order effects," as viewed by parents and teachers, to be more pronounced with identical twins than with fraternals. This suggests that these perceived differences may, in part, represent the parents' need to find some basis for individualizing and distinguishing between twins when little else is available. Birth order differences are least reported with boy/girl twins—the easiest type of twins to tell apart in other ways.

Analyzing the Data

As with all statistics, it is important to remember that research data are abstractions based on many individuals, all of whose lives are slightly different from each others'. In other words, birth order is *not* destiny! With these qualifiers in mind, you can use the research results to give your family a framework for viewing the role that birth order may be playing in your relationships.

The meaning that birth order has for individual twins varies greatly. Some children feel more comfortable establishing definite roles for themselves as "older" and "younger." They may work this out between them in some way even if they do not know which one was actually born first. For others, it does not seem to be an issue. (Though you may be sure that they will find other ways to differentiate from each other!)

The strong correlations between birth weight, heath complications and birth order, with the secondborn being at greater risk, are well-established. Beyond infancy, however, it is not at all clear to what extent these early circumstances directly influence subsequent mental and physical development. The researchers mentioned here concluded that birth order phenomena generally diminish as twins grow older. However, the La Trobe Study points out that, "At present, the effect seems to be an illustration of the 'subtle differences' between twins which may have lasting effects on the parents' perceptions," as well as on the twins' behavior.

Factors Affecting Labeling

Birth order is but one of many factors that may affect a twin's self-image and interactions with family members. Perhaps a helpful perspective on concepts like "older or younger," "outgoing or shy," or "athletic or intellectual," is to think of them as shorthand ways of appreciating and understanding each child's uniqueness. But try not to let such labels become pigeonholes that limit a child's potential growth.

When you are aware of the ways in which information can structure your perceptions, you can more consciously avoid the kind of labeling that is destructive to a child's development. The circumstances of your twins' grand entrance are simply one more chapter in the unfolding story of your family.

The next time someone asks each of your twins (or triplets or more) "Which one is the older?" listen to both of their answers. You may be surprised to learn that each of your twins has already created a private myth to explain the mystery of his birth. If he has, write it down before each child grows up and forgets it. Tuck it away in an album and in your heart. There may be just as much psychological reality and truth in those collaborative versions of their twin beginnings as there is on their birth certificates. Maybe more!

Am I a Twin or an Individual?

by Alice M. Vollmar

"How would you like it if every time you turned around at school, your nerdy twin brother was there watching you?" asks a teenage female twin of her twin brother.

Her co-twin counters, "I just don't understand you anymore. You've turned into a snot. You run around with all these kids who think they're so cool that they won't even talk to me or my friends!"

Complaints waged by twins over being a twin, such as those here, signal a child's trying to answer the question, "Who am I besides a twin?" according to Harriet Pratt, Ph.D., a licensed psychologist at Washburn Child Guidance Center in Minneapolis, Minnesota. She considers friction about twinship to be healthy in the growing-up years; in fact, she adds that it is a normal stage of development in which each twin makes an effort to establish his own separate identity. Though it may be normal and healthy for twins to accomplish this goal, the struggle to do so within their twinship can be loud and difficult for parents of twins and twins themselves.

Sandy Nieman, the mother of 9-year-old twins, Andy and Adam, says that her twins are two individuals who do not find it easy to strike a balance between being an individual and being a twin. She often hears some version of the lament, "I hate being a twin," from her boys who happen to look very much alike. "They hate looking so similar because people don't know who is Adam and who is Andy. They even got different hair cuts so they wouldn't look so much alike!" Sandy reports.

She says that she is surprised by Adam and Andy's fighting and by their not wanting to look alike. "I think I used to view them as one person, but I've changed my thinking," she says.

Her twins acknowledge that fighting is a problem between them. In fact, Adam says that it is the worst part of twinship and claims that Andy starts most of the fights, while Andy says that Adam deliberately tries to irritate him.

"It almost seems as if they are angry because the other one is always there," Sandy remarks.

Besides fighting, issues around which arguments and unhappiness often arise between these and other sets of twins include sharing possessions (and a room), friendships and dating.

Adolescence

While twinship tensions and disagreements occur at all ages, Pratt pinpoints adolescence as the time, developmentally, when a child normally questions his own identity. Therefore, that is when problems in balancing being a twin and an individual often occur. She recommends that parents of teenagers be active listeners but not jump in with answers; twins need ample room to work out their own solutions to this issue.

Feelings into Adulthood

Not surprisingly, many parents wonder if their twins' "identity crisis" will remain unresolved in adulthood. However, if twins have been encouraged to face and cope with twinship/separation issues and have been allowed to grow as independent individuals, parents can be more confident about their multiples' having positive feelings about their twinship. Conversely, twins who have been forced into constant togetherness may have a more difficult time living independently as adults, twin studies have revealed.

This latter experience has proven to be true for Catherine McGrew and Patricia Ballot, 39-year-old identical twins who have had difficulty adjusting to marriage and living apart. "The only regret I have is that our parents didn't let us become our own individuals," Catherine shares. "We dressed alike from birth until we graduated from high school; were conditioned to look and think alike; and never fought (while we were) growing up. We never really saw people fight. So now, when my husband and I have opposite ideas, I have a big problem expressing myself," Catherine remarks.

On the other hand, Dareld and Donald Nelson, 31, who were also expected not to fight or argue, enjoyed being twins as children and report a happy adulthood, living together at times and also living apart. "As kids, we'd wrestle each other to get our aggression out," says Dareld. "But when we went from our small school to a big high school, we used our bond because we got teased about being twins."

Although many adult twins say that their twinship has been a joy to them throughout their lives, some view it as a mixed blessing. In Vincent and Margaret Gaddis' book, *The Curious World of Twins*, an adult twin is quoted as saying, "Being a twin is not always a happy thing...I guess it's a resentment at being regarded as a twin, not an individual—as part, not a whole." In the same book, a male twin in his thirties commented that he wouldn't want to relive his childhood. "I hated it! My twin was the life of the party. I felt as if I had no name. I was just 'The Twin.'"

HOW PARENTS CAN HELP

To help co-twins get their individual needs met, parents need to give them the opportunity to vent their feelings honestly, advises Harriet Pratt, Ph.D., a licensed psychologist at Washburn Child Guidance Center in Minneapolis, Minnesota. "Above all else (in this situation), a parent needs to be a good listener when a child resents being a twin."

That means keeping parental judgments out of the situation and tuning into children's feelings. "Get across the idea that each person is unique and special, and look for ways to value each child individually," Pratt says. "In the case of one twin being more successful in relating to other children than his co-twin, tell the popular twin that you encourage his developing polished social skills, but be sure to value and comment on his co-twin's strengths as well."

In that way, parents can build on each twin's positive traits, thereby helping each feel good about himself. Pratt also suggests that parents brainstorm with their multiples to find ways to improve problem areas. The key seems to lie in letting twins know that it's all right to have mixed feelings at times—that it's normal to be a twin and want the freedom to be an individual, too.

WHEN TWINS WISH THEY WEREN'T TWINS: BRAINSTORMING CAN HELP

Brainstorming sessions between parents and multiples are an effective way to generate specific ideas and compromises to make a twinship problem tolerable, according to Harriet Pratt, Ph.D., a licensed psychologist at Washburn Child Guidance Center in Minneapolis, Minnesota. Below are some situations in which brainstorming can help:

- If identity mix-up is the issue, parents might sit down with each twin and say, "Let's figure out something to do about this. Do you think different hair cuts might help? How about dressing in different styles of clothing or wearing different glasses? Would you be happier being in separate classrooms or different schools? What ideas do you have about this?" The parents and twins can then have a group session to pool ideas, decide on a course of action and carry it out.
- When sharing items (or a room) causes problems for twins, their parents can tell them that they understand how hard sharing is and then work with their children to find ways to make it easier.

Parents and twins together might set up a schedule for using shared items, such as one twin using a bicycle on Mondays, Wednesdays and Fridays and his co-twin using it on Tuesdays, Thursdays and Saturdays.

Although having separate rooms may not be possible, using screens or stringing up designer sheets on a clothesline could be used to divide a room into two (or more) private spaces.

Pratt stresses that each child should have an inviolable space—a box under a bed, a desk with a lock or a closet—which is considered private. Or the family might use house space differently to create separate sleeping or studying areas.

- When one twin is eager to go his own way but his co-twin only wants to do things as a pair, parents can listen and empathize with each. To their child heading out independently, they can offer reassurance that it's acceptable to not always do things together.

The co-twin, meanwhile, needs to know that his parents care and understand how left out his twin's independence makes him feel. His parents might say, "It sounds like you feel as if your twin is abandoning you, and that's got to be a sad feeling. What can we do to help you feel better?" Parents might suggest driving the co-twin and a friend to a movie or encouraging other activities that he can do with his own friends.

Why Aren't You Like Your Twin?

by Pam Williams

Temperament theory is invaluable when used as a guideline for explaining, in a non-judgmental way, the similarities and differences between twins, between twins and classmates, or between twins, and teachers. One watchword needs to be kept in mind, however: Guard against putting your twins into a temperament type "box" and expecting their behaviors to conform to a particular label.

It is important to realize that human behavior changes according to the circumstances and the people involved; for this reason, you need to be thoughtful about informing each of your twins about his temperament type. If one of your twins questions something about his or another's attitudes, thinking process or behavior, a simple explanation of different preferences may be appropriate.

Understanding temperament theory enables co-twins to come to terms with their uniqueness, whether they are nearly identical temperament types or very divergent. Also, they will have a ready answer for the inevitable "Why aren't you like your twin?"

The theory of temperament type delves into the different ways children learn. Its origins are in the work of psychologist Carl Jung, who believed that differences in behavior are the norm and are based on certain ways each individual deals with the world. These personality patterns or preferences are based on mental habits governing what people pay attention to, what they care about and how they decide things.

One educator who deplored the effects of widespread misunderstanding of different learning preferences was Isabel Briggs Myers; she devoted her life to expanding Jung's theory into extensive profiles of personality variables to aid other educators. From her research and her own experience, she knew that children differ systematically in their perceptions of the world and in the conclusions they make. As a result, they show corresponding differences in their reactions, interests, values, needs and motivations, as well as in "what they do best and what they like best to do."

How children become aware—of things, people, occurrences or ideas—and how they then come to conclusions about what they perceived—is broken down by temperament theory into four pairs of preferences. A person usually exhibits a natural preference within each pair.

The Four Preferences of Temperament

Type Talk is a book by Otto Kroeger and Janet M. Thuesen about the following four pairs of preferences of temperament—extrovert/introvert; sensing/intuitive; thinking/feeling/ and perceiving/concluding.

The authors use the following analogy of left handedness vs. right handedness to explain a person's natural process within a particular preference: Being right-handed doesn't mean never using the left, but rather preferring the right. If the preference is strong, the left hand is used relatively infrequently. Or the preference may be slight, and the person is more or less ambidextrous.

Likewise, with personality preferences, in some people, one or more preferences is strongly dominant and quite obvious (such as Extrovert rather than Introvert). In other people, one or more preferences may be slight, and they alternate frequently in their usage.

1) The **Extrovert-Introvert** preference helps define what a child prefers to focus on: the "outside" world or his "inside" world. (The use of these terms is based on their Latin meaning.) The Extrovert child prefers to focus on people, things or occurrences as they are, while the Introvert child prefers to focus on concepts and ideas about people, things or occurrences. The Extrovert is more energized by things outside of himself while the Introvert is more energized by his internal world. Every child functions in both ways, for he must go outward to interact and inward to reflect; but he will be more comfortable with one or the other.

2) The **Sensing-Intuitive** preference defines how a child prefers to gather data: either through his five senses or through his intuition.

The Sensing child finds out about his experiences by paying attention to facts and details. The Intuitive child finds out about his experiences by emphasizing, probably unconsciously, the ideas, associations or relationships underlying the facts and the details that his senses notice.

The Sensing child (70 percent of the U.S. population appears to be Sensing) is characterized by being literal, tactile, practical, realistic and experience-oriented. The child in the other 30 percent, the often misunderstood Intuitive, excels at speculating, daydreaming, long-range planning, innovating and imagining. In *How Children Learn*, educator John Holt epitomized the strong Intuitive child when he wrote that children use fantasy to get into, not out of, the world.

3) The **Thinking-Feeling** preference describes the way that a child evaluates data. The child who prefers Thinking evaluates more on the basis of true and false, right and wrong. The child who prefers Feeling subjectively evaluates things as valued or not valued. Feelers excel at empathizing, nurturing and expressing their feelings, while Thinkers excel at ordering facts, reflecting, analyzing and reasoning.

According to *Please Understand Me* by David Keirsey and Marilyn Bates, two-thirds of all males prefer the Thinking orientation, while two-thirds of females prefer Feeling. These facts suggest an explanation for the perpetual gender war of "analytical" men vs. "emotional" women. Experts vary in their opinions as to whether this preference is genetic or environmental. Most believe that a child's temperament is inborn to some degree, but develops according to the encouragement of hindrance of his environment.

Thus, the one-third of the males who prefer Feeling, and the one-third of the females who prefer Thinking, are at a disadvantage. The boys are often stereotyped as "sissies" and are pushed into favoring their secondary, and therefore less mature, less reliable Thinking preference. The girls are characterized as unfeeling and masculine, and like the minority boys, are forced by adult or peer pressure, or by the pressure of self-image, to deal with the world primarily by their less capable preference.

4) The **Perceiving-Concluding** preference reflects the way a child makes decisions about the data he collects. (The proper Jungian phrase is Perceiving-Judging, but I prefer to substitute "Concluding" to avoid an unfavorable connotation.) The child who prefers Concluding likes best to come to conclusions or make decisions about the data he collects; he is comfortable with structure, organization and planning, and he likes things settled. The child who prefers Perceiving enjoys spontaneity, adaptability, lots of varied experiences and keeping his options open; making decisions may be difficult for him.

Learning Styles

Behavioral and educational professionals have found that the four pairs of preferences discussed above are invaluable in understanding student motivation and learning styles. The dominant mental preferences of each person actually determines his learning style. So, by analyzing student behavior and performance in the light of these four pairs of preferences, the following four learning styles—Feeling, Intuitive, Thinking and Sensing—have been characterized:

A **Feeling** child wants to communicate on a personal level with teachers and fellow students. He needs to know that the teacher cares about him and that the subject matter is something to which he can give of himself wholeheartedly.

Pleasing others motivates him to learn. The best learning environment for him is one that is accepting and nourishing, and that supplies positive, personal feedback. He enjoys group interaction and participation, democratic group processes, discussion, dramatic play, and fiction. Feelers gravitate toward the social sciences and humanities.

A parent can be alert for these characteristic problems in the Feeling-dominant child: the inability to form an attachment to a teacher or subject because he doesn't feel personally involved; rebellion or inaction because of negative feedback about his work; doing homework only if he sees the value of it; and feeling offended because of sarcasm or ridicule applied as a means of control in the classroom.

An **Intuitive** student longs to be inspired by his teachers. He learns best when his imagination is fired with intriguing ideas and plans. He is self-sufficient, serious and responds well to verbal, logical, well-reasoned dialogue. An Intuitive child tends to ask many questions, be more competent in subjects such as math and the sciences, and do homework best if it is interesting to him. Because there are few of this temperament type in a classroom, an Intuitive learner may suffer from feelings of isolation and shyness. This in turn can earn him a reputation of being arrogant, cold or unfeeling. He may also need help in developing social skills.

An Intuitive child demands competence from himself and, more than other types, may find his self-esteem is lowered by experiencing many failures. A parent can either steer this student into subjects in which he excels or see that he has after-school activities that give him the positive experiences he needs.

The **Thinking** student prefers a structured, organized environment with clearly-defined authority and rules. Facts, ideas, logic and systematic inquiry appeal to him. Having an inherent respect for authority, he trusts his teacher and his texts, expecting that the experts will help him find what is true and what is right. He thrives on stability and enjoys being responsible. Homework will usually not be a problem for a child with this learning style; it will be done in the prescribed manner and on time because it "ought to" be done this way. Clerical science and business classes appeal to this student.

"Problem" characteristics of Thinking children may include confusion if a teacher or classroom tends to be non-traditional, noisy, innovative or sponta-neous, and difficulty performing expected tasks if clear directions and sequential order are not supplied.

The majority of teachers in the lower grades have Thinking-dominant learn-ing styles, and therefore understands a child who also exhibits this learning style. However, in high schools and colleges, where the teachers tend to be Intuitives, the Thinking student will have to adjust to his teachers I intuitive-dominant methods and expectations.

A **Sensing** learner thrives on physical involvement in his learning. He prefers hands-on activities, media presentations and how-to books. He is motivated to learn what is useful and what pertains to real life. For him, to learn is to manip-ulate and to grapple with, and he much prefers mastering and practicing a skill than learning the theory of it. Unless homework is seen as useful, it tends to become a source of conflict between the Sensor and his teacher and parents. A Sensing-dominant learner is often drawn to music, art, drama, crafts, and mechanics.

Of all the learning styles, sensors are the most misunderstood and mismatched to the educational system. They are the least represented in higher institutions and have the lowest correlations between their academic ability and grade point average. The majority of students in continuation and vocational schools is Sensing-dominant.

Factors That Influence Learning Style

A child's **Introvert-Extrovert** preference will considerably influence his learning style. The more extroverted a child is, the more he will respond to verbal exchange of information and group activity. The more introverted a child is, the more he will feel most comfortable with quiet, individual activity or with contributing to a group in nonverbal ways.

It is important to understand that the child who leans toward Extroversion will verbalize in order to learn. As he talks over a subject, he is solidifying his comprehension. Conversely, the Introvert will not want to speak until he under-stands; he prefers to think through a question and formulate just what he wants to say before he ever answers out loud.

In a classroom, it is often the more extroverted child, therefore, who is quick to raise his hand to answer questions, volunteer opinions or interact in a group in any way. The more introverted child needs to understand, as do his teachers and parents, that he is neither dull-witted or slow because he takes more time to respond.

The **Perceiving-Concluding** preference also is a primary consideration in evaluating a child's attitude toward work and play. Those children who lean toward Perceiving favor a play ethic; their work can be interrupted for rest and play, and if the work process can be made enjoyable, all the better. On the other hand, those who lean toward Concluding favor a work ethic. For them, work comes before all else and must be done before rest or play.

The more a child leans toward Concluding, the more he views the following as necessary: preparation, maintenance and clean-up; being on time; having assignments done on time and in the required form; planning and making decisions; and getting things done. The more a child leans toward Perceiving, the more he emphasizes the usefulness and enjoyability of tasks (de-emphasizing preparation, maintenance or clean-up); keeping his options open and gathering more data; being flexible; trying out new things; and changing the routine.

Developing All Four Mental Processes

A child's parents and teachers should, first of all, help a child develop his own dominant learning style because this builds his self-esteem and self-confidence. Then they need to encourage the child's fuller development of the use of all four mental processes.

This gentle nurturing of a child's weaker or auxiliary processes is part of helping him grow up, and a parent often does this instinctively. For example, she may encourage her introspective, quiet child to participate in group activities; try to help an overly dramatic Feeler develop his capacity to analyze calmly; and train a "know-it-all" child in the art of listening to others' opinions.

"In type development, we assume all students need to learn good command of sensing, intuition, thinking and feeling," says Gordon Lawrence, author of *People Types and Tiger Stripes—A Practical Guide to Learning Styles*.

Temperament preferences are part of a child's psychological makeup and should be respected. At the same time, developing wisdom and maturity includes learning how to respond appropriately to the varied situations in school, as well as in life.

ONE MOTHER'S OBSERVATIONS

"My boys are Introverts who have rich internal worlds," said Jan Montgomery, a teacher, student of temperament theory and mother of fraternal twins, Ryan and Chris.

"Ryan (an introverted, intuitive Thinker) is constantly rigging battle stations, doing chemistry experiments or leading the neighborhood boys in imaginative adventures of danger and intrigue, Jan explained. "Chris (an

---

introverted, intuitive Feeler) loves to draw complex plans for tree houses, set up treasure hunts and create intricate 'creatures' on paper."

In school, Ryan is typical of his type—confident, eager, alert and ready "to get on with it." His type is also more aggressive, and he shows this by enjoying soccer games with older boys.

On the other hand, Chris exhibits the Feeler's preference for cooperation rather than competition. Jan reports that he is more sensitive than his brother.

Both boys share the introverted, intuitive child's considerable capacity for solitary, imaginative play. So what is their current attitude toward school?

"They say they don't have time and dislike the intrusion into their private plans that school represents," said Jan.

Knowing about mental preferences has enabled Jan to understand her twins' differences. Identifying Ryan as a Thinker and Chris as a Feeler gives her an explanation that she can support by concrete examples from everyday life when differences surface at school regarding divergent interests, study skills, relationships with faculty members, or strengths or weaknesses.

LEARNING LESSONS IN BEHAVIOR

As a type watcher and parent of twins, I enjoy analyzing my children's behavior in the light of Jungian theory. I am hoping to have an accurate idea of their dominant functions, and therefore, their learning styles, before they begin kindergarten next year.

My 5-year-old daughters seem fairly alike in temperament. While each can play alone contentedly, they prefer the company of one another or their older sister, suggesting a preference for Extroversion. Their sister enjoys spending hours alone with her dolls or stuffed animals (if she can keep her sisters out of her room!) and exhibits a stronger Introversion.

My twins show a difference in the Sensing-Intuitive dimension. Karen displays the Intuitive's inquisitiveness about why things are as they are, and her imagination is powerful. Linda, her co-twin, is more matter-of-fact, satisfied to know what things are. A clue to their temperaments is the difference in their answers, when pretending to be princesses, to the question, "Who are you?" Karen, never abandoning her imaginary persona, answers, "Sleeping Beauty," while Linda exclaims indignantly, "I'm Linda!"

Both girls manifest more often the Feeling process, as opposed to the Thinking. But how much of this is a reflection of their most often being with a strong Feeling mother remains to be seen.

How Could These Twins Be Ours?

by Nancy L. Segal, Ph.D.

Research concerned with the identification and explanation of individual differences among people is a fascinating process. Each person may be aware of his uniqueness as an individual, but may remain sensitive to behavioral and physical similarities that appear to "run in families." Some people recognize common features in themselves and in their close relatives, while other display relatively little resemblance to family members.

Depending upon the particular feature, a narrow or broad range of physical or behavioral outcomes may be possible from the same genotype (genetic make-up). This is because genetic and environmental influences vary in how directly they may influence human traits.

In the case of physical traits such as eye color, individuals who carry genes for blue eyes will show this characteristic in virtually all instances. The genetic effect is, therefore, very direct. Identical twins, who share all of their genes in common, would not be expected to differ in eye color.

In contrast, behavioral traits, such as IQ or mental retardation, are indirectly influenced by the genes. This represents what Anne Anastasi, a Fordham University psychologist has termed "a continuum of indirectness," meaning that many other related hereditary and environmental events occur along the way from genes to behavior. The number of steps may be different for different traits. The greater the number of steps, the greater is the number of possible behavioral outcomes.

For example, most studies show that identical twins resemble one another more on tests of IQ than fraternal twins, but differences between the members of an identical twin pair indicate the importance of environmental effects.

Heredity and Environment: They Work in Tandem

Dr. Robert Cancro, a psychiatrist from the New York University School of Medicine, Department of Psychiatry, explained, "Both the genetic and environmental contributions are equally important because they are both indispensable. The gene can only express itself in an environment, and an environment can only invoke the genotype that is present."

In other words, hereditary and environmental influences operate in an interactive fashion. This means that under various conditions, the relative importance, or contribution, of each to a particular behavior may change. If the environment is very similar for the members of a population, the observed differences between people reflect their genetic differences.

Suppose, for example, that members of a population received very similar types of instruction at school. Differences in ability between people would reflect their differences in genetic background. It is also important to consider the contribution of hereditary factors when environments are quite variable across members of a population.

Researchers have identified the following concepts to explain the important relationships between heredity and environment.

1) Genotype-Environment Interaction. Consider the case of fraternal twins. We know that, in general, fraternal twin partners demonstrate greater differences in mental ability than identical twins, even if both pair members are given the same educational opportunities and advantages. This is because fraternal twins bring different potentials with them into their environments. The important point is that different genotypes respond differently to the same environments. What may objectively appear to be the same classroom for two children may, in fact, be "different."

2) Genotype-Environment Correlation. Psychologists have, by now, documented a wide range of intellectual, vocational and recreational behaviors in which identical twins show greater similarities, as compared to fraternal twins. This is consistent with the idea that certain genotypes are more likely to be found in, or exposed to, certain environments than others.

Among our participants in the Minnesota Study of Twins Reared Apart, for example, many behavioral and medical similarities exist between reared-apart identical co-twins, despite the differences in their rearing environments. This further suggests that some genotypes are "attracted to" or may be more likely to seek out certain aspects of their surroundings than others.

Genotype-environment correlation may be further broken down into three specific principles. These principles can help to guide researchers in studying the ways in which genetic and environmental characteristics of families influence child development:

The *passive* form refers to the situation in which parents provide both genes and environment to their children. Parents who are skilled in mathematics may arrange their environments to reflect these skills by owning mathematical textbooks and games. They also may transmit some genetic potential for the development of mathematical abilities to their children.

The *reactive* form occurs when individuals in the child's environment, such as parents, teachers, or other caretakers, respond differently to children who differ in genotype by providing them with objects and experiences that are consistent with their observed talents and preferences.

The final variety, the *active* form, describes the child who seeks out particular environments that are especially well-suited to his or her inherited disposition. It is certainly possible that more than one of these principles may be operative at the same time.

An ongoing study at Harvard University is attempting to investigate the significance of these concepts. Researchers Sandra Scarr (now at the University of Virginia) and Kathleen McCartney will identify 40 preschool children, and will pair them according to age and sex. The two mothers of these children will play first with their own child, and then with the other. The theory predicts that a mother's behavior will conform to the behavior of the child. As the children mature, they can affect their surroundings actively by structuring it to suit their needs, or by seeking out objects and activities that are compatible with their natural preferences and inclinations. The researchers plan to follow these children to determine which factors influence their choice of friends and activities.

3) Emergenesis. Earlier in this article, I indicated that some family members show considerable resemblance to one another, while others show relatively few similarities. This may depend, in part, on the particular configuration of genes that each child receives from his or her two parents.

Dr. David Lykken, a researcher at the University of Minnesota and a member of the investigatory team associated with the Minnesota Study of Twins Reared Apart, explained the striking lack of resemblance between some relatives by a concept called emergenesis. This means that interactions between the various genes that influence certain traits may lead to novel behaviors, never before observed in a family. These behaviors are genetically transmitted in the sense that parents pass the genes on to their children.

The particular combination of genes from the mother and father, and the effects of the genes on one another may be responsible for the lack of resemblance between relatives, in some cases. This could, for example, explain why members of fraternal twin pairs sometimes behave very differently on some measures. It also might help explain why identical twins may greatly resemble one another for an unusual trait that has not appeared previously in their family.

A Closing Word

The majority of psychological and medical researchers would agree that both genes and environment importantly influence human development. Not all traits are, however, similarly susceptible to these different effects. The majority of studies demonstrate, for example, that mental ability may be more genetically influenced than personality characteristics. Many of these studies have been done using identical and fraternal twins, and their relatives. There is no question that the members of these families are very valuable participants in behavioral science investigations.

The following critical question was raised in an article in the British Medical Journal of February 11, 1978: Do findings concerning heredity and environment make any practical difference in the treatment of children? The answer is important.

"...Each child should be treated according to his or her individual characteristics at a given age. Trends or heritabilities of adult characteristics are as irrelevant in an individual case as are, say, the overall statistics for remission and survival of a child with acute leukemia. Medicine tries hard to be a science, and rightly so; but in the consulting room, it still feels very much like an art."

This underlines the importance of the individual needs of both parents of twins and non-twins in planning appropriately for them throughout their formative years.

RESEARCH DESIGNS

The relative effects of heredity and environment on human development can best be demonstrated by comparing resemblance between individuals who share varying degrees of genetic and environmental relatedness. Greater resemblance between people who share higher proportions of their genes in common is consistent with a genetic influence upon the behavior or physical trait under study. Ideally, however, researchers would wish to find biological relatives who have been reared in separate environments so as to "disentangle" the effects of heredity and environment. Listed below are some of the research designs used to study human individual differences.

1) Classic Twin Study. Resemblance between identical twins is compared to resemblance between fraternal twins. Greater similarity between identical twins, relative to fraternal twins, is consistent with (though not proof of) a genetic explanation for the behavioral or physical trait of interest. This is because identical twins share all of their genes in common, while fraternal twins share only half their genes in common, on the average, by descent.

2) Twins Reared Apart. Resemblance between identical and fraternal reared-apart twins is compared. The aim of the Minnesota Study of Twins Reared Apart is to determine if differences in the social life and medical life histories of reared-apart twins are associated with current social and medical life history differences. Additional comparisons between reared-apart and reared-together twins is even more informative with respect to the relative effects of heredity and environment.

3) Family Studies. Family studies examine the degree of similarity between parents and their children. It is, however, difficult to determine the sources of resemblance in parent-child pairs because both genes and environment are shared. An improvement on this design is to study adopted parents and children, as explained below.

4) Adoption Studies. Adoption studies examine similarities between adopted parents and children and, if possible, compare them with the similarities between the adopted children and their biological parents. Any resemblance between adopted parents and children is due to their shared environment, since they share no genes in common. Resemblance between biological parents and adopted away children is due to shared genes, since they do not share environments in common. The majority of studies of intelligence find greater similarity between biological parents and adopted away children, than between adoptive parents and children, supporting the influence of genetic factors on the development of intelligence.

5) Co-Twin Control Studies. Members of identical twin pairs are given different treatment or training programs, such as separate methods of learning how to read or how to solve mathematical problems. The effects of these programs on performance are later compared. In this research design, one twin serves as a "control" for the other, as the twins are genetically identical. It becomes possible to determine if one method is more successful than the other in fostering learning. Sometimes, different methods may be introduced to the twins at different times to see their effects at different stages of maturation.

6) Twin-Family Design. Adult identical twins and their families constitute, unique groups of relatives for behavioral research. This is because the children of identical twins are genetic "half-siblings," as well as first-cousins, since they "share" a parent in common. Resemblance on behavioral and physical measures can be compared for a number of different types of pairings: twins, spouses, full-siblings, and "half-siblings." Similarities between spouses provide a measure of genotype-environment correlation, referred to earlier. In other words, the extent of spouse similarity provides some measure of the twins' attraction to similar aspects of the environment.

7) Twins and Non-Twins. Comparisons between twins and non-twins are informative for several reasons. First, it becomes possible to see if the unique biological or psychological aspects of twinship importantly influence behavioral or physical development, as compared with singletons or non-twins. Dr. Hugh Lytton, a researcher at the University of Calgary, Alberta, Canada, has reported that twins develop speech at slower rates than non-twins, a possible consequence of reduced parent-child interaction of a verbal nature.

Dr. Ronald Wilson, of the University of Louisville, Kentucky, has compared the intellectual progress of identical twins and their non-twins siblings at selected stages of development. He has found that patterns of intellectual growth (that is, gains or lags in development) appear to be genetically influenced, given that identical twins show more similar trends relative to their siblings.

ESP: Does It Exist in Twins?

by Nancy L. Segal, Ph.D.

Most reports of uncanny, extrasensory communication between identical twins are difficult to prove because they are recounted after the experiences allegedly have occurred.

It has been no easier, however, to demonstrate in the laboratory that some identical twins possess powers of extrasensory perception (ESP). Moreover, no one knows how often twins make predictions about each other that prove to be incorrect.

The lack of scientific proof, however, does not deny the possibility that ESP exists in identical twins. It may be that science has not found the means to detect it. Historians of science can point to other phenomena that once were difficult to prove, but now are well accepted. At one time, for example, scientists did not know how many different types of twins there were. A twin study of intellectual resemblance, published in 1924, was the first behavioral investigation to organize twins into two types, identical and fraternal. Now with advances in genetics and embryology, this distinction is commonly acknowledged and understood.

Extrasensory Perception: What Is It?

Extrasensory perception (ESP) belongs to a branch of psychology known as parapsychology, a discipline that attempts to understand events that appear to occur outside the five known senses of vision, hearing, touch, smell, and taste.

Extrasensory perception may be organized into three classes: telepathy, thought transference between people; clairvoyance, the perception of object or events unavailable to our senses, such as stating the contents held in a closed container; and precognition, the perception of an event that will take place in the future.

Psychokinesis, the mental manipulation of objects or events, is another example of parapsychology but is distinct from ESP. In the *Introduction to Psychology*, authors Rita Atkinson, Richard Atkinson and Ernest Hilgard suggest that "willing" a particular throw of a pair of dice would be a good illustration of psychokinesis.

Brain Waves

Researchers already know that identical twins are remarkably similar in the kind of brain waves they produce. The electrical activity of the brain can be amplified and recorded by means of an electroencephalograph (EEG). These EEG recordings show consistent changes in the patterning of electrical activity, depending upon a person's activity or thought processing at the time of measurement. A brief review of this field by Zick Rubin and Elton McNeil, in *Psychology: Being Human*, indicated there are four varieties of brain waves (alpha, beta, theta and delta), each of which shows distinctive patterns. More than one type of brain wave is typically detected at any given time, although individuals vary according to which form is dominant.

The striking resemblance in the brain-wave activity of identical twins was first described in 1936 by Hallowell and Pauline Davis, researchers at the Harvard University Medical School. These investigators initially determined that certain groups of people show greater similarity in EEG recordings than others. Then they set out to determine whether the similarities were random or followed a biologic law.

Subsequently, the Davises studied eight pairs of identical twins. "Records from one twin resemble those of the other as closely as the records of the same person on successive tests," they reported. "It is particularly significant that in two instances both members of a pair of twins showed a feature which is unique in our series of over 140 records...The odds against these similarities being chance coincidences are overwhelming."

Intrigued by these results, other investigators have conducted additional studies of brain waves in twins. A substantial number have compared identical and fraternal twins.

One early study was conducted in 1945, by W.G. Lennox and his colleagues. By examining only the EEG tracings for 55 pairs of identical twins and 19 pairs of fraternal twins, they could correctly guess the twintype in the majority of cases.

The recordings were nearly the same for identical twins, but different for fraternal twins.

In Denmark, professors Niels Juel-Nielsen and B. Harvald found a strong resemblance between eight pairs of identical twins reared apart for some, but not all, brain wave characteristics they measured.

The Minnesota Study of Twins Reared Apart has routinely collected brain wave data from both identical and fraternal twins who have been reared apart. The identical twins reared apart appear to be almost as similar as identical twins reared together, and about twice as similar as fraternal twins reared together. The data of fraternal twins reared apart have not yet been analyzed.

These findings indicate that genetic factors influence brain activity because identical twins share all their genes in common, while fraternal twins share only half their genes in common.

The results of EEG studies raise an intriguing question: Do identical twins, whose brains are very much alike, display evidence of ESP?

Other Experiments

A 1965 study, in particular, is enormously provocative. In that year, T.D. Duane and Thomas Berendt of the Department of Ophthalmology at the Jefferson Medical College in Philadelphia, conducted a twin study of extrasensory induction using alpha rhythm. Alpha rhythm can be produced when an individual closes his eyes and is able to relax himself while remaining awake. Although it is distinct from ESP, extrasensory induction in this study refers to evidence of alpha rhythm in one twin (in the absence of attempts to produce it) while it is being produced in the co-twin under controlled laboratory conditions.

Fifteen identical twin pairs participated in this investigation. The twins were placed in separate lighted rooms six meters apart. They were instructed to open and close their eyes at specified times. Twins also were tested with unrelated individuals who, in turn, also were tested with one another. Two male twin pairs, ages 23 and 27, demonstrated extrasensory induction during the initial testing, and on repeated occasions later. This phenomenon was not observed in other twin partners, or between pairs of unrelated individuals.

The only feature that appeared to distinguish these two twin pairs from the other participants was that they were generally knowledgeable about biology and showed relative unconcern about the study—they were able to relax. It is uncertain, however, that these differences really can explain the observed extrasensory induction in these twins and not others. Unfortunately, there has never been an attempt by other researchers to replicate this experiment. This study suggests there may be a biological explanation for parapsychological communication between twins, but the authors deemed it unwise to draw conclusions.

In the 20 years that have passed since this study was reported, little progress has been made toward confirming the presence of ESP between twins. Few studies have been attempted, and fewer still have found evidence of the phenomenon. In addition, those studies may have little validity because of small samples and other problems with the research methods.

The Special Twin Relationship

The outcomes of the ESP studies leave researchers with the task of providing other explanations for the uncanny resemblances and coincidences that are reported in the life histories of some identical twins. It is possible that behavioral similarities, close social contacts or constant awareness of one another—even during periods of separation—may result in "ESP-like" events in the lives of identical twins.

A commonly observed aspect of twinship is the more intimate relationship shared by identical twins, compared to fraternal twins. One twin suffers a deep personal loss when a co-twin dies or when the twins are separated for some reason; they tend to reside near one another throughout adulthood (especially if they are females); and they frequently use the pronoun "we" in place of "I." Identical twins, more often than fraternals, express the view that one is and should be closer to the twin than to other siblings, according to a study by Ernest Mowrer in 1954. It is also significant that even antagonism or rivalry between identical twin partners does not appear to weaken their close affiliation.

Parents of twins and researchers can understand these observations by studying research that shows a greater resemblance between identical twins special mental abilities, personality, vocational aptitudes and interests, and medical life histories. For example, among the pairs of separated twins who have participated in the Minnesota Study of Twins Reared Apart, there are striking similarities among the identical pairs, compared to the fraternal pairs. These findings strongly suggest that genetic factors influence many of the behaviors that we measure.

It seems reasonable that the behavioral similarities between identical twins may help build and cement strong social bonds. The amazing coincidences and parallels in their lives may, therefore, be associated with their identical genetic makeup. This may contribute toward their "seeing" the world in the same way; undergoing similar life events at the same time; and knowing one another nearly as well as they know themselves. These features of identical twinships may trigger behaviors that appear to have parapsychological qualities, especially when the twins are together.

Think of your own best friend. There must be moments when a single word or glance between you tells a complete story, based upon a special shared history. This may appear somewhat magical, however, to the outside observer. That kind of communication might be more easily accomplished between some identical twins, possibly because of their common biological social background.

Related to this theme are the "giggle twins," who were identical twins reared apart and later studied by researchers in the Minnesota Study of Twins Reared Apart. These women engage in uncontrollable laughter when they are together, a behavior that is seldom exhibited when they are apart.

The important point illustrated by this example is that shared situations may stimulate similar behaviors and responses in genetically identical twins, producing communicative effects that appear to arise from unexplained sources.

--------------------------------- ❤ ---------------------------------

Color-Coding Blues

by Nancy Hedegaard

"Reddy, Bluey and Greeny" was how my 3-year-old triplet boys, Brock, Aaron and Jared, answered a stranger who stopped them and asked them their names one afternoon as we were shopping at the supermarket.

Their answer caused her to blink at me in bewilderment, but I was in no mood for a long explanation to a stranger. I smiled, pretending their response was perfectly normal, and quickly maneuvered my shopping cart around the corner. At that moment, I knew that my family's color-coding system had definitely backfired!

Color coding had seemed like a marvelous idea when I first read about it in twin-parenting publications. In fact, mothers of multiples had so highly recommended it as a method for distinguishing between both one's babies and their belongings that we gave it a try.

Here was our method of adopting the system into our household: Red was the color chosen for Brock, while blue was for Aaron and green was for Jared. Yellow was considered a neutral color and could be substituted for any unavailable color.

Soon it was an automatic response to hand the blue cup to Aaron, the green toothbrush to Jared or the red coat to Brock. Friends and relatives became familiar with the system, and before long, it was too late to turn back.

The first indication of trouble appeared when my sons began sorting their toys by color. They just assumed that all blue toys belonged to Aaron, red ones to Brock and green ones (and most yellow) to Jared.

When they played with their construction blocks, each boy would build only with blocks that were of his designated color. Their collection of miniature cars was divided among the three according to color. Even if a toy was only a small piece of a larger toy, such as a puzzle or train set, its ownership was determined by its color.

My sons rarely seemed to challenge this system they had devised or to question its fairness. No amount of intervening on my part could convince them that it was all right to play with a toy of the "wrong" color!

With the exception of coats and a few special outfits, most of the boys' clothing was not color coded. Dressing them in the mornings became a challenge in color coordination as each insisted on wearing at least one article of clothing in his assigned color.

Some days, the only items available in the desired colors were their socks or underwear. This didn't always please them! Occasionally, if one boy was especially dissatisfied with the clothing selection for that day, he would announce that his clothes were dirty and needed changing. Later, he would emerge from the bedroom covered head to toe in every scrap of clothing he could find in his color.

Erasing Color Troubles

Of course, by this time I knew that my children were a little too color conscious! At first I thought that their color loyalty was cute and clever, but I found that it quickly became a nuisance. My husband tried to convince me that our boys were just going through a normal phase, but as the situation worsened, I began to wonder.

Each boy insisted on coloring only with a crayon of his particular color. At the library, they chose their books according to the color of the covers. When we went to the carnival at the county fair, they absolutely refused to get on any rides that weren't the "right" colors!

Even worse, Brock, Aaron and Jared began calling each other Reddy, Bluey and Greeny. Soon they determined that I do the same, and they would immediately correct me if I called them by their real names. For instance, if I said, "Aaron, come here, please," Aaron would ignore me. Then Jared would promptly advise, "Mommy, that's not Aaron. That's Bluey!"

Other objects, particularly animals and cars, were also given color names. As we drove down the street, the boys would excitedly call out from the back seat, "Greeny is behind us!" or "There goes Purpley!"

I tried to be positive and look on the bright side of this color-coding mess. Without a doubt, I had done an excellent job of teaching my threesome the names of colors! For this I congratulated myself. Also, I could be fairly certain that my boys did not suffer from color blindness! Nevertheless, this obsession with colors was obviously getting out of hand.

For example, at a friend's birthday, Aaron had a fight with a little girl over the balloon she had. Since the balloon was blue, Aaron presumed that it automatically belonged to him, and he attempted to take it away from her. He couldn't understand why the rest of the world didn't follow the rules that he and his brothers had created within their special relationship. My husband and I went home from the party feeling a little embarrassed about Aaron's actions, but also sympathetic toward him since he felt truly confused and cheated. This incident helped to shed some light on our family's color-coding dilemma and gave us a glimpse into the motivation behind it.

What had started as a simple method for sorting baby items had somehow evolved into a complex system used to regulate and govern my sons' triplet relationship. By color coding their toys, clothes and other items, they were setting up boundaries and devising strategies for getting along.

In many ways, this system worked to keep peace when there was a question of ownership. Battles over toys were usually avoided because each boy respected the color rule. However, the trouble was that people outside our family did not understand or abide by this arrangement. While I didn't see the harm in allowing my sons to operate by these rules at home, it concerned me that they might have problems dealing with other children, as Aaron did at the party.

My husband and I also noticed that Jared, Aaron and Brock acted like they "owned" their colors, as if color was a tangible object that could be possessed. In their own little world where almost everything had to be shared, each boy believed that his assigned color was one of the few things that unquestionably belonged to him alone. It was part of his identity, something that separated him from his brothers.

Reaching a Colorful Balance

From these observations, my husband and I realized that it was necessary for us to step in and return some balance to this escalating situation. However, knowing how attached they were to their colors, I believed that it would be unwise to aggressively disrupt their system. One thing was certain, however:

Each boy needed to experience true ownership and have possessions of his very own.

We considered this and, since Christmas was approaching, decided we would make a conscious effort not to give our sons matching gifts. We chose toys that were totally different from one another according to each child's individual interests and talents. We made it quite clear to each child that his new toys belonged only to him, and he could choose if and when he would share them. Using stickers or a marking pen, I labeled everything from pajamas to tricycles with each boy's name or initials.

Our goal in doing so was not to eliminate color coding altogether, but to get the boys to accept different colors occasionally. After a few months of this new system, I knew that we had made some progress. When I brought home their new spring jackets, I marked their initials on the inside tags. Brock immediately reached for the red jacket, but when he saw the capital "A" on the tag, he immediately handed the jacket to Aaron without any objections.

We continue to color code some items, simply because it really is an efficient and convenient method. Fortunately, it is no longer the obsession it was a year ago, though my boys still maintain a strong preference for their own particular colors. Initially, I was concerned that this preoccupation with color might impair the development of their identities and self-images; however, at 4 1/2 years of age, Brock, Aaron and Jared have clearly formed healthy, distinct personalities. Now as I look back on this past colorful year, I see it as a small, but important, step in my sons' journeys toward individuality and separation.

Do Your Multiples Do What You Ask?

by Michael O'Connor

My wife, Sharon, our 7-year-old twin sons, Aaron and Brandon, and I were watching a syndicated television show called "Double Trouble" starring identical twin sisters. In this particular episode, one of the twins, who is an aspiring actress, wanted a part in a commercial. She talked her co-twin into attending an audition with her, and her co-twin ended up with the part. However, the twins decided to trade places so the aspiring actress could appear in the commercial.

I asked Aaron and Brandon if the sisters did the right thing.

"No," they replied.

"Why not?" I asked.

They didn't reply immediately, so their mother prompted them by asking if switching identities was kind of like lying. They agreed with that assessment.

"Would you do something like that? Switch clothes to fool your teacher?"

They both answered, "No."

"Why not?" I asked.

Aaron answered, "Because we might get caught, and then we would get yelled at."

Aaron's answer gives insight into more than how he perceives punishment in our household. It also reveals the ways he perceives right and wrong, and what his reasons for obedience are.

For more than 30 years, Lawrence Kohlberg, Ph.D., studied the moral development of children, youth and adults and discovered that people go through a predictable series of changes in the way that they perceive right and wrong, as well as what they perceive to be fair. Kohlberg referred to these changes as stages of moral development.

An understanding of the six developmental stages can help parents understand why their children obey their rules; help their children discover better reasons for obeying those rules; and learn how to find ways of motivating their children to behave in ways that are appropriate for their level of understanding, ways which will lead them to the next developmental level.

Moral development is linked to cognitive development—the ability to think about the world, structure perceptions of it, and appreciate the perspective of other people. As a result, when discussing moral development, Kohlberg did not consider discussing infants and children younger than 3 years of age. Also, the age range for each stage is relative; for example, a child may enter a stage earlier or later than the age listed, or may not progress beyond a certain level. On the other hand, some adults have never progressed beyond the level of the average 10-year-old.

Stage 1: Punishment and Obedience

This stage, which Kohlberg refers to as "punishment and obedience orientation," generally manifests itself in the preschool years, usually around the age of 4. Children who are in this stage obey their parents because adults are bigger and more powerful than them. In other words, the physical consequences of an action determine whether that action is good or bad.

Spanking, slapping a child's hand and other forms of physical punishment are typical ways that some parents use to get their children to obey them. If physical punishment is the only form of punishment used, Stage One children will likely continue to behave inappropriately until they are physically reprimanded.

However, this orientation can be used in more creative ways. For example, our daughter has always been a "people person." "Punishment" for her at Stage One involved telling her that when she misbehaved, she could not play with her friends or us. Sending her to her room to be by herself for a designated length of time was as severe a consequence for inappropriate behavior as any physical punishment could be.

Aaron and Brandon, on the other hand, are more possession-oriented. If their toys are scattered around the house and they won't pick them up, my wife and I tell them that by choosing not to pick up their toys, they have also chosen to not have them to play with for a specified period of time. Likewise, many of their fights center around possessions. If they refuse to cooperate while playing, we let them know that they have also chosen to forego the offending toy, game or book until they agree to try to get along.

Children at this stage reason that if there are no consequences to their actions, whatever they are doing must be all right. Knowing that this was true helped me understand why our children would still not do what we asked them to do just because we asked them to do it.

My wife and I also discovered that if our children think there will be no consequences to their actions, they will try to do things they are not allowed to do. For instance, when their grandparents visit, Aaron and Brandon, who are still basically in Stage One, become more rowdy than usual. They seem to think that they won't be punished because their grandparents are present. The boys usually settle down, however, after they suffer the appropriate consequences of their behavior (time out in their room) and thereby miss out on something fun.

Stage 2: Reward Motivation

Labeled as the "instrumental relativist orientation," this stage appears in the early elementary school years, around the age of 5 or 6. A good explanation of this stage is the edited golden rule. "Do unto others as they do unto you" or the more familiar phrase, "You scratch my back, and I'll scratch yours." In other words, children's obedience is based on the belief that they will somehow benefit by doing what they are told.

Stage Two children will respond well to rewards in exchange for their obedience. The school system in the United States makes extensive use of this concept in the early grades; for example, the rules of the class are explained at the beginning of the year, and children's compliance to those rules is rewarded with stickers, hand-stamps, candy or other tangible rewards. Stage One punishments, such as being sent out in the hallway or to the principal's office, are reserved for only the most serious offenders.

In our household, however, the Stage Two reward system has created some problems. In this stage, children vie fairness in terms of exact reciprocity, in other words, what one child receives, the other child believes that he, too, should receive. With two children in the same stage, one being treated differently means the potential exists for his co-twin to feel unfairly treated.

In kindergarten, Brandon and Aaron were in the same class at our request. Since they were governed by the same set of rewards, neither felt unfairly disciplined.

When they were in first grade, however, we acceded to school policy and let Aaron and Brandon be placed in separate classes. Each class had a slightly different set of rules and rewards. For example, Aaron's teacher delayed rewards until the end of the week, while Brandon's teacher gave rewards on a daily basis. For the first few weeks of school, this caused no end of grief because Aaron regularly failed to obey all the rules all week long and thus failed to get a reward, while Brandon came home every day with some prize.

We spent a lot of time talking with Aaron about the rules of his class and discussed the problem with his teacher. Eventually, we were able to get Aaron to accept the differences between the class reward systems and work within the limitations of his class. His teacher began to provide some more immediate types of rewards, which also helped to reduce tension.

Like the school system, parents can make use of children's "what's in it for me" motivation by rewarding their children—through praise, hugs, kisses and stickers, for example—as expressions of appreciation when they behave well.

Some parents have found that keeping a chart of chores that their children are expected to perform and putting a sticker next to chores completed is a good motivator for their young children. In some cases, making a contract with children is an effective way to motivate them to perform tasks. However, our family's experience with contracts is that once the contract is completed and the reward gained, the desired behavior quickly slacks off.

Stage 3: Peer Pressure

Called "interpersonal concordance or 'good boy/nice girl,'" this stage usually starts around the age of 10 or 11 and is a dominant feature of the teenage years. The classic expression of this stage is what is usually referred to as peer pressure. The various groups a child may belong to set his values. He lives up to the values of the group in order to receive its members' approval and to maintain his self-esteem.

While aspects of this stage are usually most evident in the teenage years, younger children may exhibit a good deal of this kind of behavior. When our daughter, Michelle, was 7 years old, she tended to obey in school out of her desire to please her teacher. At home, however, the reward motivation of Stage Two seemed to prevail.

A common reason for not obeying parents at this stage is the familiar refrain, "Everybody else does it." For example, bedtimes are a current conflict in our household. Michelle would like to go to bed later on school nights, saying that everyone in her class goes to bed later than she does. We have explained to her that the concern in our house is that all of our children get enough rest so that they can feel energetic the next day. But the answer that seems to satisfy her the best is simply, "This is the way we do it. Being part of the family group is enough of a reason to do things the way we do."

This external source of authority about values leads to conflicts between parents and their children. Because this stage usually accompanies children's struggles for independence, they may choose groups outside their homes as their source of authority.

At this stage, discipline options that parents used previously, such as punishment and reward, seem to have little effect on children's behavior, and responsibility to the family takes a back seat to popularity with friends. When children reach this stage, it is important that their parents talk with them and work as a team to set reasonable limits and expectations. Parents need to stress responsibility to the family, reinforce their children's self-esteem, explain their values and the reasons for them, and encourage their children to develop their own values.

Stage 4: Social Order

This stage of moral development, called "law and order," occurs when children seek to maintain the social order and show respect for authority. Children obey because they want to avoid criticism for those they see as legitimate authorities, as well as to maintain their self-esteem.

In this stage, which usually takes place during the high school years around the age of 15, children are able to adopt a wider perspective than themselves and the groups to which they relate. They realize that their actions impact on people they don't even know. At this stage, children are also able to fully understand the concept of being good citizens.

To determine if children have reached Stage Four, Kohlberg presents the dilemma of whether a girl who is shopping with a friend should report her friend's shoplifting to the store's security. In Stage Three, the typical response would be for the girl not to tell on her friend; however, a Stage Four response is based on the idea that stealing costs society as a whole, so the girl might be willing to take the chance of losing her friend in order to maintain order in society.

Of course, turning in a friend is not the only way of handling the situation. The girl could try to convince her friend to put the merchandise back or to turn herself in. Above all, however, is the concern for the broader welfare of society.

Stage 5: Individual Rights

Rarely manifesting itself before adulthood, Stage Five occurs when people understand right in terms of individual rights balanced against standards upon which society has agreed. Reasons for behaving in an obedient manner in this stage are to maintain one's self-respect and the respect of impartial observers of one's actions. The Constitution of the United States is an example of Stage Five thinking.

Stage 6: Self-Esteem

Morality reaches its highest, and least likely to be achieved, state in this stage. Like Stage Five, right is determined in this final stage of moral development. To avoid self-condemnation is the reason offered for obedience at this level.

Reaching Higher Stages

Kohlberg says that people can comprehend one stage higher than the one from which they generally operate. For example, even though a child is in Stage One, he can understand the Stage Two concept of obeying for a reward. In Kohlberg's writings, the stages are rigid; once a person advances to the next stage of moral development, he will not operate out of the lower stage.

However, we have found that our children operate out of a variety of stages at the same time, with one stage being dominant. Aaron and Brandon operate mostly from State Two, but show tendencies of both Stages One and Three. Michelle now obeys mostly from Stage Three, a sense of acceptance, but responds both to the reward system of Stage Two and the more advanced concept of "What if everyone did it?"

Parents can help their children advance their stages of development. For example, when faced with discipline situations, parents can ask their children why they should obey and then suggest that their children try to interpret the problem within the framework of the next stage.

In addition, parents can discuss situations from television shows or books by asking their children what the characters should do and why, and offer suggestions of ways to handle the situation.

By discussing situations with their children, parents can determine in what stage their children are operating, as well as try to lead them to the next stage. As soon as children begin operating from a new stage, parents should begin interacting with them from a still higher level in order to encourage their ultimately being motivated by the universal principles of justice, equality of human rights, and respect for the dignity of human beings.

Are They Close or Do They Fight?

by Harriet Simons

The position of twins within the family, their gender, their twintype and their individual personalities are factors which influence how much they fight with each other. For example, twins sometimes function as a team, fighting with other family members rather than with each other. For instance, boy/girl twins in a family with an older sister might experience a girl-girl alliance with the boy feeling at times as "the odd man out." When twins are the oldest children in the family, they might be more inclined to band together against the new arrival. However, according to White, twins may be less inclined to be abusive to newcomers than a singleton would. He reasons that since twins have never had their parents' undivided attention, the displacement is not of the same intensity.

However, several parents of twins and a younger child whom I interviewed reported that their twins fight not so much with each other as with their younger siblings. Conversely, twins may receive increased hostility from their slightly older sibling since their arrival is seen as doubly displacing, causing the twins in turn to gang up on the older sibling in retaliation.

Parents may attempt to counter these dynamics by emphasizing a family identity or team spirit. Each co-twin might enjoy having a chance to spend time privately with their younger or older sibling, and common interests should be encouraged. While some degree of sibling rivalry may be inevitable, stressing the uniqueness of each twin and relating to the twins as individuals should reduce some of the rivalry which is specific to being a multiple.

From a Developmental Perspective

It seems that the realities of twin relationships span the spectrum of behaviors varying among families, and change as the twins proceed through each developmental stage.

Their fighting can take various forms with some behaviors predominating at, but not exclusively limited to, various stages: hitting and biting (younger twins); name-calling and bickering (middle-years twins), and subtle teasing, baiting and one-upping (adolescent twins).

The Early Years

Toddler and preschool-age twins do not have a sense of the "humanness" of their co-twins; therefore, they are just as likely to bash each other over the head with toys cheerfully and without malice as they are to suck each other's thumbs. Cognitively and emotionally, they simply may not yet recognize each other's separateness. Egocentrism is normal at this age; therefore, empathy and respect for the feelings of others, be they co-twin or not, will not come until they reach the next developmental stage.

Kay Cassill, author of *Twins: Nature's Amazing Mystery*, attributes a great deal of twins' psychological relationship to their prenatal rivalry for space, position, and nutrients, a rivalry which is later exacerbated by public attention and comparisons. Twins often compete from birth for their parents' attention. For example, twins must often wait to be fed, picked up, etc., in a way in which singletons do not. While twins have never experienced being "the sole center of the universe," they do have a need for individual attention.

Pamela Novotny, author of *The Joy of Twins*, reports that parents are often disillusioned after being told how their twins would "entertain" each other only to find that it appears that fighting is *how* they "entertain" each other.

It is clear that spending time with another child who is the same age as she is—her co-twin—can be difficult for a toddler because she is dealing with the same developmental issues as the toddler with whom she is playing. For instance, it is common for 2 year olds to be reluctant to share and for 4 year olds to struggle for autonomy. Therefore, a twin may not be able to "rise above" a fight or exercise more mature judgment than her co-twin. Recognizing their twins' age-appropriate limitations, parents may need to provide close supervision while their little ones are together and have realistic expectations about their inability to get along with each other.

Many co-twins treat each other in ways in which they would not treat another person who is seen as having more clearly-defined boundaries and rights. A nursery school teacher observed twins taking toys from each other and taking the other's place at an activity, behaviors which she had never observed them exhibit toward a classmate. She felt that cognitively and emotionally, they could not yet recognize each other's separateness.

Twins also often display protective behavior toward each other even at this early age, as well. For example, one mother of boy/girl twins related that her twins dealt with their anxiety about entering nursery school by walking hand-in-hand into the classroom. In a sense, twins can serve as each other's security object.

Twins at this age are often together for most of their waking hours, sometimes epitomizing the dilemma of "can't live with each other/can't live without each other." Critics of full-time day care for preschool-age children cite the strain caused by the need for constant socializing and the absence of quiet and privacy. One mother of twins and an older sibling remarked that the time spent in nursery school was actually quieter than the time that the twins spent at home.

The lack of privacy—both physical and, it can be supposed, also psychological—has been seen as a cause of increased aggression between co-twins by many experts in the area of family relationships. For logistical reasons, twins often have the same academic and extracurricular schedules, as opposed to different-aged siblings whose school and activity schedules may be staggered. A conscious effort to schedule separate activities and the careful planning of a balance between "together" time and "private" time could reduce the strain caused by co-twins who are experiencing "over-togetherness."

If relatives or friends live nearby, scheduling separate visits to their homes for each twin could be beneficial to all parties. For example, although invitations for both twins may seem too tempting to turn down, one pair of twins surprised their mother by fighting over who got to stay home rather than over who got to go to the friend's house as she had anticipated. Parents may want to each take one twin along as they do their errands, thereby providing special "adventures" for each co-twin. Time away from each other is often helpful in providing individual space and preventing over tiredness. One mother imposes physical separation, using a timer when quarreling gets out of hand. Play areas allowing twins to play simultaneously, but separately, may also help reduce conflicts.

It is interesting to note that co-twins seem to develop their own behavioral norms and will often not perceive of their actions as fighting. In fact, it is not uncommon for the co-twin who is the "victim" to defend the co-twin who is perceived as the aggressor. It seems that some fighting in these stages—both verbally and physically—is not done in anger as much as it is out of boredom and/or as a form of playing and communication.

For example, a mother of triplets said that her triplets had gotten adept at learning just how to best annoy one another. On the other hand, as is often reported, she said that they were also supportive of one another when the "chips were down."

The issue for parents then becomes how much and what type of fighting they will tolerate. Family rules must be specific. Children may wonder, for example, if the "no hitting" rule also includes no pushing, splashing with water, and other creative forms of harassment. When twins fight, their parents can help them resolve the conflicts by exploring alternate ways of handling situations with them and explaining to them how their behavior makes each other feel.

The Middle Years

When twins enter school, competitiveness and rivalry may surface because their academic, athletic, and musical performances begin to be judged and graded.

Some twins may avoid rivalry between themselves and their co-twins by fore-going activities in which their partners excel. One mother of triplets encouraged her children to pursue different activities at different times so that they would not be competing on the same level. The fact that the triplets had different personalities and interests made this easier to achieve.

Reviewing each twin's academic progress privately, avoiding comparisons, and recognizing each twin's individual strengths can help to minimize their middle-years' competitiveness.

Many twins are separated for the first time when they enter school; this new experience may encourage them to begin to not perceive themselves as a team, but instead as distinct individuals with separate strengths and weaknesses. In many cases, placing co-twins in separate classes at school may reduce their competitiveness and decrease their fighting at home.

However, when twins are in the same class at school, they can receive the benefits of separate experiences by scheduling them in separate after-school activities; doing so may also discourage their rivalry and conflicts. It might also help each twin to believe that she does not always have to compete with her co-twin for the time and attention of her parents if she is assigned a particular block of time to report on her day at school, free from interruptions from her co-twin (and co-class-mate).

Fighting at this stage may take on a more "legalistic" tone with calls for equity and fairness. While these are issues that occur in all families, with twins there is not the rationale of age to explain differences in treatment.

To help resolve conflict between her co-twins, one mother polled her children on mutually agreed-upon unacceptable behaviors and then posted the list, thereby clearly defining what were classified as acceptable and unacceptable behaviors in their home. It is also important for parents to keep in mind that as long as the relationship between their co-twins is basically sound and the fighting between them remains within acceptable parameters, it is reasonable for them to acknowledge the fact that some level of disagreement will occur between their co-twins rather than to expect complete harmony between their offspring.

In addition, it becomes important at this stage for co-twins to establish their own peer relationships, an act which can result in reduced conflict between the co-twins. Guidelines for diminishing sibling rivalry suggest that siblings not be encouraged to share friends; however, co-twins are more apt to have friends in common, a situation which requires great diplomacy in order to avoid hurt feelings. Relationships of three are traditionally hard to maintain, and the situation of co-twins "sharing" a best friend can lead to obvious complications.

One mother reported that friends became reduced to "things" in territorial disputes between her twin daughters; she adopted the strategy of having each child invite a different friend over to their home. Some children who are friends of both co-twins might come over twice in the same week, but as the guest of a different sister each time.

Humor can be effectively used to quiet storms between co-twins at this age and can be used to bring latent fears out into the open. For example, one family resorted to a "no fighting" pact complete with a special handshake to which all family members were a party. Role-playing with twins is another way to problem-solve and provide insight into the feelings and needs of others; it encourages twins to peacefully find ways to resolve their differences.

The Adolescent Years

The crucial issue for twins, as well as singletons, during adolescence is for each young person to establish his own individual identity. This issue is compounded for co-twins, particularly identicals, because they not only need to establish their own identities as separate from their parents, but also their own identities as distinct from each other. For example, twins need to feel secure enough about themselves to make decisions independent of their co-twins; once they see themselves as individuals who are separate from their twin siblings (which may not happen until the end of adolescence), they may have an increased appreciation of their special twin relationship..

However, this road to a separate identity can be rocked with conflicts. Just as all adolescents "fight" with their parents in an attempt to define themselves as separate from them (with the younger generation believing that they are "better than" or "not like" them), twins may also try to separate themselves from each other through believing these thoughts and fighting with their co-twins to prove them. Such attempts at separation- and identity-building are developmentally appropriate, albeit noisy at times!

Because puberty and the emerging individuation of each person occurs during adolescence, these years may also be a time during which co-twins develop in different directions at different rates, thereby growing apart. During adolescence, the normal preoccupation of each twin's establishing his own identity may, to some degree, lessen the commitment to the twin relationship. Also, twins may feel the need to separate from their families at different times, causing the twin who is less interested in obtaining independence to feel abandoned. Understanding that his co-twin is trying to establish his own sense of self rather than rejecting the twinship may make the abandoned twin feel less rejected. It is also important for the so-called "rejected co-twin" to realize that relationships are constantly in flux and that the closeness to his co-twin may be re-established at a later stage.

WAYS TO MAXIMIZE TIME SPENT GETTING ALONG

Strategies that can successfully be used in a family to minimize the inevitable conflicts between co-twins will vary, depending on a family's values and their twins' temperaments. Some suggestions to try in your family include:

- Recognize and respect the degree of closeness or separateness, as well as the differences, between your twins.
- Arrange for younger twins to have time alone with you as well as time away from each other.
- Allow older pairs to make separate decisions about activities, friendships, etc., and to develop in their own individual ways.
- Express your expectations for your twins' acceptable behavior and model such behavior.
- Don't have idealized expectations about what your twins' relationship will be—that they will entertain each other or be each other's best friend as they grow older.
- Establish clear and consistent ground rules, label private property, and store shared possessions in a space accessible to both twins.
- Allow your twins to have angry feelings toward each other (so they do not get in the habit of suppressing their hostilities) while encouraging them to find acceptable ways of expressing their feelings.

MONITORING THE INTENSITY OF CONFLICTS

Parents should try to evaluate their twins' conflicts within the context of their twins' total relationship. In doing so, they need to realize that some fighting will occur between their twins, but they should intervene only when necessary in order to encourage their twins to work things out for themselves.

In addition, parents should be alert to long-standing hostility, excessive violence or fights over recurring issues, and try to eliminate the source of these disturbances, seeking outside guidance if necessary.

If fighting is incessant, violent and/or mean-spirited, it may be a symptom of deep-seated problems in the relationship and/or family that may need assistance from a family counselor to resolve.

Chaos! Is It the Only Cause of Injuries to Twins?

by Adam P. Matheny, Jr., Ph.D.

During the last few decades, accidental injuries have replaced disease as the leading cause of death and disability among children. From the latter part of infancy and throughout childhood, injuries account for more fatalities each year than all disease combined. The fatally injured children, about 10,000 per year, are but part of the picture, however. Each year, several hundred-thousand children are significantly impaired, millions of hours are lost from school and the economic and psychological costs are enormous. As we see it, children's safety is very serious business.

The general trend for accidental injuries to become *the* affliction of youth has not been a consequence of a marked increase in either hazards or victims. Rather, injuries have become significant risks to health because of the medical success in eradicating disease or sharply curtailing the effects of illness, particularly after the infant period. Injuries have become relatively more important simply because diseases have become relatively less important.

Most parents, and especially parents of multiples, have anticipated what their medical expenses would be for children's illnesses. Nevertheless, many parents have been surprised to find that their children receive the bulk of their medical care in emergency rooms where prompt attention is paid to cuts, bruises, broken bones, burns and poisonings. As one mother of much-injured twins put it, "I expected my prematures to be sick a lot, but I found out that all of us spend more time in the emergency room than in the pediatrician's office. I guess I traded one basket of worries for another."

Research on Twins' Injuries

Throughout the history of the Louisville Twin Study, researchers, including myself, asked parents of twins to review their twins' health histories every time the family visits the research center. Because the twins are seen repeatedly from their infancy to their teens, there are many opportunities to obtain virtually complete accounts of the injuries suffered by the twins, whether or not the injuries received medical attention, and also to note the circumstances surrounding the injurious event.

When we first reviewed the accumulated injury histories for hundreds of pairs of twins, several trends within the material stood out. It was obvious that there were more injuries reported for boys than for girls, the nature of the injuries changed as the twins developed, and some twins had significantly more injuries than others. In effect, there were regular patterns, rather than random events, found among the histories of injuries. We turned our attention to those patterns to see what characteristics might be associated with some twins being injured more than others.

Unlike other studies of children's injuries, our study had the advantage of using contrasts within twin pairs to link differences in the rates of injuries with differences in other respects, such as motor dexterity, mental development, and activity level. That is, if one twin was reported to have suffered more injuries than his co-twin, we could discover if the injury-prone twin differed from his co-twin in other respects.

Differences Between Twins

In our studies, we first identified the twin pairs in which there were marked contrasts for the incidence of injuries. Some pairs were remarkably different, as illustrated by the following case: a male twin was reported to have been hospitalized five times during his 15 years by being burned (1 year), ingesting gasoline (2 years), being hit by a car (4 years), breaking a shoulder (12 years), and being hit by a truck (14 years). In addition, he had received numerous black eyes, and lacerations from falls and blows to the head over the course of the same 15 years. During the same period, his co-twin had suffered only one injury, a cut on the chin at 6 years of age. Needless to say, this case was not typical for injuries between co-twins.

When we examined the behavioral characteristics of the twins with repeated injuries, we found that they differed from their co-twins in several respects. The injury-liable twins tended to have a behavioral pattern—consisting of restlessness, temperamental outbursts, impulsivity, and discipline problems—that was detectable even when some of the twins were toddlers. The behavioral pattern was not so sharply etched or persistent that one would label the twins as accident prone, but clearly some twins' actions partially contributed to their risks for being injured.

In a later study, we found that the more-injured twin also studied or attended to aspects of the visual world in a less organized or careful fashion than the other twin. For this study, we had twins scan pictures of objects displayed on a board in front of them. The twins with a history of injuries were more likely to pick out the objects in a disorganized manner and to make mistakes. This study, as well as the previous one, demonstrated quite clearly that co-twins contrasted for injuries were somewhat different, even though they were reared together in the same household.

Similar Twin Pairs

But what of the twin pairs in which both twins had repeated injuries or both twins went unscathed for years? In these instances, we recognized that characteristics of parents, family life, and the twins themselves could combine somehow to increase or decrease the chances of being injured. Preliminary studies in this direction have capitalized on our observations of the twins' parents, visits to the twins' homes, and observations or reports of the twins' behaviors during the preschool years.

When we examined the material from parents, homes, and twins, we found that the incidence of twins' injuries increased when several conditions were met. More frequently injured twins were likely to have mothers who were excitable ("high-strung"); the homes were cluttered and somewhat chaotic; and the twins themselves were more active and prone to temperamental outbursts. Each condition contributed but a small amount to the prediction of injuries; however, the combination of all of the conditions accurately identified about 70 percent of the twins injured from infancy up to entry in the first grade.

The majority of the injuries sustained by the twins during the preschool years were blows to the head, usually as a consequence of falls. Unfortunately, the blows often resulted in damage to the teeth. The next most common injuries were fractures and lacerations attendant to children falling or running into objects. Curiously enough, few twins were injured by or in automobiles or through poisonings—the two classes of injuries that receive the most public attention.

School Injuries

A major step in children's development is entry into school. We found that step coincided with changes in the reports of injuries. The total number of injuries decreased, perhaps because the classroom is less perilous than the home, but the proportion of injuries related to sports rose steadily with children's progress through the grades.

During the school years, the interplay of factors that foretold the preschoolers' injuries incorporated activities that were unavailable to our appraisals of the twins' families. For example, we were disadvantaged by not being able to observe the twins in parks and playgrounds, dozens of school settings, and in shopping malls, each with its own blend of hazards. But from interviews with parents it was clear that where children play, what they play,, and what equipment they use in their play had a bearing on the number and types of injuries.

As the children progressed in school, an increase in injuries occurred from playing in streets; in football games; and on bicycles, skateboards, and go-carts. During this time, head traumas decreased, and traumas to the limbs increased—a trend that possibly reflected changes in stature, postural control, and physical dexterity. By the time the children reached high school, contact sports and cycling accounted for the bulk of the injuries; however, serious injuries involved high-powered machines such as power mowers, power tools, heavy appliances and, most importantly, automobiles.

When we examined the connection between injuries before and during the school years, the only striking connection between the two periods was that the number of male victims exceeded the number of female victims. Other than that, there appeared to be no pronounced tendency for the injury-laden preschooler to continue to be the victim from school age on.

In effect, there did not appear to be an enduring trait of "accident proneness" that fostered repeated injuries of most of the twins throughout development. To be sure, a small percentage of the twins we studied had recurrent and serious injuries every year for 15 years. The vulnerabilities of the remainder of the twins were more limited, however. Unfortunately, at this time we cannot accurately predict which twins fit the notion of "accidental proneness" and which twins do not.

Greater Risks for Twins?

To date, we have complete records of injuries among 200 pairs of twins who have participated in the research program for at least nine years. When the records are laid out, one after the other, the cumulative effect is staggering. Within that array, almost 300 injuries of medical consequence steadily mark the progressive cadence of childhood.

We have the general impression that twins seem to be injured a lot, perhaps even more than single-born children. That impression has even been certified by some of our parents who have kept a running comparison between their twins' injuries and those of other children. Other parents, after years of tending their injured twins, have even acquired a fatalistic view that twins and accidental injuries are inseparable.

We realize that, through repeated interviews and by keeping extensive records on twins, our total count of twins' injuries may be higher than a similar account of single-born children in a less extensive examination. Nevertheless, the following reasons explain why we might expect young twins to be at greater risk.

Among the many factors thought to be associated with children's injuries, several may be directly applicable to the typical family with twins. Larger families, higher levels of stress, and tumultuous conditions within the home are correlated with an increased incidence of children's injuries.

Now consider families with twins. They are usually larger; the twins are more likely to be the last in birth order; and for a number of reasons, household hubbub is a way of life. Many twin families also are preoccupied with stresses from a burdened budget, increased work loads, and a lack of rest. There are many variations of these themes from family to family, but whatever form they may take, a day with young twins is demanding. When fatigue sets in, close watchful supervision often lapses. At those times, and there may be many such times, young twins are vulnerable.

To the accident equation, we should add the fact that twins often have only poor teachers and inept helpmates—each other—as ready participants in many activities. Parents have reported how their twins helped each other climb out second-story windows, fetch forbidden objects, or take on unsafe projects not manageable by the single child acting alone.

A parent provided us with an example: Each twin boy in a pair of toddlers could not, as an individual, engage the clutch and shift the gears on the family car. But by working together, the boys successfully put the car into neutral, whereupon it rolled down a hill and struck a convenient tree. Fortunately, this misadventure, like most others reported by parents, did not result in injury to either twin. However, there have been enough injuries reported to warrant a continual reassessment of twins' capabilities when both twins join together in a common purpose.

Whether or not twins are especially liable for injuries needs to be investigated. Whatever the outcome, present impressions are the best data at hand. The impressions indicate that the injury rates are slightly higher for twins and the rates reach their peak when the twins are between 1 and 4 years old.

After that period, the twins' risks for injury appear to be the same as the risks of single-born children. If these trends are verified by research, parents may find some comfort in knowing that their young twins' pronounced vulnerabilities are not permanent features of the twin situation.

Protecting the Child

The means to create safer environments for children has not been the central focus of our research. Rather, we have been examining the characteristics of children, parents, and places that may bear on the "injury problem."

However, with all of hindsight's sharp acuity, we can see that most of the twins' injuries could have been prevented. Slight changes in behavior or in the environment, the purchase of a different product, or a proper repair made at the appropriate time is all that would have been necessary to forestall a significant number of injuries.

There is a consensus that the most successful means to prevent injuries are those that require little or no action on the part of the person being protected. As a result of regulation, lawsuits, and public concern, safety is more likely to be built into products or materials, and hazards are more likely to be removed.

Toys that are soft, nontoxic, nonflammable, and impossible to swallow, and childproof containers of drugs and household chemicals, were designed with children in mind. Nevertheless, design can only go so far; parents must select the products and use them properly. In one form or another, the safety of children continues to be a daily demand on the practices of parents.

The development of any family regimen for safety requires learning new habits and unlearning old habits. For the twins' safety, the best time to start the process is the day that the twin pregnancy is confirmed. Well before the twins have arrived, there is ample time for expectant parents to examine how they live and what needs to be changed. Starting or reinforcing the habit of wearing seat belts, keeping clutter off stairs, putting medicines out of reach, and thinking about how the beautiful but toxic house plants might look somewhere else could be the beginning. The temperature for the hot water heater can be set lower, smoke detectors installed, and stair railings repaired, for example.

Whatever the list looks like, it can be supplemented by a number of books and pamphlets on child safety. There are many available at the public library. Parents also can develop the habit of routinely scanning periodicals especially *Consumer Reports*, that list the safety features of toys, appliances, and household products.

In this regard, information may be obtained from and shared with other parents. We think that clubs for parents of twins could provide a valuable service by creating a committee whose sole purpose is to review the literature pertaining to child safety and distribute current digests of that information to parents of twins.

When the twins are born and thereafter, parents can anticipate subsequent risks by setting the sights for safety at least six months in advance. For example, when the twins are born, the parents can take the attitude that the twins are starting to crawl, and then safeproof the household accordingly.

Some of the parents in our study have developed that approach with the added flair of going about the house as if they were seeing it from the vantage of the child. The hazards spotted from the height of two feet or less can be less obvious when one is looking from a seated or standing position. Of course, any of these efforts can be amended to suit the individual characteristics of the child.

There is no single prescription for injury prevention that will suit all families. The single requirement is that the family has a plan for safety and attempts to make the plan work. As a side benefit, parents may improve their own chances for reducing their personal risk for injuries. Any improvement in their own safe practices has the added benefit of modeling safe behaviors for their twins.

The Rhythm of Twins

by Dorothy Kroll

The goal of any parents is to help his child develop into a mature person capable of taking independent actions that will bring him happiness and pleasure throughout his life. Everything from choosing a breakfast cereal to selecting a vocation and mate involves examining alternatives, making a decision and acting upon that decision.

For parents of twins, the task of helping children develop independently is compounded by the dependence of the co-twins on one another and their tendency to develop similar interests and participate in the same activities. Parents, too, can fall into this pattern by viewing the children as a team or duo, and unwittingly reinforcing their interdependence.

As with any singleton child, each habit that a twin develops during his crucial formative years can continue into the adult years. For example, if twins learn to rely on one another in their earliest years, they are more likely to be dependent on each other in their later years. However, parents can provide opportunities for a twin to take action independently from his co-twin, and can treat each twin in a way designed to foster and encourage his independence and feelings of self-esteem.

According to Shirley Gould, author of *Raising an Independent Child*, the will to be independent is evident almost as soon as a child is born. Gould suggests that a baby should be allowed to do whatever he can safely do on his own. As he explores new behaviors, he will develop positive feelings toward exploration. Furthermore, when a baby believes that he is capable of holding his own bottle or standing on his own feet, it is this belief in himself that parents can nurture in order to lead a child toward greater independence.

According to Josephine Tingley and Rosemary Theroux, authors of *The Care of Twin Children*, one way to nurture this belief is to create opportunities for each twin to make choices—selecting clothes to wear, toys to play with, or shows for viewing—beginning around 2 years of age. As the child grows older, opportunities with more responsibility can be added, Theroux and Tingley explained, but a child must also be taught that he bears the responsibility for his decisions.

Another way parents of twins can provide decision-making opportunities for their twins is to encourage their children to have different interests. Barbara Brenner, co-author of *Raising A Confident Child*, suggested that parents begin in infancy to look at a child's preferences for foods, toys, and individual interests. According to Brenner, "Parents have to keep their eyes open. Children don't always know what they are good at; parents must look at the strong areas and encourage the child to pursue them."

Lloyd Glauberman, Ph.D., a New York City psychologist, advises parents to emphasize these different interests so that the children will associate them with something positive. Glauberman states, "Parents should encourage individual interests by praising a child. They could tell him how nice it is that he has a new friend or activity, for example, or how nice that he is doing new things."

When it comes to dressing alike—the bane of parents who have to shop for children of the same age or step on the toes of relatives who insist on buying the same clothes—Glauberman again recommends that parents stress the value of being unique so that the children see their individuality as something favorable. "When children want to dress alike, parents should say something like, 'How boring to wear the same clothes all the time. Sometimes it's fun to be different,'" Glauberman advises, "Parents should make a game of it so that the children associate being different with fun."

Judy Pasamanick, Ph.D., director of Folklore Research Center at Teachers College, Columbia University, is the mother of 27-year-old identical twin boys. Pasamanick recalled that she helped foster individualism in her sons by never buying the same toy, encouraging each to study different instruments and supporting each child in his efforts to make his own friends as well as shared friends.

Betty Reid, president of the New Jersey Association of Mothers of Twins Club and the mother of 11-year-old identical twin girls, encouraged her daughters to have separate activities and their own friends as early as preschool. "Now my twins don't want to dress alike because they rarely were dressed alike as youngsters," states Reid. "They do have a joint birthday party, but each twin sends out her own invitations."

Placing twins in separate classes in school doesn't necessarily enable each child to develop his individuality, Pasamanick suggests. She believes that many factors should be considered when making decisions about classroom placement.

Clara Loomanitz, Ed.D., director of the Early Childhood Center at Brooklyn College of the City of New York University, also stresses that independence doesn't always result when twins are separated. Loomanitz states, "When separated, children can sometimes feel isolated and threatened, which can undermine their self-esteem."

Glauberman remarks, "If you do anything well, you will feel good about yourself—that is self-esteem." If a child feels good about doing things independently, he will persist in exercising this independence.

To help a child develop positive self-esteem, a parent needs to communicate to his child that he is valued and respected. When a child makes an effort to perform a task, for example, he should be encouraged to do it and then praised if he succeeds, or encouraged to try again if he doesn't. When a child talks, he should be listened to; a child should be asked for his input during a family meeting to decide where to spend a holiday, for example. In fact, anytime there is an opportunity for decision-making, a child should be allowed to express his opinion, particularly if the decision affects him, too. When a child perceives that he is respected for his individuality, he will feel important and treasured.

Gordon Peter Miller, author of *Teaching Your Child to Make Decisions*, suggests that parents listen to their children without judging them. A child has to be understood from his own point of view, Miller adds. Parents should not try to make a child into something that he is not—he needs to be accepted for his individual personality. By accepting him and not evaluating him, the parent shows a child that he considers him to be a person capable of making his own decisions. That child will, in turn, sense that he has the ability to handle his own tasks and problems successfully.

This continual support for a child can serve to "buffer" him in times of failure. Many children who fail often believe that they somehow don't measure up to others' expectations.

In their book, *Parents' Guide to Raising Twins*, Elizabeth Friedrich and Cherry Rowland note that when parents encourage children in their different interests, it is important that the children don't feel they are competing against each other; if they do, one child will often stay away from the other child's activity because he is afraid of failing at it.

A child's own sense of importance and self-worth can be vital, as can his perception of his own failures. According to Brenner, "If a child has positive self-esteem, he will be less competitive with his co-twin who excels in something. He will also be better able to withstand failure in that subject and still feel that he is good at something else."

Childraising Styles

In addition to parents' complimenting a child on his efforts to do something on his own, there is a particular parental style that has been found to be most effective in creating independent children.

Most parents utilize one of the following three general parenting styles—authoritarian, permissive or authoritative. Authoritarian parents impose their own will on their children, prize conformity and discipline, and restrict their children's freedom to make choices. Permissive parents don't set limits for children's behavior and do allow their children unrestricted freedom. Authoritative parents, on the other hand, set standards and limits of behavior, are consistent in enforcing rules and provide children with the freedom to make decisions.

Research studies have found that authoritarian and permissive parents are most likely to foster dependent children. The children of authoritarian parents never have the opportunity to take independent actions because their parents don't reward such behavior and make all the decisions. In the permissive home, children tend to feel unimportant and unloved because they perceive their parents as indifferent and uncaring.

In the authoritative home, however, children know that their parents are in control, but trust them because they know their parents have their interests at heart. These children are rewarded and respected for voicing their own views and exercising their curiosity, and are valued for their ideas and opinions.

According to Phillip Zimbardo and Shirley L. Radl, authors of *The Shy Child*, authoritarian and permissive parents tend to make children overdependent because the youngsters feel rejected and will look to other people for approval and affection. These authors have also found that the most effective parental style is the authoritative style because it enables parents to listen to their child, talk to him, be flexible in changing rules when necessary, give reasons for required behavior, and encourage his free expression of ideas. All are elements that make a child feel he is an important person in his own right.

The emphasis on encouraging the independence of co-twins doesn't mean that the special bond between members of a set of twins should be torn apart. Whether the twins are identical, same-sex fraternal, or opposite-sex fraternal, parents can help their children become capable adults through their individual directions.

The fostering of independence is a gradual and continuous process. As co-twins feel good about being individuals, they often have a better appreciation of the closeness of their twinship.

Jealousy—Does It Put Twins in Double Jeopardy?

by Nancy L. Segal, Ph.D.

Special differences in the relationships shared by identical, fraternal same-sex, and fraternal opposite-sex twins as a continuous source of fascination for the general public, as well as twins and their families and friends. The following look at jealousy, pride, cooperation, and competition, and how these specific qualities affect different types of twins and their relationships may help explain the unique circumstances of each twin.

Twins are often asked if they are jealous of one another. My research experiences suggest that a response to this question is *not* a simple matter for twins, especially for members of identical twin pairs, because the concept of jealousy acquires a unique meaning for them. In contrast, both types of fraternal twins may be expected to respond with greater certainty to questions concerning jealousy of their twin partner.

An important point is that jealousy in any twin relationship need not be negative. Jealousy can, in fact, positively contribute to the growth and development of each twin, given appropriate attention and guidance from parents, teachers, and singleton siblings.

Jealousy: What Is It?

Jealousy, and its "cousin," envy, were recently described as two "powerful and potentially shattering emotions" by researchers, Peter Salovey and Judith Rodin, from Yale University. *Jealousy* was defined as "the thoughts and feelings that arise when an actual or desired relationship is threatened." *Envy* was described as "the thoughts and feelings that arise when our personal qualities, possessions or achievements do not measure up to those of someone relevant to us." This study was primarily concerned with romantic relationships, but the definitions of jealousy and envy are unquestionably meaningful in the context of twinship.

Different Forms of Jealousy

It is reassuring to note that "altruism and aggression" (and, perhaps, jealousy and pride) may truly be opposite sides of the same coin. Dr. Daniel G. Freedman offers the following insights into the social development of young twins: "Over the course of psychological treatment of a pair of identical twin boys, I became aware that, despite an inordinate amount of [between twin] aggression, the twins' similarity in outlook and taste on a variety of issues, their similar physical abilities and responsivity, and even their shared understanding of what it is like to be so competitive helped envelop both with a sense of inseparability. For me, this case illustrated some of the subtler aspects of altruistic relationships and the fact that aggression and altruism are not mutually exclusive."

The similar duality of cooperation and competition is echoed by Mari Siemon, a psychologist from Seattle, Washington, who wrote that, "While for most people, intimacy and competition are opposing forces, for many twins, they are so connected as to seem necessary components for a relationship."

Freedman has also raised the possibility of a kind of "tribal unity" experienced by members of identical twin pairs. This could, understandably, blur the usual distinctions between aggression and altruism, jealousy and pride, losing and winning, etc. Victory for one twin may be equally experienced by his co-twin.

The greater success of one twin does not appear to create jealousy or hostility, but rather feelings of pride, and a recognition that "I can do it, too." In this context, jealousy may be a useful human emotion because it may foster motivation and achievement.

Research on cooperation and competition suggests that jealousy probably operates differently in fraternal twinships than in identical twinships. The competitive edge that has been observed more frequently between fraternal twins than between identical twins indicates that fraternal twins have more individually defined goals and interests than identical twins. Greater jealousy between fraternal twins would, therefore, be expected.

Recent studies by Freedman and colleagues on sex differences in behavior may shed some light on the reasons for the apparent sex difference in jealousy shown by young children. In these studies, pairs of 4-year-old boys (non-relative) appeared extremely competitive when asked the question, "Who is tougher?" In the majority of cases, each boy immediately insisted on himself. At 6 years of age, however, young boys showed general agreement as to who was the "toughest" member of the class. It was further determined that male children, especially, tended to overrate their rankings on other characteristics, such as intelligence and athletic ability.

Girls, on average, behaved differently. "Try as we might, we have never found a trait or any set of traits around which girls hierarchize themselves with the same emotional intensity that boys exhibit over toughness, athletic ability, or even good looks," the researchers reported. It is, therefore, possible that jealousy assumes more subtle forms in young females that may be difficult to detect and/or that young males are, by nature, more competitive than young females.

Koch's observation of greater jealousy among male twins than female twins is, therefore, consistent with these findings. The increased jealousy within *fraternal* male twinships, as compared with *identical* male twinships, suggests some key social-interactional differences between the two types of twins as illustrated below.

Members of opposite-sex pairs were not found to be highly jealous of their twin partners. Koch did report, however, that young males may feel threatened by their sisters, probably due to the generally more rapid social maturity of females than males, and the approval that this receives from parents.

Cooperation and Competition in Identical and Fraternal Twin Pairs

A fascinating series of experiments conducted in 1934 by Helmut Von Bracken in Germany illustrates the subtleties of twin relationships that may explain twin group differences in feelings of jealousy. Though this study is now 50 years old, it is one of the best studies ever completed, in terms of illustrating the differences in social interaction across twintypes.

In the study, identical and fraternal twin pairs, in the second grade, completed two tasks (substitution of letters in words, according to a "code," and simple additions). Differences in the amount of work between the identical twins *decreased* when they worked on this task in the same room, as compared with their work output when they were alone. The explanation turns out to be simple: The "faster" twin would slow down to allow the "slower" twin to catch up with him.

Research results were quite different for fraternal twins. When they were placed in the same room, one of two things occurred: (1) either the children engaged in a fierce competition in an attempt to outperform the other; in this situation, both twins were matched in ability level, or (2) the "slower" twin realized that winning was unlikely, while the "stronger" twin sensed that winning was a sure thing. In the first case, the amount of work completed was higher when the twins were together than when they were apart; in the second case, work output showed little change across conditions.

Von Bracken concluded that the "object" in identical twinships is the preservation of harmony, while in fraternal twinships there is striving toward superiority over the partner. This same theme was replicated in a study of cooperation and competition between young twins that I conducted several years ago. Identical twins were more successful at a joint puzzle completion task than fraternal twins, who were equally matched in ability level. More specifically, a higher proportion of identical twins achieved the correct solution because they adopted a team approach to the activity. Fraternal twins, in contrast, attempted to solve the puzzle individually, despite instructions to solve it together.

It appears that in identical twinships there may be less room for jealousy because the differences between twins may be minimized by the twins themselves. Siemon noted that in many twin pairs, rivalry may be reduced by the partners' agreement to maintain equivalent levels of performance. This process may not necessarily dispense with the individuality of each twin because each has a special role to play toward achieving this equivalence.

The superior performance of one twin may stimulate the other toward greater efforts, in this case a potential danger here may be reduced motivation by the more skillful twin in an attempt to maintain equality. In that situation, parents may need to encourage their twins to pursue different interests.

It would be misleading to imply that identical twins *never* engage in competition or experience jealousy. According to Siemon, intense competition between some identical twins may sometimes work to reduce differences between them (as was observed among some fraternal twins in the Von Bracken study). Some identical twins have complained that they can become competitive, but only when compared by others. Keen rivalry or jealousy is, however, infrequently mentioned in most characterizations of identical twin relationships.

Outcomes from the joint activities of fraternal twins may set the stage for jealousy on the part of the twin who is less successful, even if he is only slightly so. Marilyn Spinner, Associate Professor of Psychiatry, at McMaster University in Canada (and the mother of infant twins), acknowledges the important role that parents may play in this regard. She encourages parents to view differences between the twins simply just as "differences," thereby downplaying a competitive or jealous spirit between the twins.

Non-Twin Siblings: Lessons for Twins

Parental attitudes and treatment of non-twin siblings can sometimes reveal useful guidelines for the treatment of twins. In their book, *The Sibling Bond*, Stephen P. Bank and Michael D. Kahn discuss five sets of siblings "who were pushed into twinlike relations with one another." These five "twin pairs," originally described in a study by Moisy Shopper, were created by parents who showed insensitivity to the individual differences between their children, sometimes in an attempt to avoid playing favorites. The results, however, were jealousy and quarreling, as the children struggled to develop a sense of self. Similar results have sometimes been reported when fraternal twins are treated as though they were identical.

The important message from Shopper's study for parents of twins is to respect the individual styles and preferences shown by each twin. To the extent that each child feels secure with his own talents and abilities, jealousy or resentment between twins will most likely be reduced. Parents with both twins and singletons should make certain each of the single children does not suffer from the extra attention that the twins are likely to receive from others. It is also advisable *not* to treat the single child as one of the twins.

Twins Speak for Themselves

Sometimes the greatest insights on twin relationships are available from twins themselves. The book, *Twins on Twins*, by identical twins, Kathryn McLaughlin Abbe and Frances McLaughlin Gill, includes expressions of the natural synchrony between identical twins, a quality which helps explain their low levels of jealousy. According to twin opera director, Christopher Alden, "The fact is obvious that we're [Christopher and his twin brother, David] both so obsessed with the same profession. We're rivals in it, to some extent, support rivals. Our creativity is always being stimulated and fed by the other."

Harriet Troxell, a gymnast and cheerleader, commented that, "A victory for my twin sister, Beth, is a victory for me. If she beats me, I'm more thrilled than she is many times."

These statements by identical twins are powerful testimony to the positive encouragement that each twin can derive from the achievements of the other. The research finding of Von Bracken and others, showing that identical twins maintain a spirit of cooperation, even in potentially competitive contexts, appears applicable in these real-life situations.

It is always possible that the twins who share their viewpoints with magazines or other public media represent a somewhat biased proportion of identical twins. In other words, it may be that we never learn about the identical twins who *do* experience feelings of jealousy toward one another. Real or perceived differences between identical twins may, understandably, result in jealous overtones.

Some very informative comments on twinship have also been made by fraternal twins. Many acknowledge warm feelings of relatedness that are similar to those described for non-twin brothers and sisters. A number of opposite-sex pairs have described valuable "protection" provided by the twin sibling. There is, however, infrequent mention of the coordinated efforts and goals that are commonly endorsed by identical twins; motivations are most typically described in terms of the individual.

Special Cases

In her book, *Twins in the Family: A Parents' Guide*, Elizabeth Bryan sensitively describes the situation of the twin with special needs, including twins affected by physical or mental handicaps, or both. Twin pairs composed of one healthy twin and one handicapped twin may pose extreme difficulties for how parents relate to the two children. Bryan cautions that jealousy and resentment will surely result if a handicapped child senses differential treatment toward the healthy twin sibling. Similarly, the extra treatment and attention often required by the handicapped child may produce feelings of jealousy on the part of the well twin.

Bryan provides some illustrative case material concerning twin jealousy in special cases. Rachel, a healthy 5-year-old, grew increasingly resentful of the "treats" acquired by her twin sister, Sarah, who suffered from cerebral palsy. One such treat involved taxi rides to school. Rachel eventually pretended to experience paralysis in an arm and a leg in order to gain the attention of her parents. Bryan emphasizes that the assistance of trained social workers may be extremely valuable in helping twins and parents come to terms with these difficult situations.

Jealousy may be expressed by a twin who loses his twin sibling because the focus of parental attention is on the deceased twin. This may be especially difficult in the case of identical twins, because the surviving twin is a constant reminder to the family of the twin who is gone. Efforts must be made to assure the living twin that he remains a valued member of the family.

Green with Envy

An examination of jealousy in twinship suggests that there are meaningful differences between twintypes. Jealousy seems reduced to a minimum in identical twinships. Success of achievement by one twin appears to stimulate comparable performance in the other, rather than the feeling that one's own abilities are deficient, or that the relationship may be threatened. Identical twins' recognition of behavioral and physical similarities may contribute to the harmony for which they are famous.

Rivalries in fraternal twinships appear more characteristic of those associated with pairs of ordinary siblings or peers. That is to say, striving toward success generally proceeds individually, with less attention to the progress of the co-twins.

A fraternal triplet, with two identical brothers, told me that, "They are more important to each other than I am to either of them." This statement underlines the qualitative deficiencies of the bonds that may be typical within identical and fraternal twinships. Strong affiliation may work to counter jealous feelings between identical twins; relatively reduced affiliation between fraternal twins may function in an opposite manner.

When a Twin Marries...

by Alice Vollmar

"A good marriage can exist only between two strong and independent people," wrote M. Scott Peck, M.D. in his book, *The Road Less Traveled*.

But how do those two people go about concocting their "good marriage?" And what if one of them is a twin? Is there some magic mix of ingredients that goes into every good marriage relationship?

"Well, it may not quite be magic, but there are fundamentals common to healthy marriages," said Dr. John McClay, a psychologist and marriage counselor in Minneapolis, Minnesota. His basic recipe for a good marriage includes:

- The capacity to be separate and, yet, close and intimate.
- A balance between being too close and too distant.
- Trust and honesty.
- Shared values and beliefs.
- Equality in the relationship (relating as equal adults and not playing out parent/child or other roles between husband and wife).

However, getting all of the those ingredients and making them turn into a stable marriage is not easy. In their article, "Marriages Made to Last" in *Psychology Today*, June 1985, Jeanette Lauer and Robert Lauer observed, "The average duration in the United States is 9.4 years."

But some couples do beat the average and create long-lasting marriages.

When Lauer and Lauer surveyed 351 couples married 15 years or longer, they asked why those couples stayed together. The response most often given was, "My spouse is my best friend." For these partners, deep friendship was born of genuine interest in one another—nonjudgmental listening, laughing together, and taking pleasure in watching each other follow his and her own dreams.

Statistics on twins and marriage are hard to come by, but experts agree that being an identical twin does make a difference in the dynamics of a marriage. Drs. Janet Kizziar and Judy Hagedorn, identical twins, commented in their book, *Gemini—The Psychology and Phenomena of Twins*, "Men and women who marry identical twins must be secure enough not to be threatened by the closeness of twins. The husband-wife relationship can be extremely close; however, it may never quite approximate the closeness of many identical twins. The divorce rate of identicals is probably slightly higher than average for this very reason."

In *Twins: Nature's Amazing Mystery*, author Kay Cassill cautions prospective mates of identical twins to anticipate possible areas of friction. The friction areas she lists include jealousy of the mate's twin, dominance/submission dilemmas, demands from the mate's twin, and being expected to replace the other twin.

One identical twin's mate said, "My husband, Tom, is the aggressive twin and is used to having Tim (his twin) agree with and follow him. Tom has gotten away with uncooperative behavior for a long time. It's been a battle to get him to do his half of the chores or pick up after himself, but he is getting better."

Tim's wife said, "Tim is cooperative, but with twins you never feel as if the twin (you are married to) is solely yours. I have felt left out when they enter their own little world and are oblivious to outside conversation. You also have to get along with two personalities instead of just one. If you don't get along with your husband's co-twin, the relationship would probably crumble sooner than the twinship!"

Tim agreed saying, "I believe the spouse of someone who is a twin and his co-twin have to be friends or the marriage won't work."

However, if the friendship criterion can be met, and if the friction areas can be worked out, twinship can offer surprising dividends. So say the mates who like being married to a twin, one of whom fondly referred to his wife's co-twin as "the sister I never had," adding that he thought it terrific his wife had such a good friend—her co-twin—in whom to confide.

Twins do enter marriage on a different footing. They already know a lot (for better or worse) about the sharing and balancing inherent in a close relationship.

Many twins, with stable marriages report that they believe they have two best friends—their spouse and their co-twin.

In these relationships, the spouse is able to accept that he is not the only significant person in his mate's life, and her co-twin conveys a special sense of appreciation to the spouse, being careful not to treat him as a "second-best friend." But all twins and their spouses, of course, do not always have such rewarding relationships.

For example, marriage did not go smoothly for Pat, a 35-year-old identical twin accustomed to sharing everything with her co-twin, Cathy—food, beverages, clothing, housework, and social activities. Until they graduated from high school, the sisters dressed alike, went everywhere together, and never argued. Their mother insisted they do things together and did not allow them to fight with each other. Pat, now divorced, said things might have been different if she had not been a twin. She wanted her spouse to go everywhere with her and do the things she and Cathy had always done together; she felt frustrated when he refused.

Pat said she resents Cathy's spouse for his overt efforts to force the two sisters to be independent of one another. She said, "He thinks I am a bad influence on Cathy."

Cathy has been married to Phil for two years and has found being away from Pat a big adjustment. "Phil has tried to discourage our twin relationship," said Cathy. The twinship is a source of friction between her and her husband, and Cathy finds it difficult to stand up to Phil and express her feelings about her relationship with Pat. She said she regrets that she did not learn the give-and-take of disagreeing in childhood.

In spite of the twinship/marriage friction, the sisters contact one another daily by phone. Pat explained, "When I was married, if my husband had died, it would have been hard; but to lose Cathy is unthinkable." Cathy commented that she sometimes welcomes the chance to be alone without having a co-twin around, but added, "If Pat is gone, and I can't reach her by phone, I feel a big loss and a sense of panic."

Pat lamented, "Life seemed so easy when we were single and it was just the two of us."

Their experiences are similar to those reported by other twins who were extremely close and interdependent in growing-up and early adult years. For such twins, problems arise out of having shared too much for too long—including the very essence of their individual beings.

Suddenly, Peck's words—"two strong and independent people"—take on heightened significance. We start life in a dependent relationship, pointed out McClay. "The task of early years is to comprehend ourselves as separate from our parents...finally culminating in emancipation as adults," he remarked. McClay said he believes that twins face the added task of separating from each other; if they do not learn to function independently, it spells trouble ahead in their adult relationships—including marriage.

Fused identity leads to dependent relationships where spouses are expected to fill in for the other twin, wrote Mari Siemon in the article, "Separation-Individuation Process in Adult Twins," in the *American Journal of Psychotherapy*. Or a twin may feel rejected when the other marries. Such twins may assume spouses will automatically know their thoughts and feelings. They also may need to "keep things even" and, thus, balance the marriage unit as they did the twin-ship unit. Some have trouble expressing anger toward the spouse. Siemon related a twin's comment: "It's as though I will destroy myself if I am angry at someone I care about."

Of course, twins are not the only people with dependency problems. Countless marriages exhibit symptoms of insecurity—unreasonable jealousy, partner's dependence on one another for approval/support, manipulative behavior, and more. However, twins are especially vulnerable because of their initial closeness.

With this in mind, parents, teachers and relatives of twins can encourage individuality by seeing each young twin as distinct and different—and reflecting that back to each child. Parents do all children a favor by gradually allowing them to make more and more of their own decisions, giving them chances to learn from mistakes and successes without condemnation or derision. Thus are sewn the seeds of independence. Adult twins also often advise parents to allow young twins to make their own decisions regarding dress, friends, and activities, as opposed to forcing them to "be" a certain way—either together or separate. These early experiences can facilitate future adult relationships.

However, twins who enjoy twinship are unlikely to give it up entirely as adults. Nor should they expect to, said McClay. Balancing marriage and twinship is not a black-and-white, "either/or" situation; rather, it often comes down to arriving at what is acceptable and comfortable for both the spouse and twin.

For Sharon and Sandra, age 39, awareness of their relationship in the twin-ship and its impact on their lives allowed them to form strong marriages and still enjoy their twinship. "So many of our formative years were together that one twin developed one side of her personality, while the other twin developed the other side," said Sandra. "Where one twin may be stronger, the other may be weaker—as long as my twin was strong, I could afford to be weaker, and vice versa. Because of this, we were at our best together.

"As time went on, we went our own ways and each had to develop the weaker side. I do feel we both chose spouses who are like our twin, which complemented our personalities. We both noticed this and have commented on it many times.

Differentiating between twinship issues and marriage issues plays a part in maintaining stable marriages for Judy and Jane, age 29. "I can talk more easily to Judy and express myself because we don't fight," said Jane. "But when it comes to personal things between my husband, Mark, and myself, it stays between us. I don't involve Judy in my marriage and Judy is the same way with me. I would say there is a special closeness with your husband that can't be shared in twin-ship."

Sometimes twins avoid the hassle of adjusting to singleton mates by marrying another set of identical twins. Such marriages can prove very stable and congenial with couples sharing houses, responsibilities, expenses, and child care.

Occasionally, there are bizarre twists to these arrangements. In their book, *Gemini*, Kizziar and Hagedorn mentioned one set of identical twins married to identical twins: "all four living in the same house and 'sharing everything.'" The authors added, "We mean everything."

They noted that some twins eschew separating/marrying for twinship in adult-hood, as did two fraternal males in their 40s who still dressed alike and lived with their parents. Siemon stipulated, "Separating depends on the kind of relationship the twins have had with each other and feelings they have about being a twin...being genetically identical is not as important an influence...as are twins' perception of similarity." In other words, if twinship was essential to the identity of fraternal twins, they, too, will have difficulty separating.

For adult twins to separate, Siemon believes a transition is needed between holding on to the old dual identity and realizing that it is no longer relevant in the same way in their adult lives. Other researchers state that such a transition is important in changing any significant relationship. That transition involves a grief process.

In an unhappy marriage McClay speculated that the twin may need to do some cutting loose and letting go. He recommended that both partners learn about the mechanics of separation and dependency to understand what might be happening.

In some cases, therapy might be helpful, added McClay: "There should be good diagnostic work at the beginning of any counseling, and the twin needs to accept that there is unlikely to be the psychic closeness of twinship in marriage," he said.

For secure and independent twins and spouses, the extras of twinship can be a plus. When life takes unexpected turns, married twins often give support to one another's families in a no-strings-attached way, as do Frances McLaughlin Gill and Kathryn McLaughlin Abbe, professional photographers and co-authors of a book, *Twins on Twins*. These sisters have provided one another with vital professional and personal help during difficult periods in each twin's life.

Whether or not to embrace a wider world through marriage can be a hard choice for twins. Because most marriages include periods of stress and upheaval, commitment to the marriage and tolerant acceptance of one another are integral to a strong relationship—even more so when marriage is paired with twinship. If twins are too attuned to each other and spouses feel left out, the marriage and twinship can be hard to reconcile. However, when twins and spouses can adapt to the intricacies of their situation, their marriages are embellished with a double measure of friendship and affection.

Dynamic Duos on the Playing Field

by Nancy L. Segal, Ph.D.

Multiples have distinguished themselves in virtually every type of athletic activity. For example, swimmers James and Jonathan diDonato were the first twins to set a world's record in any sport, and were the first two people to set a new world's record at the same time. They also were the first people to swim 10 miles doing the butterfly stroke.

Japanese distance runners, Shigeru and Takeshi Soh, took third and fourth place in the Japanese marathon in December 1983. Their finishing times were nearly identical: 2:09:11, and 2:09:17. Recently, an identical teenage trio of tennis players, Christine, Terri, and Patti O'Reilly, from Ridgewood, New Jersey, has thrilled fans along the eastern seaboard. These 15-year-olds ranked among the top 10 participants in the girls 16-and-under division of the Eastern Tennis Association. And identical twins Phil and Steve Mahre took the gold and silver medals respectively, in the 1984 men's Olympic Slalom Skiing event in Sarajevo, Yugoslavia.

Observing the same level of highly extraordinary ability in two or more individuals is truly awe-inspiring, considering how rare outstanding athletic talent is in the general population.

The examples cited above represent, however, only a handful of the multiples who have enjoyed double successes on the sports' fields. It is likely that a similar number of fraternal twin pairs also include gifted athletes. (Identical, fraternal same-sex, and fraternal opposite-sex twin pairs are each found with equal frequency in Caucasian populations.) Researchers have found, however, that it is generally *less likely* for both members of fraternal pairs to be as equally matched in athletic ability as identical twins. This explains why fraternal twin athletes generally do not attract the same degree of public attention as identical twin athletes.

Paul O'Connor, the football coach for North Central College, in Naperville, Illinois, has four and one-half sets of twins on his team, three of whom he has personally recruited. He was, however, totally unaware that two of these players were fraternal twin partners until they arrived on campus.

There are, of course, exceptions. An Italian investigator, Luigi Gedda, has described several fraternal twins who have both earned athletic distinction. They tend, however, to excel in different sports. One fraternal pair included a runner and a walker, while another pair included a cyclist and a football player.

These differences among the various twintypes raise intriguing questions concerning the basis and development of athletic skills. The biological and psychological features of identical and fraternal twinships that importantly influence sports participation and performance are reviewed in this report.

Twin Research on Sports Participation

Twin research that compares similarities in athletic interests between identical and fraternal twins has helped to highlight hereditary and environmental contributions to these behaviors. These studies include twins from many countries around the world. Hans von Grabbe, working in Germany in the 1950s, found that identical twin athletes engage more frequently in the same sports and in the same branch of a sport than fraternal twin athletes. This research included 21 identical sets and 13 fraternal sets.

A larger, more comprehensive study conducted by Gedda in 1960 provided similar results. Sports' questionnaires were completed by 351 Italian twin pairs born before 1945 that included at least one male member. This twin sample consisted of 92 identical pairs, 227 fraternal pairs, and 32 pairs for whom twin-type was uncertain. Only 4 percent of the identical pairs, as compared with 25 percent of the fraternal pairs, included partners with different sports' interests (that is, one active participant and one non-participant).

These results are particularly compelling when analyzed for twin similarity for the type of sport practiced (for example, basketball or football), and specialty within a given sport, such as walking, running, or jumping. It was found that 84 percent of the identical pairs preferred the same form of athletic activity, as compared with 49 percent of the fraternal pairs. These twin group differences are striking when it is considered that athletic activities are generally encouraged among young males.

It seems probable that identical-fraternal twin differences would be even greater among a female or mixed-sex sample because sports' interests are less uniformly promoted among females. It is important to note, however, that the 351 pairs who responded to the sport's questionnaire represent only about one-fourth of the pairs invited to participate in the research, so one may not be able to generalize the findings to the twin population at large.

Gedda called special attention to five identical twin pairs whose members had adopted symmetrical roles on their teams. Even more intriguing were three identical pairs whose members assumed positions that were opposite to one another, but that enabled them to "play in unbroken contact—as if creating a particular intra-pair competition within a general team competition." The psychological and social aspects of twinship seem to strongly underlie twins' athletic performance, and will be discussed in greater detail below.

Twin Research on Athletic Abilities

Researchers today are concerned with the specific biological characteristics and mechanisms that underlie athletic ability. Their efforts can provide important clues as to why some individuals prefer certain sports' activities to others. To the extent that these biological traits have a hereditary basis, it becomes easier to understand why genetically identical twins might show greater resemblance in sports participation and ability, relative to genetically fraternal twins.

Claude Bouchard and Gilles Lortie, from the University of Laval, Quebec, Canada, and Robert M. Malina, from the University of Texas, Austin, have contributed many informative reviews and studies of heredity and endurance performance in twins and their families. (Endurance performance is the capacity to perform during extended exercise periods.) A following sampling of their findings provides a taste of this exciting field and its growing sophistication.

Most twin studies have reported a greater resemblance in height for identical twins than fraternal twins at all ages. This indicates that height is largely determined by genetic factors. It is, however, influenced by environmental factors, such as nutrition, but is unaffected by exercise. Various body lengths, such as sitting height, leg length, and total arm length also are more similar among identical than fraternal twins, again suggesting the influence of genetic factors. Height, bone length, and skeletal breadth, while associated with endurance performance, are not its primary determinants.

Being tall is not the only physical characteristic required for basketball players, but it is certainly one prerequisite for success. This may explain, in part, why some identical twin partners, such as 6-foot-3-inch Pam and Paula McGee, who play basketball for the University of Southern California, may both be well-suited to this sport.

It is not surprising that the percentage of body fat is lower in athletes than in individuals who are relatively inactive. Studies of twins show that this characteristic is influenced by genetic factors because identical twins show greater resemblance to one another than fraternal twins. Identical twins also are more similar than fraternal twins for mean fat cell size, fat-free weight, and six skinfold measurements. It is, therefore, expected that "lightweight" identical twins, such as identical twin Olympic rowers, Bernd and Jorg Landvoigt, would both be attracted to sports in which minimal body fat would be an advantage.

Many other physical characteristics and processes associated with endurance performance also have been investigated using twins. For example, it has been demonstrated that both lung size and volume are influenced by genetic factors, although sex and body size must be taken into account. Altitude can also affect lung functioning, so it is important to measure twins at the same time, and in the same location. Lung functions in reared-apart identical and fraternal twins are currently being studied by investigators associated with the Minnesota Study of Twins Reared Apart. The results should uniquely contribute to knowledge about endurance performance.

Heart functioning also is an area of tremendous interest. Differences in heart rates among individuals appear to be influenced by genetic factors, as does maximum heart rates but to a lesser degree. Identical twins often display similar forms of cardiac abnormalities. One researcher reported a case of a pair of 20-year-old identical twin males who experienced fatal heart attacks associated with exercise at the same time. They suffered from the same type of narrowing of the coronary arteries. This case demonstrates that similar stress applied to the same genetic constitution can produce similar results.

Finally, Bouchard and his colleagues have shown that there are hereditary responses to trainability. Ten pairs of identical twins were evaluated during a 20-week endurance program. Improvement occurred at the same rate; in fact, it was found that the identical partners grew more alike with time. This should, however, not be surprising if we bear in mind that the training procedures were experienced by people with exactly the same genes. This does not imply that some people will not improve with training, but simply that different people will improve differently, and may uniquely respond to the various types of athletic programs available.

Sport fields provide, perhaps, one of the best arenas for observing some essential elements of identical twinship. This is because success often depends upon combined efforts—forfeiting individual glory for the benefit of the team. In the case of identical twins and sports such as running or swimming, where individual achievement is rewarded, competition assumes a very unusual cast. Identical twin, Ross Bonine, cleverly expressed this belief by commenting about sports in the *Sailor* Newspaper, February 27, 1984. "It's like having a race with another person but never trying to beat him."

Improved performance by one twin sets the goal toward which his co-twin will strive. A glimpse into the life experiences of some well-known twin athletes best illustrates these points.

The line between winning and losing generally is blurred for identical twins. The diDonato twin swimmers, when interviewed on the *Today Show* in 1981, emphasized that each brother would have been disappointed had his co-twin failed to complete his famous swim across the English Channel. The other identical twins appearing with them on the show agreed. Steve Mahre, in 1982, told *Sports Illustrated* that when his skiing performance is not up to expectation, he urges his brother, Phil, on to victory. Phil similarly explained that his co-twin's successes are his, as well: "It just doesn't feel as if I've been beaten when he wins."

Many twins claim that they perform better when playing alongside their twin; the resulting unity may compensate for weaknesses in performance, as well. For example, Rich and Ron Sutter, twins from Alberta, Canada, were both drafted into the National Hockey League, but on different teams. According to a coach, one twin had difficulty in adjusting to playing without his brother. National Basketball Association players, Dick and Tom Van Ardsdale, also wanted to be together; they requested a return to the same club after several years apart.

Psychologists have, in addition, consistently found greater resemblance between identical than fraternal twins across a range of mental abilities and information-processing skills. It is reasonable to expect that these similarities also are associated with twins' similarities in athletic performance, and the close social bond of identical twins.

Fraternal twins, as indicated earlier, are rarely found on the same athletic teams. Observing their social relationship on the same sports field would, however, be of high interest to researchers. From what is known about the reduced strength of their social bond and reduced similarity in mental functioning relative to identical twins, it would seem that a more competitive team spirit would be anticipated.

Aggressive/Passive Role-Playing

by Alice M. Vollmar

Identical twins Ryan and Aaron Brandt of Minneapolis, Minnesota, loved entertaining their grandmother with typical 4-year-olds' enthusiasm. "Watch me," called Ryan, executing a perfect headstand on the couch. "My turn," announced Aaron, as his headstand crumpled into a somersault. He tried again, unsuccessfully, then kicked the pillows in frustration. Ryan grinned and produced three more perfect headstands. "Quit it," warned Aaron. Ryan did another headstand, and Aaron gave him a purposeful shove, knocking him off balance.

Aaron reacted with predictable jealousy when Ryan neatly masterminded the headstand exhibition, according to his mother, who sees Aaron as the dominant/aggressive twin—the only who really pushes himself and wants to excel. "Last Christmas, Aaron worked hard to make sure his Christmas tree chain was longer than Ryan's. It was the longest chain I've ever seen. Ryan tried to keep up, but finally quit," she explained. "Aaron usually does what he wants to do. He will go outside and play with a friend by himself. Ryan never does that without Aaron; instead he is more the joker, the comic who follows Aaron's lead."

And that concerns her. "Sometimes I worry about Aaron being so dominant," she says. "I want to urge Ryan to do his own things, to not always follow Aaron."

Other parents also report feeling perplexed when the interaction between their twins looks out of balance to them, with one child always the leader, aggressor, mischief-maker, or star of the show. Their concern centers on two questions: Why does one twin become dominant/aggressive and the other more passive? And, what can or should parents do about it?

Why Aggressive/Passive Roles Develop

Dr. Keith Horton, Associate Professor of Psychiatry at the University of Minnesota, explains, "The basic dilemma with twins is that each can never get enough (nurturing) from the primary caretaker, so he turns to his co-twin, which gets very complicated."

An interdependence may develop between twins, making it difficult for each child to see himself as separate and not part of a set. If twins see themselves as a unit, they tend to develop complementary skills and roles. For example, one will be the leader and the other the follower; or one may speak for both, saying things like, "We're hungry, Mommy."

This behavior is reinforced by society and peers who tend to see twins as a unit. The problem with complementary skills and roles is that each twin needs to develop a full self-concept to go out into the world independently. Thus, an aggressive/passive interaction may inhibit their ability to function without one another later in life.

Why one twin appears to be dominant or passive seems to hinge on subtle factors. If one twin woke first, cried hardest and always got fed first, then his pattern of dominance may have begun in infancy. What twins see and hear happening to each other even as babies influence who is going to be active and who passive.

The way that identical twins' families related to the twins as well as how the twins related to each other influence aggressive and passive role-playing. If a mother calls one twin "outgoing," that twin may feel compelled to meet her expectations, for example. Or a twin may act aggressively to mask his insecurities and fears.

Adult Twins Reminisce

The following interviews with adult twins who saw their relationship as dominant or passive illustrate the nuances of twin interaction Horton described.

Calling herself more dominant than her identical twin sister, one 25-year-old said, "I always envied my co-twin. I was expected to be the outgoing, funny one. I couldn't just be myself, and my sister could."

David Smith, a 29-year-old accountant from Minnesota, described his twin sister, Debby, as the leader. "If our parents gave us instructions when we were little, they were always told to my sister. It was like, 'Debby lead David.' I always did feel like I was treated as a part of a set from my younger years through adolescence. My name was half of Debby-and-David." Smith recalls a painful time at age 24 when he finally came to terms with his own identity apart from his twin sister and figured out what he wanted to do in life.

These comments lend poignancy to Horton's advice to parents. "Avoid thinking and acting 'twins,' and focus instead on raising these two individuals who just happen to be the same age," he cautions.

"Parents of twins need to be aware of the mechanics of growing up," emphasizes this psychiatrist who views childhood's main tasks as "development of one's own unique skills, gradually separating from parents until one's sense of security is firmly placed within oneself." These tasks are complicated for twins, because each is also simultaneously trying to separate from the other.

Parents can encourage each child's talents and interests by refraining from comparing them, dressing them alike, or treating them as a pair. "The closeness of twins has a special benefit and a special vulnerability," says Horton. "Parents should help each child grow up as separate as possible."

Preventing Aggressive/Passive Role-Playing

How can parents change aggressive/passive role-playing, or is it a problem to ignore because twins leave the behavior behind as they age?

Clinical psychologist and child psychoanalyst Marvin Ack says, "Parents should not look the other way. If one twin tends to be more dominant and one passive, I would fear that the relationship would continue that way; it might become the character style to be used everywhere. One child would *always* be dominant, for instance, and one would *always* be passive. The earlier you catch the pattern, the easier time you will have changing it."

When you see a relationship like this between two people, Ack advises keeping in mind that both of them may be deriving gratification from it, although it doesn't look that way to an observer. If a submissive twin doesn't feel put upon and doesn't complain, then his self-concept most likely includes both of them. He doesn't see himself as "submissive."

Changing Role-Playing Patterns

To change or avoid twins' aggressive/passive role-playing, parents must watch how they and other family members relate to each twin and try to alternate care routines. Ack recommends that each parent regularly join in some separate activities with each child practically from birth.

Arrange playmates for your twins other than the co-twin, as well, urges Ack, and discuss problems with each child privately. "By referring to them together or disciplining them as a unit, you are creating the feeling "I am one of a pair' rather than 'I am a unique individual'," he advises.

To alter your twins' interaction pattern, ask yourself, What am I trying to accomplish now and in the future? Evaluate current practices. Then list specific methods to reach these goals.

Of course, changing an established behavior pattern takes time and alertness on the parents' part. Ray McGee, a social worker formerly with the Washburn Child Guidance Center in Minneapolis, Minnesota, tells parents to catch their kids "being good." Notice the kind of behavior you want to see repeated and downplay the behavior you wish to discourage.

If you want to encourage a passive twin to make decisions, you might visit the library, letting the twin pick out books independently. Then say, "I notice you picked out your own books today. I think you will really enjoy those."

Apply that kind of nonjudgmental commenting to any situation in which your twins make decisions and be sure to offer decision opportunities when possible. Likewise, to defuse an aggressive twin, watch for moderate and cooperative behavior (no matter how fleeting) and zero in on it immediately with a verbal "I notice you're sharing your truck, Jimmy. I like that!"

The issue, then comes down to switching the focus outward—promoting ways each of these persons can function fully, separate from one another. This lets the twinship settle comfortably into the background as a healthy and rich supportive friendship—instead of an indispensable lifeline.

AVOIDING ROLE-PLAYING GAMES

Adult twins offer the following tips which discourage and prevent aggressive/passive role-playing with twins of all ages:

- Give lots of positive reinforcement of each twin separately. Positive attention works better than punishment.
- Treat twins like any other child in the family.
- Do not compare twins, especially to other people because it robs them of making their own identity decisions.
- When you talk to your twins, single out each child. Say each name even though it may seem repetitious to you.

❤

Twins Lend Their Left Hands to Research

by Nancy L. Segal, Ph.D.

The increased occurrence of left-handedness among twins has fascinated psychologists for many years. In over 14 twin studies, including mine and those of Sally Springer and Alan Searleman at the State University of New York at Stony Brook, left-handedness was found among 15.5 percent of individuals who were identical twins and among 13 percent of individuals who were fraternal twins. In contrast, data from five studies of single individuals showed that only 8.5 percent preferred the left hand.

More recent statistics assembled by Dr. Charles Boklage at East Carolina University School of Medicine in North Carolina yielded even greater twin-singleton differences: 22 percent of identical and 22 percent of fraternal twins were either left-handed or ambidextrous, compared with only 8.4 percent of their second-degree relatives (aunts, uncles, grandparents).

The majority of identical twins are produced when a single fertilized egg, or zygote, divides into separate entities between approximately one and ten days after conception. Boklage has shown that about one-third of identical twins are "early-splitters." In other words, the zygote separates between days one and three, early enough so that the body asymmetries (left- and right-sidedness) of the twins are unaffected. Alternatively, division of the zygote occurs later for the remaining two-thirds of identical twin pairs. These twins are "late-splitters." Late splitting may (but does not always) produce left- and right-handed twin partners.

An even more provocative finding was reported by Boklage. He found that the parents of left-handed twins (who were generally not twins themselves) proved to be left-handed nearly twice as frequently as their own same-sex singleton siblings (twins' aunts and uncles) and parents (twins' grandparents).

In view of these findings, Dr. Jerry Levy at the University of Chicago has speculated that there may actually be two kinds of identical twins: one type in which early zygotic splitting occurs as a consequence of unusual factors in the uterus, and a second type involving a genetic tendency within some families to produce late-splitting opposite-handed twins and an excess of left-handed relatives. This is an exciting theory since, until now, only fraternal twinning has been thought to have an underlying genetic basis.

Mirror-Imaging

Reversals or so-called "mirror-imaging" effects are not limited to handedness. These special twin characteristics are not, however, related to a very rare condition called situs inversus, in which the internal organs of the body are mirror-imaged. Researchers have documented reversals in twins for a variety of traits: eyedness (sighting with a preferred eye, as when looking through a camera), fingerprint and handprint patterns (the left hand of one twin may resemble the right hand of his co-twin more closely than his own right hand), birthmarks and moles (these features may be present on the left and right sides of the faces or bodies of the respective twins), and patterns of hair growth (hair may grow in a clockwise direction for one twin and in a counter-clockwise direction for the other twin).

Some additional fascinating differences have been cited by other pairs. Mary Lou Hummel, left-handed twin, and adult member of Left Handers International, reports that she and her sister, Margaret, a right-handed twin, place hangers such that they face in opposite directions in the closet.

When Roger Brooks and his identical twin brother, Tony Milasi, clasp their hands, opposite thumbs are positioned on top. In fact, Roger suspects that he is truly a left-hander, even though he now writes with his right hand. As a young child, Roger had been badly burned on the left side of his body, an event that might have encouraged a "switch" in handedness.

Mothers of twins have also been successful in detecting these unusual features. One mother, a nurse, noted that her identical twin sons had more prominent veins situated on opposite arms. Several others have commented upon the opposite wear-and-tear of clothing and shoes. Late-splitting identical twins may display any, or all, of these characteristics, although why a particular combination of them appears in one set and not another remains a mystery.

Why More Twin Lefties?

The timing (early or late) of the splitting process can reasonably explain the high incidence of left-handedness among identical twins. It does not, however, apply to fraternal (non-identical) twins whose biological origins are quite different.

Both fraternal and identical twins are more highly subject to unusual birth stressors, such as premature birth, fetal crowding and hyposiz (oxygen deficiency) than singletons, events which could conceivably induce left-handedness in a natural right-hander. Some researchers have, for example, observed that second-born twins, whose births are generally more stressful than those of firstborns, include a slightly higher number of left-handers. Examination of medical records and extensive follow-up studies on many pairs of twins would be needed to establish firm links between unusual birth circumstances and left-handedness in twins.

Studies of large numbers of families have shown that left-handed parents tend to produce more left-handed children than right-handed parents. Exactly how handedness is transmitted across generations is not, however, fully understood.

Twin pairs made up of two left-handed members exist. About four percent of identical twin pairs and two percent of fraternal twin pairs are left-left sets. Left-left pairs probably arise, in a large part, from the same factors that explain the general increase in left-handedness among twins. The rarity of left-left pairs suggests, however, that the causal process may be more complicated.

Meaning of Handedness

Only recently, however, has the possible behavioral significance of opposite-handedness become a subject of serious study. Research strongly suggests that the left and right hemispheres of the brain are organized differently for left- and right-handers.

An extensive review of this area by J. Levy, in his book, *Behavior Genetics*, reveals that for the majority of right-handers, language processes are largely left hemisphere functions, while visual-spatial processes are largely right hemisphere functions. This characterizes only about 60 percent of left-handed individuals, with the remaining 40 percent showing greater resemblance to right-handers.

These findings raise a host of intriguing questions concerning the psychology of twins: Are twins' differences in handedness associated with differences in how the hemispheres of the brain are organized? If so, does this suggest differences in mental abilities between partners? Are the implications of opposite-handedness for intellectual performance the same for identical and fraternal twins? How do similarities and differences in handedness affect the social relationships of identical twins?

The available studies in this area have yielded mixed findings. For example, Helen Koch, author of *Twins and Twin Relations*, detected an association between left-handedness and intellectual superiority within right-left pairs, as compared with same-handed pairs. It is not clear, however, if this was true for identical twins, fraternal twins, or both.

A more serious problem, perhaps, is the "lumping" together of what may be very different types of left-handed twins. This is to say, if "early" and "late-splitting" identical twin sets are not studied as separate groups, then some very important differences between them may be hidden.

Unfortunately, methods for classifying different types of twins are not readily available. Inspection of the fetal membranes can be somewhat informative (early splitting is usually associated with separate membranes and placentas, while late splitting is often associated with shared membranes and a single or shared placenta), but this information is not always systematically recorded on hospital records.

--------------------------------- ♥ ---------------------------------

The Get-Along Goal

by Holly Richmond and Patrick C. Friman

While growing up, Holly and her identical twin sister, Kim, (not their real names), had a very close relationship that was, nevertheless, paradoxically rife with dislike and envy. Even into adulthood, the fighting between them ranged from mild competition to blatantly intense rivalry. Whey did they feel compelled to fight? The answer may be found in examining the twin relationship.

By virtue of being born together, the theme of twins' lives seems to be sharing. They share the same birthday; the same position in the family; extremely similar, if not the same developmental level; and in the case of identical twins, almost exactly the same appearance. Much of the feedback twins get from their environment, and from the people with whom they interact, is that they are not two separate identifies, but rather a single entity made up of two components. For example, it is not uncommon for twins to be asked, "Where is your other half?" Implicit in the idea of "halves" is that twins share a whole.

Sharing, however, is a difficult concept for children under the age of 7 to grasp because in their earliest years, they have very simplistic views of the universe. In their world, they are located at the center, and all the other people in their lives exist solely to provide them with their needs, whether these needs are physical or emotional. It is easy to see how, given this view of the world, sharing is not readily understood and is an abstract concept that must be learned.

Because sharing is such an alien idea, twins find themselves in somewhat of a predicament. They are, more or less, caught in a vicious circle. On one hand, they are two separate individuals, each one operating as though the world revolved around him as the focal point; on the other hand, their very birth demands that they share. And, twins are rarely taught to share. Most people assume that they already know how to share because they are viewed as two halves of a whole.

There also is a unique paradox about the twin relationship. The "me" part of each twin is constantly striving to overcome the other twin, win the spotlight and gain sole attention. At the same time, neither twin is willing to allow the other twin to achieve the spotlight. They sabotage each other and neither really ever feels that he has satisfactorily achieved his goal. Trying to get attention then becomes a no-win situation for both twins.

Parents may ask, "Well, isn't this true for all children when there is more than one child in a family?" Yes, it is true to some extent that all children experience competition and rivalry. However, it is not unusual for twins to feel that their very identities are on the line when they are competing and fighting for attention. Generally, single children do not seem to feel they have as much at stake.

In a relationship between two non-twin siblings of different ages, distinctions such as age, appearance and developmental differences usually act as buffers.

These differences ease the intensity of jealousy and competition between siblings because the expectation is not there, for example, for a younger child to be the "oldest," or for a 3-year-old to read as well as an older sibling.

Meeting the Expectations

For every age and developmental stage, advantages and disadvantages exist that are unique to the child who is at that particular point in life. For instance, a younger child who is jealous because an older child has a later bedtime often will have the compensation of reaping all the benefits that being the "baby of the family" brings, an identity that is uniquely the younger sibling's. Non-twin siblings simply are not compared at the same level. Younger children may feel frustrated when they can't read like their older brother or sister, but usually are consoled by knowing that when they are their sibling's age, they also will read.

With twins, this is not the case. If one twin does something better than the other, there most likely is a judgment involved, made either by the twins themselves or those around them. One twin may actually feel stupid if he can't read like his twin. After all, he reasons, they are the same age and "should" be able to do the same activities. To twins, sharing often means taking polar characteristics, as well. For example because a twin often believes he is a half of a whole, if his twin is smarter, he may believe he must be stupid, or if his twin is nice, he must be mean.

Not only do twins often look at themselves as "two sides to the same coin," but people in their environment also may find them a curious phenomenon and may want to fit their identifies into the scheme. Holly and Kim often were asked questions like "Which one of you is the nice one?" or "So, who's the smart one?" Because there seems room for only one twin to have a certain characteristic (for example, for one twin to be nice), the competition to be that twin can become fierce, especially for what society designates as the favorable characteristics. This competition usually occurs later in twins' development and may continue through adolescence and well into adulthood.

One area of competition, attention, is most apparent in the younger years. What eases the tension for non-twin siblings in this area does not often exist for twins. To look at the most obvious example, a singleton usually can be assured of having at least one day a year when he is unconditionally the center of attention-his birthday. And, birthdays are not the only time a child is the focus of attention. There are graduations, first proms, first days of school, achievements and awards, for example. These special events in children's lives, though still capable of provoking jealousy from siblings, give the "honored" child a sense of his own individual importance. And, because a child has these special individual events, he is more apt to allow siblings to have their own special times, as well.

In the case of a set of twins, however, these special days and events are usually shared. As a result, birthdays and special events may have a unique meaning for twins. For example, Holly and Kim always experienced the most friction at their childhood birthday parties. Their mother went to special efforts to alleviate the dual nature of the birthday-making two cakes, for example, so that each one of them would have their own candles to blow out at the same time. But, none of her efforts was enough to eliminate the jealousy and resentment that was present then.

Holly remembered bursting into tears during one birthday celebration because she wanted the blue dress her sister got instead of the pink one she received. Her mother was bewildered because Holly had previously told her that pink was her favorite color! The gift obviously was not the issue; her sister's getting too much attention was the problem. Holly also remembered feeling resentment when people gave her sister and her "joint" presents-one gift to share between the two of them.

As a result, Holly and Kim's behavior at their birthday parties was designed to get them the maximum amount of attention, and ideally, all of the attention. Holly would be loud and restless, often pouting and quarreling. She insisted on doing everything first. If they were given a joint present, Holly would grab it out of Kim's hands and open it. Kim, on the other hand, opened her gifts very slowly-to the point of exasperation-and would take many tries to blow out her candles. In those ways, she lengthened the amount of attention she received.

There are a variety of methods twins use to get attention. Most often they will use opposite or different methods from each other, especially twins who spend a lot of time together. When twins use the same method, it usually results in all-out warfare! For instance, if both Holly and Kim had been loud and pushy at their birthday party, they very likely would have physically fought.

Attention-Getting Devices

It is illustrative to notice that twins will play quietly alone together; but as soon as someone walks into the room, the whole atmosphere changes. What happens? Each twin immediately starts employing his attention-getting methods. That is also why these attention-getting behaviors may appear to increase in frequency when twins begin school. There is usually a scarcity of individual attention in school settings; thus, attention at school is an enviable prize.

One common attention-getting behavior or method is overachieving. A twin may go to any lengths to be a competent, I-can-do-anything-well person. This twin also will be diligent about bringing his achievements to the attention of others. More important, the overachieving twin will not allow anyone else to participate in his activity because that may jeopardize the final reward-individual attention.

In Holly and Kim's twinship, Holly was the overachiever. She would never allow her sister to help her with anything nor would she allow her to gain recognition for her own achievements. For example, they once sat down to make lists of the things each one of them did better than the other. Holly's list had 30 things on it; Kim's had five. Holly, as the overachiever, was relentless in not giving Kim recognition for any achievement at all.

Another attention-getting behavior is adopting a delicate, helpless demeanor-the runt-of-the-litter strategy. Kim employed this behavior by "having" a recurrent sore throat for several years. Each time she had a sore throat, she was permitted to stay home from school, giving her the opportunity to have her mother's unchallenged attention. When her mother took Kim to the doctor to check on her throat, he told her that she would have to have her tonsils out the next time she had a sore throat. She "mysteriously" stopped having the ailment.

Kim also used to eat very slowly, picking at her food, and swallowing very little. Her actions sometimes gave others the impression that she was weak and lethargic. Her behavior, of course, concerned her mother who would give her vitamins, cod liver oil, and special concoctions. Be needing extra care, she elicited special concern from her mother that none of the other children received.

These were just some of the methods or behaviors Holly and Kim successfully employed. Basically, twins are very observant and will, like all children, pick up on what does and does not get them attention. Their attention-getting behaviors could include making trouble, bullying, being easily scared, and acting extremely feminine or masculine, for example. In twins, these behaviors can become exaggerated and may appear as problems.

How to Deal with the Problems

Parents can never completely eliminate the feelings of jealousy and resentment twins have for one another, and one twin may always believe that the other twin gets more attention or is favored.

But a parent can always be more consistent. To a child, the world, and particularly the adult world, often seems arbitrary and fraught with inconsistency. Parents often will interact with children out of mood rather than merit. And, because it is difficult for even adults to predict when their moods will change, it becomes especially difficult for children to match their behavior to the adult's changing moods.

If one twin has done something worthy of attention, parents should give that child the individual attention he or she merits, no matter what the parents' mood. Even if the other twin feels jealous at the time, there will be more room for individual achievements for both of the twins if the reward is consistent and individual.

Sometimes, the resentment or jealousy of the twin who is not getting the attention will influence a parent to decide that paying special attention to the meritorious twin is not worth the trouble. On the contrary, this is the moment in parents' lives when their commitment to fairness and consistency should be firm. Things that children do that earn attention are the things they are likely to repeat. Withholding positive attention from a twin for fear of provoking the other is risky. It is better for parents to approve their twins' good behavior and individual accomplishments when they occur than to wait until both twins have done something that the parents can acknowledge.

Holly and Kim were usually rewarded together regardless of whether or not they had both actually achieved something. Their parents did this because they did not want one twin to feel "left out." But even if one twin did feel left out, both twins would have benefitted in knowing the real value of an earned reward. Plus, parents should know that it is possible to recognize only one twin, while still making the other twin aware that he or she is loved.

Parents should tell their twins that they love them equally, but that "equal" means that they love each of them because of their individual uniqueness, not because there are two of them. Although many parents may believe this is a trite observation, many twins think they are loved as a package deal because people can't tell them apart.

Giving the Gift of Time

One way parents of twins can show their love is to give each a small, individualized portion of their time every day-15 minutes per twin, for instance. During that time, a parent should play with each without commands, criticisms, or questions, just describing and praising the child's actions. Frequent touching is important, too. If a misbehavior occurs, it should be discussed and the session should be terminated. But, if the child's behavior is acceptable, the parent should continue to describe, praise and touch. This attention communicates love effectively because it is not deflected or diminished by criticizing or questioning. Also, the absence of commands can increase twins' sense of individuality because their parent no longer conducts the show; they do.

Feelings of jealousy and even hate for a co-twin is natural. Instead of admonishing their twins for expressing these feelings, parents should talk with them and discuss what being a twin means to each. Parents should listen attentively and avoid suggesting that one is the "bad twin," or that it is bad for them to experience the natural feelings of envy and resentment. Once they are allowed to express those, they may be more willing to look at the love they feel for each other.

The final thing parents should recognize and be ready for is that twins may retreat into their twinship when "the going gets rough." Although they will compete, even loudly, for attention and identity, they may not want to give up the anonymity of the twinship. They want to have it both ways-to have an individual identity, as well as to enjoy the safety of escaping from responsibility within the twinship.

By being firm and insisting that each takes individual responsibility, parents can help their twins gain a valuable sense of each one's own personal strength and separateness. And, not surprisingly, when they feel that, they will feel much less motivated to fight and compete.

Twins at Play

by Pat Fasanella

From infancy through toddlerhood, twins are often each other's exclusive and constant companions. Long before birth, they learn to relate to each other, becoming one another's first, and usually closest, playmates.

In an informal survey conducted in 1984 by the Wisconsin Organization of Mothers of Twins Clubs, more than 70 mothers with twins ranging in age from 2 to 21 years, expressed the following views on the friendships their children have formed both with each other and with playmates.

Several parents reported their twins first noticed each other as young as 2 weeks old, and they interacted with each other by 5 or 6 months old. While babies this young do not "play" together, they do start to form a special relationship.

They often babble and smile while "discovering" each other, for example. By the end of their first year, most twins interact and adapt to each other on a daily basis, their parents reported. Many times a relationship will develop in which one twin is assertive while the other is submissive; these roles tend to switch back and forth over a period of time.

"For months we felt sorry for Chris because his brother always picked on him," said one mother of twins surveyed, "but he's really come into his own lately and seems to be trying to make up for it all now!"

Does the Closeness Remain?

Parents overwhelmingly reported that in spite of their many confrontations, as twins approach toddlerhood, their relationship with each other usually grows increasingly close. Those with toddler twins said that their multiples usually prefer to play together rather than alone or with other children. They tend to seek each other out when separated, stick together in social situations with other children, and spend much of their time playing together.

"Sometimes my boys act as though they feel other children are intruding on their play," said a mother of 2 1/2-year-old fraternals.

Play, for toddler twins, can be a wild state of affairs, though. Their constant companionship often requires their compromising and their parents' intervening. Learning to share, even for twins, is a difficult and ongoing process.

Some parents said they bought identical toys to cut down on their toddlers' fights. Others suggested using a timer to give each twin his own turn with a particular toy. Another solution is to provide one plaything with many pieces (blocks, play dough, cars) for both of them. Many times, a few moments of quiet separation will settle the controversy.

Because of the frequent conflicts and compromises in which their twins engaged, many parents believed the children learned to share with each other earlier and more easily than singletons. "They have to," quipped one mother. "Sharing is a way of life for twins."

By preschool age, most twins have become very accustomed to being around each other, and many have definite patterns of adapting to one another. Several parents recalled incidents of one twin knowing instinctively what the other wanted when playing. Often one twin will receive a snack or special privilege and will insist that the other twin receive the same.

Preschool Relationships

Twins at this age are able to play well together for longer periods of time and usually seem to enjoy each others' company very much. While most twins have now begun to enjoy other playmates, also, the majority of parents still reported their twins often prefer to play with one another.

A mother of 4-year-old identical boys described her sons as being "very rude and sometimes mean to other children when they only want to play together."

"They know they have each other and do not feel any great need for other friends," seemed to be the echo of many parents of preschool-age twins.

It is no wonder that, at this point, many parents begin worry that the closeness and security of their twins' relationship will keep them from seeking out other friendships.

A few parents found their preschool twins able to socialize quickly and easily with other children. Many reported difficulties in this area though. In some cases, twins, though playing in a group, would still interact only with each other.

"Together, they are very outgoing," said a mother of 4-year-old identical girls, "but with other children, they become quiet and lack group participation. They have not yet tried seeking out friends within the neighborhood compared to my singleton daughter who played constantly with a neighbor friend at age 2 1/2."

Some parents whose twins have learned to work things out between themselves reported that their children are at a complete loss when faced with relating to other children.

"My twins think nothing of fighting over something between the two of them." explained a mother of 4-year-old fraternals, "but if someone at preschool takes one of their toys, they don't seem to know what to do about it-they just accept it."

In general, parents reported their preschool twins as reluctant, at first, to set aside the security of being together in order to play independently with other children. Many twins will unconsciously ignore, not notice, or refuse to join in play with others.

"My twin boys like to socialize with other children," said another mother, "but I have noticed that they will usually play with another child together, not separately. I don't think it's because they are the shy sort, it's that they really seem to rely on the other twin being there. And if it does happen that one twin leaves the room, the other twin will go look for him, so that he will not be left alone, whether there is another child in the room or not."

Sometimes it is the twins who intimidate other children. "I feel my twins think of themselves as a unit," said the mother of 5-year-old identical girls. "At times they overwhelm another youngster because the other child sees two kids, while they think of themselves as one."

Encouraging Social Development

Playgroups, preschools, and other activities that provide twins with the opportunity to interact with others can help in their social development. Some parents choose to send their twins to separate preschool sessions. Most, however, consider this too inconvenient, or find their children upset with being separated at this young age.

Even when twins attend together, teachers and group leaders can do a variety of things to encourage them to play, and relate to other children, separately. With just a little effort and foresight, a preschool teacher can make sure twins are not seated together. The simple experience of being at separate tables with separate playmates will begin fostering relationships with other children.

Most twins enjoy the security of being together part of the time, or at least "checking" on one another periodically. It is important for the teacher to make sure they are not allowed to play constantly or exclusively with each other, though. Even in the most informal playgroups, an enlightened leader can interest one twin in the activity of a playmate, such as coloring or building, then distract his co-twin with another playmate's activity.

When twins are reluctant to initiate play with other children, an adult can often introduce them separately to another playmate and suggest something for them to do together. In most cases, twins are happy to expand their circle of friends when they receive some gentle encouragement.

In addition to preschools and playgroups, many mothers reported making arrangements for their twins to visit friends or relatives separately. While one is away visiting, a special activity is planned for the twin at home.

As preschool twins mature and become exposed to more children and play situations, interesting developments take place. Making friends with others seems to become more important as children approach school-age. While most twins still enjoy each others' company, parents surveyed noticed their twins beginning to actively seek out other playmates. Some reported that one twin even insisted that his co-twin cannot be a friend, only a sister or brother.

Most early friends are mutual ones for twins, but parents said their twins often have formed separate friendships by 7 years old-especially in the case of boy/girl twins or those in separate schools.

Complications from Separation

Separate friendships often bring new problems for twins. One may feel left out, jealous or resentful because of the other's newfound relationship. Parents also told of crushed feelings when only one twin is invited to a party or after school activity.

According to those surveyed, not being invited to parties was most upsetting to these young twins just starting school. After years of their parents trying to make everything fair and equal for them, twins often find it difficult to accept unequal treatment in school and the "outside world."

In the early school years, parents dealt with the uninvited twin situation in several ways. One solution, when the party was for a mutual friend, was to call the birthday child's parents and ask that both children be included. Often, the party-givers didn't realize a twin was being left out.

When the party was for a friend of only one twin, parents found it helpful to plan a special activity for the at-home twin. Coping with jealousy was easier when one twin could go shopping, eat out, or just spend special time alone with mom or dad while his co-twin attended the party. Other parents suggested that the uninvited twin take this opportunity to have his own special friend over to play.

"No matter what you do, there are still hurt feelings when one twin feels left out," said a mother of 8-year-old identical girls. "As they get older though, it's easier to explain to them that life isn't always fair-that maybe next time the situation will be just the reverse."

As twins reached their middle years, the parents surveyed said they planned fewer special activities for a "left out" twin and spent more time talking with them about their hurt feelings.

"It's a tough thing for them when one feels excluded," a mother of 10-year-old boy/girl twins said, "but we considered it an important step in learning to live their own individual lives, and that's how we explained it to them."

In spite of new friends and new experiences, twins who enjoyed a close relationship as young children tend to continue this closeness during their school years.

As one mother expressed it, "Their twinship has imposed on them negative feelings about doing things alone, but individual class participation has forced them to become independent. They still continue to seek each others' support and approval, especially when trying new things."

A few parents related stories of twins with definite problems of over-dependence on one another; continuing to be dependent on each other into adulthood. Generally, though, most parents of school-age twins reported they believed that the special relationship their children have with each other is a help rather than a hindrance.

"When they are together, I think they get along with others easily because they feel more secure with their twin there," said one mother. "I know I feel more at ease when I have a close friend with me."

Another mother stated that she believed her twins have always found making friends easy because they learned to get along with each other so early. Even one parent of boy/girl twins who now have very different interests and friends, happily says her children still enjoy a close, special relationship with each other.

The Teenage Years

Information compiled by the National Organization of Mothers of Twins Clubs, Inc., stated that the teenage years can be a critical social time for twins. On the whole, parents said their children at this age still enjoyed being twins. Those who like their twinship the least were fraternals-and intense competition seemed to be the primary reason.

School psychologists I questioned reported that they experienced more problems with twins who were too competitive than those who were smothering each other in overdependent relationships.

At all ages, every set of twins and each individual twin have their own way of responding to social situations. Parents need to realize that the special bond that their twins share may spark many difficulties in relationships with others. It is normal for twins to depend on each other, but it is ideal for them to enjoy their twinship without relying exclusively on each other.

Coping with "The Boss"

by Irene L. Campbell

Parents of twins are often asked, "Which twin is the passive one?" The assumption is that one child must be dominant and the other passive. Oddly enough, parents who normally resent comparisons of their twins will answer such a question without hesitation.

Parents do often compare their children's personalities from the time they are very young to distinguish between their twins, and to assure themselves that their children are, indeed, developing as individuals. These parents frequently say things such as, "Jimmy is more outgoing than Timmy" or "Jane is less demanding than Fred."

Because twins are exactly the same age, minor differences between the two children often show up more clearly than between singletons. Parents who are intent on being able to differentiate between their twins are more apt to magnify such differences.

An Illinois mother of grown-up identical twin girls once said, "Over-emphasis on twinship problems can lead to an over-zealous self-analysis which, itself, can create problems."

Findings through the Glasgow Twin Study suggest that, when twins are brought up together, they sometimes adopt different roles (especially in the area of social behavior) in order to stress their individuality.

Research done by Dr. Thomas J. Bouchard, of the University of Minnesota, Study of Twins Reared Apart, shows a strong indication that twins who have been reared apart may be more similar than those raised together. Does the fact that one twin may have deliberately chosen the passive role and the other the dominant role necessarily mean that there is a problem" The answer is many-sided.

Desirable vs. Undesirable Traits

Dominant characteristics are generally seen as being desirable, while passive characteristics are seen as being less desirable, or even undesirable. The prevailing attitude in society at a certain time may well influence how a parent views his child's personality, and whether or not that parent feels that there is a problem.

Parents generally assemble a set of expectations for each of their twins. These expectations may be astute and appropriate responses to the cues received from the child, or they may be a result of the parents stereotyping each child.

In *Birth To Maturity*, Jerome Kagan and Howard A. Moss note, "The concept of maleness in our society is closely linked with the characteristics of strength, size, daring, aggressiveness and interpersonal dominance." It is possible that a parent's concern for a passive son may be generated by the fact that child simply does not fit the traditional male image.

In male/female twins, traditional sex role models are often reversed. In fact, since females mature both physically and socially more quickly than males, the girl is often the dominant one of the pair. How might this female domination affect her brother? If the boy realizes that he is not living up to "everyone's" expectation of him as a male, he may feel inadequate and inferior and resent or envy his sister. Fortunately, it seems that society may be slowly growing away from sex stereotypes.

As the male twin becomes more aware of how others view his relationship with his sister, he may become less willing to accept her "mothering." Parents often notice that their son begins to assert himself once their twins start school.

As one British mother put it, "As far as my two go, Katie has always been the leader. But of late, Alex, age 6, has begun to stand his ground a little bit more...she doesn't boss him about as much now."

Often, parents are not worried so much by the actual differences as by the lack of sameness. Most parents of fraternal twins are not as affected by this desire for sameness as are the parents of identical twins. Even twins who are the image of each other will not be psychologically identical, yet parents may still expect them to be equal to each other in every respect.

Influence by Adults

French researcher Rene Zazzo once stated, "The home environment and the parents' attitudes tend to mold children's personalities to a great extent." Modern day parents of twins, generally speaking, are now more convinced that it is important for their children to develop individuality and independence than parents in past generations. Rivalry and disharmony would appear to be a step toward that goal, yet parents constantly urge children to "get along" and become aggravated by signs of conflict. A child who is eager to please his parents may tend to "get along" by submitting rather than fighting and, by so doing, earns himself the label of being "passive."

R.D. Laing, in *The Politics Of The Family*, speaks of attribution as a basic method of setting personality traits in young children. Comments made by parents, teachers and peers can program a child to behave in a certain manner and to eventually assume certain personality traits.

A child will undoubtedly exhibit aggressive behavior, for example, if he constantly hears others saying things such as, "Johnny is a very stubborn little boy who likes to have his own way."

Comments such as, "Linda has always been shy and quiet," only serve to reinforce a child's shy or quiet tendencies. The power of "labels" in shaping a child's personality cannot be underestimated.

Role-Switching

In *Twins & Supertwins*, Amram Scheinfeld describes a phenomenon that he calls the "see-saw situation." This phenomenon, in which twins switch roles with each other, is common in at least 50 percent of twin pairs. One day, one twin will be the more aggressive or "the boss," and the next day it may be his co-twin's turn to assume that role.

Role-switching may be easy for a set of twins because of the special understanding that each has of the other. Each may be able to pick up non-verbal, as well as verbal, messages from his co-twin because of his close contact with the other.

Such role-switching can come as a real surprise to those who think they know the children well. As one exasperated mother commented, "Just when you think you've got them figured out, they fool you." This phenomenon can be particularly nerve-racking for parents who are accustomed to thinking of each child in a certain way and fitting that child into a particular personality pigeon-hole.

Confusion may result if other people have differentiated between the two children solely on the basis of personality. Others may also have difficulty developing a clear idea of the twins' separateness if the roles are continually being switched.

What happens if there is a fixed leader/follower pattern when twins start school? The passive twin (the "follower") may benefit from being separated from his co-twin. He may blossom once he is free to express himself and no longer feels he must take second place.

On the other hand, the passive twin may simply find another child to shadow. By doing so, that child is demonstrating a personality trait that, in all likelihood, will endure and one that is not necessarily dependent upon the twin relationship.

Surprisingly enough, it is often the more dominant twin (the "leader") who has difficulty adjusting to being separated from his co-twin in school. Used to being "the boss" at home, he may suddenly find himself "a small fish in a big pond" at school and lose his status as a leader.

If it does become obvious that one child is always "the boss," parents of twins should be aware of potential problems that may adversely affect their twins' development.

The Passive Twin

Unhealthy competition—a drive by the dominant twin to always be better or do better than his co-twin—can undermine the self-confidence of the more passive child. Parents can seek to prevent this by pointing out that the advantages one twin has in certain areas are generally balanced by the co-twin's advantages in other respects. If the compensating assets are not immediately obvious, it may be necessary for the parents to search out the passive child's hidden potential and then help him to develop it.

A passive twin may see herself not as an individual, but as a part of the twin unit. Such a child may think, "Without my twin, I am nothing." Therefore, she gives in constantly because she is afraid to endanger the previous twin relationship by rebelling.

The passive child needs reassurance of her own worth a person apart from her co-twin. Her parents can provide this reassurance by minimizing the "cuteness" and "specialness" of the twinship and, instead, playing up the individual qualities that make her special.

One mother expressed another potential problem in this way, "If any task is the least bit difficult, Robert knows that all he has to do is droop his lip into a pout and his brother will take over and do it for him."

The same mother explained how she copes with this problem. "Whenever a situation arises, we make a conscious effort to recognize it and give our son a few minutes of our attention and help him to see that he can accomplish it himself."

A dominant twin may demand a lot of parental attention while his co-twin does not. Parents must see that the passive, undemanding twin receives equal attention. The need exists whether or not the child can or will express it. As one mother noted, "Until she finally asserted herself, Lisa seldom asked for anything." Often the quiet member of the set-the one who rarely gets into trouble-may suffer from unintentional neglect.

One potential problem for the passive child in school is discussed by O. Weininger in his essay "Dominance in Children." As he explains it, "Every teacher knows that the child whose needs are most easily left unmet is the quiet one in the corner of the classroom whose name one never can quite remember." Just as a passive child must be encouraged to express himself at home, he must also be urged to make his needs known at school.

The Dominant Twin

A related problem occurs when the dominant twin always speaks for the more passive child. This can seriously hinder speech development in the "silent partner." If one twin will do all the talking and get his co-twin what he wants, there may be no need for the passive twin to speak for himself.

One mother said she solved the problem of the "spokesperson" by asking, "Who's we?" when one twin would say, for example, "We're hungry." The quiet child must sometimes be actively encouraged to form her own thoughts and express her own needs.

One twin who constantly "does for" or "speaks for" the other is not doing his co-twin any favor in the end. Particularly in a classroom situation with a busy teacher, others may not realize that one child is not doing his own work and learning as he should. One of the strongest arguments for twin separation in the classroom is to allow both children to develop to their full potential.

A child will sometimes insist on helping his co-twin even if his parents tell him not to do so. By defying his parents but cooperating with his twin, he can control things to suit himself and his twin no matter what his parents say.

Any comments implying unfavorable comparisons should be avoided by all who come into contact with twins. Unfortunately, many of the questions asked and comments made by others carry a negative connotation because of their implications of superiority or inferiority. This is especially true when personalities are contrasted.

Parents must guard against letting the dominant child feel that he is supervisor to or "better" than, his co-twin simply because his personality is different. Sometimes parents can, by their words or attitudes, give the impression that one of their children is more important or more valued than the other.

If a passive child accepts the idea that he is not as important as his dominant co-twin, he may submit to the demands and needs of his brother while relinquishing his own needs, for example.

Parents may have to help their dominant child to respect the rights of the passive one. In *Twins: A Guide to their Education*, by the Main Line Mothers of Twins Club, the authors say, "Domination becomes a twin problem when the leader is dogmatic and fails to let the follower assert or protect his own rights and ideas."

In her book, *Twins: Nature's Amazing Mystery*, Kay Cassill talks about her relationship with her identical twin, Marilyn. She says that there was a "thinly veiled and continuing struggle for dominance but it was balanced by concern for the other twin's feelings."

Experiencing a give-and-take relationship with a co-twin may prepare a child for the give-and-take of social contact. There is a definite "survival value" in being dominant at times and passive at others depending upon the situation. A child who had never learned to submit to another's will could run into problems in the classroom where the teacher expects to be obeyed without question.

A 1980 study of preschool children by Strayer and Strayer should reassure parents who are concerned about how their passive child will be accepted by his peers. The study concluded that social preference did not appear to be strongly related to the dominance hierarchy. In other words, the more dominant children were not always preferred for play or other social contact.

In social interaction, not only for children but for adults as well, if the wants of two individuals conflict, a compromise may have to be reached for the interaction to continue.

"DOMINANT" AND "PASSIVE" DEFINED

What do most people mean by the terms "dominant" and "passive" when referring to a child's personality? A 1976 study by Strayer and Strayer considered dominant and passive traits. In their research, the following categories of naturally occurring social conflict between two children were established: physical attacks, threat gestures, and object or position struggles (for example, over a toy or for position at the head of a line).

Strayer and Strayer then gauged the reaction of the children according to whether or not those children submitted or gave in, sought help, counterattacked, or made no response or withdrew. The child who "won" in these encounters was considered to be the more dominant child.

A person preparing a list of dominant characteristics might include such adjectives as assertive, aggressive, enterprising, adventurous, gregarious, sociable, and confident. A similar list of passive traits might include such terms as anxious to conform, eager to please, willing to be led, and strongly in need of reassurance.

♥

Addressing Attitudes About Dressing

by Terry Pink Alexander

On Christmas Eve of 1986, Jim and Annette Passaglia received early Christmas presents—the arrival of their fraternal twins, Mike and Steve. The babies were quite dissimilar in appearance. "One was blond and one was brunette," noted Jim. "So, it was and still is easy to think of them as two unique individuals."

Thinking of their twins as individuals may have been easy for the immediate Passaglia family, but it was not the automatic thinking of those in their extended family who gave the newborns look-alike holiday outfits. Should Jim and Annette have accepted the gifts of identical clothing, though they had decided before the babies were born to consider their sons as individuals when making dressing decisions for them?

These potential conflicts over how to dress one's twins for the holidays and whether or not to accept or give look-alike clothing and gifts arise in many families of multiples on an annual basis. However, according to my interviews with families of multiples, whether their twins were identical or fraternal seemed to have little bearing on whether or not they chose to dress their children alike. Instead, parents' attitudes about twinship, in general, impacted on their decision-making.

For example, 3 1/2-year-old look-alike twin boys, Marc and Erin Alfert, have never been dressed alike, according to their mother, Nova. "From the beginning, I felt it was hard enough for them as it was, just being twins, so I thought that by dressing Marc and Erin differently, they could be more like singletons," Nova noted.

Her husband, Peter, agreed. "When they were babies, we never dressed the twins alike—ever. We have given them the freedom to choose what they want to wear, and they have never expressed a desire to dress alike."

Nova added, "It's an individual choice. Some people like the extra attention; we don't."

Although the Alferts encourage their boys to choose the clothes they wear each day, the only difference in the rules Nova and Peter adhere to for the holidays is to be sure that Marc and Erin choose "nice" clothes—not things that are stained or have holes in them.

Because the Passaglia twins' birthday photo is also their holiday photo each year, choosing clothing for that once-a-year special picture could become particularly important. Yet, Jim and Annette said that as long as each twin looks nice and feels good in what he's wearing, exactly what each wears for his photo and for his Christmas/birthday celebration seems to be of little significance to the children or to themselves.

However, some parents I interviewed disagreed with this latter comment, saying that the winter holidays provided a once-a-year opportunity to capitalize on the fun of having twins. Ellen Keeshan, mother of 3-year-old identicals Hannah and Allison, noted, "In general, I only dress my identical twin girls alike occasionally; and they don't necessarily wear the same things even if they have a matched set of clothes. But for their holiday photo and for Christmas dinner, I usually try to dress them alike. Their older sister, Mia, who is 4 1/2 years old, likes to dress in the same things as Hannah and Allison for these special occasions. It makes her feel like part of the group."

Parents of boy/girl twins interviewed were just as likely as parents of same-sex fraternal or identical twins to promote look-alike attire for those special holiday occasions. Brandon and Brittany Dybdahl, 27 months old, have now celebrated two holiday seasons. Admitted their mother, Becky, "My basic feeling is that I'm proud to have twins. Since boy/girl twins look so different anyway, confusing them just isn't an issue. So, it's fun for me to play up their twinness and to dress them alike—or at least similarly. I definitely dress them alike for their holiday photos or in matching brother/sister outfits."

Paula Schiff's preferences for dressing her 4-month-old identical girls, Chrys and Gwen, alike at holiday time were influenced by her own childhood experiences. Although she is not a twin, Paula has a unique perspective on look-alike outfits.

"My mother made look-alike mother/daughter outfits for her and me until my sisters were born," Paula shared. "Then she made matching sister outfits for us, which we wore on special family occasions. That was more acceptable in those days than it is today. I wouldn't do it for myself and my children, especially because they are twins. I want them to develop pride in themselves as individuals so that others will see them as Chrys and Gwen and not as 'the twins.' I wasn't even a twin, and I shied away from the attention dressing alike brought us."

Holiday Gifts

Just as families seem to have their own distinct views on how to dress their children, they also have varied opinions on identical gift-giving for multiples. Linda Baker, mother of 9-year-old identicals Joshua and Andrew, believes, "When twins are toddlers and preschoolers, people should give them things that are similar or the same in different colors or patterns because this eliminates the competition between the children."

"But, as they get older," she noted, "they are able to handle receiving dissimilar gifts. At age 9, Joshua and Andrew never get identical things, and that is OK with them."

Marsha Rabkin, whose fraternal girls are now 8 1/2 years old, agreed. "For the holidays, I have often bought my girls the same outfits so that neither child will think I chose something more special for her sister." But, she admitted, "I know the girls won't wear the look-alike outfits at the same time. They like receiving matching clothing because they often like the same things. Ever since they have been able to dress themselves, however, one will go back and change if she discovers that she and her co-twin have dressed alike. They will never go out wearing the same clothes."

By age 8 or 9, children often have strong preferences of their own about clothes. Although the Baker boys and Rabkin girls choose to dress in dissimilar outfits for the holidays, another set of twins who recently turned 9 years old has the opposite preference.

Identical twins Kristin and Megan Harter "are at an age when they like to have exactly what their friends have, and they are each other's best friends," according to their mother, Denise. "I usually buy gifts from catalogues. I always give them the choice of what they want, and they almost always choose the same things."

The girls choose to wear matching outfits for special occasions but also have to be dressed alike five days a week because their school requires that they wear a uniform. "I learned early to respect their preferences," Denise explained. "One Christmas when they were 3 or 4 years old, I went to a lot of trouble to find pretty things that were different. When they opened their gifts, each wanted what the other had but didn't want to swap."

Marsha, however, cautions parents about giving similar gifts to twins on a regular basis. "The underlying message is that they are just alike," she noted. "But each set of twins is comprised of unique individuals who should be treated as individuals. It's like giving gifts to two siblings of different ages. You probably wouldn't give them matched gifts—even if they were close in age."

Holiday Gift-Giving

If you are considering buying look-alike outfits for infants and toddlers, first ask the twins' parents their opinion about the issue of dressing their children alike.

When buying for older children, keep in mind that look-alike gifts usually minimize competition between the twins and their perception of favoritism; dissimilar gifts usually promote greater individuality. Ask older children whether they prefer similar or dissimilar outfits before making purchases.

Holiday Trips

Whether or not to dress twins alike on their holiday vacation is also an issue for some families. According to Ayana Hassad, whose boy/girl fraternals are 3 1/2 years old, "When the children are dressed alike, it's easier to spot them if they get lost in a crowd."

But, Nova believes that dissimilar attire is especially preferable for her boys when they're on vacation because "they get stared at a lot anyway, and to dress them alike means they'll be stared at for sure."

Twin Services, a national organization serving families of twins, offers the following helpful advice about making clothing choices for infant multiples:

- The way you dress baby twins gives others a message about how to treat them. If you dress your twins alike, they may grow up feeling important only as a unit. Dressing your multiples in matching outfits may attract attention and be fun for you, but may compromise your children's ability to see themselves as separate from one another.

- For toddlers and middle-years children, let go of your emotional involvement regarding how your twins dress. De-emphasize the importance of clothing choices. If your children occasionally want to dress alike (or if they go through a stage of preferring to wear matched clothing), let them enjoy looking alike as well as different some of the time.
- Encourage older multiples to choose their own clothing each day. This will help them establish their own identities and develop their own respective tastes. Assign each child his own clothing drawer.
- Look-alike clothes promote self-comparisons and competition, especially among fraternals. Hand-me-down clothing from older siblings, relatives or family friends can be one way to discourage matched attire because there are no two-of-a-kind outfits and because the twins can decide between themselves who will claim which clothing.

SPECIAL HOLIDAY SUGGESTIONS

If you decide to dress your twins alike, keep an individual "look" to each child's outfit by:

- Choosing outfits in different colors or patterns, or choosing brother/sister outfits in the case of boy/girl twins.
- Giving look-alike co-twins some distinguishing feature, such as using different colored hair ribbons or parting their hair on different sides.
- Bringing a change of clothing for each child, and being flexible about their wearing them. If the twins are dressed alike, and if one child spills gravy down the front of her new dress, for example, it is not necessary to change both children so that they both are still wearing matching outfits.
- Dressing each child in something in which he or she looks and feels good.

CHAPTER 4

Death of a Twin

Death of a Twin

by Sheryl McInnes

The loss of a child is a tragic and devastating event for both the parents and the surviving siblings. Parents often choose not to think about this happening in their own family or among their friends.

In the summer of 1981, my own complacency was shattered by a series of events that took place within a four week period. One of my twin daughters was struck by a car while riding her bicycle. The phone call from the hospital is still a part of our nightmares. Fortunately her injuries were not fatal, but did lead to an agonizing night waiting for the results of surgery. Three weeks later, a close friend lost one of her twin sons in a drowning accident. While we were trying to absorb the shock of those two events, my son suffered a potentially fatal concussion in a diving accident.

Shock, denial, profound sadness, and relief churned through our family as we were forced to face up to fate and our own immortality.

Our family's coming this close to losing two of our children, and witnessing the grief of a friend who did lose a twin, opened up a new sense of compassion toward parents who lose a child.

It is said that death ends a life, but it does not end a relationship. How then does the loss of a twin differ from the loss of a singleton in the effect it has on the parents, the co-twin and the other siblings?

Death in Utero

Parents who lose twins through a miscarriage experience the emptiness of an incomplete pregnancy. If the mother blames herself, her grief is compounded by guilt. Friends, relatives and hospital staff often view a miscarriage as a "non-happening" and may not allow the parents the privilege of grieving. The process of mourning must be allowed to take place for both parents though, and the situation explained to any siblings, if this family is to move forward to have more children.

Premature birth is one of the leading causes of death in twins. When both babies are stillborn or die shortly after birth, all the expectations for this special type of parenthood die with them. The parents are mourning for two children along with the status of being parents of twins. If they have become involved with a parents of twins group, they may also feel they are losing new friendships. It is this triple loss that makes a twin stillbirth so difficult to cope with when so few people understand the actual scope of the loss.

The situation may be even more difficult if one baby dies. "Why this baby and not the other one?" "Did we resent the thought of two babies to care for and therefore cause this to happen?" "Did our preference for one sex cause this boy or girl to die?" These are the thoughts that may increase the burden of grief as the shock and numbness wear off and the parents begin to realize what has happened. A parent may also feel guilty and blame himself, his spouse or his other children for things they may have done or not done that led to the premature birth.

In this instance, the parents have lost the specialness of twins; but they do have a living child. People may emphasize this constantly with words like, "how lucky you are to have one healthy baby," which may not be entirely true, if the surviving twin is also in jeopardy due to complications from prematurity, or if the results of early birth will mean a permanent disability. The process of shock, denial, anger, acceptance, and eventual resolution are very similar in mourning and in coming to terms with a disabled or chronically ill child.

The parents may be in a state of turmoil, and may stand back from the surviving twin for fear of loving and losing once again. Dealing with the pain of losing a child and showing appropriate joy in their newborn baby may be totally impossible reactions to make. Parents may ignore the loss and become totally emotionally involved with the living twin, or withdraw emotionally from the living child and immerse themselves totally in grief. The father is often expected to be the strong member of this team, submerging his grief in order to carry out the details of informing the family, comforting his wife and any siblings, and dealing with the bureaucratic process of registration and burial.

Impact on the Marriage

This emotional turmoil may cause the couple to become out of sync, forcing each to be alone with their grief and anger. The other family members and hospital staff may add to this by making comments about how the couple is or is not grieving and how they feel the parents should be reacting to the living baby.

Both parents need to talk—often nothing more than listening is required in order to help. The grieving parents are very aware that words are never adequate comfort, but being able to talk about the baby is an essential part of coming to terms with the loss.

The mother may lose interest in sexual relations, further isolating herself from a source of comfort. If the father is still maintaining his "stiff upper lip," there is bound to be some misunderstanding about his feelings about the dead baby, and a wall of resentments may build between the couple. It is highly recommended by parents who have lost a baby that the couple seek grief counseling, or join a group of parents who have lost children such as Compassionate Friends, to share their feelings in a neutral setting.

It is important for family and the hospital to recognize that the baby who dies was a real person so the parents can have a clear memory of their lost baby. One mother who lost a twin shortly after birth offers the following suggestions:

See, hold, and photograph the baby who dies, if at all possible; name both babies and talk about the baby who dies using her name; save some momentos such as the crib card, a lock of hair, or a blanket the baby was wrapped in; immediately begin planning a formal funeral or memorial service; and recognize, and make others recognize, the father's grief and allow him also to express his feelings openly.

All of this will reinforce the reality of the existence and death of the baby, and allow all of the family to have a chance to say goodbye.

When the parents return home from the hospital, the true magnitude of their loss often hits again with tremendous force. If they have had to leave the surviving twin in the hospital as well, they may not be able to cope with any daily routines or the care of their children. It is essential for both parents to communicate feelings and support each other in any decision. For some couples, having family members remove the extra baby equipment before they arrive home makes it easier to adjust; but coming home to find these items gone may be devastating for other parents who consider the action a denial that there ever was another baby expected.

Once they have the other baby at home, his presence will be a constant reminder of the loss—not only the loss of a baby, but also the loss of the potential twin relationship these children might have had. Many people will have been aware that the couple were expecting twins, and every time they go out with one baby, they may have to repeatedly explain what has happened. Many of the parents' friends are uncomfortable with death, and may avoid the couple to save themselves from having to talk about the death of the baby.

The parents may initially shut out the memories of what has occurred, but months later this unresolved grief may surface in depression and anxiety that others may not realize is because of the death. It is even possible that they may shut this grief out for years, and then a different crisis will trigger the emotions that were submerged.

Some parents report that they were not able to care for, or grow attached to, the surviving baby for a period of time. The baby was seen as an intruder; someone pulling the parents away from their grief and memories of the lost baby. This reluctance to be involved with the baby led to more guilt and recriminations from other family members, isolating the parents in a "no-win" situation. Families in which this reaction occurred advise parents to find a loving alternative person to care for the baby until the parents are able to work through their grief.

Of course, each parent may react differently toward the surviving twin. The father said that he accepted the new baby and could not understand his wife's feelings about the baby who had died. Months later, the father fell apart, and it took professional help to relate his feelings of "going crazy" with the fact that he had shut out his grief.

Loss in Infancy

When a twin is lost later in infancy, the effect on the parents may be of a different nature because they have become acquainted with this little person; they may have grown to appreciate the specialness of having twins. If the death occurs after a long illness, some preparation for grief has occurred.

If a child dies suddenly, such as in the case of Sudden Infant Death Syndrome, parents often blame themselves or are blamed by others.

The Surviving Twin

The surviving twin is in the midst of this family turmoil. It is very difficult to judge the degree of any attachment there might have been if one twin dies very shortly after birth. Some parents believe that there was a conscious recognition of a co-twin by the surviving twin, and there is some evidence that adults who lost a twin at birth have some residual feelings of loss. Certainly the attitudes and emotions of the parents during the babies' early days may have some effect on how they treat the surviving twin, and this in itself may have a lasting effect.

Questions that occur frequently among parents who have lost a twin in this early period include how much detail and at what time should the other child be told that she had a twin? Most parents feel that the explanation should proceed at the appropriate age level of the surviving twin as she matures. However, there is a fine line between acknowledging the twinship and making a "shrine" out of the dead twin that will become a perpetual shadow throughout life. In that regard, one mother made the valid suggestion that a day other than the birthday should be picked as a day of memory. It would not be fair to the birthday child for that day to be clouded with sadness, she believed.

During infancy there is little sense of separateness between twins, and some parents report a period of restlessness and sleep disturbances in the surviving twin. In later infancy and toddlerhood, the twin may actively search for his missing co-twin, and may react strongly when he sees his own reflection in a mirror if the twins were identical. As with the parents, the twin needs an outlet for his feelings in order to heal. The surviving twin should be kept aware, in a matter-of-fact way, that he had a twin and be helped to express his feelings about the subject as he matures.

Childhood and Teen Years

The effect on the parents and the co-twin when a twin dies during later childhood or the teen years is very dependent on the parent-twin relationship, the twin-to-twin relationship, how the parents react to the loss, and the age of the twins.

The grieving process is similar to that when a twin dies at birth or during infancy. Parents mourn the loss of the child, the loss of a unique type of parenthood, and their dreams for their children within the twin concept.

The death of a twin is a tragedy for everyone involved, a loss that most often requires a long and complicated healing time for both the parents and the surviving twin.

Because of the burden of grief and the decisions that have to be made at the time of death, parents may fail to assist the surviving twin with his emotions. The child, therefore, could suffer two losses—his twin and, temporarily, the support of his parents.

Each parent has developed an individual relationship with each child, and each parent will react to the loss in a different way. This may lead to marital strain as the mother and the father do not meet each other's expectations for grief or support, and this family strain will undoubtedly affect the surviving twin.

If either, or both, parents have made "twin parenthood" an essential part of their own self-image and cannot resolve that part of their loss, the surviving twin may see himself as having little worth as a single child. The parents who feel that grieving is a silent, personal affair and never talk about the lost twin, or remove all evidence of his existence, may be creating a "ghost."

In this case, the surviving twin cannot express his own grief, guilt, or anger in his void. He may even see this as a silent accusation of blame for his twin's death. Unless he can get help to resolve his feelings, he may carry this "ghost" well into adulthood.

Parents often fear that they also will lose their surviving child. This is particularly acute if the twins were young. The parents may become over-protective and give the surviving twin the message that life is full of danger. The twin may become very timid and afraid of any physical or emotional separation from his parents. This growing interdependence may interfere with the formation of other relationships, especially with the opposite sex. On the other hand, some children may react to this parental "smothering" by openly defying danger and inviting parental punishment.

In some instances, parents may seek to "replace" the lost twin by transferring all of their expectations for the lost child on to his twin. They invest all of their energies into one child who now feels he has to live two lives; his own and his twin's. Even without a parental expectation for this double life, many parents do report that the surviving twin does take on some personality traits of his co-twin, or tries to fill the empty place by engaging in activities in which his twin excelled.

The other factor that would affect the parental grief reaction and the actions of the co-twin is the circumstances of the death. If the death was sudden, whether witnessed by the twin or not, he may identify with the pain, relive the event in his nightmares, and possibly feel guilt that he survived or was not able to prevent the accident.

Identifying reactions

The reactions of the surviving twin will also depend on his age and the depth of the twin relationship.

Children under 5 years of age usually have very little understanding of death and its finality. Therefore the surviving twin may insist upon having his brother's place set at the table or the Teddy bear tucked into the other bed, and may carry on conversations with his dead twin and include him in his drawings of the family, often even fantasizing about his own death as a way of finding his lost brother.

Parents must be very careful about how they discuss death. If it is glorified, or if the child is told that when he dies he will join his twin, they may be laying the ground for an attempted suicide. One mother noted that for a few months after his twin died, her son seemed to do everything he could to put himself in danger. When she drew his attention to what the consequences might be if he was not more careful, he would reply that it didn't matter because if he died, he'd be with his brother and have someone to play with again.

Speaking of death as "going to sleep" might start a series of night terrors, or the refusal of the child to sleep alone. If parents do not feel they can explain death effectively, they should seek help from parents' support groups, or books like *On Death and Children* by Elizabeth Kubler Ross (MacMillan, 1983) or *But Won't Granny Need Her Socks?: Children's Concerns with Death* by Nancy Reeves (Kendall Hunt, 1983).

A young child may also display some personality changes, such as becoming disruptive or withdrawn, or as mentioned previously, taking on the personality of his twin.

As the child matures, he will understand death better, and be better able to conceptualize time and his own mortality. The older the child is, the more he will be expected to handle his own grief. However even children in their teens will need extra support and a means of communicating their feelings. They may be experiencing tremendous guilt over past events, and the fact that they now have a greater share of their parent's attention and any material goods.

The outgoing, confident teenager may become sullen and withdrawn, and try to lose herself in drugs or alcohol. The quiet, studious twin may become a rowdy daredevil and lose interest in school. Both reactions are a plea for reassurance that the twin's death was not their fault, and that they are still of worth in this new role as a twin without a co-twin.

The twin who has a solid sense of his separate self will feel the loss as profoundly as one who does not, but the more mature twin may be able to work through the grieving process with less lasting pain than the twin with little or no separate identity.

When the twins are very dependent on each other, have a "leader" and "follower" relationship, or see their own image only as it is reflected in their twin, the death may mean a total loss of self-worth and any ability to function as an individual. If the twinship was the moving force in their lives, the surviving twin will have to seek a new meaning in life. He may become fixed in time, not wanting to grow up since this reinforces the loss as maturity forces him into situations that his twin cannot share. There may be a total denial reaction. By refusing to talk about his twin and not acknowledging the death, he can fantasize that his twin is still there. The teen or adult may feel betrayed, left alone to make life decisions and fill the void for his parents.

If the twins were at a stage in the relationship where being a twin was less than desirable or intense rivalry existed, this situation may be seen as a death wish. The surviving twin may seek to punish himself by getting into dangerous situations, creating conflict with his parents or his spouse, or by developing psychosomatic illnesses. Many twins, regardless of their relationship, express a need to seek out others who have lost a twin to share feelings that their parents or non-twin peers cannot fully comprehend.

The death of a twin is a tragedy for everyone involved, a loss that most often requires a long and complicated healing time for the surviving family members.

HELP FOR THE SURVIVING TWIN

Parents who have shared their personal experiences after the loss of a twin during childhood or the teen years offer the following advice:

- The child should be told exactly what happened in terms appropriate for his age and more details added as questions occur in later years.
- An effort should be made to explain death to the child and if the parents cannot do this, have someone else close to he child do so.
- The child should be allowed to attend the funeral or memorial service because this gives him a continuous series of events; the illness or accident, the death, the funeral, and then a gradual return to normal routine. If a child is denied this opportunity to be a part of the family, he may wonder later why he was not included.
- Care should be taken to acknowledge whatever methods of grieving the child displays, even if this is upsetting for his parents. The child should be allowed to express negative and positive feelings without judgment.
- Parents should watch for any prolonged unusual behavior immediately after the death or months later. If counseling is sought, the fact that this child was a twin should be mentioned to the counselor.
- Parents should read books about the grieving process; by understanding their own feelings, they can offer comfort to the surviving twin.
- Parents should join with other persons who have lost a child, and encourage the surviving twin to meet with other children who have lost a sibling. This mutual peer support may be very effective in resolving conflicts before they become lifelong burdens.
- The family should talk about the dead twin and share memories with the survivor, acknowledging the special relationship that they had.
- Recognize that there may be special days of sadness for many years to come. Children have anniversaries of events in their lives, too.

❤

Meeting the Special Needs of Bereaved Twins: Mourning My Best Friend

by Nancy L. Segal

The special circumstances surrounding the loss of a twin have been overlooked by many bereavement researchers. It has been suggested by some investigators and therapists that sibling loss does not lead to the same high level of grief that typically follows the loss of a child or spouse.

There are, however, several published studies which demonstrate that the loss of a twin appears to be *the most devastating type of loss for the surviving twin partner*. A brief review of this literature is presented below, followed by an update of findings and activities associated with the California State University Twin Loss Study (formerly the Minnesota Twin Loss Study).

Research Findings

The first published study concerned with the loss of a twin appeared in 1954. Professor Ernest Mowrer at Northwestern University in Chicago had high school-age twins indicate which family member would be most missed in the event of death. Mothers were listed most often, followed by twin partners and fathers, in that order. However, identical twins selected their co-twins more frequently than fraternal twins, and selected their co-twins more frequently than their mothers. This finding is not surprising in view of research indicating generally closer social relationships between identical twins, relative to fraternal twins.

In 1988, Joan Woodward, a clinical psychologist at the West Midlands Institute of Psychotherapy, Uffculme Clinic, in Birmingham, England, administered a survey to a large number of British twins. It was found that surviving identical and same-sex twins experienced twin loss more severely than twins from opposite-sex pairs.

The next study of twin loss was launched at the University of Minnesota in 1983. The decision to conduct this investigation was prompted by requests from twins who had lost twin brothers and sisters for assistance in understanding and coping with their extreme grief. In response, a comprehensive Twin Loss Survey was developed and administered to bereaved twins by Professor Thomas J. Bouchard, Jr., and myself at the University of Minnesota. This survey has been administered to twins who experienced the loss of their co-twins at age 15 years or older.

The study was transferred to the Twin Studies Center at California State University, Fullerton, in 1991. Preliminary findings from the study were published in **TWINS**® Magazine in 1985 and again in 1989. It was found that grief intensity was generally higher among surviving identical twins than fraternal twins. Furthermore, grief intensity ratings were generally higher for the deceased twin than for deceased non-twin relatives (such as parents and grandparents).

California Twin Loss Study Update

The first major paper from the Twin Loss Study, based on information provided by 70 twins, was published in 1993. The key findings were consistent with those presented in the preliminary reports published in **TWINS**® Magazine. It was found that identical twins generally recalled higher levels of grief one to two months following the loss than fraternal twins. In addition, the level of grief following the loss of a twin was higher, on average, than the level of grief associated with the loss of a parent, grandparent, aunt, uncle or cousin. At that time, very few twins had experienced the death of a child or non-twin sibling, so we were unable to include these comparisons in the paper.

Over 300 twins have now participated in the ongoing study. The participants include twice as many identical twins as fraternal twins, and many more females than males. David T. Lykken, Ph.D., at the University of Minnesota, has described a "rule of two-thirds"-that is, identical twins and females in volunteer twin studies typically comprise two-thirds of the sample. It may be that identical twins experience a greater need to seek assistance following the loss of the twin, and that females are more willing to express their feelings in a research setting.

The Twin Loss Survey includes three major components: a Grief Intensity Scale; a Grief Experience Inventory (developed by Catherine Sanders, Ph.D., and colleagues); and a Coping Scale (developed by Christine Littlefield, Ph.D.). The availability of a large number of participants enables many types of important analyses, many of which are in progress. A major task will be to compare grief intensity for the co-twin and for many types of relatives, including non-twin siblings.

A second goal is to compare scores of identical and fraternal twins on the various scales of the Grief Experience Inventory (Despair scale, Anger/Hostility scale, Somatization scale). A third goal is to identify factors that influence coping. Former Fullerton graduate student Shelley A. Blozis, M.A., found that twins who belonged to a Twin Loss Support Group (see below) reported higher levels of coping at the time they responded to the questionnaire than did non-members.

At present, efforts are also underway to identify bereaved twins who do not specifically seek research participation or clinical assistance.

Twin Study of Suicide

Most studies of twins, family members and adoptive relatives have indicated a genetic influence on suicide, though the specific mechanisms underlying suicidal behaviors are unclear.

In 1986, Dr. Alex Roy, a psychiatrist at the New Jersey College of Medicine and Dentistry, published a letter in the *American Journal of Psychiatry* requesting that colleagues identify cases of suicide involving twins. I responded to this letter, given that several such cases had been included in the twin loss study. Dr. Roy and I have been collaborating on a number of projects since that time.

The first paper from this ongoing study, published in 1991, presented psychiatric history information for 11 twin pairs (nine identical and two fraternal). Twins in two identical pairs had both committed suicide, and twins in 10 pairs had relatives who had been treated for psychiatric disorders.

These data were combined with data from three previous twin studies and with 45 twin suicide survivors from the National Academy of Sciences-National Research Council Twin Registry, yielding 62 identical twin pairs and 114 fraternal twin pairs. Both twins had committed suicide in 11.3 percent of the identical pairs, while among the fraternal pairs, 1.8 percent had done so.

Greater similarity among identical than fraternal twins suggests a genetic influence on suicidal behavior. It is important to note, however, that twins are not more likely to display suicidal behavior than non-twins.

Furthermore, while the twin partner of an identical twin who commits suicide may be at a somewhat higher risk for suicidal behavior than the twin partner of a fraternal twin or non-twin sibling, the event of suicide in both pair members was far from 100 percent. Additional twin data are being collected in collaboration with Dr. Marco Sarchiapone and fellow researchers at the Catholic University in Rome. Similarity for suicidal attempts in identical and fraternal twins is currently being compared.

The few available studies of twin loss have included adult twins. Loss does, unfortunately, also occur among young twin children and adolescents. The behavioral consequences of this particular form of loss are currently being examined at Fullerton, California.

The Legal Domain

In recent years, a number of attorneys have requested my assistance as an expert witness in legal cases involving the wrongful death, injury or custody of twins. The research on twin loss described above, as well as research on twin relationships, has proven invaluable in this regard. The first summary of courtroom cases for the general public was requested by **TWINS**® Magazine, and appeared in the September 1993 issue. The application of twin research findings in the legal domain underlines the special needs of twins, and the importance of disseminating information about twins to professionals from different disciplines.

"Lifetime Magazine," an ABC News Cable TV Production, aired a segment on April 24, 1994, concerning the use of twin research findings in cases involving the wrongful death of a twin. Twins, family members and attorneys were interviewed with respect to the special aspects of twin loss and the contributions of research findings in settling the cases. A recurrent theme was that the unique nature of the twin relationship, and the loss of that relationship, are difficult to comprehend if one is not a twin or a parent of twins.

Twin Loss Support

The Twinless Twins Support Group International was established by Dr. Raymond Brandt in Fort Wayne, Indiana. Dr. Brandt, who lost his identical twin over 50 years ago, recognized the need for surviving twins to meet and to share their thoughts and feelings with one another. An informative newsletter is periodically distributed. Some of the members have since become active at the state and local levels as well. Every Labor Day weekend, the Twinless Twins Support Group meets as part of the International Twins Association (ITA).

Please contact Dr. Brandt at 11220 St. Joe Road, Fort Wayne, IN 46835, (210) 627-5414, for additional information about the support group. Details about the ITA's meetings can be obtained from Lynn Long and Lori Stewart in Minneapolis, Minnesota, 612-571-3022.

Getting In Touch

The loss of a twin is a truly devastating event for twins and their families. Growing appreciation for the unique aspects of twinship have also helped some professionals to direct attention to m special needs of bereaved twins. A number of resources (such as support groups and reading materials) are currently available to twins, although a great deal of work remains to be done. Many twins and families may be unaware that others are confronting similar tragedies, and would welcome the support that only such families can share. Many bereavement counselors and specialists in related areas need to be acquainted with the literature on twins and twin loss.

It is also important to emphasize that while current research suggests that bereaved identical twins express greater grief intensity than fraternal twins, this is an average effect. Some fraternal twins may experience twin loss just as intensely as identical twins. Similarly, some bereaved identical twins may grieve less intensely than some bereaved fraternal twins.

Those who are interested in participating in studies of twin loss, or who know individuals who might be interested, are invited to contact Dr. Nancy L. Segal, California State University, Psychology Department, Fullerton, CA 92634, 714-773-2568.

INCREASING UNDERSTANDING ABOUT TWIN LOSS

- There are several published studies which demonstrate that the loss of a twin appears to be the most devastating type of loss for the surviving twin partner.
- The first published study concerned with the loss of a twin appeared in 1954, and asked high school-age twins to indicate which family member would be most missed in the event of death. Mothers were listed most often, followed by twin partners and fathers, in that order.
- In that same 1954 study, identical twins selected their co-twins more frequently than fraternal twins, and selected their co-twins more frequently than their mothers.
- A 1988 British study found that surviving identical and same-sex twins experienced twin loss more severely than twins from opposite-sex pairs.
- The first major paper from the California Twin Loss Study, based on information provided by 70 twins, was published in 1993.
- Identical twins generally recalled higher levels of grief one to two months following the loss of a co-twin than fraternal twins.
- The level of grief following the loss of a twin was higher, on average, than the level of grief associated with the loss of a parent, grandparent, aunt, uncle or cousin.
- The Twin Loss Survey used by the California Twin Loss Study includes three major components: a Grief Intensity Scale; a Grief Experience Inventory; and a Coping Scale.
- The greater similarity among identical than fraternal twins suggests a genetic influence on suicidal behavior; however, twins are not more likely to display suicidal behavior than non-twins.

TEACHING CHILDREN ABOUT DEATH SIMPLE, HONEST ANSWERS DISPEL TERRORS

A mother and her child, taking a walk, see a dead bird lying on the grass. "Is the bird dead?" the child asks.

The mother might answer, "Yes, he is, the poor little thing. Isn't that sad?" With that answer, she attaches a mournful tone to death. She could also say, "Yes, the little bird dies; now he doesn't hurt anymore."

Charlotte Sheehan, R.N., the parent-liaison coordinator for the Christinana Hospital in Newark, Delaware, uses this story of the dead bird when she speaks to parents about how to help their children deal with death.

"A child might ask about death in a neutral way, out of curiosity," noted Sheehan. "The response that the child receives could have a direct influence on the way the child relates to death as he develops."

Sheehan's work revolves around a topic from which many parents would prefer to shield their children. Adults sometimes shy away from the subject because they feel uncomfortable about it themselves. On the other hand, they may offer an explanation that is more than what the child is seeking.

Sheehan cites another story, one in which a little boy asks, "Mommy, where did I come from?" The mother launches into a lengthy description of sex and birth, when all the boy really wanted to know was the name of the city where he was born.

"It's important to be open, honest and to tell the truth," Sheehan noted. "Listen to the child, answer the question as it is asked and don't give more information than is asked for."

On the other hand, children are only confused by being given no answer to questions, vague responses or simple phrases that shelter them from knowing the true meaning of death. Saying, "God took him"; "He went on a trip"; "He's gone to sleep"; or "He passed away" can be confusing information for a child and can lead to his having unresolved feelings about death in adulthood.

"A child's concept of death is different from that of an adult," explained Sheehan. "So much depends upon each child's stage of development."

Children under the age of 3 can sense when family routines change because of a death, but they don't know why.

From 3 to 6 years of age, a child is beginning to understand death but also may think that it is reversible and that the dead person will return.

In the 6- to 9-year-old group, many children understand that death is final, but some still believe that the dead person will come back. However, children from 9 to 12 years of age are beginning to understand the finality of death.

An adolescent realizes that death is final, irreversible and universal. But he may also have a defiant attitude about it, saying, "I dare it to happen to me!" Adolescents' risk-taking behavior may be related to their natural developmental stage of defiance to injury or death.

Participation in Rituals

Sheehan suggests that children be allowed to participate in the death rituals, such as funerals, burials and viewings, though this suggestion is usually met with surprise and shock.

"Don't force a child to participate in death rituals," she cautioned, "but do permit a child to participate if he wishes to do so. Before attending, prepare the child for what will occur. Explain that people will be crying and why. Also let the child know that it is all right for him to cry. Afterward, discuss the experience with the child and answer any questions that he has."

HOW MOTHERS FEEL ABOUT MULTIFETAL LOSS

"It's a girl!"

"It's another girl!...Oops, no Baby B is a boy!"

"It's another boy! And one more boy."

"You have four healthy babies!"

Hearing those wonderful words on November 11, 1983, marked the most joyful moment of my life to date. For many years, I had looked forward to giving birth to a child, but the seven-month pregnancy I just endured seemed too short to prepare me for the birth of not one, but four, children simultaneously!

Yes, I had beaten the odds and delivered four healthy infants. Little did I know that eight days later, Baby C (Ryan Thomas) would unexpectedly die, causing an intensity of pain and grief I had not previously known. All of my prior training had not prepared me for this experience.

As a nurse in both adult and neonatal intensive care, and as a grief counselor, I was well-trained in the grieving process and coping strategies involved with death. I found that being able to give technical names to my feelings was of little comfort to me personally at the time of the loss of our son. I believed that no one could possibly know how I was feeling, except perhaps another parent in similar multiple-birth circumstances.

As the new mother of three surviving quadruplets, I became acutely aware of a parent's needs for special support and understanding when faced with multifetal death. The ambiguities and conflicts I was experiencing were not identified in any text. I began a study at this time in which I interviewed more than 100 mothers who had experienced a loss related to multifetal births. Additional information was obtained through interviews with high-risk obstetricians.

In contrast to single pregnancies, fetal death in multiple pregnancies presents two unique situations. The first occurs when all of the children die, either during the pregnancy itself or as neonates. The second occurs when some of the children die and some survive. Both events entail special concerns and needs.

Complete Loss

Death of all fetuses or newborns in higher-order multiple births is not at all uncommon. Yet special consideration is usually lacking to the mother who may just have lost four or five children, either all at once through a spontaneous miscarriage, or one at a time during their first weeks of life. Unlike their singleton counterparts, this multifetal mother may experience an intense cycle of grief and sorrow for one or for many children.

Whereas the grieving cycle for a singleton miscarriage lasts approximately one year (as described with other death experiences), the cycle after a multiple death is often significantly prolonged, depending on individual circumstances. It can take three to five years to completely incorporate the loss into the parents' lives, my survey showed. The specific stages of grief appear to be similar (anger, denial, guilt and depression) for either case, but each stage may be intensified according to the length of gestation and subsequent bonding which had occurred between the multifetal mother and each of her babies.

An additional factor in complete losses is the issue of the mother's self-esteem It's often low, as a result of her being unable to conceive naturally (60 percent of 450 women surveyed by The Triplet Connection had used some type of fertility drug or procedure to achieve pregnancy). The mother's ego can take a roller-coaster ride—down (from infertility), up (from successful pregnancy) and down again (from the complete loss).

Such mothers often develop either an obsessive desire to conceive again as soon as possible or an unreasonable fear of future pregnancy. These coping mechanisms may help ease the pain but cannot undo what has been done, nor replace the prior loss. The demise must be acknowledged and addressed, as it must with any other type of death.

Partial Loss

The second and more complex experience is that in which some (or one) of the newborns survive and some (or one) do not. The situation of partial loss and partial gain is unique to multifetal mothers, and it creates special problems.

The simultaneous birth and death of children causes extreme conflict. Should I be happy or sad? What right do I have to grieve when I have just received one, two, or three healthy children?

Well-intended comments like, "Two out of three aren't bad" or "You are lucky to have one healthy baby" only tend to reinforce this ambiguity. The mother may try to minimize her loss, or even worse, may feel pressured to act in a manner incompatible with her true feelings. She may fail to even acknowledge her loss, a necessary step before acceptance of the deaths can occur.

Complicating partial losses is the decreased opportunity for grieving due to the overwhelming responsibility to care for the surviving infant(s). A mother with one, two, three or more newborns may feel the need to grieve, but never find the time or peace needed to accomplish the task properly—her "survivor(s)" comes first. As a result, her own needs for grieving are postponed.

These circumstances tend to be reinforced initially by both the medical community and family, who urge the mother to bond with and manage her other child(ren). If her grief is delayed or denied, it may be experienced more intensely or in a more prolonged manner at some later date. Some mothers with partial losses reported their strongest feelings of grief occurring more than three years after the event, when they finally had the opportunity to relax and review their special circumstances.

Nearly all mothers with partial losses reported ambivalent feelings on how to label their surviving children, asking, "Should I call my two surviving triplets 'twins'?" My survey revealed that most parents never reach the point where they hear their multiples labeled by the number of survivors without some degree of discomfort.

A final factor in partial losses is the constant reminders of their missing child or children. Birthdays, holidays, hearing the lost child's name or buying objects for three instead of four serve as regular reminders of their losses.

In the circumstance of a lost identical twin, the parents will always have a "mirror image" to stir their memories. Someone saying, "Oh, what beautiful triplets you have!" may intend to be expressing a positive outlook to new parents, but can also be a painful reminder of their missing loved one.

Helping Multifetal-Loss Mothers

Nearly all the mothers who responded to my survey reported that they were unable to initially understand and discuss their feelings with anyone, for fear of being misunderstood.

Parents of twins' support group members and leaders, if properly instructed, can serve as great supports to multifetal-loss mothers. Through listening and counseling, they can be instrumental in allowing such mothers to recognize and accept their losses. Their previous involvement with multiple births enables them to be more sensitive than the general population. The following are specific suggestions to facilitate this process. Support group leaders need to:

1) encourage the parents to hold and bond with the child to the total exclusion, during those moments, of the surviving babies, whether a fetus is stillborn or dies in the neonatal period. My husband and I cherish the few minutes we had to hold and love our just-deceased son—we both feel it was vital to our grieving. Parents will have ample time to bond with their survivors, but will never have another chance with their newly-lost child or children.

2) allow the mother to acknowledge her loss. Take the time necessary to listen to her, and urge her to grieve all of her losses. If possible, coordinate quiet and uninterrupted time away from her other children to begin the grieving process.

3) label the children accurately, and help others to do so also. For example, by 1 year of age, the surviving triplets may become "twins"; but in the immediate delivery and death period, they are still triplets.

4) help others to avoid making judgmental statements like, "Two out of three aren't bad." At that moment, to the grieving mother, two out of three is bad.

5) educate the mother about the living reminders of her loss which can serve as triggers of recurring grief. Support her in these difficult times.

6) reinforce the mother's self-esteem, particularly in areas where fertility has been an issue.

7) assist the mother in locating an appropriate grief-support network. Communication with other mothers who have undergone the same experiences can be invaluable.

by Mary Kay Sainsbury, R.N., M.A.

"AM I STILL A TWIN?"

Thanksgiving Day 1985. That day will live forever in my memory as the worst day of my life. On that day my co-twin, Cindy, died at 18 years of age. Now three years and seven months later, I'm ready to share my story.

When Cindy was alive, we were often asked, "What does it feel like to be a twin?" We would always answer by saying something cute (or obnoxious, depending on our moods) to appease the questioner. We really could not answer that question, though, because we had never experienced anything except being twins. We were not singletons, had never been singletons and, therefore, could not compare being twins to not being twins. That is, until Cindy died.

In response to those who wonder what it's like to be a twin, I can now answer: It's like always having the same best friend. Now, I often wonder, am I still a twin, even though I no longer have a co-twin?

As we grew up, Cindy and I were each other's constant companion. In the early years of our education, we were placed in the same classes, but when teachers discovered that they couldn't keep us from helping each other with our schoolwork, we were separated. This was traumatic, but we survived the separation by knowing that at least we still had each other to play with after school.

In many ways, Cindy and I complemented each other. One of our mother's favorite baby stories related that when she served us chicken soup, Cindy would drink the broth, and I would eat the noodles.

Another way in which we were diametrically opposed as children was that I was an "indoor child," and Cindy was an "outdoor child." I spent my hours inside reading; Cindy was usually outside playing and would come inside only when Mom insisted that it was too dark to stay outdoors.

Cindy and I shared a room, and we would end up each day talking about the day's events. Cindy always wanted me to read a story to her; since the lamp was on her side of the room, it would not be turned off until she had heard a story, whether I was willing or not.

When we turned 16 years old, our lives were turned upside-down. In spring of our sophomore year, Cindy entered the hospital for orthoscopic knee surgery, but that surgery was never performed. During pre-operative blood testing, Cindy's doctors discovered that she had Systemic Lupus Erythmatosus, a chronic disease affecting the body's immune system.

After her diagnosis, Cindy's life changed dramatically. Her doctors strongly discouraged her from being exposed to direct sunlight, which cut out her outdoor daytime activities. Another big change occurred in her physical appearance, due to the heavy dosages of cortisone and other medications necessary to control the disease. For instance, one side-effect she found hard to cope with was excessive hair growth on her back and face.

In addition, her weight fluctuated from one extreme to the other. I can remember one week in particular: On Monday, Cindy weighted 95 pounds; she had a flare-up, and her dosage of cortisone was increased. By Saturday, she weighed 165 pounds.

Our mother made a strong effort to make sure that Cindy received the best medical attention possible—she was under the care of a team of specialists at the Texas Medical Center in Houston, Texas. Cindy's doctors gave her "at least another 20 years" to live. Tragically, they were mistaken—she died two years later.

I don't think Cindy's death affected me too much when it actually happened because she had been in a coma for a week, and I could see that she would be better off dead. I don't mean to sound insensitive; on the contrary, I knew that her body had literally fallen to pieces and that if she ever regained consciousness, she would experience an extraordinary amount of pain.

I wanted her suffering to end. It affected me very deeply to see her during the last week she was alive—she had tubes and wires coming in and out of every orifice, her head was shaved in some places to allow for the monitoring of her brain waves, and her eyes were so swollen they had to be taped shut.

At the risk of sounding morbid, I am able to recognize the good that came of Cindy's 's death. I am now much closer to my older sister, Rebecca. She is six years older than me, and we had never enjoyed a close relationship. Now, I know that there is nothing that she wouldn't do for me or I for her. Another positive result of Cindy's death is that I was fortunate to have a good friend to stand by me, something for which I will be forever grateful. Knowing that I had somebody to help me stand up if I needed it was a big comfort. Since Cindy's death, that friendship has helped me through many more difficult times.

I do not mean to say that the experience of losing Cindy has been easy for me. I think of her every day and wonder what she would be doing if she were still alive today. I have told myself again and again that she is dead, that death is not a temporary situation, and that she is never coming back. But it's one thing to say it and quite another to live it.

When someone close to you dies, it's difficult to ignore your own mortality. By witnessing Cindy's death, I feel comfortable knowing that I, too, will someday die. But perhaps the most important lesson I have learned from Cindy's death is to live each day as if it were the last. Leave nothing unsaid and nothing undone, for one never knows what tomorrow holds.

by Sandy R. Swedran

THE TWINLESS-TWIN SUPPORT GROUP

Every Labor Day weekend for more than 50 years, approximately 200 to 400 sets of twins from all over the United States and Europe have united in friendship to share with each other their extraordinary twin bond at The International Twins Association's (ITA) annual convention.

However, with the passage of time, there has also been the passing of loved ones. For those whose co-twins have passed away, their loss was paramount. Only in the aftermath of their devastation from their co-twins' deaths could they begin the struggle of finding ways to keep their twinships alive.

One arena in which their twinships continue to live is among their twin friends at the ITA. Here twins reach out to one another, offering an understanding of a life experience that transcends all else. Thus, in 1985, Raymond Brandt, Ph.D., a surviving identical twin from Indiana, in collaboration with New York twin consultants Jane Greer, Ph.D., and Marc Snowman, ACSW, ushered in new life and hope for those who have suffered the loss of their co-twins by forming a twinless-twin support group.

For some members of this group, their profound grief and bereavement is for their co-twins who have perished due to tragic circumstances. For others, their mourning is for their lost co-twins who, although actually alive, are experienced as "gone" due to the estrangement that has occurred between them.

In the exchange of their experiences, the group members are able to share their pain and offer words of comfort and support for coping. Those who have more years of coping behind them are able to convey the knowledge that "it gets better with time."

A fundamental concern for all is the identity as a twin. If their twin sibling is no longer alive, does this mean that they are no longer a twin? Without question, the unanimous agreement of the group was that they live on as a twin in identity.

The challenge for every twin is in the transition each must undergo to find comfortable ways to express his twinship status. Thus, in recognition of this task, all members of the group have related appreciation for the opportunity to begin this transformation within the twinless-twin group.

According to Nancy L. Segal, Ph.D., who was present at the twinless-twin meeting in 1987, and has done extensive research in twin loss, "A meeting of this kind uniquely meets the needs of twin survivors."

Additionally, recognizing the value gained from sharing experiences, the group has expanded its role. Present members serve as mentors for those twins who may be experiencing the imminent death of their co-twins due to illness or other life experiences.

Jane Greer, Ph.D.

CHAPTER 5

Twin Studies

Focus on Language Development

by Nancy L. Segal, Ph.D.

The observation that young twins display relatively less mature speech patterns than singletons has been the focus of lively debate. Dr. Hugh Lytton, Professor of Educational Psychology, at the University of Calgary, in Alberta, Canada, has conducted a comprehensive study of twin children, singletons, and their families in an attempt to resolve this issue. This investigation has produced in an-depth characterization of language development in young twins and singletons and an insightful description of parent-child interactions which may be associated with twin-singleton and identical-fraternal twin differences in verbal behavior.

Background

Studies of parent-child interaction in twin families, and twins' language and social development began at the University of Calgary in 1971. "Our goal was to obtain detailed information about the interactions of parents and children as they occurred in their own homes to try and find out how children developed into social beings and how parents and children affected one another," said Lytton.

The use of identical and fraternal twins additionally permitted the investigation to examine the possibility that genetic factors influenced the children's performance. Greater resemblance within identical twinships relative to fraternal twinships suggests that heredity may affect the behavior in question. This is because identical twins share *all* of their genes in common, while fraternal twins share only 50 percent in common, on the average, by descent.

These are important aims because, previously, no one had comparatively examined social-interactional features in families with twins and families without twins to relate those features to observed differences in children's language skills.

Participants in the first phase of the study were 2 1/2 years old. A follow-up study was initiated in 1978 to assess the consistency and stability of child and parent-child behaviors when the children were 8 to 10 years old. The twin sample, procedures, findings and implications from these analyses are presented below.

The Study Sample

The study included a total of 136 children (17 identical twin pairs, 29 fraternal twin pairs, and 44 singletons). The average age of the original sample was 32.4 months, with a range of 25 to 35 months. Twins were identified through birth registers maintained by hospitals in the Calgary, Alberta area. The twin sample represented almost the entire population of male twins born in Calgary during two consecutive years!

The non-twin children were recruited by child health clinics. These families were selected only if they met the criteria of having both parents available for study and a child born within three years of the "target" singleton child who was matched in age to the twins. This procedure was done to ensure "two-nests" in the social situation of the non-twin children, thereby creating an appropriate comparison group.

Of the 46 families, 43 were recontacted for the follow-up phase: 38 were available for participation. A new sample of singleton children, selected from the same classrooms as the twins, participated in the follow-up study. One child was chosen for each of the 38 twin pairs. In light of known sex differences in language skills, the inclusion of both males and females would have meant conducting separate analyses and, therefore, doubling the size of the sample. For that reason, only males were chosen as participants in this study.

Test and Procedures

Methods used in this study included the continuous recording of children's social and verbal behaviors (individual behaviors, interactions between twins and between siblings, and parent-child interactions); impressionistic behavioral ratings of family members by observers; observations of twins and singletons during experimental playroom sessions; administration of a standard vocabulary test; and parental interviews and questionnaires.

Families were observed in their homes on two afternoons in successive weeks at approximately three hours before the children's bedtime. Both twins (or the single child) and at least one parent were required to remain in the observation area.

The children's behaviors being observed included their expressions of displeasure, approaches to parent, and percentage of time engaging in active behavior; the parent's behavior focused on their use of warmth and reasoning, consistency of rule enforcement and displays of affection.

An observer positioned a microphone close to his mouth and softly "translated" the ongoing activities into a special code. A second observer was present on the second day to interview and rate the mother. Mothers also maintained a 24-hour diary in which they entered hour-by-hour events that affected the child, as well as their own reactions to these events. Fathers (if available) completed questionnaires that, together with their observed social and verbal behaviors, enabled the impressionistic ratings described above.

Compliance, attachment, and independence, as shown by twins and singletons, were recorded in the playroom setting. (Twins were studied separately and mothers were present in all cases.) This was accomplished by presenting various tasks to the children and observing, for example, the extent to which assistance was solicited from the parent.

The Peabody Picture Vocabulary Test (PPVT) was also administered to twins and singletons. Dr. Jerome Sattler, Professor of Psychology at San Diego State University, in San Diego, California, describes this test as estimating a person's verbal intelligence, in a non-verbal way, by measuring his hearing vocabulary or "receptive knowledge" of vocabulary.

The follow-up phases of the investigation included both home and school visits. Verbal and non-verbal behaviors at 9 years old were assessed by evaluations based on interviews with mother and fathers, teachers' ratings, and tests. These were compared with previous results at 2 1/2 years old.

Findings at 2 Years Old

Outcomes from the University of Calgary twin study are available in a volume entitled, *Parent-Child Interaction: The Socialization Process Observed In Twin And Singleton Families*, by Hugh Lytton, Ph.D., New York, Plenum Press, 1980. Given the tremendous scope and depth of this investigation, a comprehensive treatment of its many findings is not possible here. Selected results and their implications are, therefore, summarized below.

1) Twins demonstrated less verbal proficiency than non-twins, as indicated by a relatively reduced amount of speech (both rate per minute and percentage of total actions). Their speech was also rated as relatively less mature.

2) Identical twins scored below fraternal twins in vocabulary skills, rate of speech, and rate of speech by mother and father to child. The educational level of the mother was higher among fraternal twins, and was associated with identical-fraternal twin differences in language behavior.

3) Overall verbal exchanges, displays of affection, verbal commands or suggestions, statements of approval, and rule enforcement were offered less frequently by parents of twins than by parents of single children.

4) Relationships between birth history factors (pregnancy complications, for example) and language development in the identical and fraternal twin groups were not found. The only exception to this is that the fraternal twins had higher Apgar scores. Apgar scores reflect the infant's physical status at 1 minute and 5 minutes after birth; these evaluations are sometimes also made at later intervals. These scores, which range from 1 to 10, are based on heart rate, muscle tone, respiratory effort, response to stimulation, and skin color. A higher score is associated with a more favorable condition. Birth history data were, unfortunately, not available for the non-twin participants.

5) Twins displayed a higher rate and percentage of attachment behaviors (for example, seeking attention and physical closeness) than did singletons. Parents of twins and singletons did not, however, differ in their encouragement of independent behaviors. Dr. Lytton and his co-workers have suggested that the reduced displays of affection shown by parents of twins may lead to less mature behaviors on the part of their children.

The Findings (Follow-up Study: At 9 Years Old)

1) Mothers showed greater stability in behavior than their children across the two times of measurement. They were especially consistent in displays of warmth, use of praise, rule enforcement, degree of restrictiveness, and amount of play with child. Children maintained similar levels of verbal competence from 2 to 9 years old, but showed some change in their social characteristics.

2) The "cognitive competence" of the child, based on ability and achievement, was best predicted by child's verbal facility at 2 years old, the mother's level of education, her tendency to encourage mature behavior, and her ability to avoid supplying material rewards for good behavior.

3) Twins and singletons, as groups, were similar in height, weight, vision and hearing, as measured at 9 years old. In contrast, the twins had lagged somewhat behind the singletons in these traits at 2 years old. Twins and singletons were equally skilled in non-verbal abilities at the time of follow-up, but the twins, on average, were slightly less competent in verbal skills and in academic achievement. More twins than non-twins had received speech therapy between 2 and 9 years old.

4) The verbal lag displayed by identical twins at 9 years old was not adequately explained by the twin relationship. This may possibly be due to relaxed pressures on parental time, and the twins' greater access to social contacts outside the home. The identical twin-singleton difference in verbal ability at age 9 years old was, however, associated with both the twin mothers' slightly lower educational level and the twins' greater early exposure to biological stressors . It's interesting that the twin-singleton difference in verbal ability at 2 1/2 years old was not related to birth history events but to the home social situation. Fraternal twins did not show reduced verbal ability, relative to singletons, at 9 years old.

5) Members of identical twin pairs showed greater resemblance in height, weight, non-verbal IQ, and speech facility than did member of fraternal twin pairs. These results suggest that genetic factors influence the expression of these behaviors.

The close social relationship shared by twin children appears to have an important effect upon the nature and quality of interactions between parents and children, as measured in home settings.

Reproductive and Health Characteristics
by Nancy L. Segal, Ph.D.

Differences in reproductive and health characteristics between families with twins and families with only singletons, as well as related issues, have been the focus of an extensive series of studies directed by Dr. Grace Wyshak at the Center for Population Studies, Harvard University, Cambridge, Massachusetts.

Wyshak's studies began in 1964 with an analysis of the inheritance of fraternal twinning. Since that time, she and her colleagues have pursued investigations of twinning rates, fertility and longevity, and other health characteristics of twins, relatives of twins, and individuals not related to twins. The findings from this research illustrate that twins and families with twins appear to be a unique portion of the population.

Wyshak has attempted to survey large populations of twins and other individuals by a variety of methods to ensure that her study provides a good amount of quality data. She has, for example, examined records from the Genealogical

Society of the Mormon Church, Salt Lake City, Utah, that provide life history data on 9,719 families with one, or more, sets of twins. The 29,967 children from these families included 11,921 twins and 17,688 singleton siblings who later became parents themselves. (There are over 4,000,000 records in the Mormon Church which date back to the 18th and 19th centuries!)

Mothers of Twins Clubs across the United States have provided over 4,000 participants for studying maternal health and reproductive characteristics. Several population registries in Connecticut have furnished additional information on nearly 4,000 mothers of fraternal twins and triplets, and nearly 4,000 mothers of singletons, for studying relationships between fraternal twinning and the prevalence of specific diseases and allergies.

Gathering Survey Material

Investigators engaging in population survey research generally do not meet their participants directly. They utilize available information which has been systematically recorded, often over a number of years, or they distribute questionnaire forms to individuals whose social or medical backgrounds are appropriate for the research question at hand. These methods allow large quantities of information to be obtained in relatively brief periods of time.

The Harvard University investigators have been creative in their efforts to collect data. Family records maintained by the Genealogical Society in Salt Lake City included an asterisk (*) next to the names of many children, indicating that they eventually became parents and have separate records containing their own family information. This enabled the researchers to determine the frequency of twinning among this generation.

Members of Mothers of Twins Clubs sent forms that asked the average length of the menstrual cycle, age at first birth, height, weight, and other reproductive and birth history events. A comparison group, composed of mothers of singletons, was assembled by asking the mothers of twins to select an unrelated woman, close in age, whose family did not include a multiple birth. Responses given by these two groups of women were then compared.

Studies of allergies and diseases in mothers of twins and mothers of non-twins proceeded differently. A sample of 3,982 women, born between 1885 and 1935, who had delivered fraternal twins (only opposite-sex twins, or triplets or more), were identified from records compiled by the Connecticut Twin Registry, Connecticut Tumor Registry, and Connecticut vital statistics. Causes of death were noted and compared with a group of 3,982 mothers of singletons.

A key question in this study was whether or not mothers of fraternal twins show a higher frequency of breast cancer or cancers of the reproductive system, relative to mothers of singletons. This possibility was suggested by the observation that Japanese women, who have a low rate of fraternal twinning, show a low rate of breast cancer. Evidence for differences in susceptibility to other diseases also was compared in these two groups, given that differences in reproductive and health characteristics were observed.

Findings

Wyshak's studies have generated results that should influence thinking, practice, and research regarding the health and reproductive life histories of twins and their relatives. Summarized below are some of the findings that may be of greatest concern to families with twins, and to individuals associated with twins and their families.

Results present in 1, 2 and 3 area based on data from church records:

1) Fraternal female twins and their singleton female siblings show an increased rate of twinning, relative to the population frequency. In contrast, male fraternal twins and their singleton male siblings do not show an increased number of twins among their children.

2) Twins were shown to produce fewer children than their parents and non-twin siblings. Possible explanations include the observation that newborn twins, on the average, are smaller and somewhat behind singletons in physical development, and (fraternal) twins tend to be born to older mothers who may provide less optimal intrauterine environments.

3) Parents of twins (both mothers and fathers) have a fertility and longevity advantage over parents of non-twins, as well as their own twin and non-twin children. Parents had less than one child more, on average. Life span was slightly greater for fathers than sons, but daughters tended to live longer than mothers. Life span, however, appears to be increasing, so that twins and their siblings may eventually be expected to outlive their parents.

Results presented in 4, 5 and 6 are based on responses from members of Mother of Twins Clubs, and mothers of singletons:

4) Mothers of multiples reach natural menopause at a slightly earlier age (49.36) than mothers of singletons (50.60 years). Mothers of opposite-sex twins reach menopause earlier (47.99 years) than mothers of same-sex twins (49.77) years.

5) Fraternal twinning rates increase with advancing maternal age. Though fraternal twinning also rises with increasing birth order, this effect is not as strong.

6) Mothers of multiples differed from mothers of singletons on most health and reproductive characteristics under study, yet these differences were not large. The average age of these women was 34 years, and women in both groups had been married for an average of 13 years. Results are presented separately for mothers of singletons, and for mothers of twins, as follows:

SS = mothers of same-sex twins (identical and fraternal twins combined);

OS = mothers of opposite-sex twins;

T+ = mothers of two, or more, twin sets;

T = mothers of triplets.

- Maternal age at first birth was lower among mothers of singletons (22.6 years) than mothers of twins (SS = 23.3 years; OS = 23.4 years; T+ = 23.4 years; T = 23.2 years).

- Interval between marriage and first live birth was longer among mothers of multiples (SS = 1.9 years; OS = 2 years; T+ = 1.7 years; T = 1.6 years) than mothers of singletons (1.6 years).

- Length of the average menstrual cycle was shorter among mothers of twins (SS = 28.5 days; OS = 27.7 days; T+ = 27.6 days; T = 28.3 days) than mothers of singletons (28.9 days).

- Weight over height difference (pounds divided by inches) was greater among mothers of twins than mothers of singletons.

- Age at onset of menstruation was one month earlier among mothers of twins (SS = 12.65 years; OS = 12.53 years; T = 12.58 years), and three months earlier among mothers with two or more sets of twins T+ = 12.42 years), relative to mothers of singletons (12.71 years). A general trend toward a younger age at menarche was noted.

- Number of marriages was higher among mothers of twins (SS = 1.06; OS = 1.07; T+ = 1.05; T = 1.12), relative to mothers of singletons (1.05). Number of marriages is a sociological event. It is interesting to note that frequency of sexual activity has been associated with greater frequency of fraternal twinning.

- Pregnancy loss is greater among mothers of multiples than mothers of non-twins. Mothers of fraternal twins have greater difficulty conceiving and are more likely than mothers of singletons to seek drug assistance to improve the chances of pregnancy.

- Mothers of singletons take longer to achieve menstrual regularity, around the time of beginning mensuration than mothers of multiples (SS = 5.4 months; OS = 4.3 months; T+ = 2.8 months; T = 2 months).

Results presented in 7 are based on a recent review of the effects of fertility drugs on multiple births:

7) Fertility drugs are associated with multiple births in 50 percent of the cases. Some major complications include ovarian cyst formation and ovarian enlargement. The severity of these effects appears to be reduced if clomiphene, rather than gonadotrophins, is administered.

Results presented in 8 are based on data provided by population registries:

8) Mothers of fraternal twins may be at a greater risk for cancer of the pancreas, but not breast cancer, or other forms of cancer, than mothers of singletons. They may, in addition, have an increased risk of developing diabetes, endocrine disorders, and allergies, relative to mothers of non-twins. These results are consistent with previous evidence:

- Women with pancreatic duct cell cancer show increased gonadotrophic activity. High levels of gonadotrophic hormones have been detected in mothers of fraternal twins.

- High levels of follicle-stimulating hormone (FSH) have been found in the urine of post-menopausal women and in diabetics.

Future Directions

The Harvard University twin studies have successfully highlighted a number of important areas for future research. Some intriguing issues include the incidence of twinning among the grandchildren of fraternal twins, the role of gonadotrophic hormones in twinning, and the appropriate use of fertility drugs and dosages among different women.

Most importantly, perhaps, is the need to seriously investigate the long-term health and reproductive characteristics of mothers of twins. The associations found between fraternal twinning and disease susceptibility are important from the point of view of prevention. Additional research efforts are, of course, required before these findings can be accepted definitely.

It is also critical to remember that the findings reported here reflect data obtained from groups not individuals. Given that some findings were based on populations which may differ substantially from one's own, a cautious interpretation is advised.

---------------------------------- ♥ ----------------------------------

Twin Survivors of the Holocaust

by Nancy L. Segal, Ph.D.

The first international conference of twin Holocaust survivors took place from January 27 to February 6, 1985, with visits to Auschwitz and Birkenau in Poland, and Yad Vashem, the Holocaust memorial and research institute in Jerusalem, Israel. (Yad Vashem means "hand and name" in Hebrew.) A major purpose of this meeting was to document the brutal medical experimentation conducted on twins in Nazi concentration camps by Dr. Josef Mengele, from 1943 to 1945. A second aim was to reunite the surviving twins for them to share life events and memories with one another.

This conference was organized by C.A.N.D.L.E.S. (Children of Nazi's Deadly Laboratory Experiments Survivors), founded in 1983 by one of the surviving twins. January 27, 1985 marked the 40th anniversary of the liberation of Auschwitz and Birkenau (the camps in which the twins' experiments were performed) by Russian troops.

I attended this reunion of twin Holocaust survivors with approximately 80 of the twins and their families. We participated in dedications, memorial services, and public hearings about the experiments. During the visits to Auschwitz and Birkenau, the twin survivors and their families related many of the events that had occurred 40 years before. In addition, there were opportunities to inspect barracks and crematoria, and to re-enact the famous "death march" out of Birkenau at the time of liberation.

At a visit to the Auschwitz museum, we saw a large collection of archival material about the individuals and activities in the camps that is available to the public. It included lists of twins' names and identification numbers; log books that included names, ages, countries of origin, and dates of entry into the camps; various medical documents; and numerous photographs. Among the photographs was an especially disturbing picture of little twins raising the sleeves of their tattered garments to display their identification numbers. A list of about 20 different body measurements made on the twins as part of the research program including height, weight, and head size was available, also.

A three-day public hearing on the war crimes committed by Mengele was the central event of the second half of the conference. This took place at Yad Vashem, in Jerusalem, Israel. Thirty twin and non-twin survivors provided insightful and moving testimony about the different psychological and physical treatments they experienced in the camps, as well as the lasting effects that in many cases are as stressful—for example, many experience severe depression or poor health. Their statements were tape-recorded and will be housed permanently at Yad Vashem. Events like these were tremendously meaningful to the twins, many of whom had not seen or heard from other Holocaust pairs in the 40 years since they were liberated.

The Twins' Reunion

I witnessed a wonderful meeting on the airplane flight from Paris to Tel-Aviv of two such twin survivors. Frank Klein (a member of an identical twin pair) and Marc Berkowitz (a member of a fraternal, opposite-sex twin pair), both twins at Birkenau, suddenly met and embraced warmly in the aisle. The genuine joy they exuded upon recognizing one another made for a truly marvelous moment.

That incident illustrated a profound theme of the reuniting survivors—most critical to the twins was recognition by another twin. As children, they had been cruelly separated from their families. After the war, they found themselves in a variety of living situations, such as adoptive homes, orphanages, or displaced-persons' camps. While in the camp, the other twin children were, in essence, a "family" to them, due to the shared experiences that only they could truly understand. For that reason, this reunion was tremendously important to the twins.

"I came to find out about myself from someone who knows me, " said one survivor. Another related, "For years no one understood—the memories are bitter, but when I see old friends, they become sweet." Yet another explained, "I came to show this to my son so he would understand and remind the world that it should never happen again. The (twin) children are still part of my life."

Feelings like those spoke powerfully to the need for communication among the twins of the Holocaust. C.A.N.D.L.E.S., therefore, should be a vital organization in the years to come.

Life Histories

Eva Moses Kor and her identical co-twin, Miriam Moses Czaigher, grew up with their parents and older sisters in Cluj, Rumania. They arrived at Auschwitz at 9 years of age, where they were immediately plucked from the warmth and security of their family to serve as subjects in Mengele's twin experiments. Kor tearfully recalls the moment at which she was separated from her mother for the last time—she did not realize until later that they were never to meet again.

Kor received a series of injections that caused a high fever. She spent several weeks in the camp infirmary, close to death, and she continually worried about her twin sister. Her sister grew weak and thin from malnutrition, and eventually displayed a lack of interest in living, a common consequence of prolonged confinement in the concentration camps. Her condition improved when Kor was able to secure a bit of food for her.

Following the war, the twin sisters returned to their hometown. Their family was gone—their father, mother, and two older sisters had all perished in the gas chambers at Auschwitz. The sisters left for Palestine to begin a new life.

Today, Kor is married, has two children, and is a real estate agent in Terre Haute, Indiana. Czaigher lives in Israel with her husband and three children, and is a nurse. Each heads the organization of twin Holocaust survivors in her respective country.

Peter Greenfeld continues to search for his twin sister, Marta (or Miriam), from whom he was separated at 4 years of age. Born to Jacob and Helen Kleinman, in Prague, Czechoslovakia, on April 14, 1940, little Peter had fallen asleep in the snow during the march out of the camps, but was rescued by a Mr. Greenfeld who took him home.

Three days later, the man passed away, leaving Peter to be raised by his daughter.

A Case of "Pseudo-Twins"

Ephraim Reichenberg is *not* a twin. He did, however, bear a striking resemblance to his older brother, Menashe, causing Mengele to mistake them for twins. Despite their claim to be ordinary brothers, Mengele refused to believe them and assigned them to the twins' barracks along with three other pairs of twins. Ephraim was chosen to serve as a "messenger" for Mengele. He was assigned to collect the young female twins when they were needed for experiments.

Menashe had a beautiful singing voice and was often called upon to entertain the Nazi officers. Mengele was curious as to why only one "twin" in a pair should display such talent. Ephraim was forced to undergo a series of injections into his neck that caused swelling, difficulty in speaking, and shortness of breath. In 1967, doctors in Israel detected growths on his vocal cords. His condition gradually worsened, and the vocal cords were cut. Today, he functions successfully by speaking with the assistance of a special device that was ironically developed by German scientists. He is living in Israel with his wife and two children.

These few cases demonstrate the tremendous inner strength of the survivors, both as individuals and as twins. There are many other stories that show that kind of courage.

The Twin Research: A Pseudo-Science

In previous reports in **TWINS®** Magazine, I have emphasized the importance (for research purposes) of accurately classifying twins according to twin type—identical or fraternal. According to the "classic" twin method, greater resemblance between identical twins, relative to fraternal twins, is compatible with, yet does not prove, a genetic influence upon the behavioral or physical trait under study. This is because identical twins share 100 percent of their genes in common, while fraternal twins share 50 percent of their genes in common, on the average, by descent.

In his book, *Doctors of Death*, Phillipe Aziz states that, "Scientific curiosity concerning twins was not new, but acquired an unforeseen aspect in the context of Nazi ideology, for twins constitute living proof of the essential importance of heredity. All medical books of the National Socialist period insisted on the resemblance, physical and psychological, between identical twins—those born of the same egg and possessing the same hereditary patrimony. The dissimilarity of fraternal twins was carefully emphasized." Producing proof of the hereditary transmission of human characteristics was critical to the Nazi theory of the superiority of the Aryan people.

Mengele did not organize the twin pairs according to twin type. The result is that the "data" collected by him are of no scientific value. This conclusion was based on interviewing the twins, and inspecting copies of twin lists and data sheets. Also, it is known that three "non-twin" pairs were included, and there may have been more. The location of much of the recorded material is unknown, as well, and correspondence between Mengele and his collaborators has been destroyed. Members of the panel at the hearings in Jerusalem also concluded that the experiments were worthless.

Lessons for Research

The Nazi extermination programs and twin research were part of a horrifying and unthinkable period in recent human history. It is the responsibility of all people everywhere to be sure that such events are never repeated. The C.A.N.D.L.E.S. twins remind us that scientific methods can be abused. All twin research should be conducted in a way that will benefit the twin participants, as well as the field of investigation. A spirit of mutual respect between researchers and twins is a necessary precondition for valid scientific study.

SYSTEMATIC EXTERMINATION

Historically, a large-scale program of racial discrimination (outlined in the Nuremberg statutes of 1935) against the Jewish people was undertaken by the German Nazi party. Plans were made to systematically exterminate all Jewish people living in Europe, in addition to other individuals (for example, those who were mentally defective, or who were judged to be "inferior" to the Aryan people). Auschwitz and Birkenau, as well as other concentration camps, were established for that purpose.

The Jewish people were informed that they would be "resettled" in work camps where living conditions were quite favorable. They were, instead, delivered to the Nazi death camps where those who were considered to be "unfit" were disposed of by Xyclon B, a strong, fast-acting poisonous gas that causes death by suffocation. About 12,000 people could be killed simultaneously by this procedure. The bodies were then burned in specially designed furnaces, called crematoria.

It is estimated that 4 million people perished in Auschwitz and Birkenau alone, and that a total of 10 million people perished in all of the camps. Six million of these people were Jewish; 1.5 million were children.

THE MEANING OF BEING A TWIN

An estimated 1,500 pairs of twins (mainly children) were the unfortunate victims of horrifying medical experiments conducted by the Nazis during World War II. When Auschwitz and Birkenau were liberated in 1945, only 157 twin children (from both intact and non-intact twin pairs) were alive. These children were weak from continual exposure to hunger and cold and deeply frightened by the painful physical and psychological torments they had suffered. Many were sick, some nearly to the point of death, as a result of these treatments. One of the twin survivors said that actually 167 children were escorted out of the camps, but that 10 died along the way.

Being a twin or triplet at Auschwitz or Birkenau spelled a critical difference between life and death. Twins were separated and spared for purposes of experimentation, while non-twin children were directed to the gas chambers where they were immediately killed. Other family members, if considered "physically fit" by the Nazi doctors, were placed in various barracks throughout the camp, and were usually forced to perform hard labor, such as moving heavy rocks or digging trenches under insufferable conditions.

The twins, in contrast, were kept together in special barracks. They were provided with somewhat better food and clothing to maintain them as "guinea pigs" for the experiments. Their situation was, however, terrifying and life-threatening. As one twin explained, "We were healthier, but not safer."

The twins received numerous injections of unknown substances, blood transfusions (both within and between pairs), exposure to radiation, and injections of dye into the eyes to determine the influence of such treatments upon eye color. In the event that one member of a twin pair died, the twin sibling generally was killed to enable comparative examination of body structures.

The South African Twin Study

by Nancy L. Segal, Ph.D.

Drs. Phillipa Clark, Zita Dickman, and Penelope Krige, from the Department of Psychology at the University of Natal, in Durban, South Africa, have completed a modest, but very revealing series of studies on social-interactional features in infant twinships. The aim of this research, titled the South African Twin Study, was to compare the "quantity and quality of parent-child and child-child interaction" within twin pairs, and between pairs of twins and pairs of singletons. The study was organized into the following parts:

Study 1 was a long-term analysis of the social interaction between the members of one pair of identical male twins who happened to be the only children in their family. The twins were observed every two weeks during free play periods between the ages of 8 months and 32 months.

The children were observed with their mother during the first half of each 15 minute session, and by themselves during the second half. Researchers videotaped the twins as they played with toys, such as simple puzzles and a wooden train.

Study 2 was a comparative analysis of the social interaction of singleton and twin pairs, both with their mothers and with each other. Participants included five pairs of twins and five pairs of singletons. The singletons were paired up only after they had played together at least once weekly for three months before the study. The singletons thus were familiar with one another so their relationships could be more comparable to that of the twins. Two age groups, 9 to 13 months and 14 to 19 months, were included.

Participants were required to engage jointly in a specific task—the use of a hand-operated see-saw—so researchers could obtain a sampling of cooperative behaviors. To keep the see-saw going, each player had to push down the arm of the toy, then allow the partner a turn, thus maintaining a continuous rate of activity. Each child played the game with his mother, and then with the twin partner or a peer.

Findings of Study 1

If parents sometimes feel it is impossible to give each twin all the attention he needs, they are no different from the mother in this study. The first three minutes of film showed, in fact, that she shifted her attention 26 times from one twin to the other.

There was also evidence that she would look at one twin while stretching out a hand to the second twin. This "juggling" act" may be common not only for families with twins, but also for families with several young children closely spaced in age who must be creative at times to interact effectively with both their children simultaneously.

Observations of the twins' social interaction away from the mother represent an attempt at capturing the essence of the close bond between twins. The bond is well-known, but definitions and descriptions often are inadequate. It was found that in play periods involving specific toys, the twins displayed a level of communicative competence typical of most children their age.

However, their communicative skills seemed especially advanced in other situations, as they attempted to distract and console one another during times of distress—by banging on the table, moving into closer proximity, vocalizing, and making eye contact at 8 1/2 months of age.

The fact that this behavior was demonstrated at 8 1/2 months may be significant in light of researchers' knowledge of the nature of twin relationships. Many child development researchers have indicated that social interest on the part of one infant for another generally does not emerge until 10 months. There is evidence, however, that twins may develop social awareness of one another at an earlier age. Pediatrician T. Berry Brazelton noted, for example, that identical twin girls he studied displayed awareness of each other very quickly: "As early as 3 and 4 months of age, when one baby was out of the room, the other seemed disoriented and looked around as if watching and waiting ... When one twin made a noise, the other startled; when one cried, the other tended to join in, as if to soothe her or to back her up."

More elaborate examples of distracting and consoling behavior were displayed by the twins at the age of 1 year, 6 months. One twin might, for example, attempt to distract his brother by offering a toy. The twins also appeared to gain mutual comfort by maintaining close physical proximity and alternately consoling one another. The important point emphasized by the researchers was that the twins provided one another with such a sufficient level of emotional support that they were able to remain in the playroom without their mother.

Three different forms of play behavior were observed. Solitary play, one child being absorbed in activities that are unrelated to the activities of his partner, was displayed most frequently throughout the study. Joint play, when children engage in a common activity so that the actions of one may affect the actions of the other, occurred most often during months 14 to 19. Cooperative play, involving actions that, according to the investigators are "interdependent and complementary" and occur as a series of continuous behaviors, were observed during months 20 to 31.

The quality of the twins' verbal communication is also important to consider. They made noises back and forth themselves by 11 months of age. This form of verbal behavior is generally not observed in peers until later.

Findings of Study 2

Mutual gaze, smiling together, vocalizing, and game-playing were compared in this study. It was found that mother-child pairs consistently exceeded child-child pairs in the frequency of these four types of behaviors. The investigators said that the findings suggest "cooperative activity is fostered by a socially competent adult."

Twin-singleton differences are, however, important to consider. Mother-twin pairs showed less mutual gaze than mother-singleton pairs, and a tendency toward reduced mutual smiling. Twins vocalized less with their mothers than did singletons, although mothers' frequency of speech was higher for singletons than for twins only in the older (14 to 19 month) age group. Mother-singleton pairs in the younger group, and mother-twin pairs in the older group displayed more game-playing than their counterparts.

In analyses involving the twin and peer pairs, the twins showed less mutual gaze than non-twin pairs, but higher frequency of mutual smiling. The twins showed less verbal behavior with their mothers than the non-twins. The younger pairs of peers and older pairs of twins engaged in the greatest amount of game-playing.

The investigators make the important point that while the twins showed generally reduced social interaction with the parent, as compared with the non-twins, they were equally successful on the given task. This may have been possible, however, due to the essentially nonverbal nature of the game.

Practical Implications of the Studies

The findings highlighted by the studies above suggest several important implications for social development in twinships. First, it would seem that separation from parents or involvement in novel situations may be less difficult for twins than for singleton children because of the constant presence of a familiar partner which may reduce the threat of the novel event or experience. This sentiment has been echoed by many adult twins who regard being a twin as a very positive aspect of their lives.

This apparent advantage can, however, be offset by a built-in disadvantage— the difficulty young twins often experience when away from each other. One implication of the research is that not only should twins be allowed to fully enjoy their special bond (which, in some cases, may mean relying on one's co-twin for support in unfamiliar places), but they should also be prepared for inevitable periods of separation.

Parents may wish to arrange occasional periods alone with each of their twins to relieve the strain associated with attending to the wishes of two children simultaneously, as well as improve the quality of each twin's speech. Both clinical and experimental evidence exists to prove that the quality of twins' speech may be improved if they are separated some of the time.

Partners in Crime?

by Nancy L. Segal, Ph.D.

Physical and behavioral resemblances between twins fascinate researchers and the public alike, and example of partners in crime are no exception. While prisoners at the Nebraska penitentiary, Carey and David Moore were observed switching cells in the prison; they were eventually detected due to a weight difference. Twins Luis Pedro and Pedro Luis Ajete-Terra caused great confusion in a Minneapolis court. One had committed a traffic violation, while his twin brother was charged for cocaine possession. Difficulties arose, however *both* twins claimed to be Luis Pedro.

The examples cited above raise the difficult question: Are some people "born" criminals, or are criminals fashioned from their social and cultural surroundings? The genetic and environmental underpinnings of criminal behavior have been widely debated by psychologists, sociologists, educators, and the general public. Richard J. Herrnstein, Ph.D., professor of psychology and James Q. Wilson, Ph.D., professor of government at Harvard University, co-authors of the 1985 book, *Crime and Human Nature*, emphasize that both genetic and environmental factors influence criminality:

"The causes of crime lie in a combination of predisposing biological traits channeled by social circumstances into criminal behavior. The traits alone do not inevitably lead to crime; the circumstances do not make criminals of everyone; but together they create a population responsible for a large fraction of America's problem of crime in the streets."

In other words, a complex blend of heredity and environment may result in criminal activities, with neither one being solely responsible. Furthermore, there are no genes for criminality. There seem to be certain behavioral characteristics (such as aggressiveness or lack of impulse control), which appear to have a partial genetic basis and which may underlie criminal tendencies in specific situations. Low IQ scores and abnormal EEG (electroencephalographic) patterns have also been observed among criminal populations with greater frequency than among the general population, but the precise role of these features in criminal behavior remains unresolved. It is also important to appreciate that a lower IQ or an atypical EEG pattern is insufficient, in and of itself, to produce criminality.

Twin and adoption research has provided us with the most reliable information we have concerning the genetic and environmental influences on criminal behavior. The major contribution of these studies has been to focus attention on the important and often unappreciated, role played by heredity. Twin researchers have, for example, observed greater resemblance between genetically identical twins, relative to genetically nonidentical.

Sarnoff A. Mednick, professor at the University of Southern California, and colleagues have reported a higher correlation between adopted-away boys and their biological parents in the conviction for property crimes than between these same adopted boys and the adoptive parents who raised them.

This same relationship was *not* upheld in the case of violent crimes. Michael Bohman, M.D., at the Sweden University School of Medicine, and colleagues reported that many of the biological parents of adopted-away, non-alcoholic petty criminals also had histories of petty crime, but were not alcoholic. The risk of criminality in alcoholics, however, was associated with the severity of alcoholism, rather than with the criminal behavior of biological or adoptive parents.

These findings, provided by different investigators using different study populations, converge on the common conclusion that genes are implicated, to some degree, in criminality. Identical twins are *not* necessarily partners in crime, however, as evidence by the much less-than-perfect correlation for criminality observed between these twins.

Some Crime Statistics

Wilson and others have noted that crimes are committed more frequently by males than by females. Behavioral geneticists John Fuller, Ph.D. and the late William R. Thompson, Ph.D., warn, however, that this apparent sex difference could reflect a greater male propensity toward crime and/or a reduced likelihood of female incarceration.

The age at which crime occurs most commonly is 18 years. Individuals with very high offense rates tend to show "delinquent" or "aggressive" behavior by the time they enter the third grade. David Rose, Ph.D., professor of psychology at the University of Oklahoma notes, however, that most adolescent delinquents are not destined to become adult criminals.

Twin Research on Criminality: Early Studies

Many of the early studies on twins and crime were conducted in foreign countries, and consequently, some of the information presented below is based on reviews by other investigators. J. Lange's 1929 study, "Crime as Destiny," conducted in Germany, was the first twin study of criminality. It was also the first twin study to strongly support the influence of genetic factors on criminal tendencies. Lange found that 77 percent of identical twins, as compared to 12 percent of same-sex fraternal twins, and 10 percent of opposite-sex fraternal twins, displayed similarities in criminal behavior.

These results are quite striking, yet this work has been criticized for its methods of subject selection and the procedures used for determining twin-type, both of which may have inflated the percentage of similar identical pairs. A second series of studies, carried out in Germany by F. Stumpfl in 1936 and 1937, utilized a sounder methodology.

In his informative review of this area, David Rosenthal, Ph.D., reported that Stumpfl's major contribution was his attempt to organize the severity of crimes or antisocial orientation in terms of five different levels: overall resemblance in criminality, resemblance for one or more offenses, resemblance in type of crimes committed, resemblance in social orientation and resemblance in personality traits.

It was found that identical male twins showed greater similarity in overall criminality than fraternal male twins, but that the size of the difference was less than in some previous studies, suggesting a more modest genetic influence. Resemblance was very high identical twins for social orientation and personality traits, relative to that for fraternal twins. In the context of criminality, Rosenthal suggests that individuals with certain personality characteristics may be more likely to encounter friction with the law. An unfortunate flaw in Stumpfl's research is the failure to conduct blind assessments. In other words, Stumpfl himself evaluated the twins' behaviors and was, therefore, aware of their twintype.

Early researchers in the United States provided data concerning developmental aspects of criminal behavior. A. Rosanoff, L. Handy and I. Plesett, in 1934, identified twins who were either adult criminals, juvenile delinquents, or children with behavior problems. They found that resemblance was greater between identical twins than between fraternal twins for all three groups, but that the greatest difference occurred in the adult crime group.

Based on these findings, Fuller and Thompson raise the joint possibilities that genetic factors associated with criminal behavior may surface in the adult, but that childhood and adolescent difficulties may be more environmentally influenced. It should be recalled, however, that individuals with extensive criminal records have reportedly displayed delinquent tendencies as young children. The need for twin studies of criminal behavior, which include long-term follow-up evaluations, is clear.

Twin studies of criminal behavior have been conducted in Holland, England, Finland, and Japan during the years 1933 to 1967. Fuller and Thompson's combined analysis of the data from studies and of these works examined above reveals that criminality and delinquency are observed in identical twin partners three times as often as in fraternal twin partners. A more recent and comprehensive review by Professor Lee Ellis, from the State University of North Dakota at Minot, indicated that in 13 twin studies of criminality, identical twins resembled each other more than twice as often as fraternal twins. These results furnish some support for genetic influences.

Only five reared-apart identical twin pairs, in which one or both twins showed various criminal tendencies, have been identified from the 121 previous cases. Information provided by the respective investigators is variable in depth and detail. In some cases, differences in criminality seem to be apparent between twins raised in very different types of social environments.

Current Research

David Rowe, Ph.D., is well-known for research on criminal behaviors in adolescent twin pairs. In 1986, he published findings from the Ohio Twin Project, which included 265 twin pairs. The sample included 107 identical female pairs, 61 identical male pairs, 59 fraternal female pairs and 38 fraternal male pairs. The twins were in grades 8 through 12, with an average age of 17.5 years. The twins completed questionnaires, concerning the frequency with which they performed delinquent activities (e.g., stealing and vandalism), as well as deceitfulness, perceived parental rejection, anger, impulsivity, and value placed on school achievement.

Evidence of genetic influences on self-reported deviance were found, as reflected by the greater similarity within identical twinships than fraternal twinships. Males showed a higher frequency of delinquent acts than females, an observation consistent with previous studies. Deceitfulness, anger, and impulsivity as associated with delinquent behavior.

Similar analyses were also conducted using a sample of 43 opposite-sex twin pairs. Opposite-sex twin partners showed reduced resemblance, relative to same-sex fraternal pairs, for commission of delinquent acts. The finding of some resemblance, however, suggests the operation of genetic influences associated with criminal activity common to both sexes.

Rowe also examined the effects of the twins' interaction as possibly influencing criminal tendencies. Twins were found to influence one another because the greater the percentage of twins engaging in a delinquent act, the more often it was performed with the twin partner. Rowe, therefore, proposes that delinquency might be reduced by working closely with the "more conforming" pair partner.

Implications and Future Research Directions

Critics of behavioral-genetic studies of criminality have argued that uncovering a genetic influence on such behaviors may lead to the unfortunate labeling of such individuals. It should be emphasized, however, that through twin research and research involving other types of biological and non-biological relatives, investigators can begin to identify the bases of criminal behavior. These efforts constitute an important step toward developing programs to assist families at risk.

Rowe emphasizes that occasional delinquency should not necessarily cause concern. In contrast, serious or frequent criminal acts on the part of adolescents may warrant professional attention. He asserts that genetic explanations of criminality may help to relieve parents of guilt feelings concerning their children's activities, but emphasizes their need to assume responsibility for helping children to control their behaviors.

Identical twins may occasionally appear to be "partners in crime" even when they are innocent. A frequent example concerns their providing similar answers to test questions in the classroom. In order to avoid false and unfair accusations, it is important to know that identical twins, on average, behave in very similar ways, a phenomenon associated with their genetic identity. The occasional dramatic examples of twins as "co-conspirators" can convey the misleading impression of twins as "double-trouble." The important truth is that twins are no more predisposed toward crime than non-twins.

Twin Studies of Anorexia Nervosa: A Research Update

by Nancy L. Segal, Ph.D.

Anorexia Nervosa, an eating disorder most commonly (but not exclusively) observed among young women, was first described by Dr. R. Morton about three centuries ago. Approximately 95 percent of the affected individuals are female. The key identifying features of this condition include self-induced weight loss and consequent amenorrhea (stoppage of menstruation).

The relative importance of genetic and environmental influences on the appearance and course of anorexia nervosa are of tremendous importance to psychologists, psychiatrists, and the concerned public. Studies of identical and fraternal twins and triplets are proving very informative with respect to singling out factors that may trigger, or prevent, the onset of this disorder. Cases involving identical twin pairs with only one affected twin are especially useful in this regard: Careful analysis of well and ill twin partners can dramatically highlight life events that may be associated with the development of, or resistance to, anorexia in predisposed people.

Anorexia Nervosa: Descriptive Characteristics

Individuals with anorexia typically display considerable preoccupation with body weight. Loss of appetite is rare, the term *anorexia* (which implies appetite loss) is not strictly correct. Weight loss is accomplished by reduction in food intake, and often supplemented by extensive exercising, use of laxatives or diuretics and induced vomiting. Underweight people may show hypothermia (low body temperature), bradycardia (resting pulse of 60 or less), lanugo (coat of fine body hairs) and other symptoms. The disorder appears to be more common among sisters and mothers of affected individuals, relative to individuals in the general population.

Approximately one-third of anorectic patients are overweight prior to becoming ill. The most common sequence of events includes a single episode of weight loss, followed by a return to normal body weight. Severe cases may, however, necessitate hospitalization to prevent death due to medical complications associated with starvation and abnormal eating behavior. Follow-up studies indicate that between five and 18 percent of anorexia nervosa cases are fatal. Rate of recovery is usually best if the disorder develops at a younger age (prior to 18 years of age).

Twin and Family Studies: Genetic and Environmental Influences

Most studies report that anorexia nervosa occurs with equal frequency among both twins and non-twins. Recent work by Paul Garfinkel, M.D., and David Garner, Ph.D., at the University of Toronto, however suggests that twins might be at slightly greater risk for developing anorexia nervosa than non-twins. Comparing resemblance for anorexia between genetically identical twins to resemblance between genetically non-identical, or fraternal, twins is still an important first step toward unraveling the bases of this perplexing condition.

Genetic influences on anorexia nervosa are suggested, but are not yet conclusive. Dr. A.J. Holland and colleagues assert that a genetic vulnerability might be a predisposition to a particular personality type; to psychiatric illness, in general (and, in particular, to affective disorders); to a disturbance of body image; or to a hypothalamic disorder. Thus (identical) twins carrying one or more vulnerability factors would both have the potential for developing anorexia nervosa under conditions of stress. Others factors such as earlier life experiences or particular life events may be different for each of the twins, thus influencing the expression of the disorder.

Dr. A.H. Crisp and colleagues at St. George's Hospital agree that "there are potentially many strands of genetic contribution to anorexia nervosa," and that "the way that these come together and become reinforced or muted by the nurturant developmental experience" is relevant to anorectic episodes. A fearful, unassertive, and protected child might, for example, feel especially threatened by "new-found puberty 'fatness'" and adapt to adolescent pressures by refusing to eat.

Several common stress factors have been implicated in the onset of anorexia. In his review, Holland notes that a neurotic personality, fears surrounding impending sexuality, various adolescent coping capabilities, family conflicts, and body image disturbances are cited in published studies and case reports.

Several twin studies of anorexia are currently available. The greater resemblance of identical twins than fraternal twins, and the greater risk of first-degree relatives of affected individuals supports (although does not prove) that the genes play a role in anorexia. The influence of environmental effects is highlighted by the finding that (1) not all identical twins with anorexia show similar symptoms, and (2) not all identical twins with the disorder have affected twin partners.

Dr. Hiroyuki Suematsu identified seven identical twins with anorexia nervosa. In two of the seven cases, both twin partners were diagnosed as having anorexia, while in the remaining five cases only one twin partner had the disorder. One of the dissimilar pairs was male. Even in the two cases in which both twins were affected, the symptoms differed, such that one was diagnosed as "genuine" and the other as "secondary." It was concluded that genetic influences on anorexia were, therefore, not supported. The two similar cases were, however, the first reported occurrences of anorexia in both members of a Japanese twin pair.

Holland studied 34 twin pairs and one triplet set. Thirty pairs were female and included 16 identical twin pairs and 14 fraternal twin pairs. In nine of the 16 identical twin pairs, and in only one of the 14 fraternal twin pairs, both twins had severe anorexia. This twin group difference is consistent with a genetic interpretation.

Close examination of the dissimilar twin pairs revealed no association between anorexia and birth order, birth weight or educational success. In seven of these pairs, however, birth difficulties were identified: In five cases these difficulties generally affected the ill twins, and in two cases they affected both twins. Most anorectic twins from dissimilar pairs reached menarche second and tended to be the less dominant twin. Holland notes that these relationships are suggestive, but warns that they are based on very modest size samples.

In further analysis of these same twins, Crisp reports that in identical pairs with two affected twins, the age of onset for the twin who first becomes ill (15 years) is much younger than for his ill twin partner (17.3 years). These twins also develop anorexia nervosa earlier than anorectic identical twins, fraternal twins with nonanorectic twin partners, or anorectics in the general population.

Twins in the single similar fraternal pair developed the disorder at ages 15 years and 17 years, respectively. He suggests that this might reflect the "special vulnerability of identical twins when faced with puberty." As indicated above, both Holland and Crisp regard the origins of anorexia nervosa as largely unresolved.

An Interview with Elke D. Eckert, M.D.

Elke D. Eckert, M.D., is a psychiatrist with a special interest in the genetic and environmental bases of eating disorders.

Dr. Eckert has observed that anorectic patients appear to fall into two groups: bulimic and non-bulimic. (Bulimia is an eating disorder characterized by periods of binge eating—rapid consumption of large quantities of food during specified periods—following by purging.) The bulimic anorectics are often impulsive and promiscuous and have been known to steal. Non-bulimic anorectics seem to be less socially mature than bulimic anorectics and may be fearful of "growing up." Such refinement of patient populations is a step toward defining the events associated with the cause and course of the disease.

Ideally, Dr. Eckert would like to identify all twins born in a given location, within a given period, and to then identify those diagnosed as having anorexia nervosa. This method would ensure that the members of the affected sample did not represent a biased sample. She would, in addition, like to follow a group of young twins through the age at risk so as to study anorectics *as they actually develop the disorder*. Information obtained in this way is more accurate than information obtained through recall.

Unanswered Questions and Future Directions

The majority of investigators converge on the common conclusion that genetic factors may be implicated in the onset of anorexia nervosa, although certain stressful life events seem to be important. The specific nature of the genetic influences, however, has not yet been identified. Selected life experiences, while apparently associated with this disorder, do not necessarily result in anorexia in everyone.

Anorexia nervosa, like many other behavioral and medical conditions, appears to reflect unique combinations of genetic and environmental influences. It is, therefore, critical that readers not immediately generalize the current research findings to their own situations. Anorexia nervosa, despite the increasing attention paid it, is still relatively rare in the population.

It is unfortunate that no adoption studies of anorexia nervosa have been completed. Adoption studies, by examining individuals who have been reared by unrelated individuals, can uniquely "separate" genetic and environmental influences.

Crisp recently identified a family which included an anorectic adoptive father and two unrelated adoptive daughters who eventually developed anorexia. his discussion of this case focused on the "anorexogenic household" as the source of the disorder. That is to say, in this particular family a parent had anorexia, the children experienced conditional love and rejection, and discussion of sexual matters was avoided. It would, however, be of great interest to study adopted-away children whose biological parents and siblings had been anorectic. There are no documented cases of anorexia among identical twins reared apart, although Holland mentions a pair of identical twins who both developed the disorder while living apart in different countries, one concealing this from the other. Similar cases would provide compelling support for genetic influences.

Nancy S. Nowlin, M.D., at the University of Kansas, supports the development of a national registry for identifying twins with anorexia. She emphasizes the likely possibility that dissimilar twins may otherwise miss detection by the medical community. Exclusion of dissimilar cases can lead to misleading interpretations of genetic and environmental influences on this disorder.

The need for researchers to apply uniform diagnostic criteria, and to document the methods by which twintype was determined, is also critical. Failure to comply with these procedures in the past may partly explain the lack of definitive findings.

DIAGNOSING ANOREXIA NERVOSA

The specific diagnostic criteria for anorexia nervosa vary across research centers within the United States and abroad. The criteria established by the American Psychiatric Association and applied by researchers in the United States are reproduced below:

- Refusal to maintain body weight over a minimal normal weight for age and height, e.g., weight loss leading to maintenance of body weight 15 percent below that expected; or failure to make expected weight gain during period of growth, leading to body weight 15 percent below that expected.
- Intense fear of gaining weight or becoming fat, even though underweight.
- Disturbance in the way in which one's body weight, size, or shape is experienced, e.g., the person claims to "feel fat" even when emaciated, believes that one area of the body is "too fat" even when obviously underweight.
- In females, absence of at least three consecutive menstrual cycles when otherwise expected to occur (primary or secondary amenorrhea). (A woman is considered to have amenorrhea if her periods occur only following hormone, e.g., estrogen, administration.)

Researchers in Japan and in England have developed similar diagnostic schemes, although there are some differences, Drs. Hiroyuki Suematsu, Tomifusa Kuboki and Etsuro Ogata, at the University of Tokyo, in Japan, identified 10 criteria for Anorexia nervosa in their 1986 twin study. In addition to those listed above, they include (1) loss of more than 20 percent of standard body weight, (2) hyperactivity, (3) denial of the illness, and (4) absence of known physical or psychiatric disorder. Patients are classified as "wide criteria" anorectics if they show numbers 1, 2 and 4, and as "typical cases" if, additionally, they are female; display abnormal eating patterns and amenorrhea; exhibit a disturbance of body image and a history of weight loss; and the disorder develops before age 30.

Dr. A.J. Holland and colleagues at the Maudsely Hospital in England listed intense fear of fatness, self-induced weight loss and amenorrhea as the three major criteria for anorexia nervosa in their 1984 twin study. Individuals were classified as "severe" if their body weight remained below 75 percent of their weight prior to illness, or if the course of the disorder necessitated three or more hospital admissions.

Nature vs. Nurture: Who Is Happy?

by Nancy L. Segal, Ph.D.

Psychologists have spent years trying to identify the factors that affect human happiness. What they've found is surprising: Most things that we believe should permanently influence feelings of happiness, such as marital status or religious commitment, do not have lasting effects.

In fact, according to David Lykken and Auke Tellegen, professors in the department of psychology at the University of Minnesota, "religious conversion or being born again' is said to be a joyful experience, but its effect on mood may not be more lasting than being promoted or winning the lottery."

Everyone wishes to be happy and most people try to structure their lives with this aim in mind. However, it often seems that the joy we experience at achieving certain goals doesn't boost our mood indefinitely. Instead, it's short-lived.

Lykken and Tellegen published a 1996 article, "Happiness is a Stochastic Phenomenon, " in the journal, *Psychological Science*. This paper reports findings from a twin study of subjective well-being, based on over 1,000 pairs of identical and fraternal twins reared together, and more than 100 pairs of identical and fraternal twins reared apart.

Measuring Happiness

All participants in the study completed the Minnesota Personality Questionnaire. The MPQ, developed by Tellegen, includes items that measure a person's standing on 11 different personality scales, such as traditionalism and social closeness.

Scores on the well-being scale reflect the tendency to feel good about one's self and one's place in the world, while the stress-reaction scale is a measure of negative emotionality. Happiness researchers, David Myers and Edward Diener, have suggested that subjective well-being (SWB) includes both positive and negative feelings. It's for this reason that in the present study, SWB was calculated as WB-SR, or the difference between the well-being and stress reaction scores.

Many Factors Irrelevant

Several sets of analyses were conducted. First, it was found that educational attainment (i.e., highest grade in school), marital status and even income did not have a major impact on either well-being or on subjective well-being.

Furthermore, religious commitment, as measured by the traditionalism scale of the MPQ, was unrelated to happiness. In other words, people who are highly involved in religious activities do not report greater happiness than those who are uninvolved.

Next, the researchers compared the similarity of the identical and fraternal twins to see if there was evidence of a genetic influence on happiness. Most interesting was the finding that identical twins reared together were much more alike than fraternal twins reared together, which is consistent with a genetic effect. The identical twins reared apart were as *similar* as the identical twins reared together. This is a very important finding because it shows that events and influences in the same home have very little effect on happiness level.

Another significant result was that the similarity between the fraternal twins was quite low, as compared with that of identical twins. This suggests that many different genes are associated with one's level of happiness. Recall that identical twins share all their genes and, therefore, will share unusual gene combinations.

In contrast, fraternal twins share only half their genes and so will tend not to share the unique combinations and configurations of genes that underlie complex traits such as happiness. Overall, the data shows that about 50% of the variation that we see in happiness is influenced by genetic factors. The other half is influenced by environmental factors.

The Results

A subsample of the twins who were about 20 years old at the first testing period completed the MPQ a second time 10 years later. This allowed the investigators to examine the stability of happiness. Specifically, what was done was to compare twin 1's score at time 1 with twin 2's score at time 2, and vice versa. The similarity was considerably higher for identical twins than for fraternal twins. That's to say, the happiness of one identical twin was a better predictor of the twin partner's happiness at a different time than was his own marital status, educational attainment or income! This means that the stable part of our happiness level is also affected by genetic factors.

Happiness in the Real World

What do the findings from this twin study of happiness mean for everyone else? Everyone undergoes various daily fluctuations in how happy they feel. These changes are largely due to the many unplanned favorable and unfavorable events that happen to all of us throughout our lives. However, all of us appear to have our own special set point, or characteristic level of happiness, and it is this particular point around which the unplanned events cause us to vary.

Many people have believed that positive or negative fortunes have the effect of altering happiness in a significant way, but this has been shown to be largely untrue. The twin study suggests, instead, that our basic moods or dispositions lead us to seek out certain experiences people or events. For example, a contented individual may savor social gatherings, while a discontented individual may prefer to withdraw from others. In the words of the investigators, the proper interpretation is "from mood to behavior" rather than the other way around.

More Take-Home Messages

There are some additional important take-home messages for twins and families. Parents raising identical twins can expect general similarity in their level of happiness. In the event that large differences are observed, efforts should be made to discover the cause. Perhaps a difficult situation at school or with peers has persisted for one twin and not the other. In contrast, parents of fraternal twins should not be surprised if their children differ in how happy they seem, despite sharing the same family and school—such children differ genetically and will, therefore, differ in personality traits that are tapped by measures of well-being. Of course, behavior similarity is not always predictable from genetic relatedness, and so some identical pairs are expected to differ somewhat, while some fraternal twins may be similar.

We should not feel discouraged or confused when the efforts we make on behalf of those who are discontented fail to raise their spirits as much as we would like—but we can keep trying. Similarly, we should not feel let down because the exhilaration of our accomplishment has faded all too quickly. The twin research reviewed in this article should help us make sense of these events.

Anyone interested in further information about twin research on human happiness should review the original article by David Lykken and Auke Tellegen, published in *Psychological Science 7* (1996), 186-189.

———————————————— ♥ ————————————————

Australian Focus on Reading, Language, Individuality

by Nancy L. Segal, Ph.D.

The La Trobe Twin Study of Behavioral and Biological Development began at La Trobe University in Melbourne, Australia in 1978 in response to parents' requests for information on twinning. Its primary aim is to understand age-to-age changes in mental ability and social behavior in children between 3 and 15 years of age.

According to the project director, Dr. David Hay, "In the same way that no two single-born children are exactly alike, neither are any two twins or sets of twins. What holds true for one family and their twins may not apply to the next."

Some unique features of this investigation include study of siblings and cousins, and the influence of the twin relationship on intellectual and social development. The La Trobe Twin Study also provides information and services to parents of twins and medical and educational professionals in the community.

The Study Sample

The twins in this study are identified using the same resources as those used by researchers in the United States: Mothers of Twins Clubs, maternity wards in hospitals, infant welfare centers, and preschools. Though only six years old, the study now includes a total of 1,626 children (471 twin sets, nine triplet sets, 492 brothers and sisters of twins, 157 cousins, and eight survivors of twin pairs in which one twin had died).

Dr. Hay notes that except for families moving far away from the Melbourne area, nearly everyone enrolled in the project has continued to participate. In this respect, the Australian twins and their families are no different from participants in the other studies reviewed in **TWINS®** Magazine who share an unusually high level of enthusiasm for research due to their interest in the special twin situation.

Tests and Procedures

In this study, children are tested once each year within two weeks of their birthday. The physical, behavioral, and social information obtained for each child is listed below:

Physical measures include weight, height, head circumference, facial photos, skinfold thickness on arms, pulse, blood pressure, color vision, visual acuity, depth perception, hearing, and fingerprint patterns. The photographs are used to study the developing bone structure of the head. Blood pressure is monitored to identify children who may be at risk for high blood pressure or hypertension in adulthood. Tests of vision and hearing may provide insight into performance on mental ability tests.

Behavioral measures include language comprehension; vocabulary; memory; information-processing; spatial ability; learning ability; concepts of left and right; and hand, eye, and foot preferences.

Social measures include questionnaires completed by twins (ages 8 years and over), siblings of twins, parents, teachers, and testers. It is estimated that approximately 1,500 to 2,000 items are completed by each family! The material obtained covers four stages of childhood; information from parents (demographic data, family stresses, children's progress during the last year, and experience of having twins); data from children (experience of being a twin or having twins in the family); reports from teachers (behavioral and social adjustment); feedback from testers (behavior and attitudes of children); and material on younger children (infant and toddler temperament scales and behavioral style questionnaire).

Findings

Investigators associated with the La Trobe Twin Study faced the difficult task of examining twins who lived many miles away from their laboratories. To simplify this process, they rebuilt an ordinary mobile home to include separate testing areas for each twin and equipment for carrying out the various behavioral and physical assessments.

Today, investigators can simply drive to homes or schools and test each twin separately and simultaneously.

Reading and language problems as well as the individuality of twins are key concerns of this study that have been extensively researched. (Reading disability refers to specific reading problem displayed by children who show competence in other intellectual functions. Approximately five percent of school-age children show some form of reading difficulty.) The researchers have found that male twins show delays and deficits in language and reading skills that are not observed among female twins or singleton children. Findings pertaining to these areas during different developmental stages are summarized below:

Infancy (18-24 months): Male twins were eight months behind female twins and singletons (both males and females) in language expression, six months behind in language comprehension, and three months behind in symbolic play, such as using a table cloth as a tent or pillow. The suggestion that twins' lower social interaction with parents may underlie these behaviors is *not* an adequate explanation because twin girls do not display such problems. Hay and colleagues have suggested that differences between male and female brain organization may be the causes of this situation.

Early Preschool Years: Observations of children in playgroup settings revealed that twins with better fluent and expressive abilities were also more socially skillful. In contrast, this same relationship was not observed among non-twin children. In other words, single-born children with well-developed language abilities did not always display comparable social skills.

Primary School Years: Reading and language problems were found to either disappear or grow worse during this time. Approximately 75 percent of the twin boys were not showing satisfactory progress, and many required speech therapy. The specific language problems observed involved accuracy, not comprehension; the twins were knowledgeable about words, but were unable to translate written material into spoken material. These children were, however, performing at above average levels in other school subjects.

It is very likely that preschool language problems contribute to later difficulties in reading. Parents of one-third of the male twins in this study recalled earlier language difficulties. In fact, 92 percent of the twins in this group did eventually develop reading problems in later years.

Secondary School: Little research on special mental abilities in adolescent twins has been undertaken; therefore a comparison done by the Australian Council of Educational Research between the performance of 10-14 year old twins and singletons is quite informative. Students completed tests of literacy and numeracy and the results were made available to the La Trobe Study researchers. It was found that 71 percent of singleton boys (who generally score behind singleton girls throughout development) did catch up by 14 years of age, while only 42 percent of twin boys demonstrated comparable skills. In contrast, twin girls were only slightly behind singleton girls in these areas of mental ability.

It is also important to note that among the singleton children and female twins, the tests administered measured distinct numerical and language skills. In the case of the male twins, however, performance on some numerical items seemed closely related to language skills. The numerical difficulties of these twins were, however, much less pronounced than their language difficulties. Providing these twins with appropriate problem-solving strategies may afford an effective solution.

Future of the Study

A major aim of this project for the coming years is to compare the twins and their siblings with their singleton cousins. The present data show that twins (especially females) often perform better than their siblings, which contrasts with the "twin deficits" in ability reported elsewhere. One suggested explanation for the discrepancy is that the singleton siblings *with* twins in the family are scoring lower than singletons *without* twins in the family due to a possible detrimental effect from the amount of parental attention given to twins.

Other goals include studying relationships between birth history events and mental ability levels for firstborn and secondborn twins, and understanding how adolescent twins cope with critical life events during this important period.

Infant Temperament Report: The Louisville Twin Study

by Nancy L. Segal, Ph.D.

Twenty-four years ago, the Louisville Twin Study was organized as an international investigation on child development designed to identify key hereditary and environmental influences underlying intellectual and physical development.

In 1975, the Louisville Study began concentrating more exclusively on infant temperament and sociability because of three factors: increased professional interest in the infant's characteristics and how they affect the caretaker; observations indicating that twins' early temperamental or behavioral project, the New York Longitudinal Study, demonstrating stability in certain behavioral styles over time.

In the Louisville Study, tests of mental and physical ability are administered to twins at these ages: 3 months, 6 months, 9 months, 1 year, 1 1/2 years, 2 years, 2 1/2 years, 3 years and once each year thereafter. The study of temperament in infant twins requires visits at 3, 6, 9, 12, 18, 24 and 30 months of age.

Key questions that researchers are attempting to answer include: What factors influence temperamental characteristics like emotional tone, attention, body activity? Are there relationships among these different behaviors at particular points in time? How and why do behavioral features change during development? What roles in hereditary and environmental factors play in shaping and modifying mental, physical and temperamental characteristics?

The Twin Pairs: Where Do They Come From?

Participants are identified by means of birth records provided by the Board of Health in the Louisville, Kentucky area. The twins range in age from 3 months to 15 years, and the families represent a wide sampling of social and economic groups. A total of 476 twin pairs have been studied in the project and 3,500 visits to the research project office have been made by twins.

New Findings

Some of the discoveries of the Louisville Twin Study include:

1) Identical twins show substantial agreement in the timing and direction of changing behaviors, as indicated by adaptability scores obtained at ages 9 months, 12 months, and 18 months. In contrast, fraternal twins do not display the same striking resemblance. Boy-girl pairs tend to show some very apparent personality differences, although in some cases the same-sex fraternal twins may show even greater differences. For example, fraternal boy-boy pairs differed the most in temper and irritability, while fraternal girl-girl pairs differed most in crying and expressing affection.

2) Identical twins display more similar patterns of "spurts" and "lags" in mental development than fraternal twins, from as early as 12 months of age. "Spurts" and "lags" refer to periods of gain and stability in intellectual growth, respectively. This suggests that changes in these behaviors are largely (although not exclusively) governed by genetic factors.

3) Large differences in birth weight between identical twins are not necessarily associated with large differences in intelligence later in life. Ten pairs of twins who differed in birth weight by 1 1/2 pounds or more achieved similar IQ scores at age 6 years.

4) Twins, on the average, are somewhat lighter in weight and shorter in length than non-twins from birth through their 4th birthday.

5) Identical twins actually display larger differences in birth weight and birth length, relative to fraternal twins. This may seem strange because identical twins share all of the genetic inheritance. After one year of age, however, identical twins

become increasingly alike in weight, while fraternal twins become increasingly dissimilar. After 2 years of age, height differences tend to disappear within identical twinships, but seem to become more marked within fraternal twinships. The early reduced resemblance between identical twins is explained, in part by their unique, unusual birth factors, such as crowding in the uterus and shared circulation. The effects of these factors tend to diminish with time.

6) Identical twins produce more similar scores on standard IQ tests than fraternal twins, a result which may be largely due to their more similar genetic background. Relative strengths and weaknesses in special mental abilities also appear to be more similar for identical twins than for fraternal twins when measured at age 6. The degree of identical twin resemblance in mental ability profiles is, however, not as great as that for IQ suggesting that nongenetic factors are also at work.

7) Same-sex fraternal twins and opposite-sex fraternal twins show about the same degree of resemblance on tests of IQ, when measured periodically between 3 months and 6 years of age. The only exception occurred at 9 months of age, at which time the same-sex twins were considerably more similar on this measure. In both groups, similarity in IQ increased between 3 months and 3 years, but later decreased between 3 years and 6 years.

8) Adequacy of the home environment, mother's temperament, mother's intellectual skills, maternal mood and temperament, and father's education have been found to be associated with twins' IQ scores at age 6 years.

Genetic Influences on Tourette Syndrome

by Nancy L. Segal, Ph.D.

Tourette's Disorder (TD) is a neuropsychiatric syndrome, chiefly characterized by involuntary motor and vocal tics (twitches or rapid movements). The disorder begins between 2 and 15 years of age and often appears first as eye blinking. Three times as many males as females are likely to be affected.

This disorder first came to the attention of the psychiatric field in 1825, when J.G.M. Itard described a case of a female patient who displayed multiple tics and shrieks. Itard regarded the case as representing an unusual form of seizures. It was not until 1855 that this condition was given its name by Gilles de la Tourette, who published a paper describing nine such cases.

Research findings on TD have undergone informative changes as knowledge of this disorder has progressed. In 1978, Gerald S. Golden, at the University of Texas, noted that, "Tourette syndrome is generally considered to be a rare sporadic condition."

A decade later, the majority of researchers now suggest genetic influences on the disorder, as evidenced by resemblance between twins and other relatives. In 1985, David E. Comings, Ph.D., at the City of Hope Medical Center in California, and colleagues, stated that TD is a "common genetic disorder with 1 percent of the population estimated to be gene carriers and 50 percent of these expressing the gene as either Tourette syndrome or motor or vocal tics." In a recent issue of the *American Journal of Human Genetics*, Comings suggested that some cases of depression, phobias, and other behavior and mood disorders may be associated with the same genetic defect responsible for TD.

According to Comings and associates, TD is a psychiatric, as well as a neurological, disorder. In a 1985 study involving 250 patients, 61 percent displayed problems and/or difficulties with violence and anger. Obsessive-compulsive behaviors were observed in 32 percent of the cases, and Attention Deficit Disorder (ADD) with hyperactivity was present in 54 percent of the cases.

There are other movement disorders that should be distinguished from TD. Atypical Tic Disorder includes tics that cannot be classified in any of the categories. Atypical Stereotyped Movement Disorder includes behaviors such as head banging or small hand rotations. In contrast with the symptoms of TD, these movements are both voluntary and sudden in occurrence. In addition, the symptoms do not appear to be activated by stress.

Twin and Family Studies

A growing number of twin and family studies have suggested genetic influences on the development of this disorder. A key problematic issue, however, is that the development of this disorder may be under some genetic control.

It is, consequently, not possible to disentangle the hereditary and environmental effects that are relevant to this condition. Environment does seem to play a role because not all affected identical twins show similarities in the development of the illness; and in some cases, twin partners may be unaffected.

In other words, since identical twins share all of their genes in common, any differences between them must be environmental in origin. E. Robert Wassman, M.D., and associates, at the Cornell Medical Center in New York City, have suggested that there may be an acquired form of TD "in which environmental factors are crucial."

The majority of research on TD in twins has been published in the form of single case histories or reviews of multiple case histories. Reports of greater resemblance between identical twins than between fraternal twins is consistent with a genetic influence on TD. Richard L. Jenkins, M.D., and Howard B. Ashby, M.D., from the University of Iowa College of Medicine, explain that when both twins are affected with TD, the chances are higher that the case will receive medical attention than if only one twin were affected. The finding that a disproportionately high number of identical twins and a disproportionately low number of fraternal twins resemble one another for TD is persuasive evidence of the role of genetic factors.

A. Arlen Price, Ph.D., at the University of Pennsylvania in Philadelphia notes, however, that the number of published cases is small and was often unsystematically identified. Only a few studies have systematically gathered twin data on TD through national surveys.

Price (formerly associated with the Department of Human Genetics at Yale University) and colleagues mailed questionnaires to over 8,000 members of the *Tourette Syndrome Association* and identified 42 twin pairs in which at least one member was diagnosed as having TD (two triplet sets composed of an identical twin set and fraternal co-triplet were each treated as two pairs and a "sib"). An additional case provided by the Yale Child Study Center brought the final sample to 43 pairs. (Several of these pairs were included in previous case reports, as would be expected from a systematically conducted national survey.) The sample included 30 identical twin pairs and 13 fraternal twin pairs.

When very strict diagnostic criteria were used, both twins in 53 percent of the identical twin pairs and 8 percent of the fraternal twin pairs were diagnosed as having TD. When the diagnostic criteria were broadened to include "any tics" in the twin partners, both twins in 77 percent of the identical twin pairs and 23 percent of the fraternal twin pairs were diagnosed as having TD.

The researchers concluded that these findings suggest a "substantial" genetic influence on the development of the disorder. They emphasize, however, that as yet unspecified nongenetic factors (i.e. various environmental exposures or periods of enhanced vulnerability during development) may influence the onset and expression of TD, as witnessed by identical twins with unaffected twin partners. It may be that affected and unaffected twin partners both have a predisposition to TD, but that certain events (possibly stress-related) associated with the onset of symptoms may be experienced by only one twin.

Family study data should enhance understanding of research on the genetic and environmental features of TD. It is observed more frequently among male relatives (about 19 percent) than female relatives (about 8 percent) of affected individuals, as reported by Drs. Kenneth K. Kidd and David L. Pauls, at the Yale University School of Medicine in New Haven, Connecticut.

The pattern of transmission (for example, who passes the disease susceptibility to whom across generations) has not yet been discovered. Ten years ago, it was suspected that TD occurred more frequently among Jewish people of Eastern European ancestry. More recent evidence by Comings, based on a larger and more diverse sample, showed that this was not the case because Eastern European Jews represented only 10 percent of the 250 cases in his study.

Further Research, Remarks and Resources

Twin and family studies have, so far, provided valuable insights into the origin, course, and progress of TD. Investigations using larger numbers of twin pairs, as well as introducing adoptive parent-child pairs and adoptive sibling-sibling pairs, would furnish important additions to current research programs.

Parents should be alert to symptoms in their children that may signal the presence of TD. Comings advises that when learning disorders, attention-deficit disorders, or significant emotional or learning disabilities are observed in children, parents should be questioned about the possibility of tics or vocal disturbances in the child and in other family members.

TD may interfere with normal school progress, even in very bright children, because of children's inabilities to settle down and fully concentrate, the compulsive need to re-read sentences, and related factors. Ridicule by peers and reduced self-esteem may eventuate in school phobia. Parents can help children overcome their fear of school by *not* giving in to their wishes to remain at home.

The presence of tics does *not* indicate TD in every instance. Researchers report that simple, transient tics may occur in six to 12 percent of children. It is, therefore, very important to consider all aspects of a child's behavioral development in decisions concerning medical attention and treatment.

HOW TO DIAGNOSE TOURETTE SYNDROME

The specific diagnostic criteria for Tourette Syndrome, established by the American Psychiatric Association, are:

1) Age at onset between 2 and 15 years

2) Presence of recurrent, involuntary, repetitive, rapid, purposeless motor movements affecting multiple muscle groups.

3) Multiple vocal tics.

4) Ability to suppress movements voluntarily for minutes to hours.

5) Variations in intensity of the symptoms over weeks or months.

6) Symptoms occur for more than one year.

Indiana University Twin Studies: A Multiple Birth Event

by Nancy L. Segal, Ph.D.

The many-faceted research programs on twins currently in progress at Indiana University (IU) originated from several sources over 22 years ago. Two of the program founders, Joseph C. Christian, M.D., Ph.D., (currently chairman of the Department of Medical Genetics at IU and program director) and his research fellow, Dr. Ke Won Kang, began what is part of today's twin studies at the university by collecting a roster of volunteer twins for participation in research on disease and disease susceptibility.

According to Dr. Christian, "...The comparison [of identical and fraternal twins] is a natural comparison that answers many important questions about the relative importance of genetic and environmental influences on human diseases and risk factors." (Editor's note: Dr. Christian was referring to the fact that identical twins share all their genes in common, while fraternal twins, on average, share half their genes.)

The twins involved in the early studies were identified through records of Indiana families with inherited disorders. Advertisements and word of mouth successfully led to the discovery of additional twin pairs. The researchers also capitalized on the many twin pairs enrolled in the various IU branch campuses. (Editor's note: It is estimated that approximately 400 college-age twin pairs are available for study at a given point in time.)

The Half-Sibling Study

Walter E. Nance, M.D., Ph.D., joined the twin research program at IU in 1969. He was active in the development of the Half-Sibling Study, in which a large variety of psychological, physical, and medical data was obtained from adult identical twins, their spouses, and children.

Given that the children of identical twins are genetically equivalent to being half-siblings (as well as first cousins). these unique family constellations are informative as to how genetic and environmental influences affect human development. Dr. Nance was also involved with the inception of numerous other twin projects concerning mental abilities, placentation, fingerprint patterns, and facial characteristics.

Dr. Nance and an associate, Sam Rhine, Ph.D., completed research on an unusual variant of twinning called superfetation, which refers to multiple conceptions occurring during different menstrual cycles. Evidence of this process in humans includes delivery of full-term infants separated by weeks or months, and the birth or abortion of twin infants discordant for developmental status.

In 1979, Drs. Rhine and Nance described a family which included six twin pairs born in four consecutive generations, all of which included one normal twin and either a stillborn twin, macerated fetus, or premature infant. They suggested that either the mother or the father could transmit a gene responsible for superfetation; this would explain how twinning might be passed down through the father's side of the family.

The Investigators and Their Studies

The first IU publication, which appeared in 1969, reported twin analysis of blood lipids, including cholesterol. Since then, approximately 300 scientific publications have been completed. It is now estimated that more than 4,000 twin pairs are enrolled in the Indiana University Twin Panel.

The separate twin studies at IU are too numerous for presentation in full detail, but a broad sampling of past and current investigations and findings are provided below:

- A study of variability on blood pressure was completed by psychologist Richard J. Rose, Ph.D., in 1980. Over 110 twin pairs, between 14 and 30 years of age, were given instruction in how to measure their blood pressure at home. Measurements were repeated six times daily over a period of two to four weeks.

It was determined that identical twins showed more similar changes in blood pressure than fraternal twins, pointing to a genetic influence. Individuals with increased variability in blood pressure show greater susceptibility to sustained high blood pressure levels, so it is important to understand how genetic factors may be implicated.

- Relationships between twin development and placental type have been of great interest to IU researchers. Linda Corey, Ph.D., and colleagues at the Medical College of Virginia and at IU demonstrated that birth weight resemblance in twins is influenced by the proximity of the placentas.

Rose and colleagues, in collaboration with Dr. Irene Uchida at McMaster University in Ontario, Canada, found that identical twins with two chorions were no more alike than fraternal twins on a test of perceptual ability and spatial relationships, whereas identical twins with a single chorion were much more similar. This may reflect differential environmental effects, in utero, for identical twins with two chorions.

Other studies involving twins and their families have addressed genetic and environmental influences on physical growth measures; blood pressure response to dietary change, interests, and attitudes; personality characteristics; cardiovascular disease; dental traits; and alcohol use.

"Special Deliveries"

The IU Twin Panel publishes a periodic newsletter entitled "Special Deliveries." Currently edited by Daneal Qualls-Holston, this newsletter includes descriptions of ongoing research projects, research findings, recent information on twinning, titles of publications and presentations by staff, and notices about upcoming projects and how twins and their families can become involved.

Reared-Apart Twins: The Most Intriguing Varieties of Twinship

by Nancy L. Segal, Ph.D.

The special relationship shared by twins evoke feelings of mystery and fascination in those who view it from the outside. Twins have, for this reason, been the focus of numerous novels, plays, films, and other artistic works. Twins easily lend themselves to being opposing sides of a common whole, making them convenient devices in situations involving compromise or struggle.

Identical twins comprise only one-third of the twin population in the United States, yet this unique minority attracts greater interest than the larger two-thirds of fraternal twins. In a society which prizes individuality, the sight of two identical individuals runs counter to people's expectations. The general harmony and synchrony demonstrated by most identical twins suggest a private set of rules and practices (almost a "mini-culture") which exclude the rest of the world. Many identical twins claim that only other identical twins can truly understand the nature of their relationship. Translating the true spirit of the identical twin bond into artistic works is, therefore, a challenging task.

Fraternal twins, or non-identical twins, may be of two varieties: same-sex or opposite-sex. These twins share the same genetic relationship as ordinary siblings, which is half their genes in common, on average . It is a frequent misconception that twins are *always* alike. Fraternal twin sisters or twin brothers may be quite different in behavior and appearance, sometimes causing others to question if the pair really is a pair of *twins*! Opposite-sex twins also do not conform to common conceptions of twinship because of their obvious differences.

The scientific world has also been intrigued by the various types of twinship. The role of genetic and environmental influences on human behavioral and physical development is highlighted by studying similarities and differences between reared-apart identical and fraternal twins. Twins are a natural living laboratory for this type of research. Differences between identical twins must be due to environmental effects, while differences between fraternal twins may be associated with both genetic and environmental factors. One consequence of scientific work is the demystification of observations that, at first glance, appear beyond explanation.

In March 1979, Thomas J. Bouchard, Jr., Ph.D., professor of psychology at the University of Minnesota, launched the Minnesota Study of Twins Reared Apart. The aim of this study is to determine how differences in the life histories of reared-apart twins may explain current medical and social life history differences between them.

Bouchard clearly delights in this work. "Apart from my two children, this is the most important thing to which I have helped give birth. Like a child, this study has been a package of both joys and tribulations—and like most people who love children, I would do it again without any hesitation.

A Supreme Partnership

The research staff and twins maintain a most supreme partnership. Reared-apart identical and fraternal twins probably represent the most intriguing varieties of twinship. While resemblance may be anticipated between identical twins reared together, it is less expected between people who have never met.

However, the reared-apart identical twins who have participated in the study have displayed some striking similarities. The medical life histories (for example, the timing and expression of specific symptoms, such as weight gain or headaches) of reared-apart identical twins have proven to be similar, even though they were raised apart until adulthood. It has also been observed that the mental abilities and personality characteristics of these twins are very much alike.

The greater resemblance between reared-apart identical twins, relative to reared-apart or reared-together fraternal twins, suggests that genetics play a more important role in behavior than was previously anticipated. This interpretation, while of a scientific nature, hardly dampens the tremendous excitement which has permeated this study since its beginning. In fact, nine years and 90 reunions later, the investigators are as enthused as ever.

Bouchard emphasized, "Working with our many wonderful participants has made me truly respect the tremendous range of differences that may be observed in human behavior—and has made me more fully appreciate the unique individuality of each and every twin."

The crucial message in this comment is that the special talents and preferences of every child must be carefully considered in decisions involving child-rearing and education. Each child brings into this world his or her own set of behavioral potentials that warrant special nurturing from the opportunities and encouragement made available in their homes and communities. A practice that may work optimally with one child may prove unsuccessful with a sibling.

The twins, in turn, have a great deal to learn about themselves, as well. It is important to recall that many of the reared-apart twins are adoptees who have never had access to information concerning their biological relatives. When finally confronted with a co-twin, they can begin to find answers to questions such as, "Where does my red hair come from?" or "Is my nearsightedness associated with heredity, or is it solely due to poor lighting?" The twins also derive considerable satisfaction from knowing that they are contributing to science in important ways.

Reared-Apart Twins: How Rare?

Approximately 10 pairs of reared-apart twins are identified each year. This number, however, really represents the frequency with which reared-apart twins visit the laboratories of the University of Minnesota.

No one really knows how often twins are separated at birth. Many of the participants in our study did not know that they were twins until they were located by their twin siblings or until they were grown women and men and their adoptive parents told them they had a co-twin. Some of the twins did not even know that they were adoptees!

It is perfectly possible that other "unknown twins" are closely passing one another on the streets as their lives proceed in tandem. Some twins will live their entire lives without meeting, so we will probably never know just how often twins really are reared apart. The fact that some twins will never be reunited is unfortunate when we consider the happy partners with whom we have worked over the years.

I occasionally receive letters from twins in search of their twin siblings. These twins explain that they are sometimes mistaken for other people or are "seen" in places which they have never visited. Such events may be very informative clues (some of our reunited pairs have met due to such occurrences), and I encourage the twins to follow them up, if possible.

Some leads may prove disappointing. I find, however, that people are quite enchanted when the suggestion of their being a twin is raised because there is a special, indescribable quality to being a twin.

Elsewhere, I have written that people seem generally unenthusiastic at the prospect of a first meeting with a cousin or other distant relative. In contrast, a meeting with a parent creates a high level of interest and excitement. The idea of being a twin (especially an identical twin), however, brings an unmistakable gleam to the eye. The thought of confronting one's exact likeness is an opportunity that seems difficult to resist.

The Family Connection

The many joyous reunions that have occurred between reared-apart twins are poignant reminders that twins do belong together and that it is unwise to place them apart. The majority of the twins who have been reunited have developed lasting relationships, though identical twins appear to have a more immediate closeness and familiarity with one another.

A pair of identical female twins from Scotland, who met for the first time at the age of 64, are now sharing a home. A member of a fraternal female twin pair and her husband provide comfort and company to the twin sister who is widowed. The "Jim Twins," identical male twins from Ohio, are enjoying their twinship and searching for a writer to translate their lives' events and reunion into a book. Family get-togethers are never the same for families of reunited twins because they may include newly acquired in-laws, nieces and nephews and, in some cases, new sets of adoptive parents.

It is important to point out that for various reasons, some reunited twins do not go on to pursue the twin relationship. All of the twins, however, have valued the opportunity of meeting their twin siblings. Sometimes a brief encounter with a co-twin may effectively satisfy the curiosity surrounding one's biological past.

The Search Goes On...

Reared-apart twins appear to come in clusters. In other words, three pairs may be identified in a given week while, at other times, several months may pass before we hear of a reunion. It is possible that at any moment, a twin in search may stumble across the critical information that ultimately will result in a meeting. Twins may be unaware of the work of the Minnesota Center for Twin and Adoption Research and may search unsuccessfully for many years.

One of the participants in our study wept as she watched a television program about the Minnesota Study of Twins Reared Apart because the address of the center was not given; all the while, her twin sister's file was sitting in our desk drawer! Twins in search should write to: The Minnesota Center for Twin and Adoption Research, 75 East River Road, Elliott Hall, University of Minnesota, Minneapolis, Minnesota 55455.

In conclusion, Bouchard noted that his studies of reared-apart twins "have had more influence on the behavioral science field than we had anticipated. The impact has been positive, in that it has opened people's eyes to the many mysteries that are, as yet, unsolved."

THE FIREMEN TWINS, MARK AND JERRY: BEYOND BROTHERS

Identical twins Mark Newman and Jerry Levey were separated at three days of age and were reunited when they were 31 years old. They share an impressive list of similarities: Both are very tall (6 feet, 5 inches and 6 feet, 6 inches, respectively), are volunteer firemen, wear aviator-type eyeglasses, have similar moustaches, are balding, have an unquenchable thirst for Budweiser beer, wear belts with large buckles and carry key rings attached to the right sides of their belts. (This list is by no means exhaustive.)

Researchers at the University of Minnesota have studied other pairs of identical twins reared apart who also greatly resemble one another, but in different ways. There have, for example, been identical females who wore seven rings, three bracelets and a watch; and identical males who read magazines from back to front, wore elastic bands around their wrists and enjoyed sneezing loudly in elevators.

Mark has stated that finding his brother after 31 years simply felt as if Jerry had only been away on vacation for a while. In other words, the basis of a close relationship was present almost at the moment of meeting, leaving the brothers the task of merely filling in the details. He adds, "He (Jerry) is me—we don't need to find out about each other because we have lived our separate lives in parallel." They agree that their lives have not changed dramatically—each still has his own family, occupation and friends. Feelings of "someone being out there" or "something being missing" have, however, been satisfied.

The question of whether separated twins necessarily experience a sense of loss is often raised; and the answer to that question is "no." First, not all of our twins have described a sense of loss or incompletion. Secondly, many non-twins complain that some pieces of their lives are not in place. The key point, however, is that following reunions between identical twins (as in the case of Mark and Jerry, and many others), the "missing piece" is finally found.

Perhaps we are all looking for identical twins or someone with whom we can share complete trust and understanding. It is worth noting, for example, that fantasizing about having a twin is not uncommon. There are numerous examples in which the establishment of "twin like" relationships has proven especially supportive to people in times of stress. The advantage of having a built-in, lifelong anchor and support is a hallmark of most identical twinships.

Mark observes that he has always questioned the reasons for his adoption. His reunion with Jerry nearly two years ago has, however, made him wonder why he is still alive after having narrowly escaped several life-threatening situations as a volunteer fireman. "Maybe it was intended that I should meet up with Jerry. When you see an exact likeness of yourself, it makes you wonder about destiny, about the scheme of things. Nothing really phases or surprises me."

Fears and Phobias: Findings from Twin Research

by Nancy L. Segal, Ph.D.

The regularity and intensity of some fears over the course of the human life cycle, such as the fear of strangers and fear of the dark, have been well-established.

Richard J. Nally, Ph.D., of the Chicago Medical School, recently prepared an extensive summary of studies concerning the origins of fears and phobias. He noted that the fear of snakes generally develops in early childhood, but that the particular characteristics of snakes which induce fear are unknown. He encouraged researchers to construct various snake models to present to children of different ages in order to learn what cues may produce fear. Such studies would also help to identify methods for preventing or overcoming fears.

In another recent paper, Gregory Carey, Ph.D., at the University of Colorado, and Irving Gottesman, Ph.D., at the University of Virginia, emphasized the importance of twin studies for understanding genetic and environmental influences on phobic disorders and other behavioral disturbances.

Twin studies of common fears and phobias, especially in children, are unfortunately few in number. One study of young twin and non-twin pairs has examined children's perceptions of other children's fears. Several studies have compared the resemblances between identical and fraternal adult twins, and suggested that some fears may be genetically influenced. Finally, fears and phobias have been discussed in published studies of reared-apart twins and are currently being investigated by researchers associated with the Minnesota Study of Twins Reared Apart.

What Are Fears and Phobias?

Fears and phobias have sometimes been used interchangeably in both behavioral science journals and in the popular literature. Attempts have been made, however, to distinguish between them. Svenn Torgersen, Ph.D. of Oslo University in Norway, (whose research on twins will be discussed here) informs us that,

"Phobic fears, in contrast to normal fears, are elicited by relatively harmless situations and objects." Phobias seem, therefore, inappropriate or exaggerated responses to the events with which they may be linked.

A large population survey conducted in 1969 by Stuart Agras, M.D. and colleagues at the University of Vermont showed that about 75 people in 1,000 experience mild phobias. He noted that some common fears, such as fear of animals and heights, have a high rate of occurrence during childhood, but generally decline in adolescence and early adulthood. Other common fears, such as fear of death, illness, injury, separation and crowds, are most widespread during the late adult years.

Children's Perceptions of Other Children's Fears

The way in which children perceive their own fears and the fears of other children was examined by Eve Lazar, in 1969, at Columbia University's Teacher's College. Participating in his project were 43 members of same-sex twin pairs and 104 non-twin children. The children ranged in age from 7 1/2 years to 9 1/2 years. Everyone provided information about his or her own fears by responding to 24 items in a fear checklist. Twins additionally answered for their twin partners, while non-twins additionally answered for two classmates, one friend and one acquaintance.

The specific questions of interest were: 1) Do children believe that their own fears are unique or shared by others? 2) Is perceived similarity (or dissimilarity) in children's fears and the fears of others associated with closeness of the relationship? 3) Is accuracy in children's perceptions of other children's fears associated with closeness of the relationship?

An interesting finding to emerge from this study was that children do not regard their own fears as unique. Participants reported that they believed that their own fears were generally similar to the fears of others. Secondly, the findings showed that twins assumed greater similarity between themselves and their twin partners than themselves and acquaintances. Friends and acquaintances did not, however, differ substantially from one another in perceived similarity.

The investigator suggested that the fact of twinship per se, rather than closeness of the relationship, might explain the relatively high level of perceived similarity between twins. In other words, she suspected that twins might feel similar to one another just because they are twins, regardless of the quality of their social relationship.

I believe that this explanation is unjustified. The failure of the investigator to identify identical and fraternal twins, and to examine their answers separately, limits interpretation of these data. There was, furthermore, no adequate measurement made of the closeness of the twins' relationship.

A substantial number of studies using young and adult twins has demonstrated a generally closer bond between identical twins than fraternal twins. To the extent that the twin sample was primarily composed of identical twins, one could speculate that the social relationship did influence perceived fear similarity. The underlying basis of the twins' greater perceived similarity in fears must, therefore, await further investigation.

Lazar also found that twins did not show greater accuracy in predicting the fears of their co-twins than did the pairs of acquaintances. This seems somewhat surprising, given that identical and fraternal twins would be expected to know one another better than mere acquaintances. In a separate study, Lazar found that older children (in the fifth and sixth grades) were better predictors of other children's fears, than the younger participants in her initial study. It is therefore possible that the young twins in her study were unable to understand or articulate the fears experienced by their twin partners.

Studies of Adult Twins: Norway

In 1979, Torgersen reported the results of a twin study on common phobic fears. The major purpose of the study was to examine the relative contributions of genetic and environmental factors in the development of fears and phobias. Additional aims were to consider the relationship between phobic fears and personality and to explore the influence of phobic fears upon emotional and social adjustment. His findings were based upon interviews and questionnaires administered to 50 identical twin pairs and 49 fraternal twin pairs between the ages of 20 and 71 years.

First, the twins were questioned about events in their childhood histories, closeness with the twin partner and general interests. Next, a personality inventory was given to the twins to complete at home. Finally, the twins were asked to classify their strength of fear produced by 51 items, such as crowds, mice, blood, eating with strangers, and sharp objects.

Identical twins were more similar than fraternal twins on all phobias, with the exception of separation fears, suggesting a genetic influence on their strength and content. Torgersen explained that identical twin differences in separation anxiety were very strongly related to differences in emotional and social adjustment: The twin with greater separation anxiety had achieved a lower educational level and poorer occupational and marital adjustment and expressed more neurotic symptoms.

Identical twins were, therefore, not more similar than fraternal twins in separation anxiety. Fraternal twins showed a very high degree of difference in how they rated animal fears and mutilation fears. Even though fraternal twins share the same rearing environment, the dissimilarity of their answers in some categories suggests that they experience situations and events quite differently. Fraternal twins share half their genes in common, on average, so that differences between them may be explained by both genetic and environmental factors. The difference genetic make-ups of fraternal twin partners may be associated with their dissimilar experiences in the same home.

Torgersen identified certain characteristics in identical twins who received higher phobia scores than their twin partners. The more fearful twin tended to be second born, shorter at birth, more dependent, more reserved, and less self-confident in childhood. There is some evidence that second born twins, on average, may be more highly subject to birth hazards than firstborn twins, though continued research in this area is needed.

Some correlation between phobic fears and some personality traits was also observed. For example, dependence, lack of self-esteem and self-doubt were associated with all five types of phobias, suggesting that individuals who express such traits may be more fearful than those who do not. Personality studies of phobic patients have produced similar findings.

Studies of Adult Twins: Indiana

Two studies of adult twins were conducted by Richard J. Rose, Ph.D., and his associates at Indiana University. These studies were published in 1981 and 1983. In the first study, 151 college-age twin pairs and 66 pairs of these twins' parents completed a 51-item fear survey. The twin sample included 91 identical pairs and 60 fraternal pairs. The fear items were rated on a 7-point scale, ranging from *No Fear* to *Terror*.

Identical twins showed greater resemblance than fraternal twins in how they answered the items in the four categories, suggesting that fear responses (as measured by the Indiana University team) may be genetically influenced. An analysis of 10 specific fear items, such as snakes and thunderstorms, was additionally informative. A genetic influence on all items was observed, with the highest being for death of a loved one and the lowest being for deep water.

The second Indiana University twin study examined developmental and genetic influences on the acquisition and persistence of fears. The 51-item survey described above was completed by over 2,600 individuals between 10 and 64 years of age. This sample included more than 400 same-sex twin pairs.

First, it was shown that people in different age and sex groupings responded differently to items in some of the categories. Fear of water increased substantially for females after age 24 years, and increased fairly steadily, but less dramatically, for males after age 34 years. Fear of dangerous places consistently increased with age for both men and women, but the change was not substantial.

A twin analysis was conducted separately. The most intriguing finding to emerge concerned differences between twins in the age group of 19 years and below and twins in the age group of 20 years and above. It is important to note that twins in the younger group were generally living together, while twins in the older group were generally living apart. Identical twin resemblance increased slightly in the older sample, while fraternal twin resemblance decreased substantially in the older sample for items concerning loved one's misfortune and personal death. Rose commented that this study might be the first demonstration of age-related changes in genetically-influenced attitudes.

The observation of greater behavioral resemblance between identical twins living apart, as compared to identical twins living together, has been reported previously. Gordon Claridge, Ph.D., at Oxford University in England, found that identical twins who had lived apart for five years tested more alike on some ability and personality measures than identical twins who had always lived together. Claridge suggested that when identical twins live apart from one another, they can express their genetic potential without influence from the twin or twin relationship. Fraternal twins in the Indiana study showed some similarity only when they were living together and able to influence one another directly. Not all studies of identical and fraternal twins living apart and living together have, however, produced consistent results concerning relative behavioral similarity and dissimilarity.

Identical Twins Raised Apart

Comparison of adult identical and fraternal twins who have been reared apart from an early age provides a unique opportunity to examine genetic and environmental contributions to fears and phobias. Three early studies of reared-apart identical twins (by Profs. Horatio Newman, Frank Freeman and Karl Holzinger, 1937, at the University of Chicago; Prof. James Shields, 1962, in England; and Prof. Niels Juel-Nielsen, 1966, in Denmark) did not systematically gather data on fears and phobias. Some relevant material is, however, available in the case histories.

Fear of heights was described by twins, Rodney and Barry. Twins Dora and Brenda both maintained a fear of falling, although they differed in their attitudes toward physicians. Other fears jointly experienced by reared-apart identical twins included childhood fear of the dark and nightmares, childhood fear of pulling the chain that flushes a toilet, and fear of illness. Similarity of fears and phobias is impressive in reared-apart twins, but becomes even more so when the particular fear is rare or highly specific, such as fear associated with a toilet chain.

The Minnesota Twin Study

The Minnesota Study of Twins Reared Apart began in March 1979. Very early into the study, psychiatric interviews began providing evidence of genetic influences on the onset and expression of fearful behaviors. Six out of nine pairs of identical reared-apart twins were alike for the presence or absence of fears and phobias. Among these six twin pairs, three were alike for expressing no fears, while the remaining three were alike for expressing common multiple fears and coping strategies. Our most illustrative example concerns a pair of female twins who had a strong fear of the ocean. The twins dealt with this situation by backing into the water slowly up to their knees before turning around—this solution was developed *independently* on the part of each twin! Members of this particular pair also feared fast driving.

Researchers associated with the Minnesota Study of Twins Reared Apart administer an extensive fear questionnaire to all participants. Spouses of reared-apart twins also complete the fear questionnaire to better understand the frequency of common fears among the general population.

The available twin studies suggest that there are genetic influences on the development and persistence of common fears and phobias. It is important to appreciate, however, that the *degree* of genetic influence differs across the spectrum of various fears, and that many fears can be lessened by appropriate treatment programs or other intervention. Identical twins tend to share more fears than fraternal twins, but the expression of a given fear by one twin does not always signify the eventual expression of the same fear in the other twin. Results from large studies apply to groups as a whole, not to individual twins or twin pairs. Behavioral scientists are still a long way from fully understanding the development, maintenance and modification of common fears and phobias. Continued research with twins and adoptees will hopefully provide valuable insights.

Expressive Behaviors in Twins

by Nancy L. Segal, Ph.D.

Human behavior evolves from a very complex interaction among genetic and environmental factors. In other words, behavior does not only reflect the impact of objects and events in one's surroundings, but also reflects the types of environments to which an individual is attracted; this, in turn, may partly reflect one's hereditary predispositions. The manner in which the individual interacts with the environment to make it personally meaningful may, therefore, represent a unique blend of genetic and environmental influences.

Throughout the course of human history, researchers have attempted to answer the question: why are we the way that we are? Comparative studies of identical and fraternal twins have proven enormously valuable in this quest, by furnishing clues to the genetic and environmental processes underlying a wide variety of behavioral, physical and medical characteristics.

Twins: Some Fascinating Findings

In her 1981 book, *Identical Twins Reared Apart*, Susan Farber provides this short summary of findings concerning expressive movements in reared apart twins: "Though this section is the briefest in the chapter, the overwhelming similarity of gestures and mannerisms is one of the most pronounced observations of almost all studies."

The observation that the way we sit, stand, walk, speak, laugh and gesture may be influenced by hereditary factors is, possibly, of the most provocative findings to emerge from studies of twins, especially twins raised apart from early in life. Identical twins share all their genes in common, as compared with fraternal twins who share half their genes in common, on average, by descent. Greater resemblance between identical twins than fraternal twins is, therefore, consistent with (but not proof of), a genetic influence on the behavioral or physical traits being measured.

The quality and timing of vocal and gestural characteristics have not been extensively compared between identical and fraternal twins because these behaviors are very difficult to precisely measure. But interest in human expressivity is growing and twin studies are proving to be obvious ways of uncovering genetic and environmental influences on body movements.

In this article, I will draw upon findings from a number of published and ongoing studies (especially the Minnesota Study of Twins Reared Apart) that are concerned with the "how" of human behavior, such as how quickly or slowly a person speaks, or how vigorously, or leisurely a person walks. Responsive behaviors are closely associated with a person's unique identity.

Professor Sal Maddi, at the University of Chicago, calls this identity the "Johnian quality of John"—that special quality that distinguishes someone from other people. An important exception to this concept, however, may be found in identical twins. Therefore, I will attempt to show how, in terms of expressive behaviors, identical twins may be uniquely alike.

Body Posture

Individual differences in body posture and movement have often been regarded as learned behavior. Findings of similarity in body posture among identical twins reared apart (which suggests a genetic influence on this behavior) are, therefore, often greeted with amazement by some of our colleagues and members of the general public. We should appreciate that most people have favored positions for sitting and standing, preferences which are associated with how our bodies are constructed.

The monumental efforts of Dr. Claude Bouchard and his colleagues, at Laval University, in Quebec, Canada have shown that the physical characteristics and capacities of identical twins are more alike than those of fraternal twins. It should, therefore, not be terribly surprising to find that identical twins often assume similar postures. The fact that we frequently observe this phenomenon among identical twins reared apart suggests that different rearing environments, even different cultures in some cases, are not strongly related to body posture. Body posture is, in addition, a trait that does not receive a great deal of attention or training, so that identical twin similarity becomes even more impressive.

Case reports of identical twins, reared together and apart, contain numerous references to similarities in body posture. The Minnesota Study of Twins Reared Apart is one of the few twin studies attempting to systematically "capture" this interesting aspect of behavior by a variety of methods. On the first day of a pair of twins' week long assessment, Professor Thomas J. Bouchard, Jr., the Project Director, takes a series of unposed photographs of the reared apart identical and fraternal twins.

According to Bouchard, the twins are simply asked to stand with their backs to the wall. The (identical) twins seldom notice that they assume the same posture and hold their hands in the same way.

Gestures and Mannerism

Similarities in mannerisms and gestures observed among reared apart identical twin sets (from the Minnesota Study of Twins Reared Apart and other investigations) include intense nail-biting, rocking when tired, and making "puffing" noises while lost in thought. The very specific nature of these behaviors is striking, and may understandably be interpreted as "uncanny coincidence."

In *Identical Twins Reared Apart*, Farber noted, for example that, "Even if twins had ample reason for nervousness, the issue is not why they had nervous habits, but why they should express them motorically in such consistently similar ways."

Videotaped interviews provide an excellent method for recording gestures and mannerisms. This is because they allow for repeated analyses of behavior by many judges. Participants in the Minnesota Study of Twins Reared Apart undergo a series of individual and joint interviews during which they are asked to discuss their life histories and to provide opinions on a variety of topics. They are permitted to smoke and to sip coffee or other beverages if they wish, so as to obtain a representative sampling of behavior. Twins are videotaped in a number of ways: whole body shots, and close-ups of the face, hands and feet. They are additionally requested to walk, shake hands with the interviewer, throw, catch and draw. Participants are encouraged to speak as freely as they wish about the wide range of topics and issues that are presented.

Twins complete an activity called REFACT (Requested Facial Action Test). This procedure was devised by Paul Ekman and Wallace Friesen, at the University of California, in San Francisco. Twins are asked to show specific emotions on their faces and to perform certain facial movements, such as smiling, frowning and lifting an eyebrow. Responses are videotaped, and these tapes are currently being analyzed. To the extent that greater similarity is found within the identical twinships, relative to the fraternal twinships, we might gain additional insights into the contribution of hereditary and environmental influences on gestures and mannerisms. It is possible, for example, that common muscular characteristics underlie similar facial movements and expressions.

Participants also view an emotional reaction film. This film consists of several segments which become increasingly "difficult" to watch, and so elicit a variety of reactions from people. This type of analysis has never before been done using twins, and is sure to prove extremely informative with respect to relative similarity in identical and fraternal twins reared apart.

Voice

A recently reunited pair of identical male twins informed us that on their reunion night, they telephoned the father of one of the twins to tell him the exciting news. The twins took turns speaking with him, yet the quality of their voices was so similar that the father was unable to distinguish between them. Observations such as these are not uncommon among identical twins. In her summary of studies of twins reared apart, Farber emphasized that the "pitch, tone and overall characteristics of the twins' voices were so stunningly alike that almost all investigators made mention of the similarity." The twins even laughed alike.

One important difference between the reared apart identical twins, however, concerned stuttering. There was, unfortunately, insufficient information available for detecting a strong relationship between stuttering and birth or family history. More recent studies of twins reared together, by Pauline Howie, at the University of South Wales, in Australia, have found greater resemblance for stuttering among identical twins than fraternal twins, consistent with a genetic influence on this behavior.

There are, however, identical twin pairs in which only one twin displays stuttering, but the critical environmental factors have not yet been identified. (Identical twins share all of their genes in common so that any differences between them must be explained by prenatal or postnatal environmental events.) Most studies in this area have detected a higher proportion of stutterers among males than females.

Voice samples of twins have not been systematically collected and analyzed. Researchers associated with the Minnesota Study of Twins Reared Apart have been gathering voice samples in standardized fashion during the videotaped interviews discussed above. (Twins are asked to read several paragraphs out loud.) From the anecdotal material summarized so far, greater similarity between identical twins than fraternal twins is the anticipated finding.

What Lies Ahead

Expressive behaviors is an exciting and very rich area for research using twins. I believe that the major contribution in this field will eventually be the scientific demonstration and explanation of a wealth of observations on twins that has been accumulated over the years.

Activity in this field seems to have paralleled improvements in video camera technology. Video cameras enable the gestures and mannerisms of twins to be "taken apart" because they furnish a permanent record that can be repeatedly examined.

In a study of non-verbal interaction in identical and fraternal twins, recently completed by Barbara Mausser, at Hahnemann University, in Pennsylvania, young twins were videotaped during separate play periods, and the behaviors were later evaluated by judges. The sample was, unfortunately, too small to yield definitive conclusions, but larger scale studies are likely in the future.

Most importantly, perhaps, the fact that this study was conducted by an individual involved in creative arts and movement therapy demonstrates that twins are valuable research subjects to professionals in many diverse fields.

Parents who have collected moving pictures of their twins over the years are the owners of extremely valuable information. These films should allow mothers and fathers to determine if changes in expressivity occur in synchronized fashion within identical pairs. Similarities and differences within same-sex and opposite-sex fraternal twinships can be explored in this way. If researchers were to gain access to these films, it is possible that the relative roles of heredity and environment on some very subtle and meaningful aspects of human expressivity might be better understood.

Twins in Sweden: Reared Apart and Together

by Nancy L. Segal, Ph.D.

The Swedish Adoption/Twin Study of Aging (SATSA) has been gathering psychological and life history data on twins reared apart and on twins reared together since May 1979. The study is carried out in the department of environmental hygiene at the Karolinska Institute in Stockholm, Sweden.

The Swedish researchers include Dr. Nancy L. Pedersen, Dr. Lars Friberg, Dr. B. Floderus-Myrhed, and Dr. Jennifer Harris. The American investigators involved in the study include Dr. Robert Plomin, Dr. Gerald E. McClearn, Dr. John R. Nesselrode, Dr. Cindy S. Bergeman, Heather Chipeur, and Christine McCauley, from the Institute for the Study of Human Development at Pennsylvania State University in University Park, Pennsylvania.

Comparison of twins reared apart to twins reared together is an important research procedure because the incidence of twins reared apart is relatively rare, leading researchers to sometimes question how representative they are of twins, in general. If it can be proven that reared-apart twins resemble reared-together twins with respect to various psychological and physical traits, investigators may be confident that the findings based on studies of twins reared apart can be generalized to the broader population of twins.

For the SATSA Study, both members of 698 twin pairs, separated before the age of 10 years, received extensive questionnaires concerning their early childhood circumstances. Specific questions included the age at separation, reasons for separation, extent of contact with one another following separation, frequency of current contact, characteristics of the adoptive home, and biological relation of the parents who reared them. Half the twin pairs were separated by 1 year of age, and 80 percent were separated by 5 years of age. Twintype (identical or fraternal) was determined by responses to a physical resemblance questionnaire.

Areas of Study

Swedish reared-apart twins were compared with Swedish reared-together twins for **similarity in height and weight.** In general, the reared-apart twins did not differ substantially from the reared-together twins, though there were a few discrepancies; fraternal twin correlations for height were somewhat greater than expected, and the reared-apart fraternal twins from the older group showed less resemblance that the reared-together fraternal twins.

Measures of height and weight were obtained by self-report (rather than by direct measurement by investigators), a procedure which may introduce some inaccuracies into the data. An alternative explanation of the discrepancies noted above might be the misclassification of some identical twin pairs as fraternal because of misinformation.

Reared-together twins in the older group generally showed greater resemblance than reared-apart twins for **consumption of coffee; total alcohol, beer, wine and spirits; as well as heavy alcohol consumption; and smoking habits.** The reared-together twins were found to be much more alike in their degree of heavy alcohol consumption than the reared-apart twins.

In contrast, reared-apart fraternal twins in the older group were generally more alike than reared-together fraternal twins on these measures, especially for total alcohol consumption. This finding was unexpected and may possibly be explained by the misclassification of some identical twins as fraternals.

Identical twins reared apart in the younger group did not differ in resemblance for dietary and smoking habits from all the identical twins. However, resemblances for dietary and smoking habits for fraternal twins reared together in the younger group was generally greater than for fraternal twins reared apart.

Overall, resemblance for consumption of coffee and alcohol, and for smoking habits, was greater for twins reared together than for twins reared apart. Genetic factors appear to influence resemblances in these behaviors, but increased behavioral similarity for some measures among twins reared together may reflect the effects of a common rearing. Additional analyses of these data will be informative.

Twelve different mental ability tests were completed by Swedish fraternal twins reared apart. These 12 tests were organized to examine twin **similarity in general ability, memory, spatial ability and verbal ability/perceptual speed.** Testing was completed in groups of two to three individuals, and the majority were tested on the same day to avoid within-pair communication about the items.

The reared-apart fraternal twins in this sample showed substantial resemblance in general mental ability, a result consistent with evidence from other studies. In contrast, these twins showed more moderate resemblance for each individual test category that comprises general ability (memory, spatial ability and verbal ability/perceptual speed).

Resemblance across individual test categories between fraternal twins reared together was somewhat higher than for fraternal twins reared apart, but the difference was not substantial. Memory was the category reflecting the lowest resemblance for fraternal twins, regardless of rearing status.

Age at separation proved to be the only factor associated with twin similarity for verbal ability/perceptual speed. The result was, however, not in the anticipated direction. Earlier age at separation was related to increased twin resemblance. This would suggest that early shared environmental experiences do not necessarily lead to later resemblances in special mental abilities. The investigators caution that this finding is based on a small number of reared-apart fraternal twin pairs (only 29) so that additional analyses are required to confirm the findings.

Analyses of personality similarity in SATSA's twins reared apart are reviewed here by identical twin Christine McCauley, a member of the research team. The following information compares these findings with results from earlier studies of separated twins, and with ongoing studies of reared-apart twins in Minnesota and in Finland.

The Swedish and Finnish studies found less evidence for a genetic influence on some personality traits than did reared-apart twin studies conducted in Illinois (1937), England (1962) and Minnesota (1988). Because the twins in Sweden and Finland were systematically identified through population registries, they may be more representative of twins in general (since they include twin pairs who are both behaviorally and physically similar and dissimilar), while twins identified by other means (such as mistaken identity) may include a higher proportion of very similar pairs.

Swedish twins reared together were more alike than Swedish twins reared apart on some personality measures, such as extroversion and neuroticism. The age at separation and degree of separation were not found to be related to personality similarity. The only factor associated with some measures of personality similarity was length of time between separation and reunion; twins who met shortly after separation were more alike in neuroticism and impulsivity than twins who met for the first time later in life, or who had never met.

In contrast, the Minnesota twins reared apart and reared together were equally similar across 11 personality traits, suggesting that a common rearing does not influence personality similarity. Twins reared apart and together were also equally similar for neuroticism and extroversion in a study conducted at the University of Chicago in 1937, results consistent with those reported by the Minnesota study. However, twins reared apart were more similar than twins reared together in a 1962 British study.

WHAT AFFECTS PERSONALITY— HEREDITY OR ENVIRONMENT?

The Swedish Adoption/Twin Study (SATSA) is an ongoing study that focuses on twins during the last half of the life span; the average age of the participating SATSA subjects is 59 years old. Subjects in the project are a subset of the Swedish Twin Registry which includes information on approximately 25,000 same-sex twin pairs in Sweden. The nearly 700 pairs of twins from the registry who were reared apart in different families are the focus of SATSA.

The SATSA project utilizes both twins and adopted individuals to determine genetic and environmental influences on behavioral traits in areas of development, such as physical and mental health characteristics, family and social environments, and daily activities. Another primary area that the project focuses on is personality, including one group of personality traits called EAS (Emotionality, Activity Level and Sociability).

A substantial amount of genetic influence on these traits has been detected in studies of young children. Similarly, when the EAS traits were analyzed in the SATSA sample of middle-age individuals, a large degree of genetic influence was also apparent, leading researchers to conclude that approximately one-third of the variability among personalities in late middle age is associated with genetic differences among them. However, the degree of observable genetic influence was less than that observed in the younger samples included in previous studies.

Although genetics appears to influence personality, the environment has been observed to play an approximately equal role as genes. The most dramatic finding in SATSA and other studies is that the majority of variation in personality is due to environmental experiences that family members do not share. In other words, experiences that do not make family members similar to one another—the non-shared environment appear to influence personality more than shared experiences.

by Christine McCauley

Genetic/Environmental Effects on Dental Health

by Nancy L. Segal, Ph.D.

Twin methods are becoming increasingly appreciated by researchers in a wide variety of medical fields, including dentistry. My examination of the research in this area revealed an extraordinary number of dental characteristics for which resemblance has been compared in identical and fraternal twin pairs.

Greater resemblance within identical twinships, relative to fraternal twinships, suggests a genetic influence. Knowledge of how genetic and environmental factors affect dental health is vital to individuals responsible for treating dental problems and for planning preventive programs.

The information presented below, chosen from a large number of available twin studies of dental characteristics, was selected because of its usefulness to parents with young twins.

Dental Cavities

A study of genetic influence on the total number of caries was conducted by Dr. C.G. Fairpo, in the department of child dental health at the University of Leeds in England. Study participants included 100 identical twin pairs and 120 same-sex fraternal twin pairs ranging from 5 to 15 years of age.

According to Dr. Fairpo, genetic influence "may show its effect in a general susceptibility (or resistance) to dental caries as reflected in the total number of teeth affected in each twin." The DMF index, developed to compare the number of caries both within and between twin pairs, is the number of decayed, missing and filled permanent teeth. This formula was modified for use with twin children between the ages of 5 and 8 years who have primary molars.

In Dr. Fairpo's study, the identical twins showed greater resemblance than the fraternal twins, indicating that genetic factors influence susceptibility to dental caries. This was true for both permanent and primary teeth. This finding agrees with reports from some, but not all, earlier studies.

Dr. Fairpo suggested that contradictory results across studies may be due to differences in research methods used, and in the twins' ages. He noted that his results raise additional questions, such as whether genetic influences operate on individual teeth or on specific areas of individual teeth.

Dental Characteristics and Oral Clefts in Twins

Because oral clefts occur in approximately one in 1,000 live births among Caucasian populations and twinning occurs in approximately 1 in 80 births, clefts are infrequently observed in twins.

However, twin studies reveal important information about oral clefts and other dental abnormalities. For example, Elizabeth Bryan, M.D., a consultant pediatrician and senior research fellow at Queen Charlotte's Hospital in England, noted that research data has shown that identical twins are five times more likely than fraternal twins to resemble one another for cleft palate, an opening in the roof of the mouth. She observed the fact that at times, however, only one member of an identical twin pair has an oral cleft. According to Dr. Bryan, while both twins may have a genetic predisposition for this trait, prenatal environmental effects may differentially affect their facial growth and development.

The implications of oral clefts for dental age and for tooth formation in twins were investigated by Drs. Marjatta Nystrom and Reijo Ranta, in the Institute of Dentistry at the University of Helsinki in Finland.

In their study, twins with cleft lips showed advanced dental age, as compared with non-cleft-lipped twins, a finding that contradicts previous research. The investigators suggested that this contradiction among the findings may be due to the smaller number of twins included in the later work, as well as to different data collection procedures.

Asymmetry in tooth formation was not observed more often in identical twins than in fraternal twins, according to their study. However, a greater severity in the oral cleft was associated with increased asymmetry in the formation of teeth.

Dr. H.L. Bailit, at the human genetics branch of the National Institute of Health in Bethesda, Maryland, and colleagues, have suggested that dental abnormalities, increased asymmetry, delayed development and cleft may all be associated with adverse prenatal factors affecting organisms which are susceptible to stress.

In other words, there may be a breakdown in the system responsible for protecting the developing organism; improper nutrition or exposure to toxic agents may, consequently, harm the fetus to some degree. In a review of the literature on congenital malformations in identical twins, Dr. Bryan noted that the splitting of the fertilized egg may disrupt the normal development of the embryo, causing susceptibility to unfavorable environmental agents.

Dental Studies of Twins Reared Apart

Twins reared apart as infants and reunited as adults provide a powerful research design for examining genetic and environmental influences on medical and psychological traits. Resemblance between identical twins raised in dissimilar adoptive homes persuasively demonstrates the effects of identical genes.

The Minnesota Study of Twins Reared Apart, at the University of Minnesota, has been conducting dental studies since 1980. The investigators include Joann Boraas, D.D.S., John Conroy, D.D.S., and Michael Till, D.D.S., from the department of pediatric dentistry at the University of Minnesota. Similarity in a number of dental characteristics has been evaluated in 44 reared-apart twin pairs and in three reared-apart triplet sets.

According to the investigators, identical twins were similar to one another in the number of teeth present, percentage of teeth and surfaces restored, percentage of carious or restored teeth, tooth size and malalignment. In contrast, fraternal twins showed reduced resemblance on these measures, with virtually no resemblance in malalignment. These results suggest that genetic factors are influencing these characteristics. Such findings are especially impressive in view of the differences in diet and professional care in some co-twins' cases. Some measures, such as arch width of some teeth, were similar for both identical and fraternal twins. Other measures, such as overbite, were dissimilar for both identical and fraternal twin pairs. Dr. Conroy emphasized that the study provides fresh evidence that heredity plays a role in many aspects of dental health.

Recently, a study of periodontal (gum) disease in reared-apart twins has been initiated by researchers at the University of Minnesota.

Implications of Twin Study Findings

The finding that some dental characteristics may be influenced by genetic factors is vital to the establishment of treatment programs that are effective for different people. It is important to appreciate, however, that the findings may not apply equally to all populations.

For example, cross-cultural dental studies using twins, by Dr. R.S. Corrucini, from the anthropology department at Southern Illinois University in Illinois, and Dr. K. Sharma, from the anthropology department at Panjab University in India, found differences in some dental patterns between American and Indian samples.

It is also important to note that genetic influences do not imply that dental caries or other conditions are unavoidable. Proper diet and regular care contribute greatly, of course, toward ensuring good dental health.

CAN DENTAL SIMILARITY INDICATE TWINTYPE?

It is intriguing to consider whether the degree of dental similarity between co-twins accurately assigns them as a particular twintype—identical or fraternal. In order to address this question, a second objective measure of twintype must be available in order to compare the two sets of results.

In a 1963 study, A. Lundstrom found 94 percent agreement between twintype as determined by similarity in dental characteristics and similarity in various physical traits, including blood groups. A more recent study by Charles E. Boklage, Ph.D., from the University of East Carolina, and colleagues, found that assignment of twintype based on dental studies agreed with assignments from blood-typing for 86 percent of identical twin pairs and 92.2 percent of fraternal twin pairs.

Based on these findings, it appears that dental similarity is an accurate, but less than perfect, method for distinguishing identical and fraternal twin pairs. Blood-typing remains the most accurate procedure that is easily available.

COMING TO TERMS

Some acquaintance with dental terminology is necessary for understanding the research in this field:

- **Caries** is another word for cavities.
- **Dental age** represents dental maturity and is determined by the states of formation of permanent teeth.
- **Cleft lip** results from incomplete closure of the lip during development.
- **Cleft palate** is an opening in the roof of the mouth. Both of these features are present at birth in affected individuals.
- **Craniofacial morphology** refers to the form and structure of the skull and face.
- **Occlusal variation** refers to differences in the meeting of opposing teeth in the upper and lower jaws.
- **Orthodontics** involves changing the dental and skeletal form of individuals by specific clinical procedures.
- **Spatial position** refers to the angle or inclination of selected teeth.

Alzheimer's Disease: The Valuable Role Twins Play

by Nancy L. Segal, Ph.D.

In recent years, some progress has been made with respect to understanding the nature and transmission of Alzheimer's disease, though no cause of Alzheimer's has been proposed and no cure has been found. Several research teams have relied on twin studies to provide insight on critical issues because they are known to be quite valuable for identifying genetic and environmental factors associated with the origins of disease, age of onset and expression of symptoms.

This is accomplished by comparing resemblances between genetically identical twins and genetically non-identical (or fraternal) twins. Greater resemblance between identical twins, relative to fraternal twins, suggests a contribution by genetic factors. Identical twins share all of their genes in common, so that differences between them must be explained by environmental effects. Cases in which only one identical twin is affected with Alzheimer's can prove informative because the well twin may provide important clues as to prevention.

Thirteen twin studies of Alzheimer's are now published in the medical literature. The first single case study of Alzheimer's in identical twins was reported in 1955 by E.A. Davidson and colleagues. This was followed by a larger study of 54 twin pairs, published in 1956, by Franz J. Kallman, M.D., at the New York Psychiatric Institute. Reports from Dr. Kallman's study indicated that both twins were affected with Alzheimer's disease in 43 percent of identical twin pairs and 8 percent of fraternal win pairs. More recent analyses by L.E. Nee, M.S.W., at the National Institute of Health, and colleagues found that both twins were affected in seven out of 17 identical twin pairs (41 percent) and in 2 out of 5 fraternal twin pairs (40 percent).

The greater resemblance between identical twin pairs than between fraternal twin pairs in these studies suggests that genetic factors influence the onset and expression of Alzheimer's disease. Environmental factors also play a key role, however, because a substantial proportion of the identical twin pairs included both affected and unaffected members. As indicated above, behavioral differences between genetically identical twins must be associated with environmental factors. It is possible, however, that with time, some of the unaffected identical twins will display Alzheimer's symptoms. Nee and colleagues have observed that delayed expression of Alzheimer's in one twin primarily occurs among female twin pairs.

A large-scale study of aging twin veterans is currently underway by John Breitner, M.D., at Duke University Medical School.

Dr. Brietner's study aims to 1) determine the causes of the disease; 2) identify the factors influencing its course; and 3) specify methods for its delay or prevention. The plan is to use the 9,000 male twin pair veterans enrolled in the National Academy of Sciences Twin Registry. Twin pairs whose members have Alzheimer's will receive yearly examinations over a five-year period. This procedure should prove especially informative in the case of identical twin pairs with one affected member.

Preliminary study of the registry twins has been conducted, using 442 twin pairs (or 884 individuals) living in North Carolina and in neighboring states.

Questionnaires mailed to the twins to request their participation in research yielded 678 positive responses. Telephone interviews with these 678 twins identified 125 people whose health histories suggested Alzheimer's; these twins were further examined through interviews with family members. Eighteen twins with probable Alzheimer's were then invited to the medical center for comprehensive physical examinations. Examinations performed on the identical partners of these twins suggested some early symptoms of Alzheimer's disease.

This preliminary study suggests that over two percent of twins in the registry may be affected with this illness, a percentage which could provide some valuable information on the many aspects of the disease.

DIAGNOSTIC CRITERIA

Reproduced below are the diagnostic criteria for Alzheimer's, as indicated in the 1987 *Diagnostic and Statistical Manual of Mental Disorders (DSM-III)*:

- Dementia involving a multifaceted loss of memory, judgment, abstract thought and other higher cortical functions, and changes in personality and behavior.
- Insidious and gradual onset with a generally progressive deteriorating course.
- Exclusion of other specific causes of dementia by history, physical examination and laboratory tests.

WHAT CAUSES ALZHEIMER'S DISEASE?

Charles Embry, M.D., and Steven Lippman, M.D., at the University of Louisville School of Medicine in Louisville, Kentucky, note that several explanations for the onset of Alzheimer's disease have been proposed, but that none has been identified with certainty. The theories refer to genetic factors, exposure to viruses or toxic substances and defective immune systems.

John Breitner, M.D., has indicated that several investigators have observed associations between head trauma and Alzheimer's disease, though other investigated environmental risk factors have not been confirmed. Albert Heyman, M.D., at the Duke University Medical Center, did not find differences between Alzheimer's patients and unaffected individuals with respect to animal contacts, smoking behavior, drinking behavior, and unusual dietary habits. Alzheimer's patients did, however, show an increased history of head injury, and female patients showed a higher frequency of previous thyroid disorders.

KNOWING YOUR FAMILY'S HEALTH HISTORY

The brains of Alzheimer's patients reveal characteristic plaques and tangles. Melvin Konner, M.D., at Emory University in Atlanta, Georgia, defines plaques as "large, dark bodies now known to be agglomerations of dead nerve endings" and tangles as "abnormally twisted tubular structures within nerve cells." He notes that these features were first identified in 1906 in microscopic studies of the brain of an Alzheimer's patient by Alois Alzheimer, M.D., a German physician. Recent studies by David Hinton, M.D., and colleagues at the University of Southern California, suggest that a unique form of eye damage may be associated with Alzheimer's and could possibly help in arriving at accurate diagnoses.

It is also important to become familiar with one's family health history because Alzheimer's is known to occur in families. In a 1984 interview, Leonard Heston, M.D., in the department of psychiatry at the University of Minnesota, indicated that the brothers, sisters and children of Alzheimer's patients generally have a 33 percent chance of developing the disease at some point in their lives. The chance of becoming affected increases, however, if a close affected relative develops the disease in his or her forties.

It is important to realize, however, that having a close relative with Alzheimer's does not mean that all other family members will eventually become affected; it simply means that such individuals may be at somewhat greater risk for developing the disease than an individual without affected relatives.

Down syndrome has also been identified as a factor that increases predisposition to Alzheimer's disease. Dr. Heston has noted that individuals with Down syndrome (caused by an extra 21st chromosome) who reach 40 years of age will most certainly develop Alzheimer's, as well as leukemia. He has also reported that families with Alzheimer's patients have a higher risk of producing children with Down syndrome and leukemia; this risk appears, however, to be extremely slight.

A 1984 study by Albert Heyman, M.D., and colleagues, at the Duke University Medical Center in Durham, North Carolina, confirmed the association between Alzheimer's and Down syndrome families, but failed to detect a relationship between Alzheimer's and leukemia.

❤

CHAPTER 6

To Separate or Not to Separate

In Search of a "Self"

by Jane R. Hirschmann

Mary likes to spend time alone with each of her 4-year-old identical twin daughters. With this in mind, she plans a short outing with each of them once a week. Today, she is going out with Beth.

They get on the elevator of their apartment complex at the 17th floor; it stops on the ninth. Mary's friend, Mrs. Jackson, gets on, looks at Beth, and says, "Oh, how cute they are. Your girls always wear the nicest outfits."

Mary thanks Mrs. Jackson, but explains that there is only one child in the elevator, so there is no need to speak in the plural.

Mrs. Jackson looks indignant and replies as she exits, "But *they are* cute."

Mary and Beth start walking down the block and are greeted by another neighbor who asks Beth, "Where's your sister?" She explains the day's situation and off Mary and Beth go. On their outing, they are greeted by many more acquaintances who ask them the same question, "Where's your sister?" No one says, "Hi! How are you Beth?"

On the way back home, a playmate of Beth's sees them. The child's mother asks Mary if the "the twins" can come over to play. Mary says, "Of course, Beth and Sue can play with Sam."

When Mary got home and reflected upon her outing with Beth, she realized how very difficult it is for her twins to feel a sense of individuality. They were always referred to as a unit—"the twins." Often they were spoken to in the plural sense, as if they really were two peas in a pod. How can I respect the uniqueness of their twinship while helping each of my girls establish a sense of self apart from that close bond? she asked herself. Is it ever worth trying to educate the people who seem to find it difficult to relate to my twins as two separate people?

For Mary and other parents of twins to answer these questions, they need to understand how a child develops a sense of self and to think about the psychological steps most singletons take to develop into their own distinct personalities. Dr. Margaret Mahler, child psychoanalyst, wrote extensively about the psychological birth of the human infant. She described the road from oneness to separateness that all infants travel as they move toward selfhood.

This road of life begins with a close symbiotic tie to the mother. The infant's task over the next few years is to move from this close dependency and oneness with mother to a more separate and independent existence, both physically and psychologically. The closeness and trust that the infant has with her mother allows that infant to move gradually into the world. When things get scary or if there's rough going during a child's exploration, she comes back to her mother for warmth, love and support. Eventually this "refueling" gives the child the courage to go out once again to conquer the world.

In this process, the child develops a sense of herself as separate from her mother, which is different than the earlier notion of being one with her mother. Naturally, this process is a gradual one that takes place with forward and backward steps. There are pauses, struggles, accomplishments and frustrations—all necessary in the process of developing a sense of self.

Twins, like all children, must go through a psychological birth. But the interesting thing is that many twins have two primary attachments—one with their co-twin and one with their mother. When most singletons begin to move away from their mothers, they move off alone. A twin, on the other hand, may turn to her co-twin to lessen the blow. In a psychological sense, a twin may remain in a state of oneness with her co-twin, making it difficult to attain a distinct sense of self. Is it necessary for the twin to break this attachment to allow for the individualization the singleton develops as she begins to separate from her mother?

Breaking the Attachment

The answer to this question is a complicated one. One should never, nor should he want to, break the special attachment that exists between twins. Yet, all children need to emerge from a state of oneness (with their co-twin and their mother) to learn who they are and who they can be a s unique individuals. Therefore, twins need an environment where they will have the opportunity to be separate from each other in both a physical and psychological sense, so that each can go through a process of health separation and individualization from her parents.

While respecting the unique bond that is inherent in the twinship, parents of twins can provide opportunities where each child can grow as an individual. They can start by educating the community; tell their friends that they should refer to their twin children by name, for example, and discourage them from speaking (and thinking) of the children as "the twins." They also can avoid talking to their twins in plurals, and look for characteristics that are unique to each child without always making a comparison to the other. Parents of twins are continually asked, "Which twin is the extrovert and which one the introvert (or quiet vs. noisy, or well-behaved vs. poorly behaved)?" This type of polarization should be avoided.

Parents of twins can plan separate time with each child and encourage separate playmates so that each child has the opportunity to meet peers on her own terms. They also should allow them to have their own special possessions that they don't have to share. Twin infants don't need to be seated facing each other in their stroller all of the time; each should be allowed to face out and view the world from her own perspective. Not giving twins rhyming names and matching clothes, and if possible, placing them in different classes, after school groups, and camp bunks, will give each twin the opportunity to grow on her own, as well.

As parents of twins attempt to create a climate where their twins can be individuals, they should remember that there will be times when their twins will need and want to merge into the twinship (dress alike, for example). I advise parents to allow this to happen. An identical twin, Jack, wanted to dress like his co-twin, Bill, on the first day of school, for example. His mother was going to try to dissuade him until she realized it was his way of dealing with his fear of school and being in a different class than Bill.

Another example is when one set of 5-year-old twins went trick-or-treating on Halloween. This was their first Halloween experience where they wore costumes and went around with older children to strangers' homes. Their mother was shocked to hear them say to people who opened doors to them, "We're twins!" It finally dawned on this mother that, to her daughters, there was safety in numbers!

Relying on Twinship

Often when twins are facing a new anxiety-producing situation, they may rely on the twinship for safety. This is much the same as a toddler running to her mother's lap for security, or a child who decides to take a favorite stuffed animal from home to school as a way of feeling secure in a new situation. Basically, parents need to be attuned to their children's needs at the moment; for parents of twins, that may mean an awareness of when the reliance on the twinship is a return to home base.

To some, it may look like twins are more autonomous at an earlier stage. For example, when they are left by their mother, they may not experience the same separation anxiety appropriate for their age because they have each other. Yet, the reliance on the twinship can slow the separation process down. As you help your twins individualize you might see them go through stages that a younger child has gone through earlier.

It may be that the separation from the parent will occur after the partial separation from the twinship. And I say partial since there will always be a unique bond that won't (and shouldn't) be altered between twins. Parents of twins can only provide an environment where the individuality of each twin is allowed to flourish.

———————————————————— ♥ ————————————————————

How Much Togetherness— How Much Separation?

by Judith O. Hooper

If you are considering how much togetherness is appropriate and healthy for your middle-years multiples, here are some practical pointers to help you make an informed decision.

First, it is important for you to remember something which is so obvious that parents often forget to think about it. Your children are not simply "twins" or "triplets"; each is a unique individual who happened to be born as one baby of a multiple birth. Every human being born is unique. Being a co-twin is not a unique experience. But being Fred Jones, born, along with co-twin Jane Jones, on a certain date to certain parents living in a certain place, is a unique experience.

As you weigh your children's needs for togetherness and separation, be sure you remember to think about each individual child and his or her specialness.

Secondly, be aware that by the time your children have reached the middle years of childhood, a level of togetherness has evolved which is comfortable for them. This means, among other things, that making a radical change in the level of togetherness they experience is going to be quite difficult.

If one child wants and needs a change in the co-twin relationship, that is an important reason for you to intervene. If one twin is constantly dominating his co-twin, for example, or if they exclude all others from their relationship, you need to try to change these interaction patterns.

If, however, your concerns about their togetherness come from remarks made by "Grandma" and "Uncle Fred," or from some expert advice you have read on how multiples "should" interact, you need to remember that you know your children better than anyone. You will know, or sense in that mysterious way that parents can, when all is not well with your children. Until then, relax, smile at Grandma and Uncle Fred, and change the subject.

After carefully assessing your children's relationship in terms of their unique needs, you may decide to make some changes in it. By the middle years, many twins have developed their individuality to the point that they are naturally led to separate friends and activities. You can encourage this natural separation by gently noticing, reinforcing and praising each child's unique talents and interests (never by comparing or belittling).

Parents are likely to be much less concerned if multiples spend little or no time together. No doubt healthy separateness is more positive for children than dependent clinging. Nevertheless, being a twin or a triplet is a special gift, and co-twins speak of a closeness and a shared understanding that is profound and moving. If your children are not friends, try to think about why they are not. How could you encourage and promote enough togetherness so that they can give their special bond a chance to grow and develop?

As mentioned above, you are the world's greatest expert on your children. Trust your awareness of their needs to decide how much togetherness and how much separation is right for them.

❤

Voices of Classroom Experience

by Laurie S. McCreery

There are many advantages—expounded upon in virtually every source dealing with multiples' education—associated with separating twins in the classroom. However, very little attention has been paid toward the negative aspects of separating twins in school.

Had my husband and I been able to foresee some of the difficulties we encountered as a result of separating our fraternal twin sons, Tripper and Jamie, in kindergarten, we would possibly have kept them together. We share our experiences here so that they might be instructive to other parents.

Before making the decision to place the boys in the same or separate class-rooms, we discussed the issue with admissions officers and our pediatrician. We also learned that the public school's policy was to automatically separate twins unless the parents requested otherwise. All of these professionals supported plac-ing the boys in separate classrooms for reasons customarily cited, such as indi-vidual development and separate identities. We were convinced that the boys should be separated.

The difficulties which sprang from this decision were twofold. First, their kindergarten classes did fundamentally the same activities, but at different times. Consequently, Tripper came home from school the second week in September with a paper bag puppet which his brother's class would not make for another two weeks. No amount of explanation, understanding or making puppets at home would compensate for Jamie's hurt feelings of being "left out." This type of "crisis" recurred with both boys throughout the year.

Secondly, one class was taught by a teacher with a more dynamic, outgoing, enthusiastic personality than the other. While one of our twins came home every day bubbling about what his teacher had said or done, his co-twin began to feel as though he'd been "short-changed" on teachers and was missing something. His attitude was reflected in his daily performance, and he gradually lost all enthu-siasm and interest.

The parents of the other set of kindergarten twins (boy/girl), who had also been separated, had also noticed the differences between the kindergartens. We spoke to the teachers about the difficulties we were having, and they tried to rectify the situation. Unfortunately, the child in the "quiet" classroom was never fully convinced that his brother was not having more fun, adding to the stress both were already under in adjusting to kindergarten.

In conclusion, my husband and I both firmly believe in the importance of estab-lishing and maintaining the separate individualities of our boys. However, they are twins—and no amount of psychology will ever change or fully comprehend the special bond that is shared by twins. In this respect, they are totally different from singletons.

In hindsight, we would have kept our boys together for at least kindergarten. Five year olds find it difficult enough adjusting to the school situation. If placed in separate classrooms, twins have the added burden of learning to adjust with-out their co-twin. We believe our experience shows that sometimes the results are counterproductive.

The ABC's of Classroom Assignments

by Fran Bevington

Every spring (or summer), school personnel have the task of selecting the appropriate classroom for each child in their schools. But in the cases concerning triplets (or more), school personnel must also take into consideration whether each co-triplet will be in a separate class, in the same class as both his co-triplets, or whether a combination of two together and one separated will result.

Occasionally, when a school only has a small number of classrooms, choices are limited. But much more often, two or three classrooms are available at each grade level and the decision is based on desirability rather than necessity. Many professionals agree that three categories, "The ABC Factors," (academic, behavioral and companionship) should be considered by parents and school officials when determining classroom assignments for multiples.

The Academic Factors

The underlying rationale of any school placement decision is concern that each child feels comfortable proceeding at his own level rather than feeling pressured to compete with his co-triplet. Even when triplets are identical, there can be variation in each of the inherited intelligence determinants due to intrauterine and environmental influences. Fraternal multiples can also exhibit very similar or different levels of intellectual development.

Keeping these possibilities of individualizing intellectual differences in mind, parents and teachers are the most valuable observers of school readiness in a child. Regarding the decision about whether or not to enroll a child in kindergarten, most school districts conduct required or optional pre-kindergarten testing, usually done in the spring when children register for the next school year. For example, the Mesa Public Schools in Mesa, Arizona, administer a test called the Readiness Skills Inventory to discern if a 5-year-old child is ready kindergarten.

According to John E. Anderson, Ph.D., of the University of Minnesota, an authority on child psychology and development, the father of two pairs of adult twins and the grandfather to another twin pair, "The problem of separating or keeping twins together in school depends upon characteristics of the twins themselves. If they are nearly equal in ability and have common academic interests, there is no reason to separate them. But if they differ markedly in ability, with one co-twin or co-triplet advancing more rapidly or more slowly, it may be advisable to separate them or even place them in separate schools."

Mesa Public School psychologist Louise Goldstein adds another factor for parents to consider when evaluating the academic abilities of their multiple children—the factor of language development. "Separating all three children in a triplet set may help foster individual communication skills," she noted, "especially since language development is often delayed in twins or other premature children."

The Behavioral Factors

Just as triplets can differ academically, they can also exhibit very different personality styles. One child in the trio may be much more aggressive or passive than the other two, for example. Goldstein believes that it is important for each multiple to cultivate his own personality without being overshadowed by his co-triplet.

Terrie Keck, a first grade teacher in Marlowe, Oklahoma, and an identical triplet herself, agrees with Goldstein and notes that the dominant child should not be placed in the same room with the least dominant, if at all possible.

When deciding on classroom placement for your multiples, you, as the parent, are the best source of information for school personnel regarding the personality type of each of your children. In a preregistration conference with the school principal and/or teachers, it is important that personality differences are made obvious and clear to all involved in the decision-making process. This can eliminate conflicts which may occur if triplets or quadruplets enter classrooms without regard to their behavior patterns.

The Companionship Factors

Frequently, multiples develop very close and sometimes very dependent bonds with each other. Boy/girl triplet combinations often provide obvious evidence of this.

For example, my two boys, Shane and Sean, have interests so similar that their relationship is much closer than that between each boy and his co-triplet sister, Ashley. When one of the two had difficulty with another child in preschool, he would simply call for his brother, and the two would then gang up on that one child. Their preschool teacher recommended that Shane and Sean be placed in separate classrooms the next year; during that year, each was able to develop his own social coping skills.

Too much interdependence among triplets is a behavioral style that Keck would like to see corrected by appropriate class placement. Based on her own experience as an identical triplet and as a teacher, she recommends all children in a set of multiples be placed in separate classrooms whenever possible. This she believes, encourages individuality.

On the other hand, the companionship encouraged by placing twins together can be beneficial for the educational development of some co-twins or co-triplets, according to Otha Davis, principal of Garfield Elementary School in Springfield, Virginia. Although one set of triplets at his school was separated into three different classrooms, Davis cited a special case in which twin boys moved to the United States from a foreign country. They were placed in the same classroom in Garfield School because their parents, principal and teacher believed that the two children would benefit from the mutual support.

Davis noted, "Sometimes it is valuable to place multi-birth children together, such as in times of tragedy or family stress, because they may truly need the support of one another."

When analyzing the ABC Factors listed above, parents and administrators need to remember that classroom placement can vary from year to year and that school success can be found in any of the possible combinations, as these following families exemplify:

- **Molly, Nellie and Anna Sandman, triplets from Lockeford, California, have been in the same classroom each year for all five years of their schooling.** Bert Sandman, the girls' father, remarked that each of the girls achieves at about the same level academically and works cooperatively in studying at home, even providing support for one another academically.

- **Joey, Andy and Marguerite Timm have been separated during each of their three school years.** Their parents, Damon and Diane Timm of Chandler, Arizona, believe that the three children have individual interests, so separating them in school is a logical outgrowth of their very different personalities.

- **Eight-year-old Jonathan, Joshua, and Naphtali Gunther of Highland, California, have been "placed" differently from year to year.** Because their school has only two classrooms per grade level, one of the identical boys has previously been paired off with his sister. But in the current school year, Jonathan and Joshua are in the same room while Naphtali is in a different classroom. Sheila Gunther, the triplets' mother says the "two and one" combination works well, and the child in a separate classroom does not feel left out.

Success in school depends, of course, on more than just classroom placement. Parents of multiples must do their best to smooth the way for their multiples' adjustments to and acceptance of their teachers, as well as their "fate" of being with or without their co-triplets in a classroom.

Multiples, especially as they get older, will have their own opinions on classroom placement, and these are not to be totally disregarded. But by checking where one's multiples stand on the ABC Factors checklist, having open discussions with educators about each grade level's teacher and classroom availabilities, and using parental instincts to guide the process of fitting the arrangements to each child, school placement choices can be made with confidence and to the benefit of teachers, students, and parents alike.

Mixing Individuality with Education

by Patricia Ireland and Peggy Pizzo

Adolescent twins have greater need than average singletons to strengthen their identity and autonomy in and out of their school environment. Besides the usual developmental push toward identity formation and self-reliance, an adolescent twin feels extra pressure to distinguish his identity from that of his twin and to move toward greater ability to function on his own.

During adolescence, twins must sort out, not only who they are in respect to all other people, but also—and most especially—their uniqueness and individuality in respect to each other. For many twins, this means clearly learning and feeling comfortable with the fact that one may be different in many ways from the other, and that they may be alike in some ways. Growing twins and their parents sometimes panic when twins indicate some similarities, thinking that this means that the twins have failed to establish their individual identities. This is not so—what makes any individual unique is his particular constellation of qualities among which may be some qualities he shares with any number of other people.

In addition to carving out their separate identities, adolescent twins need to learn that they are increasingly able to manage and direct their own individual lives, not only apart from their parents but apart from each other.

Therefore, if it is important for all adolescents to have access to various options and choices in their schools, it is even more important for twins to have this access. Each twin needs an opportunity to discover as freely as possible in a noncoercive atmosphere, a variety of intellectual and vocational roles, ways of interacting with other people, and learning styles. If the options and choices a school offers are too few, a twin may find himself constantly colliding with his co-twin in a way that limits his "space" and psychological freedom, including freedom from coercion from a twin.

This need for access to extensive diversity, however, does not mean that adolescent twins should necessarily be sent to separate schools, or that it is cause for alarm if your twins choose some similar educational and extracurricular activities. The key word is "access," for as Drs. Judy Hagedorn and Janet Kizziar point out several times in their book, *Gemini: The Psychology and Phenomena of Twins*,

twins should neither be forced together nor forced apart, but consistently encouraged to follow their own paths—even if these paths sometimes take them in similar directions. There is nothing wrong if both twins choose to play in the school band or to study advanced algebra, for example, as long as they are choosing to do so freely and honestly, have had chances to opt for other things, and see their choices as integral parts of their own separate developing identities and not as decisions they must make together in order to feel "safe."

"Early adolescents need to try on a wide variety of roles," Dr. Joan Scheff Lipsitz said in her study of young adolescents, *Growing up Forgotten*. Lipsitz is the founder and director of the Center for Early Adolescence in the School of Education, University of North Carolina, Chapel Hill.

According to Lipsitz, adolescents are primarily oriented toward their need to develop a strong sense of who they are—unique and individual human beings. In order to do this, adolescents need to be able to explore and "test out" a great variety of choices and options in educational settings.

Opportunities to experience what's involved in being a mathematician, artist, scientist, or writer, for example, are what help kids discover for themselves where their talents, interests and identities best lie. Similarly, a wide variety of extracurricular activities enable teenagers to determine the degree to which the words "athletic," "competitive," "philosophical," "cooperative," and "political" describe who they are, and who they are becoming.

In the same way, different educational formats, such as classroom lectures, small group work, internships, work experience, and group projects give adolescents a chance to identify their strongest and weakest cognitive and learning styles as well as other aptitudes. By testing out different educational formats, adolescents learn to utilize self-knowledge as they move toward their future and to relate this knowledge to their growing sense of the larger world.

Within these formats, adolescents' identity formation will thrive better if they are given opportunities to experiment; to experience "real life" situations; to learn by reflecting, singly or in groups, on these experiences; to discover insights and concepts on their own instead of always being told about them; and to express their experimental, changing sense of themselves, even if that sometimes means a different style of clothes or hair color every week. Research shows that schools that are overly regimented, authoritarian, or insistent on uniformity or rigid consistency, backfire educationally and produce drop-outs rather than scholars.

Besides these instructional modes and approaches, an adolescent also needs varied interactions with a diversity of other people, as well as periods when he can be alone in order to best perceive, contemplate, embrace and integrate his "differentness." Finally, since decisions and choices are what most reveal and strengthen identity, they need to be able to ponder decisions and make choices from among elective courses, extracurricular activities, educational formats, and curricular directions to maximally benefit from these opportunities.

Schools or parents who offer children no options, or make all the decisions and choices for them, are frustrating the adolescent's fundamental need to form a clear sense of who he is. Adolescents who are frustrated this way often cease to cooperate, as a kind of self-protective measure.

Though it's unlikely that the right school or schools, or combination of school and extracurricular activities, will produce cries of, "I love school!" from your adolescent twins, well-considered decisions in these areas can result in happier, more school-oriented children.

———————————————————— ❤ ————————————————————

Helping Teachers Avoid the Unit Approach

by Barry E. McNamara

Since I became a parent of twins, I have realized that many people seem to think of twins as public domain—making all kinds of comments to them and their parents such as, "Better you than me," "How do you manage" and "I'd die if I had twins," about the relative ease or discomfort involved in helping them grow up. I believe that teachers in particular must become aware of the effects of twins being addressed and responded to as a unit—a pattern that erodes each twin's sense of self-acceptance and individuality.

Through today's parent education programs and teacher in-service training, many educators, as well as parents, often have increased opportunities to become aware of the effects that their verbal responses have on children's behavior. When interacting with co-twins in a school setting, educators also need to keep in mind the negative effects of certain methods of responding to co-twins.

Whether they receive positive or negative comments about being a twin, the central question surrounding the nurturing of each twin is individual identity. Can students who are co-twins see themselves as valuable, contributing, worthwhile members of their class because of the reinforcement given to each one's efforts? Or does each see himself as inextricably united to his twin sibling because he only receives reinforcement as a member of this set? Comments such as, "You and your brother are so smart" or "You and your sister are so cute," can reinforce this latter notion.

This is not to suggest that there are only negative aspects of being a twin, or that one's twinship is something that should be denied. But, I repeat, to increase the self-acceptance of each co-twin, each needs to be judged and reinforced based on his individual efforts and achievements and not solely as a member of a twin set.

One way teachers may undermine this goal is by attempting to find some characteristic (psychological intellectual and/or physical), however inconsequential, that differentiates the two students. Often, the act of labeling a student by saying, "Mary's the verbal one" or "Sue's the shy twin," causes it to be a "self-fulfilling prophecy." The differences between the co-twins may simply be due to a teacher's perceptions or may be strengthened by them. By not labeling each twin, teachers are giving each the chance to emerge as a unique individual.

Practically speaking, it has been well-documented by research studies on twin behavior that twins will shift from being "passive" to being "aggressive" or from being successful in one academic area to being less proficient. For example, once a teacher notes that one of the twins is better in reading comprehension than his co-twin, the co-twins may flip-flop in their performances. This fact should caution educators and parents against the arbitrary labeling of students' behavior and attempts to find differences between twins.

The goal of reinforcing the individual identity of co-twins is also undermined when teachers give twins the impression that they don't know who each is or can't distinguish between them. They may make comments to the twin pair such as, "I can never tell you apart" or "I'll never get you straight."

Unfortunately, when teachers simply cannot tell co-twins apart, being able to do so often becomes a badge of merit. Instead of staring at the twins and trying to "guess" names, a teacher needs to ask the children their names and attempt to recall their names in the future by associating one of the twins' names with that person's face.

Like singletons, children who are twins need to be responded to by their educators (and everyone else) as individuals. The fact that they happened to be born at the same time should not diminish this basic human need.

———————————————— ❤ ————————————————

Facing the Separation Dilemma: Part I

by Marion P. Meyer

What are parents' responsibilities in building a solid foundation for twins' education? Twin rearing is mainly the responsibility of the parents, but the impact of outsiders cannot be ignored. As the twins reach puberty, they begin to assume some of the responsibilities of shaping their own lifestyles. It is our job as parents to teach them right from wrong and give them the tools to become happy, well adjusted, useful adults.

Encouraging the development of unique personalities and individuality does not deny the twinship. It does help avoid the hazard of overdependence. This is the reason for the persistent request to dress the twins differently most of the time.

One reason for dressing twins alike all the time is to ensure the public response to one's specialness in being a parent of twins. This concept is difficult to accept but is nevertheless true. If babies are always dressed alike and therefore always create excitement when they go out, they, too, will quickly learn to depend on this impact as a means to reinforce their impression on the group.

If your children have been given most of their clothing in pairs that are alike, encourage them to wear (or dress them in) different outfits most of the time. Duplicate outfits of clothing do not need to be worn at the same time.

One expert, Edith Neisser, states in her book, *Brothers and Sisters*, "If twins enjoy being dressed alike, and most of them do, they need not be deprived of that pleasure. But if they are *not* always urged to wear identical outfits, each child will tend to rely on herself and her innate strength rather than the magical powers of twinship in meeting daily contact with the real world."

As the children become toddlers, be sure that they have exposure to and experience with groups of children. This can be in a religious school, an organized play group, or a day care center. Time away from mother is very important. Encourage separate playmates as well as shared playmates. Let each twin have the chance to play outside at home or to visit a friend or relative alone. Plan separate outings with daddy! These experiences will be helpful to the child and will help the parent to know and to enjoy each twin as an individual.

Gradual Separations

The gradual separations will not be easy to accomplish, and the first visits away from home alone may not be completely successful. If both parents will take the time to do special things at home and away from home with each child, these gradual separations will be successful. This is another small step toward the goal of individual development which is recommended by so many professionals.

Dr. Herbert Collier, father of fraternal boy/girl twins, psychologist, and author of *The Psychology of Twins* recommends "Identical twins, tending to be more dependent on one another, should probably be weaned from each other gradually from a very early age...If occasional separations are made prior to the start of school where one twin has the opportunity to be apart from the other twin on weekends or even briefly during the course of the weeks, then over dependency is not likely to occur."

In other words, all experts tend to agree that occasionally being apart is good for each child. The separations should be very short at first, and with one of the parents or a familiar baby sitter or relative.

Preschool or Day Care

Preschool play experience or day care centers can be a good experience if both parents and teachers encourage gradual individual development and minimize the "pair" activities. At home it takes a special effort on the part of the mother to do different things with each child. Within an organized play group it is easier to make opportunities for each twin to play with other children and have brief separate activities.

Neither parents nor the teachers should rush the process of individual development. Adults provide the opportunity and encouragement, the child must make his own progress. Most twins, like most singletons, will be shy entering into a new situation and will tend to rely on each other to help them adjust. Care should be exercised to let this be an advantage and not become a crutch. Singletons must make this adjustment to group activities alone; a twin will have his co-twin to help him grow towards independence. As the children have different experiences, they will share them, and each child's experience is expanded because of this. If the first attempts at separation do not work, wait a while and try it again.

If the children attend a day care center or nursery school, separate activities can be encouraged after the children make the adjustment to being a part of the group and away from home.

Parents of twins (or more) have the same choices to make as do the parents of singletons, with the additional factor of having to consider the needs of two children of the same age. Another factor in carrying out this decision is the availability of schools with different classrooms within the same or a nearby school. School policies on the placement of twins must also be considered.

One underlying theme remains. Do not wait until it is time to register your children for school before deciding whether you want to place them in separate classrooms or keep them together in the same room.

PRACTICAL WAYS TO ENCOURAGE SEPARATION

Specific ways to enhance the individuality of each child are:

- Think of and treat the babies as two people.
- Plan for the babies arrival as two separate and different individuals. Avoid rhyming and like-sounding names. It might seem cute at the time of birth, but it could be confusing to the babies and yourself.
- Refer to and call each by his own name in order to establish they are two people and not one pair. If new parents make a conscious effort to think of and speak to the children separately and by given names, they will have accomplished the first steps in reaching their goals.
- Parents must have the courage to insist that playmates, neighbors and relatives call each twin by his own name. At first parents may be embarrassed to correct outsiders who ask, "Where are the twins?" but the end result does make this sacrifice worthwhile and, in the long run, the outsiders will respect your concepts.
- Even when the babies are small, assign each to his own sleeping place.
- Have some clothing and toys for each baby to help him establish pride of ownership.
- Have some toys to share to enhance the twins' natural tendency to share with each other.
- Spend some time alone with each child each day.
- Learn to recognize the subtle differences in each twin.
- Start the practice of dressing them differently for ease in identification.

Facing the Separation Dilemma: Part II

by Marion P. Meyer

Parents of twins must take the same choices about schooling as parents of singletons, but also must consider the special needs of two children of the same age, the availability of a school with different classrooms within the same grade, and school policies on the placement of twins.

Before parents register their twins for school, they should decide whether to separate them in different classrooms after consulting with the school principal about the availability of more than one classroom per grade, the school's policy on separation, as well as an assessment of the twins' individual needs and abilities.

Making the Decision

If the children are fraternal twins of vastly differing appearance, development, abilities, and interests and have had some separated experiences, they most probably will make better progress in separate classrooms, It is important for parents to understand that a more docile, "follower" twin needs to have his rights protected and have the chance to speak for himself; therefore, separation of twins who have an aggressive/passive relationship may be advisable, too.

According to research at the Gesell Institute, extremely dependent, shy, immature twins who cling to each other and have trouble adjusting to school may need to be together. The contradictory nature of the findings suggest that parents should decide for themselves how to let the twinship be an advantage for their children.

Planning for Separation

If parents are leaning toward separating twins in school, they must make a conscious effort to always think of the twins as individuals, dress them differently at least part of the time, refer to each by his given name rather than "the twins," spend time alone each day with each child, and encourage separate activities part of the time. If the twins adjust to these measures, they usually can attend school (even kindergarten) in separate classrooms with very little difficulty. Following preparations such as these and progressive separations, twins do not usually need the "crutch" of the twinship to adapt to school. They are usually able to make the adjustment like a singleton child.

Even with planned preparations for separation, one or both may pine for the other during the adjustment period. If the parents, principal and classroom teachers agree in the preregistration conference, school rules regarding complete separation of classroom activities may need occasional relaxation. If one twin needs the temporary support of the other, he could look through the window at the co-twin or join his co-twin during playtime, recess, or snack time, for example.

A Personal Perspective

In my twin girls' grade school, the second kindergarten classroom was directly across the hall from the first. During the first month of school, the more shy twin often looked over to the other room to feel secure that her sister was all right. Each class had separate playground areas, but the teachers would let the lonely twin seek out her co-twin during the first months of school. By their 5th birthday in late October, the adjustment had been successful with each child. They didn't even want a joint class birthday party!

Both parents and teachers may work toward the goal of separation, but, unlike this case, emotional disturbances may occur in one or both of the twins that may seem severe enough to postpone placing them in separate classrooms. This is the time, advises the Main Line Mothers of Twins in their book, *Twins: A Guide To Their Education*, to wait patiently and try separation the following year.

If the grade school where you live has only one classroom per grade or the classes are set up by ability so that separating the twins may cause one twin to be grossly misplaced, your twins' classroom teacher may be challenged by trying to promote the individuality of each twin.

Make a special effort to help her by dressing the twins in different outfits, which will encourage her and the other children in the class to think of each twin as a unique person. A teacher in this situation will usually place the children in different parts of the room and in different work groups.

The Same Class

With extra patience and effort, a teacher with a set of twins in her classroom should gradually encourage small separate activities as the children adjust to the school experience. Later, she can challenge each child to work at his own level and progress at his own rate. Of course, no teacher or parent should ever compare the performance of each twin in front of the children or the class.

It is the parents' responsibility to check frequently with the school to see how their children are progressing during this adjustment period. Even in different classrooms, the children may have similar assignments and be smart enough to divide up the homework. "You do the math, and I will do the spelling" may work out for the clever twin who understands the math, but is a dismal failure for the child who thinks the spelling words could be learned by osmosis!

During this same adjustment period, teachers need to keep the parents informed of the progress at school and point out even trivial areas that could become potential problems. Prevention, it seems, is crucial to avoid later conflict. Teachers must be sure that each child speaks for himself, learns to use a singular pronoun when speaking of himself, and begins to make contact with other children in the room.

Author Anne Corrigan writes, "Teachers need to be aware that though twins are separate people, they do have a special bond. Parents should realize this and try to respect this bond and still create a self-sufficiency in both children."

When children are in the same classroom, the teachers may find that the two are never apart. They may even sit "alone" together and not try to make any friends or to participate with the group.

According to *Twins: A Guide To Their Education*, "When the twins finally do make a friend, even if it is the same one to be shared, the teacher may use him as a wedge, seating him between the pair, thus separating them. Later, she can try to break up the trio as often as possible by assigning separate partners for tasks and games. Separation during the rest period may be the last stage of this gradual drawing apart."

Teacher Communication

Whatever decision is made, there must be a close, supportive alliance between the parent and teachers.

Whenever teachers asked me how to tell my identical girls apart, I would point out the subtle physical differences or the barrette color-coding and then say, "Get to know each child; then you will readily identify her by her personality. If you are confused when you see one in the hall, talk to her a minute. If you are still uncertain, then you can be sure it is the co-twin and not the child in your classroom."

A sensitive teacher can observe when the children are ready to pursue separate activities part of the time without her forcing the issue. Psychologist Dr. Herb Collier, a father of boy/girl twins and author of *The Psychology Of Twins*, writes, "Far too often, twins can become much too dependent on each other because they tend to play together while at home and may not reach out for other playmates. If they are in the same classroom at school, separating identical twins in the primary grades is probably beneficial because it allows each child to feel more unique and assists him in developing his own identity as a person."

According to the authors of *Twins: A Guide To Their Education*, if kindergarten provides the child's first real school experience, it is important that he has the opportunity to respond to this new experience in his own way, to have his teacher observe him as an individual rather than as one-half of a whole. Some parents may choose to put each twin in his own school if each has very different abilities. For example, if Mary is very bright and Sally of more average ability, Sally may feel more comfortable in a school where Mary is not around to be compared to academically; if Sam has special physical or psychological problems and Tom does not, Sam may have a better school experience in a specialized school.

The First Day of School

Once the decision is made to separate the twins in school, be sure to present the facts to the children in a positive, constructive way. Allow them to express their concerns over starting to school. Be aware that there can be difficult adjustments even though you feel very comfortable with your decision and have made careful preparations to implement it.

An experience we had with our twins confirmed my belief that parents must also help teachers confront problems. On the first day of school, two very happy and excited girls left my car and ran into the school. "Don't come in, Mommy, we're big girls," they shouted.

I waited in the school lobby, quite at a loss of having my babies leave home. Just as I decided it was time to go home and enjoy my "freedom" for the first time in five years, one of the teachers came running down the hall in a panic. Somehow the girls had gone into the wrong classroom. The mistake was not discovered until one of the girls objected to being called by the wrong name.

The teacher said, "Please help! We don't want to make them cry, but they are in the wrong class!" With great trepidation, I went into the room, took the twin by the hand and said, "Naomi, you are in the wrong room. Let's go over and get Ruth and switch classes." The only people upset were the three adults; each child just wanted to be sure her teacher knew who she was.

Research and personal experience have shown that high school experiences and adult separation of twins will be greatly influenced by the success or failure of gradual separations in the early years and grade school.

THE SEPARATION GOAL: INDIVIDUALITY

Results from The National Organization of Mothers of Twins Clubs, Inc. survey of teachers of twins show the overwhelming majority of teachers believe separating the children reduces competition and dependence between the twins, gives twins experience away from each other, and allow each child to be thought of as an individual.

Teachers Should:

- Avoid comparing or confusing abilities and performance of each child.
- Be able to tell the children apart.
- Be aware of role switching and, if it occurs, how it may affect the teacher-child relationship.
- Be aware that even independent twins will have a special kinship and bond.

Parents Should:

- Maintain a close working relationship with the teachers.
- Schedule separate conferences for each child, even when they are in the same classroom.
- Encourage development of independence while protecting the special twin bond.

❤

Same or Separate Classes?

by Barry E. McNamara and Francine J. McNamara

Parents of twins may be confronted with many issues regarding the education of their children. However, whether to place them in the same class or different classes is a primary decision that should be considered long before the children enter school. The purpose of this column is to discuss the concerns surrounding this issue and to provide information that will enable parents of twins to make an informed decision about separation for their family.

To place twins in the same class reinforces society's stereotype of twin children as a "unit," with little attention being given to their individual attributes. Therefore, we support the notion of placing twins in different classes to reinforce the individual student's identity in the world of schools.

Researchers have suggested that when twins are placed in different classes, educators are forced to see each student as an individual. No doubt, they will continue to be compared by school personnel. However, these comparisons will be greatly reduced if each child has his "own" teacher. Over the years, we have "interviewed" a number of adult twins and asked their opinion about their own experiences; invariably they have reported that the opportunity to be treated as an individual, in one's own classroom, with his own teacher, far outweighed any of the negative consequences associated with separation from his twin sibling.

One individual recalled having to check the validity of the first grade teacher's comments by turning to her sister and inquiring, "Is she right?" It was obvious that if both children were to succeed in school, they had to be placed in different classes. They were—and they both agreed that it was the best thing that happened to them.

Separating Early

We are not insensitive to the negative aspects of this separation. For many twins, this may be the first time they will spend considerable time away from their co-twin. Therefore, we believe that parents should provide "separate" experiences as early as possible.

At the same time, they should impress upon school personnel that while they may support separate classes, they want the process to be one that is sensitive to the needs of their children.

For example, we are appreciative of teachers who spend the time to get to know our daughters as students in their classes—students who have individual personalities, wants and needs, but who happened to be born at the same time. Comparing any student to his sibling has been considered a poor educational practice for years; to engage in this type of behavior with students who are twins is clearly inappropriate.

As children progress through the elementary grades, they may be grouped by ability for specific subjects, such as reading, math or science, which may again bring up the separation issue. On the junior and senior high school levels, there may be a limited number of courses available to the twins and, once again, parents are faced with the dilemma of choosing the same or different classes. Clearly, if most of their time spent in the early grades of school is in separate classes, they probably have established their own identities as students, therefore, placement in the same reading group or driver's education class is not going to make a big difference. However, parents of twins, and twins themselves, have to encourage teachers to view them as individuals and reinforce teachers in their efforts to do so.

We recognize that a number of variables may compound this issue, not the least of which is the size of the school district. In this era of declining enrollments, it is not unusual for schools to have only one kindergarten class per morning and afternoon session. Therefore, parents' schedules may necessitate placement in the same class unless they are willing to send one child to another school.

We know of parents of twins who did send their children to different schools and found it to be a successful alternative to same-class placement. This also may occur in the middle and upper grades when the availability of a particular course is limited and both children want to be enrolled, or in the more "sticky" situation when parents feel that one teacher is far superior to the other.

While we believe strongly in the notion of separate class placements for twins and have done research clearly indicating the positive effects of that arrangement, we are cognizant of the fact that there will be those who feel this is detrimental to their children. Parents who appreciate this thinking should monitor the educational progress of their children and evaluate whether the placement decision is interfering with or facilitating their growth—both academically and emotionally.

Ultimately, it is our responsibility as parents of twins to be the primary advocate for our children. School personnel often take cues from us—if we don't treat our children as individuals, how can we expect others to do so?

—————————————— ❦ ——————————————

When Is Separate Schools the Answer?

by Barry E. McNamara and Francine J. McNamara

One of the central questions raised regarding the education of twins is class placement. Should twins be placed in the same or separate classes? To briefly summarize our position, we believe that the optimal placement is in separate classes. This position is taken with the realization that there are variables that may make the decision more difficult than it appears. However, there is evidence to suggest that, generally speaking the individual needs of each twin will be better met when each is "on his own."

When to Consider Separate Schools

Parents of twins should consider placing their children in different schools if the needs of each child cannot be met by the same school. The most obvious situation in which this may occur is when there is only one class per grade, thereby eliminating the option of placing twins in separate classrooms. Also, one of the twins may have special needs, which would be best served by classes especially for those children with learning disabilities or language disorders, for example, that are provided in a special school.

Some parents of twins may also see an unhealthy amount of attention paid to their children because they are "twins." This attention may result in the children being perceived as a "unit," lacking any value as individuals. Clearly, this type of environment is not conducive to individual growth; therefore, the notion that they be placed in two different settings should be considered. Finally, if it is in the best interest of one twin to be retained, perhaps a different setting would diminish the stigma associated with such a decision.

None of the above is intended to suggest that being a twin is something to be embarrassed by, ashamed of or denied. Quite the contrary is true. As parents of twins ourselves, we celebrate the fact that we were blessed with the births of two children. Our twin daughters' relationship with each other is truly special and has added a dimension to their lives that would not exist if each was a singleton.

Yet, it is important to remember that twins are two individuals; in the educational field, this fact is often forgotten. When it appears impossible for a set of twins to receive this kind of treatment at one school, then parents of twins should examine their option of separate school placements.

Positive Aspects of Separate School Placement

Co-twins will naturally feel less competition, experience less pressure on the twin relationship and be the subject of few comparisons when they attend different schools. Each of them will also tend to be perceived and treated more consistently as an individual and be allowed to progress at her own rate. This will be particularly true if each twin is in need of special education services, remedial services or services for children who are gifted/talented and these services were not available in his/her other school.

Parents may find that a new school is a better "fit" for one of their twins. That is, one school's philosophy of education—favoring a flexible vs. a rigid environment, for example—may be more compatible with a particular child's learning style. This ability to match the needs of the student and the school placement is not as simple as it sounds, yet it can yield very important results.

When twins are placed in different schools, they will often begin to develop different friendships. This will allow them to see that they are valued for their own unique qualities—not merely for their unique status as a twin. For the twin student who is always "behind" his brother/sister academically and socially, this new status can be very important. Grading, evaluations, class ranking, extracurricular performance, etc., are difficult enough for all students. When twins are placed in educational settings where this is heightened, the results can be extremely negative. Be selecting separate schools, this can be eliminated, or at the very least, greatly reduced.

Negative Aspects of Separate Placement

Some of the negative aspects of this separation are logistical. The schools may be a long distance from one another; transportation may not be readily available; and/or the schedules may necessitate a radical change in family work patterns. These are important considerations, but we believe that they can be overcome if the needs of each child are being better met.

More substantial concerns are not as easily remedied. For example, the quality of one school may be inferior to the other. We worked with parents who, after much deliberation, came to the conclusion that separate schools were necessary. However, they had a hard time reconciling the fact that one school was clearly superior to the other. They stuck with their decision to separate their children, but this continued to be an area of concern for them.

This decision can also pose a problem if it is done late in the child's education so that a child feels that he is "losing" all of his friends. It's hard being the "new child in school" at any age; but during the early school years, the adjustment is usually more rapid than in the upper grades.

The parents' goal in educating their children should always be to provide an educational program that meets the needs of each of their twins. When this cannot be achieved by both twins attending the same school, other options, such as sending each child to his "own" school, need to be explored.

The Team Approach to School Separation

by Barry E. McNamara and Francine J. McNamara

It happened again just last month. In fact, when discussing the topic of education with parents of multiples and/or educators, it is always the first or second question asked: "Should twins be placed in the same or separate classes?"

We will briefly share our views on the "same vs. separate classes" dilemma, and, as importantly, will provide you with a way to "fight" your children's school system if your personal opinion differs from the system's policy.

School Policy

Prior to their twins' first day of school, parents need to inquire about the school's policy regarding class placement for multiples. While most school districts that we've researched have the same policy (separate classes), only a handful of them actually have a written policy statement on this issue. If there is a written policy statement, parents need to find out if it is mandatory. If it is, they can then ask the board of education to provide them with all supporting documentation for its policy.

In many instances, a school's policy, whether for or against separation, may not necessarily be supported by research or discussion; instead, the school district's personnel may have selected its policy because it seemed like the reasonable decision to make.

Fighting the System

Once parents know the school district's stance, then they can gather their own "team" of experts to reinforce theirs. For example, they could ask their twins' pediatrician, local hospital, or university personnel with backgrounds in psychology or education for their personal opinions and articles that support their view.

The school system, like any organization, has a chain of command. If parents follow its chain, then they can proceed in a logical manner; if they don't, chances are good that someone will send them "back" to the link they've missed. Therefore, while it may appear to be a waste of time to proceed in a step-by-step manner when presenting their case, it really isn't. The chain to follow is:

school principal
•
**assistant superintendent
for instruction**
•
superintendent of schools
•
board of education

We suggest that parents meet with their children's principal sometime during the spring of the prior school year; for example, if their children's school has registration in August, they need to talk to their principal during the previous April to let him know of their placement preference for their multiples.

If parents are not pleased with the response they receive, then they can meet with the assistant superintendent for instruction. This individual has the power to overrule the principal's decision or at least can try to work out a compromise.

If they are still unhappy, parents need to confer with the superintendent of schools. The person in this position has the responsibility and power to address parents' concerns; in addition, the superintendent also has access to all of the school district's resources.

If parents are still not getting the result they desire, they can go directly to the Board of Education. To begin this process, they need to write a letter to each board member that clearly outlines their concern, send copies to their local legislators (they are usually quite involved in legislation regarding schools) and request a meeting with the board.

While it is important for parents to address the issue of same vs. separate classes, they will also have to handle many other issues throughout their multiples' educational years. As we have said many times, parents are their multiples' best advocate, so they need to select their "battles" carefully, consider the possible consequences of their actions and begin to forge a good relationship with their children's school personnel before, not after, problems arise.

IN OUR OPINION...

For us, the answer to the same/separate classes dilemma is a simple one:

We believe that separate classes are preferable because they foster each twin's independence and sense of self.

Although we are sensitive to situations that may necessitate keeping multiples in the same class (special needs, small school districts and convoluted schedules, for example), we still strongly believe that each co-twin is better off in his own class.

At the very least, having ownership of his own class will help each co-twin establish peer friendships and relationships with teachers on an individual basis as he discovers that he doesn't have to deny his twinship to develop his individuality.

If multiples have difficulty adjusting to their classroom separation, their parents need to investigate the source of their discomfort and implement strategies to try to ease their transition. If dependence on each other continues to be an issue, we think that the multiples' parents may want to seek professional guidance to help their children adjust to the separation more successfully. We are continuously amazed by the strength of the twin bond and believe that this should be fostered; however, when it interferes with a twin's ability to act in an independent manner, it is no longer a productive factor in his life.

Separation Decision-Making

by Linda Andrews and James E. Andrews

Over the past several years, we have done a lot of reading about twins in which the authors have stressed the importance of encouraging co-twins to each build a sense of individuality and separate identity. This encouragement was recently reinforced by the outcome of our separating our sons in school—separating them into different schools, that is. Here's why we chose this course for our sons:

When we moved from Florida to Maine, we bought a home in an area in which our children's school was very small and contained only one class of each grade. Therefore, the decision was "made" to keep our identical twin boys, Sean and Brian, together for kindergarten.

As the year progressed, we began to notice our already less aggressive twin, Sean, retreat more and more into himself. He fell behind not only in matters directly related to school, but in outside activities as well, even displaying a lack of enthusiasm for activities he previously had enjoyed. It became apparent to us that if Sean believed that his brother would do better than he at a certain task, he would refuse to even try to do it.

Despite our ongoing praise and attempts to build his self-confidence, he continued to retreat. Toward the end of their kindergarten year, the boys were introduced to reading. From the start, Brian tackled it with enthusiasm and confidence. Sean decided that he had no interest in reading and was not even going to attempt it. We believe that his brother's doing so well with this new challenge contributed to Sean's negative attitude toward it.

We felt that for Sean's emotional well-being, we had to break these patterns that were being established. After talking with the boys' principal, guidance counselor, and teacher, we made the decision to send our children to separate schools. We also decided that it would be best for our less aggressive twin to remain in a familiar environment.

For our boys, the separation has worked out well. Sean has made great strides academically, and has a new sense of self-confidence and a more positive attitude about life. Initially, the separation was hard for both children because no matter how separate or independent each twin felt, there was a comfortable sense of familiarity that came from having his brother close by. We were blessed, however, with caring insightful teachers in each class, and this made a big difference in our boys' adjustment to their separation.

Choosing the "Right" Preschool

by Barry E. McNamara and Francine J. McNamara

Selecting a preschool for your twins can be as a simple or as complex as you decide to make it. Nowadays, there is increasing pressure on parents to provide the "right" educational opportunities for their children from preschool through college. Indeed, there are some parts of our country where getting into the "right" preschool is as difficult as getting into an Ivy League College.

The purpose of this column is to help parents choose an appropriate preschool for their child or children, based on the principle that, whether it is a preschool or college under consideration, students should attend the school that wants them. With the wide variety of preschools available in most parts of the country, a good match can almost always be made between students and schools.

Factors to Consider in Selecting a Preschool

Philosophy. Perhaps the most important consideration when selecting a preschool is that particular school's philosophy of education. Are what the director and staff of the prospective preschool think important, also the values and expectations of the inquiring parents? For example, there are schools that are very academically oriented, geared to teaching preschoolers to read and to compute. Some parents may find this concentrated academic approach inappropriate for a preschool-aged child.

Parents need to be comfortable with how each of their children's preschool experience will benefit the "whole" child—not merely how it will develop specific skills. Preschools often are grounded in a specific theory of child development; parents need to inquire closely about each before commiting their child to one.

Physical setting. The classrooms and play areas of a preschool should be clean, bright and cheerful. The area should be well-stocked with appropriate materials and toys. Most preschool classrooms have various centers around the room where children can play and learn at a level commensurate with their abilities.

The physical setting should promote and provoke a child's curiosity and desire to learn. "Serious or contemplative settings are not appropriate for preschool-aged children; learning should be fun! Young children learn best when relaxed, comfortable and motivated by their own natural curiosity.

Staff. The director and staff should be certified (or licensed) to teach preschoolers. It is important to assess professional qualifications of both the director and staff members, usually through an interview with the director. Is there a high turnover rate among the staff? Are teachers provided with assistants? In general, parents need to know if the director and staff are not only competent, but also dedicated to their work and the school.

Finally, parents of multiples need to find out if the preschool staff has experience with twins. How will same/separate class issues be resolved? Is the staff sensitive to twin-specific concerns?

Other considerations. Parents of prospective students need to visit the school under consideration at least several times, scheduling each visit for a different time of the day. Do the children and staff appear happy? Is learning taking place in a reinforcing and motivating environment? Is there too much pressure on children to excel? Most schools allow—even encourage—parents to bring their children in for a "trial run." This is an excellent way to find out if a specific child and school "match" well with each other.

Parents should also inquire as to the amount of parental involvement permitted or encouraged. Some schools, such as cooperative preschools, require considerable participation, whereas others may frown upon this. Parents should pick a preschool consistent with their views on this matter.

Same or Separate Classes?

A major question for parents of twins regarding their children's educations is whether to place the twins in the same class or separate classes. There is a strong case to be made for placing twins in separate classes with separate teachers during the school years.

However, there are exceptions, and one of those is preschool education programs. The major reason for the exception is one of logistics. Until recently, there has usually been, in most preschools, only one class per age group. Twins, of necessity, have remained in the same class.

A second reason to make an exception to the "separate classroom" rule is that many preschool-aged twins have always participated in activities together, and to abruptly separate them in a school setting may be upsetting.

However, if both of their twins are in the same classroom, parents need to be concerned about the following issues surrounding their offsprings' individuality: How will the teacher monitor the interaction of the twins and their relationships with other children? How will she make sure that each child is treated individually and not as one of "the twins?"

Parental Expectation

Parents send children to preschools for a host of reasons. It is important for parents to recognize that even the best preschool program is not a substitute for parental participation in the education of their children. The parents' role is critical if children are to acquire a love of learning. They need to provide encouragement and reinforcement, and be appropriate role models for their children. They cannot abdicate these responsibilities to schools, especially at the preschool level. Parents still need to spend time reading to their children, discussing topics of importance, and letting them know that the acquisition of knowledge is important.

Nor can children's skill development be ignored. A school cannot begin to provide the appropriate social skills to a preschooler if it is operating in a vacuum; it can only reinforce those skills and values learned in the home. Preschool can be a wonderful complement to good parenting—but never a substitute.

IN OUR OPINION...

All the guidelines in the world can't replace the "feel" you get for a school. If you think there is a good fit between your values and that of the school, consider the points noted here. Remember, you are a consumer and you should be pleased with the preschool. If the school cannot answer your questions adequately, move on to another school. Most importantly, the school may lack experience with twins, and you can be assured that issues regarding competition, separation and individuality, for example, will come up throughout the school year.

It is better to discuss any of these and other issues before they occur and open lines of communication from the start, rather than wait for a problem to arise. Your role as an advocate for your children is just beginning, and the preschool years are a good place to put that role into play.

Support Around The World

A Directory of Organizations Serving Multiples and Those Who Care for Them

Australian Multiple Birth Association, Inc. (AMBA), founded in 1974, is a self-help, voluntary organization concerned with the well-being of multiple-birth children and their families. AMBA, c/o The National Secretary, P.O. Box 105, Coogee N.S.W. 2034, Australia, or call (049) 46 8030.

The Center for Study of Multiple Birth, a public charity organized in 1977, stimulates and fosters medical and social research in the area of multiple births. CSMB, Suite 464, 333 E. Superior St., Chicago, IL 60611, or call (312) 266-9093.

Center for Loss in Multiple Birth, Inc. (CLIMB) is a non-profit organization offering a newsletter, support and information resources for parents who have experienced the death of one, both or all of their children during a twin or higher-order multiple pregnancy, at birth or during infancy. CLIMB, c/o Jean Kollantai, P.O. Box 1064, Palmer, AK 99645, or call (907) 746-6123.

INFACT Canada is a nonprofit organization that promotes, protects and supports breastfeeding. Fore more information, contact: INFACT, Infant Feeding Action Coalition, 6 Trinity Square, Toronto, M5G 1B1 or call (416) 595-9819.

The International Society for Twin Studies is an international multidisciplinary organization, established with the purpose of furthering research and social action in all fields related to twin studies, for the mutual benefit of twins and their families, and of scientific research. Adam P. Matheny Jr., Ph.D., c/o The Louisville Twin Study, 2301 S. 3rd St., Louisville, KY 40208, or e-mail at apmath01@ulkyvm.louisville.edu.

International Twins Association, Inc., is a non-profit organization promoting the spiritual, intellectual and social welfare of twins throughout the world. ITA, c/o Lynn Long or Lori Stewart, 6898 Channel Road, NE, Minneapolis, MN 55432-4621; or call (612) 571-3022.

Mothers of Supertwins (M.O.S.T.) is a non-profit organization that serves the needs of families expecting multiples or those already the parents of triplets, quadruplets or quintuplets. MOST, write to P.O. Box 951, Brentwood, NY 11717, or call (516) 434-MOST, or e-mail at mostmom@nyc.pipeline.com.

Multiple Births Foundation provides professional support to families with twins and higher-order births by educating professionals through study days and newsletters, and by serving as a resource center. Multiple Births Foundation, Queen Charlotte's and Chelsea Hospital, Goldhawk Road, London, England, W6 OXG, or call (0181) 383-3519, or e-mail at mbf@rpms.ac.uk.

The National Organization of Mothers of Twins Clubs, Inc. (NOMOTC), is a non-profit nationwide network of parents of multiples clubs which shares information, concerns and advice, and focuses on education, research and support. Its services include: MOTC's Notebook (a quarterly newspaper); a Multiple Birth Data Bank (an information registry); a club development kit; the Cope/Outreach Program; and an annual convention. NOMOTC, P.O. Box 23188, Albuquerque, NM 87192-1188, or call (800) 243-2276.

Parents of Multiple Births Assn. of Canada (POMBA) is a non-profit organization whose purpose is to act as a general information source; to be a liaison between parents and agencies, health caregivers and educators; to publish multi-birth information; and to conduct and/or participate in research. POMBA, 240 Graff Ave., Box 22005, Stratford, Ontario, Canada N5A 7V6, or call (519) 272-2203, or e-mail at pomba@cyg.net.

Sidelines is a nonprofit organization providing education, referral information, support and advocacy services for women experiencing complicated pregnancies. For more information, call Candace Hurley, Executive Director, at (714) 497-2265 or Tracy Hoogenboom, (719) 488-0266, or e-mail at www.earthlink.net\~sidelines

Special Children is a nonprofit support network for parents raising multiples with special needs. For more information about available services and the organization's quarterly newsletter, contact Sharon Devo, P.O. Box 8193, Bartlett, IL 60103, or call (708) 213-1630, or e-mail spclchldrn@aol.com. Sharon Devo, P.O. Box 8193, Bartlett, IL 60103, or call (630) 213-1630, or e-mail spclchldrn@aol.com.

The Triplet Connection is a support service for expectant and new parents of higher order multiples which provides information on preventing pre-term birth as well as networking opportunities. The Triplet Connection, P.O. Box 99571, Stockton, CA 95209, call (209) 474-0885, or e-mail at triplet@inreach.com.

The Twin to Twin Transfusion Syndrome Foundation, Inc. is a nonprofit organization dedicated to providing educational, emotional and financial support to families and caregivers before, during and after pregnancies diagnosed with TTTS. For more information, write Mary Slaman-Forsythe, executive director, 411 Longbeach Parkway, Bay Village, OH 44140, call (216) 899-8887, or e-mail at tttsfound@aol.com.

The Twins Foundation is a non-profit, membership organization that is building a national twin registry, providing a quarterly newsletter to members and providing an informational clearinghouse on twin-related matters. The Twins Foundation, P.O. Box 6043, Providence, RI 02940-6043, or call (401) 729-1000, or e-mail at twins@twinsfoundation.com.

Twin Hope, Inc. is a nonprofit organization providing service to families, educating the public and broadening the awareness of twin-to-twin transfusion syndrome and other twin-related diseases. For more information, write to Jill MacNiven at 2592 W. 14th St., Cleveland, OH 44113, or call (216) 228-8887.

TWIN SERVICES is a non-profit agency providing publications in English and Spanish to multiple-birth families all over the United States; in northern California, classes and respite child care are also offered. Twin Services, P.O. Box 10066, Berkeley, CA 94709, or call the TWINLINE (510) 524-0863, or e-mail at twinserv@aol.com.

Twinless Twins Support Group is a membership of twins of all ages whose co-twins are deceased or terminally ill. New Members are continually adding breadth and depth to the group's skills in coping with the pain of separation in a bond which seemingly cannot be broken even by death. Twinless Twins International, c/o Raymond W. Brandt, 11220 St. Joe Road, Fort Wayne, IN 46835, or call (219) 627-5414.

Twins and Multiple Births Association (TAMBA), supports multiple-birth families through local clubs and special support groups. The organization offers several publications as well as the TAMBA TWINLINE, a confidential telephone helpline.

Books Available from TWINS® Magazine

Discipline Without Shouting or Spanking
by Jerry Wyckoff, Ph.D. and Barbara C. Unell, Simon & Schuster

Exploring Twin Relationships: Is Being a Twin Always Fun?
by Betty Jean Case, Tibbutt Publishing

Having Twins
by Elizabeth Noble, Houghton Mifflin

How to Discipline Your 6 to 12 Year Old
by Jerry L. Wyckoff, Ph.D. and Barbara C. Unell, Bantam Doubleday Dell Publishing Group, Inc.

The Joy of Twins
by Pamela Patrick Novotny Random House, Inc.

Mothering Multiples
by Karen Kerkoff Gromada La Leche League International

Mothering Twins
by Linda Albi, Deborah Johnson, Debra Catlin, Donna Florien Deurloo, and Sheryll Greatwood, Simon & Schuster

Multiple Blessings
by Betty Rothbart, William Morrow & Company, Inc.

On Becoming Babywise
by Gary Ezzo and Robert Bucknam, M.D., Questar Publishers, Inc.

Pregnancy Bedrest
by Susan H. Johnston, M.S.W., and Deborah A. Kraut, M.I.L. R., Henry Holt & Company

The Parents' Guide to Raising Twins
by Elizabeth Friedrich and Cherry Rowland, St. Martin's Press

The Premature Baby Book: A Parents' Guide to Coping and Caring in the First Years
by Helen Harrison, St. Martin's Press

The Psychology of Twins
by Herbert L. Collier, Ph.D., TWINS® Magazine

The Stork Brought Three
by Jean P. Hall, TWINS® Magazine

Solve Your Child's Sleep Problems
by Richard Ferber, M.D., Simon & Schuster, Inc.

365 Ways to Help Your Children Grow
by Sheila Ellison, Sourcebooks, Inc.

The Twinship Sourcebook
by the editors of TWINS® Magazine, published by TWINS® Magazine

Twenty Teachable Virtues
by Barbara C. Unell and Jerry L. Wyckoff, Ph.D., The Berkley Publishing Group

Twin Care
Twin Services, Inc.

TWINS Special Reports:
*Health & Safety for Infant Multiples
Tips & Tools for New Parents
Feeding Multiple Babies
Premature Twins and Triplets,*
published by TWINS® Magazine

Your Pregnancy After 30
by Glade B. Curtis, M.D., F.A.C.O.G., Fisher Books

Your Premature Baby
by Frank P. Manginello, John Wiley & Sons, Inc.

We Are Twins, But Who Am I?
by Betty Jean Case, Tibbutt Publishing

Index

The T♥INS Magazine Bookshelf
Dedicated to making your life with multiples more enjoyable!

T♥INS Magazine

The magazine created just for you! **TWINS** is the only international magazine created with your unique multiple-birth parenting needs in mind. Imagine the joy and comfort you'll get when every issue brings you practical hints, inspiring stories, invaluable child development information, and the latest research results about giving birth to and raising multiples.

It's the best of both worlds—expert advice from professionals and from parents who understand your needs ... and care! **$23.95 a year**

Twice as Funny ... TWINS *David Lochner*
A book of cartoons

Twins can be double the trouble ... and double the laughs. This delightful cartoon book will have you chuckling over the misadventures and predicaments that only twins can get into! Expect to find plenty of laughable, just-like-us cartoon strips!
$10.95

Published by **TWINS** Magazine

The Stork Brought Three *Jean P. Hall*
Secrets of successful coping for ALL parents of multiples

You may have twins instead of triplets, but you're sure to enjoy this touching, humorous first-hand account of pregnancy and the first year when the stork brings three. Easy to read and sure to bring a smile, this inspiring tale emphasizes the two essential ingredients for raising multiples—patience and a sense of humor. You'll also learn from the practical steps this mom took to make life manageable.
  $12.00

Published by **TWINS** Magazine

The Psychology of Twins *Herbert L. Collier, Ph.D.*
A practical handbook for parents of multiples

Twins *do* have different natures. They differ from singletons and, just as importantly, from each other. Herbert L. Collier is a psychologist and father of twins who draws on firsthand experience dealing with multiples. He is a therapist for many families with multiples. For the parent who wants to understand and value each child as an individual, this book presents an outstanding framework for what goes on inside the heads of multiples ... as well as the psychological dynamics of successful families with twins.
$13.95

Published by **TWINS** Magazine

The Twinship Sourcebook *From the editors of* **TWINS** *Magazine*
Your guide to understanding multiples

The leading source of information for parents of multiples—**TWINS** Magazine — brings you this handy, one-of-a-kind guidebook to help you understand and cope with twins, triplets, and more. Compiled from the pages of **TWINS**, it's your day-in, day-out reference as your multiples grow from birth through adulthood. *If you have only one book on the subject, this is the one to have!* An ideal gift to suggest to your friends and family!
$14.95

Published by **TWINS** Magazine

TWINS Magazine Special Reports

Health & Safety for Infant Multiples
From choosing a pediatrician to ear infections and diaper rash, every parent of multiples will benefit from the simple, essential advice about the health of their babies. 40 pages

Tips and Tools for New Parents of Twins and Triplets
When "twinshock" hits new parents, it hits hard. This compilation of special articles will be a godsend to new parents of multiples when their babies are young, providing practical, encouraging advice about coping with day-to-day challenges. 52 pages

Feeding Multiple Babies
The simple questions—such as to breastfeed or bottle feed, weaning, handling colic, and many more—become more complicated when there are two or more baby appetites to deal with. Full of useful insights from mothers who have been there! 40 pages

Premature Twins and Triplets
This wonderful collection of articles helps frightened parents deal with the big and little traumas they must face as their small, prematurely born multiples enter life with extra health problems. 44 pages

$14.95 For Two ($5.50 ea. additional)   Published by **TWINS** Magazine

20 Teachable Virtues   *Barbara C. Unell and Jerry Wyckoff, Ph.D.*
Practical ways to pass on lessons of virtue and character to your children
Barbara Unell, founder of **TWINS** Magazine and mother of twins, and Jerry Wyckoff reveal practical ways to teach your children to care about others … and themselves. A great guide to help you pass on the lessons and values that are most important to you and your family. $12.00

The Premature Baby Book *Helen Harrison, with Ann Kositsky, R.N.*

A Parents' Guide to Coping and Caring in the First Years
Exactly what parents need to know to deal with the emotional, medical and practical issues facing them after the birth of a premature baby—communicating with doctors and nurses; dealing with shock, denial, anger, guilt and fear; preparing for when the baby comes home; ongoing concerns; and much more.
$19.95

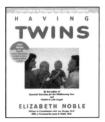

Having Twins   *Elizabeth Noble*
A parent's guide to pregnancy, birth, and early childhood
This 430-page book is bursting with details about multiple pregnancy, the birthing experience, postpartum concerns, and caring for twins at home. This revised edition includes new chapters on prenatal psychology, premature delivery, twin bonding and the experience of loss. $16.95

To place your order, call 1-800-328-3211 or use order form

On Becoming Babywise   *Gary Ezzo and Robert Bucknam, M.D.*

How 100,000 new parents trained their babies to sleep through the night the natural way

The title tells only part of the story contained in this easy-to-read, common-sense guide. The whole book is bursting with practical, realistic steps every family can take for happier babies that won't leave parents frazzled. "I cannot argue with the success of *Babywise*. It provides infants with needed structure and stability and brings the joy and love so needed in our homes today.. Parents constantly tells me, 'It changed our lives.'" - Janet Dahmen, M.D. **$9.99**

Multiple Blessings   *Betty Rothbart, M.S.W.*

**From pregnancy through childhood,
a guide for parents of twins, triplets, or more**

Sure to make the life of new parents easier, *Multiple Blessings* places a human face on the many issues confronting parents of multiples. This volume is fact-filled, interesting, and often humorous in its advice to parents. You'll use the dozens of practical ideas designed to make your daily routine easier.   **$12.00**

The Joy of Twins   *Pamela Patrick Novotny*

Having, raising, and loving babies who arrive in groups

This handbook for parents covers everything from the scientific facts about twins to practical parent-to-parent hints about how to cope with a task that is at once thrilling and exhausting— raising two babies at once.   **$16.00**

Twin Care

A handout collection for parents

This special collection of helpful articles is from the Parent Education Series created by Twin Services, the nonprofit support organization for parents of multiples. The short, topical articles emphasize practical tips every parent will appreciate.
Published by Twin Services   **$19.95**

The Parents' Guide to Raising Twins

**From pre-birth to first school days—the essential
book for those expecting two or more**

Elizabeth Friedrich and Cherry Rowland

Readers will tap into a wealth of practical tips and advice from doctors, nurses and dozens of other parents of twins. The authors, both mothers of twins, deliver a bounty of useful guidance.   **$10.95**

Mothering Twins

**Advice and support
from five moms who've been there and lived to tell the tale**

Five mothers of twins offer a superb collection of it-worked-for-me solutions to the many situations unique to caring for twins. These insightful moms speak from the heart—and the head—in terms other mothers will understand.

$13.00

To place your order, call 1-800-328-3211 or use order form

Pregnancy Bedrest *Susan H. Johnston, M.S.W., and Deborah A. Kraut, M.I.L.R.*

A guide for the pregnant woman and her family

Discusses all the facets and frustrations of a pregnant woman's life when bed rest is suddenly required. The authors offer dozens of practical suggestions to make the restricted confinement more comfortable and manageable. **$14.95**

Your Pregnancy After 30 *Glade B. Curtis, M.D., F.A.C.O.G.*

The author of *Your Pregnancy Week-by-Week* provides sensible, reassuring information tailored to the specific needs of women who conceive after 30. Health, nutrition, prenatal testing, counseling, work-related and lifestyle issues are just some of the topics covered. **$12.95**

Your Premature Baby *Frank P. Manginello, M.D., and Theresa Foy DiGeronimo, M.Ed.*

Everything you need to know about the childbirth, treatment, and parenting of premature infants

Many twins and multiples are "preemies," adding to the childrearing burden of their anxious parents. This book helps lessen parents' fears with an essential guide to facing the challenging and often costly ordeal of giving birth to and caring for premature babies. It's loaded with valuable facts and calming advice. **$15.95**

Discipline Without Shouting or Spanking

Jerry Wyckoff, Ph.D., and Barbara C. Unell

Practical solutions to the most common preschool behavior problems

Every parent of 1- to 5-year-olds contends with children who sometimes whine, refuse to eat, throw tantrums, etc. Barbara Unell, founder of **TWINS** Magazine, and Jerry Wyckoff help parents discipline children without damaging their self-esteem or curtailing their natural curiosity about the world. **$6.00**

Solve Your Child's Sleep Problems *Richard Ferber, M.D.*

Does your child have difficulty falling asleep? Wake in the middle of the night? Suffer from night fears? Based on six years of intensive research in a top medical facility, this handy book is packed with insights, tips, sample problems and solutions, and a bibliography of children's "go-to-sleep" books. **$12.00**

Exploring Twin Relationships *Betty Jean Case*

Is Being a Twin Always Fun?

New from Ms. Case, this wonderful book uses extensive research and personal case studies to describe the dynamics among identical twins, same-sex fraternal twins, and different-sex fraternal twins, plus twins' relationships with siblings, parents, etc. **$14.95**

We are Twins, But Who Am I? *Betty Jean Case*

A truly remarkable work, this eye-opening book is by a twin, about twins, and for twins—yet it's also filled with insights into the psychology of twins that parents will relish. Based upon hundreds of surveys of twins of all ages and types.

Hardcover $18.95

Books for Children

Baby Boo *Random House*

An enticing starter book for parents to read to their infant and pre-reader twins. A small, padded fabric book, *Baby Boo* is just right for baby hands. Each set of pages has pictures of two babies—surely twins!—with brightly colored fabric flaps meant to be lifted to find one baby hiding underneath. Non-toxic, washable, 10 pages. **$6.99**

Curious Kids Go to Preschool

Ingrid Godon

A wonderful picture book to help pre-schoolers develop their vocabularies. For multiples 2 to 5, 22 pages. **$13.95**

Born Two-gether

Jill Brennan

A delightful look at the joys and dismays of twinship written by a mom of twins. Photos show twins in 11 settings from birthday parties to dressing alike, showcasing life as a twin from a twin's point of view. For multiples 2 to 7, 40 pages. **$9.95**

Twin Pickle *Ann Doro*

Playful rhymes carry you through a day of crazy antics with fun-loving Jenny and Ivory, identical twin girls. Wonderful illustrations. For multiples 2 to 7, 25 pages. **$14.95**

Twins *Monica Colli*

A story about twin rivalry and a first-hand opinion of how it feels to be a twin and mistaken for your sister. Small square size with simple text and colorful illustrations. For multiples 3 to 8, 24 pages.

$6.99

The Plant That Kept On Growing

Barbara Brenner

When critters gobble up all the vegetables growing in their garden, Will and his twin sister are afraid they'll never win the 4H garden prize. Then they're surprised by the one mysterious plant the critters left behind. For multiples 3 to 6, 32 pages.

$3.99

Two Dog Biscuits

Beverly Cleary

When the neighbor lady gives 4-year-old twins Jimmy and Janet dog biscuits, their mother insists they find a dog to feed them to. But the twins just can't seem to find the right dog .... Fun illustrations. For multiples 3 to 7, 32 pages.

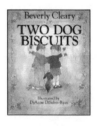

$10.25

On the Trail with Miss Pace

Sharon Phillips Denslow

While spending the summer at a dude ranch, identical twin boys, Bill and Phil, meet up with their teacher, Miss Pace, and a cowboy legend named Last Bob. The four team up for fun adventures. Filled with imaginative illustrations. For multiples 4 to 8, 36 pages.

$15.00

To place your order, call 1-800-328-3211 or use order form

One Up, One Down

Carol Snyder

An amusing look at the life of a big sister of twins. It celebrates the antics of twins and acknowledges older singleton siblings who feel a little left out. Filled with clever plays on words and cute illustrations. For singletons and multiples 4 to 8, 32 pages. **$15.00**

The Twins Strike Back

Valerie Flournoy

Natalie and Nicole are identical twins and best friends who are tired of their cousin and older sister teasing them about being twins—they just want to be treated like individuals. To teach them a lesson, Natalie and Nicole devise a clever trick to play on them. For multiples 5 and up, 29 pages. **$5.00**

Tatterhood and the Hobgoblins: A Norwegian folk tale

Lauren Mills

A fairy tale of twin girls very different from each other—one beautiful and one wild and boyish—who love each other very much. Together they embark on exciting adventures that celebrate their differences and teach readers never to judge on appearance alone. Beautifully illustrated. For multiples 5 and up, 32 pages. **$5.95**

Triplet Trouble

Debbie Dadey and Marcia Thornton Jones

Best friend Sam Johnson knows triplet trouble when he sees it! He and the Tucker triplets set out to see who can bake the best cookies. But when no one wins the contest, they all learn a valuable lesson about togetherness. For multiples 7 and up, 54 pages. **$2.99**

The Valentine's Day Mystery

Marion Markham

Clever twins Kate and Mickey Dixon want to be detectives when they grow up. Soon after arriving at their neighbor's Valentine's Day party, a mystery unfolds before them, and they help solve the case of the missing ruby pin. For multiples 7 and up, 48 pages. **$13.95**

The Adventures of Mary-Kate and Ashley: The case of the Sea World Adventure

The trench-coat twins Mary-Kate and Ashley are serious kid detectives. Their motto: "We'll solve any crime by dinnertime" and that they do! While on a Sea World vacation, the twins solve the case of a mysterious body discovered in the woods. For multiples 7 and up, 80 pages. **$3.99**

The Great Pony Hassle

Nancy Springer

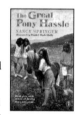

Two sets of very different 10-year-old twin girls come together when their parents marry. All four girls love ponies, but only one girl gets a pony. It teaches lessons of sharing, individuality and acceptance. For multiples 8 and up, 76 pages. **$3.99**

To place your order, call 1-800-328-3211 or use order form

TWINS BOOKSHELF ORDER FORM

❑ **YES!** I'd like to subscribe to **TWINS** Magazine . . . and save 20% off the newsstand price. Please start my 1 year bi-monthly subscription for only $23.95 – a savings of $6.05.

AMOUNT DUE

$ _____

❑ Sign me up for a 2-year subscription to **TWINS** Magazine for only $39.95. I want to save 33% off the newsstand price – a savings of $20.05!

_____

Please send me the following books:

LIST BOOKS:

	PRICE	x	QUANTITY	AMOUNT DUE
_____	_____	x	_____	_____
_____	_____	x	_____	_____
_____	_____	x	_____	_____
_____	_____	x	_____	_____
_____	_____	x	_____	_____

SUBTOTAL _____

Sales Tax (Colorado residents only, add 3.8%)   _____

Regular Shipping & Handling   No. of books _____ x $3.00 per book (Count any number of Special Reports as one book)   _____

Express Shipping   No. of books _____ x $7.00 per book   _____

MINIMUM ORDER OF $12.00   TOTAL AMOUNT DUE _____

SOURCE

PAYMENT MUST ACCOMPANY ORDER

❑ Payment enclosed (Payable to **TWINS** Magazine)   ❑ Bill my MasterCard   ❑ Bill my VISA

_____   _____
Card number   Expiration date

_____   _____
Name on credit card   Signature

_____   _____
Name of recipient   Phone

_____
Address

_____   _____   _____
City   State   ZIP

Send your order to: TWINS Magazine • 5350 S. Roslyn St., Ste. 400 • Englewood, CO 80111
Tel: 888-55-TWINS (toll free) 888-558-9467 Fax: 303-290-9025

SOURCE

Discipline Without Shouting or Spanking – $6.00

Exploring Twin Relationships – $14.95

Having Twins – $16.95

Joy of Twins – $16.00

Mothering Twins – $13.00

Multiple Blessings – $12.00

On Becoming Babywise – $9.99

Pregnancy Bedrest – $14.95

Psychology of Twins – $13.95

Solve Your Child's Sleep Problems – $12.00

The Stork Brought Three – $12.00

The Parent's Guide to Raising Twins – $10.95

The Premature Baby Book – $19.95

The Twinship Sourcebook – $14.95

20 Teachable Virtues – $12.00

Twice as Funny ... Twins – $10.95

Twin Care – $19.95

TWINS Special Reports first two – $14.95

✳ Extra Special Reports – $5.50

    Health & Safety for Infant Multiples

    Tips & Tools for New Parents

    Feeding Multiple Babies

    Premature Twins and Triplets

We Are Twins, But Who Am I? – $18.95

Your Pregnancy After 30 – $12.95

Your Premature Baby – $15.95

CHILDREN'S BOOKS

Baby Boo – $6.99

Born Two-gether – $9.95

Curious Kids Go to Preschool– $13.95

Harry & Tuck – $14.00

One Up, One Down – $15.00

On the Trail with Miss Pace – $15.00

Tatterhood and the Hobgoblins – $5.95

The Adventures of Mary Kate & Ashley – $3.99

The Great Pony Hassle – $3.99

The Plant That Kept On Growing – $3.99

The Twins Strike Back – $5.00

The Valentine's Day Mystery – $13.95

Triplet Trouble – $2.99

Twin Pickle – $14.95

Twins – $6.99

Two Dog Biscuits – $10.25